A History of Russian Cinema

Birgit Beumers

BERG
Oxford • New York

English edition
First published in 2009 by
Berg
Editorial offices:
First Floor, Angel Court, 81 St Clements Street, Oxford OX4 1AW, UK
175 Fifth Avenue, New York, NY 10010, USA

Berg is the imprint of Oxford International Publishers Ltd.

Library of Congress Cataloging-in-Publication Data

Beumers, Birgit.
A history of Russian cinema / Birgit Beumers.—English ed.
p. cm.
Includes bibliographical references and index.
ISBN-13: 978-1-84520-214-9 (cloth)
ISBN-10: 1-84520-214-7 (cloth)
ISBN-13: 978-1-84520-215-6 (pbk.)
ISBN-10: 1-84520-215-5 (pbk.)
1. Motion pictures—Russia (Federation)—History. I. Title.

PN1993.5.R9B48 2009
791.430947—dc22

2008036678

British Library Cataloguing-in-Publication Data

A catalogue record for this book is available from the British Library.

ISBN 978 1 84520 214 9 (Cloth)
978 1 84520 215 6 (Paper)

Typeset by JS Typesetting Ltd, Porthcawl, Mid Glamorgan
Printed in Great Britain by the MPG Books Group, Bodmin and King's Lynn

www.bergpublishers.com

Contents

Illustrations

Cover illustration:
Andrei Zviagintsev's *The Return*, courtesy of Intercinema XXI, and personally Raisa Fomina.

Chapter 1

Chapter 2

Chapter 3

Chapter 4

Chapter 5

Chapter 6

Chapter 7

Chapter 8

All images are courtesy of the *Iskusstvo kino* archive, except for image 1.3, which is reproduced here with the kind permission of David Robinson, and image 8.4, which is courtesy of Intercinema XXI.

Acknowledgements

I would like to thank, above all, Tristan Palmer for venturing on this project and for his incredible patience. My thanks also go to Julian Graffy and Richard Taylor for their help, and to Denise Youngblood for her useful comments. For the illustrations I am deeply indebted to the *Iskusstvo kino* archive, especially Lena Plotkina and Liudmila Mishunina. Special thanks to Raisa Fomina of Intercinema XXI for permission for the cover image. I would also like to thank the anonymous readers for their helpful suggestions.

Note on Transliteration

Transliteration from the Cyrillic to the Latin alphabet is a perennial problem for writers on Russian subjects. I have opted for a dual system: in the text I have used the Library of Congress system (without diacritics), but I have broken from this system as follows: (a) when a Russian name has a clear English version (e.g. Maria instead of Mariia, Alexander instead of Aleksandr); (b) when a Russian name has an accepted English spelling, or when Russian names are of Germanic origin (e.g. Yeltsin instead of Eltsin; Eisenstein instead of Eizenshtein); (c) when a Russian surname ends in -ii or -yi, this is replaced by a single -y (e.g. Dostoevsky instead of Dostoevskii), and all Christian names end in a single -i; (d) when 'ia' or 'iu' are voiced (at the beginning of a word and when preceded by a vowel) they are rendered as 'ya' or 'yu' (e.g. Daneliya, Yuri) – with the addition of the name Asya to avoid confusion with the continent, Asia, and the accepted spelling for Ilya (instead of Ilia). I have also spelt the name Gherman with an added 'h' in order to avoid confusion with the adjective 'German' and used the accepted spelling 'Ermoliev'. The voiced 'e' has been prefixed (e.g. Yevgeni and Yelena, and not Evgeni and Elena) at the beginning of a name to make the difference clear to Elem or Eldar; when preceded by a soft sign in name endings it has been rendered as 'ie' (e.g. Soloviev). This lengthy description serves to outline the system invented to make the reading as user-friendly as possible while remaining consistent. In the scholarly apparatus and the transliterated film titles in the text I have adhered to the Library of Congress system (with diacritics).

Introduction

A history of Russian cinema is, no doubt, much needed. Jay Leyda's vivid account of Russian cinema captures developments until just after the Second World War and remains an invaluable reference for students and scholars alike. However, the development of cinema in the second half of the twentieth century remains largely unmapped, although several excellent studies have been published on specific themes or periods.

This history is designed to provide a chronological overview of developments and trends, experiments and searches, traditions and conventions in cinematic art. The history of cinema is connected to political, historical, cultural and social developments. The aesthetics of films are singled out where these have had a profound effect on film history or when they characterize the work of a particular filmmaker.

Any 'history' is necessarily shaped by the historian's eye for detail, and here historiography becomes selective: not in its chronology and linearity, but in what it includes and what it excludes. This book focuses on fiction films while addressing documentaries and animation in a cursory manner, sketching only the major phenomena in those important areas of film art. The cinemas of the former Soviet republics are included until 1991, when national cinematographies emerged and the 'histories' of Kazakh, Kyrgyz, and other cinemas began to be rewritten.

In each chapter I outline first the historical and cultural context (detailed in the timeline at the volume's end) before investigating the major films and themes of the period. I elaborate on those films that have made an important contribution to cinematic or cultural history, both in Russia and beyond, while referring to lesser-known films to provide the wider picture. There will no doubt be films that could or should have been mentioned, that could have been explored in more or less depth. Here we return to the point about selectivity: the choice of 'key films' is without doubt subjective and, maybe, disputable. And yet – who would have thought thirty years ago that a key film of the 1960s for today's film historians – and part of almost every curriculum – would be *The Commissar*, unshelved in 1987? Who would have been able to predict twenty years ago the significance for the history of Stalinist musicals of *New Moscow*, retrieved from the archives in the early 1990s? Who would have predicted the wealth of pre-Revolutionary cinema before it was uncovered in 1989? Subjectivity and selectivity mean little when compared to the tricks that history can play. Film histories are written and rewritten not by film scholars and historians, but by time itself, and these histories often tell more about the present than about the past.

The book contains a bibliography and a timeline, as well as a list of Russian films at international festivals that serves to highlight Russian cinema's role on an international level. I have chosen to refrain from a filmography, as I provide full details of the films in the text.

A history of Russian cinema must begin with pre-Revolutionary cinema, which is often excluded from film histories, treated separately from the main body of Soviet film – which, it is true, advanced cinematography across the world with its revolutionary (and Revolutionary) methods of montage promoted by Vertov, Eisenstein and others. It was in the pre-Revolutionary era that Russian cinematographers were already at the forefront of discoveries, from Władysław Starewicz and his experiments in puppet animation, to Yevgeni Bauer with the magnificently decorated interiors for his melodramas. However, pre-Revolutionary cinema has been neglected in Soviet and Russian film histories and restored largely thanks to the Eighth Festival of Silent Film at Pordenone in 1989, resulting in the catalogue *Silent Witnesses*, as well as the pioneering work of Denise Youngblood, who has published widely on the cinema of this period. The restoration of old films still continues: a recent example is the restoration by film scholar Nikolai Izvolov of Lev Kuleshov's *Engineer Prite's Project* (1917) at the original projection speed.

It is usually Soviet cinema of the 1920s that is perceived in film history as the cradle of cinematic art and experiment. In the early Soviet years, the 'Kuleshov' effect described the process of conflating the meaning of images through their juxtaposition; Eisenstein developed and implemented his montage theories; the Petrograd Eccentrics (FEKS) dazzled with circus-like performances and expressive acting; and Vertov laid the foundations of documentary film art. These filmmakers (as well as others) have made a tremendous impact on the development of cinema and of film theory, even if their careers changed dramatically under the ideological constraints in Stalin's Russia of the 1930s.

'Socialist Realism', prescribing the vision of reality as progressing towards a socialist future, halted all experimentation. The constraints of Socialist Realism required filmmakers to varnish reality and show life in a positive light that would allow people to trace the path to the bright (communist) future, whilst the reality consisted of forced collectivization, famines and the Purges. At the same time, there was an appeal for 'movies for the millions' to make cinema accessible to the masses. The Soviet musical tradition of Grigori Alexandrov and Ivan Pyriev in the 1930s and 1940s responded to this call, and in no way lagged behind that of Hollywood's musicals, although the ideological message of Soviet musicals often seems quite ridiculously contrived from today's perspective. Many of these musicals remain unknown to the Western eye – only a few of the classical Soviet musical comedies are available with English subtitles.

The Second World War (or the Great Patriotic War, as it is called in Russia), the victory and the subsequent isolation of the Soviet Union during the so-called 'Cold

War', brought cultural and cinematic life almost to a standstill. Only the Thaw, announced during Khrushchev's 'Secret Speech' of 1956, could revive Soviet film art. The Socialist Realist model hero turned into a human being, and individuals in domestic settings with everyday problems returned to the screen. Above all, films that reviewed the Soviet war effort in entirely humanistic terms garnered international prizes: Kalatozov's *The Cranes Are Flying* and Chukhrai's *Ballad of a Soldier*. The re-emergence of cinema was followed by the arrival of a new generation of filmmakers and with them, of the *auteurs* of Soviet cinema, although their films soon ran into trouble with censorship. Nevertheless, Soviet cinema once again ranked highly on the international festival circuit, while Soviet art-house cinema became associated with dissident voices who preferred complex visual metaphors rather than simple and plain narratives – at a time when Socialist Realism was still the prescribed mode of creative work. Thus were the characteristic features of the films of the masters of post-war Soviet cinema: Andrei Tarkovsky, Kira Muratova, and later Alexei Gherman Senior.

The film industries in the Soviet republics blossomed during the 1960s, influenced by the great avant-garde filmmakers who had worked in cities such as Alma-Ata (Almaty) and Frunze (now Bishkek) during the wartime evacuation. Many of the national film studios began to develop their own style to tell their own (hi)stories. The 1970s saw political and cultural life stagnate as depression grew over the impossibility of change. However, in the 1980s cinema got back on its feet, starting with Menshov's Oscar-winner *Moscow Does Not Believe in Tears* and the emergence of yet another young generation of filmmakers preparing the ground for the second 'thaw': Gorbachev's glasnost and perestroika.

During the Gorbachev era international interest turned towards Soviet cinema, as numerous previously banned films were 'unshelved', shedding a new light on the horror of Stalin's Purges, but also speaking a new language about the bleakness and desperation of contemporary society, of people frustrated and crippled by years of suppression or stagnation.

With the collapse of the Soviet Union, Russian cinema underwent a turbulent period as the state-run film industry had to be transformed into a commercial industry. It was not until the late 1990s that the first signs of a new industry emerged. In the new millennium, the industry recovered once the social and economic stability of the Putin era had facilitated the growth of a solid infrastructure. Russian filmmakers could at last connect with their audiences and create a balanced diet of commercially successful and art-house films. The landmark for this resurgence of new Russian cinema was the first Russian blockbuster, *Night Watch*, which was followed by a host of commercially successful films from 2005 onwards.

This book covers the development of Russian cinema over a hundred years, from 1908 until 2008. The division into chapters is guided by the general division of Soviet history – into pre-Revolutionary Russia, the 1920s, Stalin's Russia, the Thaw, the Stagnation, Gorbachev's glasnost, the Yeltsin period, and the Putin era. However, some important dates that are pertinent to the film industry have necessitated slight modifications to this general division: thus, the chapter on early Russian cinema extends beyond the 1917 Revolution until 1919, the year of the nationalization of the industry; the chapter on the 1920s ends with the advent of sound and the establishment of Soyuzkino in 1930 as a controlling body for production and distribution; the chapter on the Thaw reaches into the Brezhnev era until the final symptoms of the end of an era became evident with the trial of Andrei Siniavsky and Yuli Daniel in 1967; and the chapter on Stagnation ends with the breakthrough of *Moscow Does Not Believe in Tears* rather than including the short terms of office of Andropov and Chernenko. The chapter on the Thaw groups films in thematic sections rather than temporal brackets to reflect the simultaneity of the diversification of cinematic styles and themes that is characteristic of the Thaw. The post-Soviet period has been divided into Yeltsin's turbulent 1990s and the Putin era because, at the time of writing, the changes in cinematic and cultural life are already significant enough to merit such a chapter organization.

The book thus ends, historically, with the election of Dmitri Medvedev as president on 2 March 2008; cinematographically it ends with the highest-grossing film so far in Russian history, *Irony of Fate: The Continuation*, which was released on New Year's Day 2008 and grossed US$50 million at the box office. In terms of cinematic history, the book marks the centenary of Russian cinema celebrated on 15 October 2008.

–1–

The Beginnings of Russian Cinema (1908–19)

> Yesterday, I was in the kingdom of the shadows. If only you knew how strange it is to be there. There are no sounds, no colours. There, everything – the earth, the trees, the people, the water, the air – is tinted in a grey monotone: in a grey sky there are grey rays of sunlight; in grey faces, grey eyes, and the leaves of the trees are grey like ashes. This is not life but the shadow of life … I must explain … I was at Aumont's café and I was watching the Lumières' cinematograph – moving photographs.
>
> Maxim Gorky, 4 July 1896[1]

This chapter looks at the impact of the new medium on Russian culture before exploring Russia's own film production begun in 1908. Until the outbreak of the First World War in 1914, Russian filmmakers explored a range of genres, from documentary to historical feature, filmed theatre, literary adaptation and animation. During the First World War the genre of melodrama dominated Russian cinema, and the chapter analyses closely the work of Yevgeni Bauer in this genre, before considering the impact of the October Revolution of 1917 on cinema.

The Arrival of the *Kinemo*, 1895–1907

Maxim Gorky's reaction to the invention of cinematography reflects the amazement, confusion and bewilderment that the new medium caused, not only in Russia. When cinema was demonstrated for the first time in France on 28 December 1895 in Paris's Grand Café, by the brothers Auguste and Louis Lumière, showing ten one-minute-long films, the new medium of the so-called cinematograph was first and foremost an 'attraction'. A few months later, as part of the Lumières' tours of their new invention across Europe and the United States, the cinematograph arrived in Russia. On 4 May 1896, the cinematograph was presented at a fairground in the Aquarium Park in St Petersburg (nowadays the territory of the city's film studio, Lenfilm). In Moscow it made its debut at a fair in the Hermitage Theatre and Gardens on 26 May. The first Russian shows featured short films made by the Lumières, including their film demonstrating the arrival of a train at a station, with passengers waiting on the platform to board the train (*Arrival of the Train at La Ciotat*, 1895), which is alleged to have inspired fear, because the train advanced from the back of the screen towards the audience, as though it could ride straight into the spectators.

The cinematograph was exhibited in Russia by Francis Doublier, a 17-year-old laboratory worker from the Lumière plant and one of the company's envoys sent out to spread the news of their invention, which consisted of an apparatus that functioned as camera and projector simultaneously. Doublier's arrival in Russia coincided with Tsar Nicholas II's coronation, scheduled for 14 May 1896, which was captured on film by the cameraman Charles Moisson, who joined Doublier for the occasion.

By March 1897 the cinematograph was touring Russian towns, acquainting the people with the new attraction and providing cheap entertainment. For the first years, thus, the cinema featured as sensation, or an attraction, for the masses. Films were mostly shown in booths at fairs and exhibitions rather than in stationary venues. In 1903 two 'electric theatres' opened in Moscow. Stationary cinemas became more widespread, thus attracting also a different audience: the urban middle class and bourgeoisie.

The Russo-Japanese War (1904–5) spread a defeatist mood in the country, which was intensified by the 1905 Revolution that further heightened the atmosphere of despair. Moreover, urbanization was increasing as famines had affected the countryside in the early 1890s, and the peasants moved to the cities in order to earn a living. The countryside was depleted of its workforce, posing further problems for agriculture. The authorities tried to stop the process of migration by imposing excessively high taxes on peasants working in the cities. In January 1905, Father Gapon led a peaceful demonstration of workers in the streets of St Petersburg, protesting against this high taxation. The tsarist officers panicked and opened fire: the crushing of this demonstration, known as Bloody Sunday, led to a wave of protests across the country, including strikes and the mutiny on the battleship *Potemkin*. That event would later make its way into cinematic history through Sergei Eisenstein's *The Battleship Potemkin* (Bronenosets Potemkin, 1925). The events of Bloody Sunday sparked the 1905 Revolution, which brought about a number of concessions, such as the introduction of democratic structures through the establishment of a parliament (Duma), whilst control over the army remained firmly in the hands of the tsar. The tsar's lethargy in undertaking substantial reforms of a political and economic scale weakened his power and gave rise to growing political opposition: assassinations were on the rise. Thus the new century saw a climate of despair at failed, but much-needed political and economic change, and of humiliation after the defeat in the Russo-Japanese War. The sense of entrapment and isolation would be intensified further through the First World War (1914–18).

Cultural life tried to deflect attention from the depressed economic and political climate of the period. The Silver Age, as the period from the 1890s to the 1910s is commonly known (with reference to the 'Golden Age' of Alexander Pushkin and Mikhail Lermontov at the beginning of the nineteenth century), dwelt on Russia's cultural glory, setting high artistic standards which opposed the growing mass entertainment that had gripped Russia in the 1890s – with cabarets, vaudevilles, circus, Petrushka's puppet theatre, fairground attractions and music-hall entertainment for the lower classes. The Silver Age was characterized by a withdrawal from reality (and the realism of nineteenth-century literature and art), searching for values elsewhere, notably in transcendental realms or other, distant cultures, as is evident in the interest in the exotic and oriental, in mysticism and symbolism. It shared with its Western counterpart, the *fin de siècle*, the interest in themes of extreme beauty combined with decay and decadence, found in Gustav Klimt's women depicted in erotic poses with such an abundance of decorative detail that the scene is almost obscured, or Aubrey Beardsley's drawings of repulsive or disturbing acts, such as the decapitation of Jokanaan in Oscar Wilde's *Salomé*, embellished with ornaments and décor to the extent that even the disembodied head appears beautiful. The erotic, beautiful feminine contains both decadent and mystical attributes – a theme that would later inspire filmmakers such as Yevgeni Bauer. Cinema here offered the possibility of creating a transition between the elitist themes and tastes of the Silver Age artists and the mass audience of popular entertainment. Thus, while cinema as an invention could attract both the common people and the tsar's family – followed by the aristocracy and bourgeoisie, cinema as an art form would also have the potential of drawing on both 'high' and 'low' art forms in forming its creative agenda, addressing the different tastes of its audiences.

At the end of the nineteenth century, France had a clear monopoly on the Russian film market. The companies Gaumont and Pathé exhibited their films, as no rental system existed. The cinema programmes usually lasted forty-five minutes, presenting a range of films; initially people could move in and out during the programme, but as time went on they had to wait for the beginning of the programme and the foyer became a necessary part of the cinema, which until then could be a makeshift installation in somebody's apartment, as was frequently the case. The attraction of the cinematograph grew rapidly: cinemas increased in number and size: seats numbered around twenty-five at the beginning and reached up to 800–1,000 by 1917. In 1908 a law established guidelines for the distance between cinemas and their number, which had reached a total of seventy-five in Moscow. By 1910 there were eighty-four cinemas in St Petersburg, rising to 130 by 1913. Before the war there were 1,400 cinemas in Russia, all with seating capacities of 300–800. In contrast to the exhibition sector, which was concentrated in St Petersburg, the production of films was centred in Moscow, the economic capital, where fifteen studios could be counted in 1913.[2] As the cinema grew from a room in a private apartment to a venue with an auditorium and a foyer, the 'electric theatre' became a venue that could break boundaries of social class, of gender and of the private and public divide. The cinema bridged the gap between high and low culture by bringing in both lower-class audiences (at fairs and in cinemas on the urban periphery) and the bourgeoisie (cinemas in the city centres); often cinemas would have boxes for the upper classes, while the stalls were reserved for the bourgeoisie and the balcony for the simple people – a division reinforced through ticket pricing.[3] Gradually, entire cinemas would have their distinct audiences composed of different classes, depending on their programmes, location and interiors – and ticket prices. New, purpose-built or specially fitted cinemas opened, such as the Kinofon in the Solodnikov Arcade in Moscow in 1903 or the Grand Parisian on Arbat and Sretenka Streets in 1906. In the same year, one of the ballrooms of the new Metropole Hotel was converted into the cinema Moderne, showing films to the upper classes. The Artistic cinema (*Khudozhestvennyi*) on Moscow's Arbat opened in 1909; it had been designed by the leading architect of the period, Fedor Shekhtel (Franz Schechtel, 1859–1926), whose art nouveau architecture has left numerous traces on the Moscow cityscape.

In the first years of cinemas, there were numerous accidents, largely because of the fire hazard of the nitrate film stock and the heat produced by the projector. In 1906 a floating cinema on the boat *Red Star* on the Volga, seating 800, went up in flames before it could be put to proper use. Another major incident was the fire in a cinema club in Bologoe (between Moscow and St Petersburg) in 1911, which led to new safety legislation. Until then, cinemas were often hastily equipped, with a few chairs and a piece of linen hung in lieu of a screen, and they would be there one day and gone the next. Cinemas suffered from unreliable electricity sources (especially outside the capital) and until 1908 oxygen burners were frequently used to supply the light bulb and the projector with electrical current, thus increasing the fire hazard and producing a flickering projection on the screen.[4] Whilst the projectionist was initially in the first row, in stationary cinemas he was moved into a (fireproof) booth at the back, thus enhancing safety. Censorship was applied only to images of the tsar (because it was unclear how they would be presented in the context of a programme), pornography and, after 1905, to demonstrations and events of the French Revolution that could lead to political agitation. The Church, opposed to the cinema in general, also restricted the demonstration of religious themes on screen.

Gradually the cinematograph could no longer rely on its sensational novelty alone, but had to present programmes with a variety of films. It was no longer sufficient to show scenes of life and have the audience admire the new technology alone. Russian audiences were perturbed to exclusively see images filmed in foreign countries instead of seeing their own culture.[5] It became clear that Russia had the potential for its own domestic production. Russia had cameras, laboratories and the facilities to make its own films, and numerous Russians had gained experience in working for the French companies with businesses in Russia.

Russian Film Production, 1907–14

The breakthrough for Russian film production came in 1907, when Alexander Drankov (1880–1949), an official Duma photographer, opened an office in St Petersburg and announced that he would make films that would offer authentic views of the country. Pathé and Gaumont immediately followed suit, opening their own production studios in Russia. Russian film production thus began on a professional level (set aside here the fact that amateur film cameras had been used since the arrival of the cinematograph by Russians, but the films were not normally shown to the public).[6] Drankov possessed enormous skills as a businessman and had a good understanding of the entertainment business and marketing. By 1908 he had produced some seventeen films, which he sold both in Russia and abroad, in a series entitled 'Picturesque Russia', offering glimpses of life in the country and thus catering for the call for images of Russia on the silver screen.[7] These short documentary films about the lives of ethnic groups, regional habits or great figures attracted audiences' curiosity.

In 1908 Drankov produced the first Russia feature film: *Stenka Razin* (Ponizovaia vol'nitsa, dir. Vladimir Romashkov, Drankov Studio) was released on 15 October 1908 – the date normally given as the birthday of Russian cinema. The film told of the popular folk hero and rebel Stenka Razin, but it focused on his emotional life: it

Figure 1.1 Poster for *Stenka Razin.*

is effectively a ballad about the drunkard Razin's infatuation with a captive, a Persian princess, who detracts his attention from the fight against oppression. Therefore, his men devise a scheme to make Razin jealous. Overcome by emotion, Razin throws his beloved overboard. The film exploits the exotic settings that were so popular in Romantic literature, capturing from a series of angles with the statically positioned camera how the boats float on the Volga as the crowd watches from the shore. This sequence of images recalled the style of images in a *lubok* (a coarse woodcut used for printing illustrated stories for the masses). The score for the film was specially composed by Mikhail Ippolitov-Ivanov; this was an outstanding innovation at the time, if we bear in mind that most cinemas of the period employed only pianists to accompany the films. The use of specially composed music highlights the importance of the occasion: the folk songs written for this first Russian film were intended for the audience to hum along to. As Yuri Tsivian has convincingly argued, pianists functioned mainly as gap-filler between the living audience and the dead screen world: 'Music made the "cold" medium inhabitable'.

> The uncanny feeling that films somehow belonged to the world of the dead was prompted by mutually contradictory signals … coming from the image. Some of them drew attention to the lifelike quality of film, others rejected life: the presence of movement made the image look strikingly lifelike, while the absence of sound and colour turned it into a haunted frame. Furthermore, the early spectator was aware of the fact that the fleeting moment on screen was in fact something that could be endlessly repeated, and this awareness helped to project the picture into eternity. A game on film turned into a game in the world of the dead.[8]

Russian film production soared and new companies emerged. The Baltic-German Paul Thiemann (Pavel Timan, 1881–?) had worked for the Russian arm of Gaumont until he left the company in 1909 to set up his own studio, together with the tobacco merchant Friedrich Reinhardt, who brought in the capital. Thiemann & Reinhardt first distributed films made by the Danish Nordisk, the Italian Ambrosio and the American Vitagraph companies, before producing its own films. To this end, Thiemann hired directors such as the former army officer and amateur actor Vladimir Gardin (1877–1965) and Yakov Protazanov (1881–1945); the latter had spent time in Paris after inheriting a large sum of money and had subsequently worked for Pathé in Moscow. Both directors left the studio when the anti-German campaigns made business difficult for Thiemann during the war; Thiemann subsequently hired Viacheslav Viskovsky (1881–1933), Vladimir Uralsky (1887–1955) and Vsevolod Meyerhold (1874–1940). Moreover, Grigori Libken, the owner of a sausage factory in Yaroslavl, began to buy, collect and rent films, setting up one of the first Russian 'film exchanges' where films could be leased for theatrical display by cinemas.

The former army captain Alexander Khanzhonkov (1877–1945) opened his trading company in 1908; by 1912 he had transformed it into a stock company, the first of its kind in Russia. Khanzhonkov competed with Drankov until the latter retired from film production temporarily between 1910 and 1913, when he joined forces with the entrepreneur Alexei Taldykin and his costume firm. Khanzhonkov's role for Russian film production is unique in that he skilfully recruited young Russian talents – directors, designers, animators and actors, and made films that aimed at an aesthetic development of cinema. His first production, *The Gypsy Camp* (Drama v tabore, directed and filmed by Vladimir Siversen, Khanzhonkov 1908), was a documentary-style film with real gypsies performing the story of an attempted abduction from a gypsy camp – with local colour and exoticism in abundance. *A Sixteenth-Century Russian Wedding* (Russkaia svad'ba XVI stoletiia, Khanzhonkov 1908) was directed by Vasili Goncharov (1861–1915) and filmed by Siversen; it captured the ancient forms of the wedding ritual, re enacted by Alexandra Goncharova (1888–?) and Andrei Gromov (1883–?).

In response to Drankov and Khanzhonkov, Pathé Moscow produced a film on the Don Cossacks to compete in – and conquer – the Russian market with a domestic product. Subsequently Pathé embarked on its own series of films about 'Picturesque Russia'. Moreover, Pathé drew on the French practice of showing famous actors in the cinema, and introduced the *film d'art* to Russia, first in its French form and later in a Russified version: for the Russian operation, André Maître and the Franco-Dane Kai Hansen directed films in Russia for Pathé and began to recruit a Russian crew. Pathé's first Russian-produced films, released in 1909 and directed by Hansen and Goncharov, dealt with historical figures such as Dmitri Donskoi and Peter the Great.[9] One of the films of this series is *Princess Tarakanova* (Kniazhna Tarakanova, dir. Hansen and Maître, Pathé Moscow 1910), a dramatized historical event. Count Orlov, adviser to Catherine the Great, suspects the princess of laying claim to the throne. The princess is arrested, incarcerated, and dies in her dungeon. The typically static camera captures movements within the frame, but the stunning contrast of light and dark is used skilfully for psychological ends: darkness reigns for the prison scenes and increases with the fatal ending. The emotional world of the characters is reflected in the world that surrounds them. The directors used the device of introducing the characters at the beginning of the film, hinting at the growing importance of actors' faces for the cinema. Moreover, special attention was paid to the sets, which were built by the production designer Cheslav Sabinsky (1885–1941), a set designer at the prestigious and innovative Moscow Art Theatre (headed by the pioneer of psychological stage acting, Konstantin Stanislavsky and founded in 1898), who tried to move away from flat and painted sets towards sets with proportion, depth and real objects. The film reveals the reliance on the fixed position of the camera, where close-ups were perceived as vulgar, since they left no distance between the face on the screen and the viewer. The close-up was used only towards the second half of the 1910s, when the audience had got accustomed to the proximity of the screen. Likewise, the trailing or tracking shot was avoided for psychological rather than technical reasons, as it could potentially disorientate the viewer. Lateral tracking was gradually and slowly introduced, and films relied instead on crosscutting (for example, from speaker to listener and back) to give depth to the narrative.

So far cinema had chronicled events, shown episodes from the lives of historical figures, or taken the role of an ethnographer exploring the habits and ways of life of other people. Dramatized historical events, such as *Princess Tarakanova*, were the first step towards telling longer stories, before cinema turned to classical literature and began to illustrate literary plots: the adaptation, or *ekranizatsiia*, was born. The Russian classics, ghost stories and romantic tales proved especially popular, partly because they were well known and partly because there was no need to obtain consent from the author. Moreover, none of these published works aroused the attention of the censor, who disliked contemporary events as they could cause turmoil. The most popular adaptations were based on the works of Alexander Pushkin, Nikolai Gogol, and Anton Chekhov.

The dark, mystic and supernatural that had inspired Romanticism formed a fascinating theme for cinema. The folk legend 'Rusalka', rendered in a poetic version by Pushkin, tells the story of a miller's daughter who is seduced and abandoned by a prince, on whom she takes revenge as a water spirit when he returns years later. *Rusalka* (dir. Vasili Goncharov, Khanzhonkov 1910) consists of two parts: the first sees the miller's daughter fall for the prince, who is forced to marry another woman. Eight years lapse until the prince returns: the miller's daughter, who turned into a water spirit (a *rusalka*) after taking her own life, seduces him, with her fellow spirits, to the bottom of the River Dnepr. The ballet-like movements of the water nymphs as they lured the prince to the other world lent themselves to filmic presentation; moreover, the supernatural and folk elements were highly suitable for the interest in the non-real that characterized a period marked with the hardship of everyday life and the collapse of an entire value system. The use of inter-titles was crucial for the understanding of temporality in this film (the eight-year lapse), and would become instrumental in describing events in those years. Later titles would render the narrative through snippets of dialogue. Pushkin's story 'The Queen of Spades' (Pikovaia dama, 1834) was penetrated by the supernatural and was adapted by Petr Chardynin (1873–1934) for Khanzhonkov in 1910, starring Gromov and Goncharova.

The supernatural also extended to the contemporary world, as shown in *The Secret of House No. 5* (Taina doma no. 5, dir. Hansen, Pathé 1912) which explores the *ménage à trois* of the courtesan Else, her gentleman-lover Darsky and their friend Wechsel. When Darsky falls for another woman, Else and Wechsel – inspired by a newspaper report – devise a punishment for Darsky: at a party they speak about a house inhabited by a ghost and provoke Darsky to announce that this is all nonsense and that he will stay in the house to disprove the story. In the house, Else poses as a living portrait and steps from her frame to scare Darsky (production design by Cheslav Sabinsky), while Wechsel robs and shoots him, masking the murder as suicide. Suspense is created through crosscutting between the room where Wechsel and Elsa prepare the plot and the room where Darsky spends the night, although the film discloses the supernatural and the ghost theme as human invention. The supernatural is no longer the result of folk beliefs, but instead cinema uncovers the ploys and tricks behind supernatural stories.

In adapting literature, filmmakers were often inspired by poems of themes from the classics. *The Brigand Brothers* (Brat'ia razboiniki, dir. Vasili Goncharov, Khanzhonkov 1912) was based on a poem by Pushkin. The film used a flashback to invest the main character with additional psychological depth. In a tavern a brigand (Arseni Bibikov) tells the story of his life: the ensuing flashback serves to explain the current state of the brigand. He and his younger brother (Ivan Mozzhukhin) were orphaned, but the children found a new master and both fell in love with the master's daughter. They were chased away when a calf was trampled to death as a result of the younger brother's negligence. The daughter follows them, and so does the master. In a scuffle, the elder brother kills the master. Thereafter the brothers wander through the land and become robbers; the elder brother often murdered his victims. When the younger brother dies, the elder shows mercy to his old victims. The film created a psychological portrait of a man of the lower echelons of society and showed his downfall into a criminal life. Society of the time offered no scope for social mobility: orphaned children were simply left to fend for themselves. Films begin to address issues of social injustice, as is also evident in *The Daughter-in-Law's Lover* (Snokhach, dir. Alexander Ivanov-Gai and Petr Chardynin, Khanzhonkov 1912), which deals with the practice of fathers or fathers-in-law sexually abusing their daughters and daughters-in-law. Ivan (Mozzhukhin) and his wife Lusha lead a quiet life, but Ivan's father (Bibikov) forces himself on Lusha. When she gets pregnant, she hangs herself out of shame. The film tells, on the one hand, the tragic fate of a young woman. On the other, it addresses a social malpractice that was often quietly tolerated in the countryside. These films also see one of the first stars of early Russian cinema appear on the billboard: Ivan Mozzhukhin (spelling his name as Mosjoukine after his emigration to France, 1889–1939).

Before the rise of the actor as star of the silver screen, however, Khanzhonkov ventured on the first large-scale historical epic on celluloid and the first full-length Russian feature: *The Defence of Sevastopol* (Oborona Sevastopol'ia) was premiered in 1912. A former army captain from a Cossack family, Khanzhonkov possessed enough skills and expertise to command armies of actors in the scenes that re-enacted the battle of Sevastopol, that brave act where the Russian army defended the city against the Allied forces during the Crimean War – and suffered a terrible defeat (1854–5). Moreover, he had enlisted competent consultants who turned the film into a powerful chronicle of events, and the experienced cameramen Alexander Ryllo and Louis Forestier.

Russian cinema had explored the genres of documentary, historical accounts and epics, and literary adaptation. Before becoming a fully-fledged artistic medium it had to assimilate two further important genres: comedy and melodrama. The length of early films (lasting around ten minutes) lent itself to the genre of the comic sketch. Such sketches were produced early in Russia's cinema history, but they would gain even more importance after the Revolution when they developed into the form of agitational sketches (*agitka*) that were used for Revolutionary propaganda (see Chapter 2). In the 1910s these short – and longer – sketches entertained the audiences with situational comedy, as *Romance with Double Bass* (Roman s kontrabasom, dir. Kai Hansen, Pathé 1911), based on a story by Anton Chekhov. It is set in the countryside, where first a bass player and then a lady have their clothes stolen by some ruffians while swimming in a lake. A true gentlemen, the bass player offers the lady his bass case to hide in, but as he goes to find help, the case is found and transported to its destination: a concert hall in the nearby town. Here it is opened – and an embarrassed lady in her swimming costume climbs from the case. Similarly, *The House in Kolomna* (Domik v Kolomne, dir. Chardynin, Khanzhonkov 1913) is a comic sketch about a man who cross-dresses and disguises himself as a female cook in order to be close to his girlfriend, who works as a maid in a household under the supervision of an old and strict housekeeper. The success of these comic films led several studios to promote their leading comedians: Khanzhonkov promoted Arkasha (Arkadi Boitler) and Drankov marketed Antosha (Anton Fertner). *Antosha Ruined by a Corset* (Antosha korset pogubil, dir. Eduard Puchaski, Lucifer 1916) showed husband Antosha's repeated attempts to get rid of a corset forgotten in his flat after a party he held in his wife's absence.

The concern with emotional dramas of young women forced to sacrifice their love for the sake of arranged marriages became a dominant theme in early Russian cinema, although the genre of melodrama would flourish fully in the films of Yevgeni Bauer (1865–1917). *The Peasant Lot* (Krestianskaia dolia, dir. Goncharov, Khanzhonkov 1912) explores the impossibility of love for a young peasant woman. During an idyllic harvest scene Masha (Alexandra Goncharova) and Petr (Mozzhukhin) are introduced: they are in love, and the parents consent to the marriage. Then fate strikes a harsh blow: the house of Masha's parents burns down and the marriage is called off as the girl has lost her dowry. Masha finds work as a maid in town. Surprisingly, she is no stranger to high-society life: just like the two ladies of the house, she too looks at her appearance in the mirror and imitates their demeanour. Neither is Masha the naive country girl who is easily duped and abused by her master: she fends off his advances. In crosscutting to Masha's home, the viewer sees the hardship her parents suffer in the aftermath of the fire. At the same time, Goncharov shows Masha's emotional turmoil by illustrating her thoughts. He thus provides a psychological motivation for Masha's next action: to surrender to the landlord's advances for a large sum of money, which she takes back to her parents. However, her love for Petr, who is now married to a harsh and unkind woman, is irretrievably lost: Masha marries an old man. Although the film closes with a harvest scene that brings together the peasant community, things are no longer as idyllic as they appeared at the beginning. The circumstances of peasant life are stifling.

An influential film, although made outside Moscow (in Rostov) is *The Merchant Bashkirov's Daughter* (Doch kuptsa Bashkirova, aka Drama na Vol'ge, dir. Nikolai Larin, Libken 1913), which also tells of marriages arranged for financial benefit and of the impossibility of romantic love. The merchant's daughter Nadia loves a young man, the clerk Yegorushka, but her father must not know: he has arranged for Nadia to marry a rich merchant, whom she does not love. Nadia's mother helps the girl meet with her lover in secret – a famous frame shows them embracing while they stand in an archway overlooking the river and the town. They break the moral rules of the time. When Nadia's father returns home unexpectedly, the two women hide Yegor under a mattress, where he tragically asphyxiates. The women ask a peasant to help dispose of the body, which is dumped into the river in a barrel. However, the peasant blackmails Nadia, demanding jewels and later raping her. Nadia overhears him boast of the rape in the tavern; she locks the rapist and his audience in the tavern and sets it on fire. The film, allegedly based on a real story (therefore the title had to be changed to *Drama on the Volga*), uses a provincial setting to provide a comment on the predicament of women in society: Nadia is unable to make her own decisions and run her life; her mother is stifled by her husband. The changing role of women in society, and society's attitude towards women, is perhaps one of the most significant themes in early Russian cinema. When cinema moves its plots to the cities, it brings the women's question much closer to the majority of Russian audiences, with films such as *The Wet Nurse* (Kormilitsa, dir. Chardynin, Khanzhonkov 1914), which explores the fate of the maid Duniasha, who is seduced by the master's son, Georgi. Their affair is betrayed and Dunia is fired and rejected by her family. She earns a living as a wet nurse – for Georgi's child from a marriage with a noblewoman. When Duniasha confides in the infant's mother, the noblewomen leaves her unfaithful husband. *The Wet Nurse* is untypical for the time in that the film sees justice done, and has a happy ending for the poor maid. It gives women the chance of an independent life – at least if they are noblewomen.

The two-part film *The Keys to Happiness* (Kliuchi schast'ia, dir. Gardin and Protazanov, 1913), based on Anastasia Verbitskaya's best-seller, told of a new woman, Mania, who tries to navigate the new world and ends up killing herself. This popular film set the template for the new woman who either failed in the world that surrounds her, or else was not understood and appreciated by men who refuse to accept change, a model that would play a significant role later.

As cinema was exploring the various genres possible in documentary and artistic films, the art of animation arrived in Moscow's Khanzhonkov studio. In 1912 Khanzhonkov brought to Moscow Władysław Starewicz (1882–1965), who had attracted attention as designer and photographer in his native Kovno (now the Lithuanian Kaunas, then Poland). Starewicz made a series of feature films for Khanzhonkov, but he gained even wider acclaim as the master of puppet animation. His animated films, such as *The Cameraman's Revenge* (Mest' kinematograficheskogo operatora, Khanzhonkov 1912), *The Dragonfly and the Ant* (Strekoza i muravei,

Khanzhonkov 1913), and the part-animated, part live-action film *The Lily of Belgium* (Liliia Bel'gii, Skobelev Committee 1915), were parables of modern life set in the world of insects and flowers. Moreover, they were fine and subtle parodies and satires on the dominant cinematic genres of the time, from melodrama to costume spectacle.

Starewicz's interest in filming insects, first in documentaries and then in the form of puppets, turning them into anthropomorphic figures with clear human features, made his art innovative and ahead of his time. In *The Cameraman's Revenge*, he set a tale of marital relations in the world of beetles, among the characters of Mr and Mrs Zhukov (*zhuk* means 'beetle'). Starewicz endowed the insects with human agility and emotions, thus abstracting a tale of adultery and making it laughable rather than condemnable, because it pertains not to the world of human civilization. The moral codes of both worlds condemn adultery, but the setting in a non-human world distances the tale. The betrayed beetle-husband takes his beetle-wife to the cinema, having forgiven her affair with a painter; they see a film about an unfaithful husband – Mister Zhuk. The husband with high moral demands on his wife has himself committed adultery. Starewicz's *The Dragonfly and the Ant*, based on Ivan Krylov's fable, exposes the laborious ant as the responsible working creature and contrasts it with the lazy, bohemian dragonfly, who entertains and plays all summer but starves in winter as it has neither supplies nor the support of the animal community. Starewicz's puppet animation created human movement with insect figures, and reduced human emotions to a puppet-house world that made them laughable by inverting the visual enlargement (close-up) of human emotions on the silver screen.

Starewicz's *The Lily of Belgium*, made for the Skobelev Committee (established in 1914 for the production of films to support the war effort), is a more reality-grounded film: it tells in drawn animated images the story told to a little girl by her grandfather after she has plucked a lily. The film's inset drawn images thus illustrate the girl's imagination during her grandfather's narrative. In this early piece, the role that animation could play is defined in a precise manner: to render the rich and colourful images of children's imagination and fairy-tale worlds. *The Lily* also makes clear the educational potential of the animated film: after the instructive story, the girl kisses the lily on its stem the next time she is in the garden, and neither plucks it nor removes it from its root. The girl has learnt to observe the rule of nature and respect the flower, which symbolizes peace in the grandfather's tale, which links the destruction of nature with the horrific images of the First World War.

The Art and Commerce of Cinema

Once Russian film production had been fully established, the public interest in cinema increased and a critical debate began about the art form labelled the 'tenth muse'. Cinema's role was discussed in particular in relation to the theatre. The interest in cinema by leading writers and playwrights of the time was used as a gauge to measure cinema's value. Leonid Andreev and Lev Tolstoy were cited, and Tolstoy's appearance on screen served as an endorsement of the 'tenth muse' – despite his wife's initial outrage at Protazanov's film, which she perceived as a caricature. *The Passing of the Grand Old Man* (Ukhod velikogo startsa, dir. Yakov Protazanov and Yelizaveta Thiemann, Thiemann & Reinhardt 1912) captured the figure of Lev Tolstoy on celluloid, combining documentary footage with re-enactment of his last days.

The psychologism of the Russian theatre school dominated early Russian cinema's acting techniques as well as the structure of films, as is evident in such psychological dramas as *The Brigand Brothers*. Therefore the relationship between literature and the writer on the one hand, and the new medium of cinema on the other, informed many programmatic statements by leading literary figures of the time.

The writer Leonid Andreev, an ardent supporter of the cinematograph, delineated cinema from theatre with the words 'The great cinema! … It copes with everything, conquers everything, conveys everything. There is only one thing that it does not convey and that is words, and there lies the limit to its power, the boundary of its might.'[10] Cinema allowed the capture of reality in an authentic, truthful and realistic way and as accurately as possible. In this sense, cinema could do more than theatre, whose power relied on words. However, the discourses of the avant-garde artists, such as the poet Vladimir Mayakovsky or the theatre director Vsevolod Meyerhold, were less concerned in their assessment with the new cinematic medium than with theatre: they compared film and theatre to draw attention to the need for theatre to reform, to define its remit, to stop attempting to convey a photographic image of reality. Instead of shackling the actor in a set overburdened with realistic detail, theatre should leave realism to the cinematograph and focus on the theatrical art: 'Theatre has brought itself to ruin and must bequeath its inheritance to cinema. But cinema, which has made naive realism and artistic quality into a branch of industry like Chekhov and Gorky, is opening the way to the theatre of the future, the unshackled art of the actor' (Mayakovsky, 27 July 1913).[11] The hyper-realism of the image – with its great detail that is not focused on one aspect of reality as is, for example, the painting (which selects) – provides too much information and leads to confusion: 'The image was too perfect to be true'.[12] Whilst warning the cinema against imitating the theatre, as it had done in some early films that captured stage performances on film, Meyerhold emphasized that cinema should find its own language – something he hoped to do with his first feature film *The Portrait of Dorian Gray* (Meyerhold 31 May 1915).[13] This film (which is not preserved) is described in terms of 'bold black-and-white masses' and striking contrasts: 'One of the most vividly original episodes was a scene from *Romeo and Juliet* shown as reflected in the large mirror of the loge behind the watching Dorian.'[14] This indicates Meyerhold's concern with expressive devices to render a character's state of mind, a method he would develop in his theatre after the Revolution.

By the mid-1910s cinema was still struggling to establish itself as an art form rather than purely commercial entertainment, and it was through art films that it could prove its status. In France the cinema had, in the so-called *film d'art*, drawn on well-known stage actors. Khanzhonkov first showed these films in Russia and scored an immediate success. In early cinema (1908–12) the majority of films were documentaries and only a third were acted; of the art films 53 per cent were adaptations, 26 per cent historical, 13 per cent melodramas and 8 per cent comedies.[15] The foreign detective series, such as *Fantômas* (Louis Feuillade, Gaumont 1913–4) with its pursuits and adventures, disguises and criminal violence, *Nick Carter* (Victorin Jasset, Eclair 1908–9) and *Zigomar* (Jasset, Eclair 1911), or *Nat Pinkerton* (Pierre Bressol, Eclair 1912–14) proved immensely popular and vouched for the serial form as a way of continually drawing audiences. Thus, the adventure series *Sonka Golden Hands* (Son'ka – zolotaia ruchka, Drankov, eight parts, 1914–16) exploited the serial form for Russia and combined it successfully with the adventure genre in episodes about the thief Sonia Bliuvshtein. Drankov, and later Libken, catered largely for second-rank cinemas, providing entertainment for the masses; they continued in these serials the *lubok* style of early Russian cinema, where the screen events are coarse illustrations of a simple story made for attraction and amazement.[16]

The imported *films d'art* brought to Russia the first foreign stars, focusing the audience's attention on the actor: the French comedian Max Linder, the Danish actress Asta Nielsen from the Royal Theatre Copenhagen, the Dane Valdemar Psilander (with the nickname 'Garrison'), and later the Polish ballerina Apołonia Chałupiec, who gained fame working with Ernst Lubitsch under her assumed name Pola Negri (1897–1987). However, Russian actors and actresses of the imperial theatres were not allowed to act in cinema, and the screen was therefore taken largely by lesser-known second- and third-rate actors.[17] Thus the reputation of a stage star could not assist the promotion of a film in the early years of cinema. However, cinema quickly created its own stars. Ivan Mozzhukhin became a name that guaranteed success for Khanzhonkov until he left for Ermoliev in 1916. Leyda argues that Vladimir Maximov (1880–1937) made a career largely because he was seen as a copy of Psilander[18] and, considering Maximov's roles after the Revolution (he left cinema in 1920s for the stage), Leyda's suspicion may well be correct.

In 1914, Iosif Ermoliev (1889–1962) produced his first film. From a merchant family, Ermoliev had studied and worked in the finance section of Pathé Moscow before venturing into film production on his own. Under his elephant logo he managed to assemble the leading directors and actors of the time: Protazanov and Mozzhukhin, as well as Olga Gzovskaya (1889–1962), an actress of the Maly Theatre and later primadonna of the Moscow Art Theatre,[19] who first appeared in cinema in 1915 and joined Ermoliev from 1916–18 when she left, with Vladimir Gaidarov (1893–1976), to go to the Rus Studio before both emigrated to Berlin in 1920. After their return to the Soviet Union in 1932, Gzovskaya was banned from

Figure 1.2 Building of the Khanzhonkov Studio.

working on the stage and only had a few film roles. Upon his return, Gaidarov worked at the Pushkin Theatre (formerly the Alexandrinsky) in Leningrad. Both fates are indicative of the harmful effect that a stay abroad had on people's lives during the 1930s, as will be discussed in Chapter 3.

By 1915 Khanzhonkov had developed his studio into one of the leading ventures in pre-Revolutionary Russia: he had hired the directors Petr Chardynin and Yevgeni Bauer, and kept some fifty actors and five cameramen on the payroll; his studio had affiliations all over Russia. His greatest coups were the recruitment of the ballerina Vera Karalli (1889–1972), who came to the cinema after an injury on stage (and emigrated in 1918); and the silent film star Vera Kholodnaya (née Levchenko, 1893–1919). However, Mozzhukhin left Khanzhonkov in 1916 for Ermoliev's studio when Chardynin cast another actor in a role he wanted. Russian cinema was growing both as an art and as an industry when the First World War struck.

From War to Revolution, Entertainment to Agitation, 1914–17

In July 1914, Austria-Hungary and Germany declared war on Russia. By 1915 defeats abounded and the frontiers were closed for trade. This meant the closure of foreign film distribution offices in Russia, and ultimately a shortage of film stock, which had been imported from Germany. The war also led to a crisis in imports of foreign films, because film contained nitrate and was thus classified as strategic commodity. Pathé closed its Russian office in 1915 as rising anti-German sentiments led to houses being set on fire, and Thiemann – with a German-sounding name – came into a precarious position, while his business partner Reinhardt left Russia.

The rare foreign imports (facilitated by Ermoliev's company, for example) were the preferred viewing of the upper classes: almost 80 per cent of films shown prior to 1914 had been foreign. During the war, Russian film production increased along with the proportion of Russian films shown in cinemas.

When Protazanov joined Ermoliev, he developed his potential as director. His outstanding work with actors is evident in his adaptation of *The Queen of Spades* for Ermoliev's studio in 1916. The role of Hermann was played by Mozzhukhin – by 1916 the leading star of Russian cinema. Protazanov employed flashbacks and visions to present the narrative in a non-linear manner, as a complex psychological web with insights into the characters' minds. In the tradition of Russian theatre, which dwelt on the relevance of the psychological motivation for the character, early cinema too began to rely heavily on psychology and motivation for action. When the gamblers toast, there is a flashback to the countess's youth in Paris, where she lost a huge sum of money and her husband refused to pay up; the flashback continues to show how the Count Saint-Germain told her the secret of the three cards that she must play to win and pay off the debt. In the flashback, Protazanov carefully juxtaposed the frilly and ornamental style of Louis XV's France with the ascetic style of Nicholas I. He also used a spliced frame for Hermann's vision of the gambling table as he is in the countess's house trying to extract the secret from her, thus underlining his split personality. Or he would use unusual camera positions, for example filming Hermann from Liza's window as he stands and waits outside her house; or following Hermann and filming from behind. Finally, the portrait of the countess merges with the image of a playing card as her portrait on the wall turns into a spade. Thus Protazanov enshrined several typical features of early Russian cinema in this film: the use of flashbacks to create depth of character, and the psychology-driven narrative for cinema. *Queen of Spades* is also a good example of the development of the genre of literary adaptations in a relatively short space of time. Protazanov continued making highly successful adaptations of the classics, such as *War and Peace* (Voina i mir, directed with V. Gardin, 1915) and *Nikolai Stavrogin* (1915), starring Ivan Mozzhukhin.

The war situation imbued the country with a depressive atmosphere as the Russian army suffered defeats. At home, the assassination of Rasputin in 1916 showed the beginning of mistrust in the imperial family, leading ultimately to the abdication of the tsar in 1917, which destroyed the 'empire' both physically and symbolically.

Production companies began to deflect from the war reality by focusing on melodramas centred on women and by adapting literature. The unhappy endings, which were so typical of Russian melodramas of the period, may be interpreted in terms of genre, but they were also an indirect reflection of a reality where women lost their men in the war. The melodrama was an emotionalized version of coping with the new role of women. Culturally, the decadence of the Silver Age period contributed to the key function that the 'new woman' assumed on screen. But the period also saw the rise of primitivism and abstract art (cubism and futurism),

Figure 1.3 Ivan Mozzhukhin as Hermann in Protazanov's *Queen of Spades*.

fragmenting a static or mobile reality into geometrical forms. These avant-garde art forms stood in sharp contrast to the melodramas that were obsessed with wealth and property, with emotion and *byt* (everyday life), just as in the post-Revolutionary period constructivism and montage would oppose the realist fashion of linear narratives.

Mirages (Mirazhi, dir. Chardynin, Khanzhonkov 1915) was one such film of a 'new woman'. Marianna (played by Vera Kholodnaya) is a young woman with artistic talent who reads books to the millionaire Dymov (Bibikov). When Marianna meets his son (Vitold Polonsky, 1879–1919), she is gradually more and more drawn away from her safe home and her fiancée Sergei towards the 'dark forces' of the artistic, Bohemian world: Marianna gives in to Dymov Jr. and when he drops her, it is too late: rejected by her family, she kills herself. The film followed the typical pattern for early Russian melodramas: a woman is lured into a different life and finds herself exploited and rebuked by that new way of life, ending up as a social outcast and belonging neither to the old (her family) nor the aspired, new society as represented by capital and the liberal arts.

Yevgeni Bauer and the Melodrama, 1913–17

The uncontested master of melodrama and of films about the predicament of women was Yevgeni Bauer, without doubt one of Europe's best directors of the era. Bauer was working with Khanzhonkov when he discovered Kholodnaya among the extras and gave her the lead in *Song of Triumphant Love*. He later also cast the ballerina Vera Karalli, and brought to the screen Mozzhukhin's wife Natalia Lisenko (1880–1969, emigrated in 1920), Vladimir Maximov, and Vitold Polonsky. Bauer attempted to render the inside world of characters through visions and dream sequences, rather than through flashbacks, to provide explanations and motives, and therefore did not depend on a psychological acting style.

Bauer's melodramas captured the decadent lifestyle of the time and dwelt on psychological rather than physical action, upon which American cinema was based. The importance of production design for Bauer (and his frequent collaborator Sabinsky) was crucial; indeed, Bauer had trained as painter and set designer under Shekhtel (the architect of the *Khudozhestvennyi* cinema). Both Bauer and Sabinsky wanted to move away from flat, painted sets towards three-dimensional spaces that would convey volume. Bauer was obsessed with decorative columns and curtains that created depth, and with staircases that would create a sense of height. Bauer's sets were artistically arranged, placing doors or windows at the back of the traditional box set and breaking up the rectangular space with statues, columns and staircases. He deployed carefully chosen accessories of modern life, from phones, clock and lamps to cars and trains; thus, a wristwatch sported by a woman signalled her emancipation. The excessive use of objects is indicative of the luxurious lifestyle of his fictional characters, displaying their wealth in the same way that aristocrats had some of their possessions painted in portraits and still lifes to capture their property on canvas. It is almost as though Bauer was fixating for posterity the wealth and lifestyle of a passing epoch.

Bauer's first film, *The Twilight of a Woman's Soul* (Sumerki zhenskoi dushi, dir. Bauer, 1913), picks up the theme of marriage and rape, of a woman's status in society defined through marriage and her fall through male violence, from the earlier film *Drama on the Volga*. The young countess Vera (Nina Chernova) leads a protected life, but wishes to help the poor: for this purpose she leaves her safe home and visits, among others, the ruffian Maxim Petrov. He lures her into his abode and rapes her; then Vera kills him. Rachel Morley has astutely commented on the

Figure 1.4 Yevgeni Bauer.

role of Vera as an 'urban Little Red Riding Hood', who visits the wild barbarians with a basket of medicine.[20] Vera ventures into another world and kills the wolf as he tries to devour her, but the film does not find the happy ending of the fairy tale. Vera marries Prince Dolsky, but when she tells him about her past, he blames her for the rape in a way that shows the rigid and stale social conventions of the time. Vera leaves Dolsky and becomes an opera singer. One day, Dolsky sees her on stage under her new name, Ellen Kay (a Western name suggesting the lifestyle of an emancipated woman), performing in *La Traviata*, but when he approaches her, she refuses to take him back. Dolsky kills himself. Apart from the use of angles (for example to underscore the imminent danger as Vera approaches Maxim's abode), the film highlights Bauer's concern with depth of the set through the use of curtains which provide perspective, but also have the symbolic function of showing Vera's seclusion from reality at the beginning and her gradual venturing into the outside world. Moreover, Vera is a strong woman who takes action (she kills Petrov) and who is capable of telling her husband about her disgrace. When it turns out that Dolsky is imprisoned in old values, Vera leaves him – for a new life. She is perfectly capable of leading a life without a man in the world of high arts. The strong woman moves into a new social age, while the man stays behind: he appears too weak to accept the new role of women. As Louise McReynolds has argued, 'The essence of melodrama is not so much that it rewards virtue as that it exposes evil in the moral universe constructed by daily life'.[21]

These Russian melodramas juxtapose the new, emancipated woman who strives for a full and independent social life with the old-fashioned men who view women as an object of beauty and decorum. Once women depart from the assigned role, men are scared and appear weak when confronted with female activity. This pattern applies to a number of films of the era, such as Bauer's *Child of the Big City* (Ditia bol'shogo goroda, dir. Bauer, 1914), which features not an aristocratic, but a lower-class heroine, one of those women who 'try to use men to escape their tedious lives'.[22] Maria's (Mania's) mother dies of consumption in a filthy basement, an opening sequence that gives an impressive idea of the living standards of the working class in Russia. Nine years later Mania (Yelena Smirnova) has become a seamstress who is often caught daydreaming, an activity rendered cinematically by having her look out on to the Moscow streets; likewise Mania enjoys window-shopping. The gentleman Viktor Kravtsov (Mikhail Salarov) longs for an unspoilt, different kind of woman companion: together with a friend he inspects photos of women. The use of photographs to evaluate women's beauty reflects the extent to which women were objectified: the photo captured a static image that the moving camera would bring to life: here, cinema uses photographs to make a critical comment on the old medium that froze life in an immobile view. In the street Viktor and his friend invite Mania to a restaurant: her behaviour at the table marks her different social class. But Mania quickly adapts to the new lifestyle and turns into Mary (another Western name used to indicate a transformation); she soon appears in extravagant dresses and moves elegantly in Viktor's circles. Mary dances a tango – a dance shown here for the first time on Russian screen;[23] she flirts and stretches on the chaise longue. Her financial needs, however, soon exceed Viktor's possibilities and leave him financially ruined. The new woman can climb the social ladder through men, but she can also bring about a man's downfall. When Viktor suggests that they go away and live modestly, Mary responds that, if he cannot afford her, he should find another woman. Love may not have been on the cards in arranged marriages, but it is also not the motivation for the new woman to live with a man. Viktor, however, loves Mary and is plagued by the pain of loss: Bauer equips him with a psychological dimension through visions of Mary in another man's arms. Viktor cannot bear this and, as Mary looks at herself in the mirror while flirting with her new lover, Viktor enters the room and fires at her – but hits his own reflection in the mirror: Viktor hates himself, not Mary. A year later, Viktor lives in a small, dark room and wears a shabby coat. Viktor makes a last attempt to see her: he crosses a bridge (physically and symbolically between the worlds of poverty and money) with the Cathedral of Christ the Saviour looming in the distance. Upon receiving a note of his arrival, Mary sends him three roubles and refuses to receive him. Viktor kills himself on the steps of her house. Another man has fallen victim to a woman's whims and passions. But Mary then has the arrogance and cold-heartedness to step over his body to go to Maxim's restaurant, with the words that 'Meeting with the dead brings happiness'. In *Child of the Big City*, Mania-Mary adapts to the rules of high society, making use of men to climb the social ladder; she is also a femme fatale or a vamp who sucks the blood from the weaker man to advance in society. Bauer's sets juxtapose the world of poverty (the basement, Viktor's poor room), with that of glamour and high society, where the interiors are overburdened with detail and objects, thus showing the seductive effect of luxury.

In *Silent Witnesses* (Nemye svideteli, dir. Bauer, 1914), Bauer juxtaposed the urban and rural way of life, and offered an insight into the cross-section of the house, from servant quarters downstairs to private rooms upstairs, and complete with a doorman at the public entrance. The Kostritsyns' maid Varia wants to go back home to her husband and children, but Kostritsyna refuses to let Varia go, as she is about to depart for the Crimea and needs the maid to look after her son, Pavel. The doorman's granddaughter Nastia (Dora Chitorina), a young and curious woman who observes the life upstairs attentively, agrees to take Varia's place. She notices Pavel's love for Ellen, who is indifferent towards Pavel as she has an affair with Baron von Roehren. When Pavel is distraught, Nastia comforts him; when he is sick, she calls Ellen. Whilst Ellen rebukes Pavel, Nastia tries to get rid of a suitor in the kitchen: Bauer thus juxtaposes amorous relationships on the upstairs/downstairs level with the servants echoing the love life of their masters. This allows him to make effective use of the staircase, one of Bauer's favourite decorative elements. When Nastia comforts the drunken Pavel, who gets her drunk as well, he seduces her. Forced by her father to marry Pavel Kostritsyn, Ellen continues her affair with the baron under Pavel's nose. Nastia, who has fallen in love with Pavel, watches with sadness. Nastia represents moral order in a decadent society where extramarital affairs are the order of the day and marriages are arranged for financial reason only. Nastia's love for Pavel is also a sign of her aspirations to higher society. Bauer creates three interior spaces: the entrance hall to the Kostritsyns' apartment, with the front door and the staircase as exits and entrances that link inside and outside spaces; the servants' quarters with a staircase at the back that leads to the 'upstairs' world, and a door at the side for exit and entrance to the street; and the Kostritsyns' apartment, with the door at the back that allows for movement in the frame to be captured by the statically positioned cameras. Bauer also borrows a device from the French *films d'art* with well-known actors, namely to introduce the characters with portraits to facilitate recognition. Moreover, Bauer uses an ingenious and novel way of presenting the new invention, the telephone: he splits the frame, showing both speakers simultaneously.

Apart from his melodramas, Bauer made several short, comic films that followed the pattern of comedies of the early 1910s. *The 1,002nd Ruse* (Tysiacha vtoraia khitrost', dir. Bauer, 1915) stars Bauer's wife Lina, a great comic actress, in the role of the clever wife whose husband tries to control her with the help of the book *1,001 Pieces of Oriental Wisdom for Husbands* – in allusion to the Arabian fairy tales of 1,001 nights. Trick seventy-eight explains the usefulness of observing the wife through the keyhole. Stunningly, Bauer here uses the shape of the keyhole to reshape the cinematic frame and allow the spectator to imitate the husband's view. When husband and wife go for a walk, a rare panorama shot of Moscow is faintly visible in the background. Back at home, the wife sends her husband off into bed in order to receive her lover in her boudoir right next to the husband's bedroom. The wife smokes a hookah and drinks alcohol – both characteristics of the 'new woman'. Suddenly the husband wakes up and the lover hides – in a classical slapstick move – in the cupboard. This hiding place is so obvious that the husband does not even look there. The book of wisdom cannot cover the inventiveness of the woman's mind, capable of inventing ruse 1,002. Another short comic film, *First Love* (Pervaia liubov', Bauer 1915) starred Bauer's children and those of the actress Vera Glinskaya. A little girl lies in a hammock while watching her mother and a friend getting dressed and ready to go for a walk. Once alone, the girl imitates their demeanour and dresses up to go for a walk to meet a boy in the neighbourhood who is already waiting for her. On the way, however, she stumbles over an obstacle: a frog. She tries to chase the creature away, throwing her umbrella, purse, socks and shoes at it – but to no avail. Finally she runs home and plays with her pigeons, having forgotten about her rendezvous. The two women find a heap of things on the path and underneath – a purse in the shape of a frog. *First Love* is an amusing vignette about the aspirations of children to behave like adults while they remain deeply rooted in their childhood, forgetting immediately what they had set out to do. The film employs crosscutting between the women and the girl to underscore the mimetic aspect of the little girl's behaviour, and between the girl and the boy waiting to provide the narrative with a goal – that the little girl abandons. In this sense, it mocks the girl-meets-boy plot that is typical of the melodrama, and thus parodies the genre.

The theme of women's role in a collapsing society of a country undergoing political and social upheavals continued to inform Bauer's melodramas. *Dreams* (Grezy, dir. Bauer, 1915) explored the psychological effect of a wife's loss of a loving husband. Sergei Nedelin's dead wife Yelena is first pictured in a coffin, and later seen on framed photographs before she is memorialized through the tresses which her husband cuts: she is objectified, and therefore manageable. Nedelin is besotted with his dead wife and believes he recognizes her in a woman in the street – Tina, an actress who plays in Meyerbeer's *Robert the Devil* (Tina is played by the same actress as Yelena). Her part in the opera is that of a woman who rises from the dead, emerging from a coffin – the supernatural element of the fictional opera plot is woven into Nedelin's obsession with his dead wife as he sees the woman he believes to be her rise from the dead (albeit on stage). Next he obtains a photo with her autograph – a replacement for Yelena, but in the form of a frozen image. For Nedelin, Tina is an animated portrait of his dead wife. Therefore he wants to have her painted in Yelena's clothes: women are manageable only as an image fixated on canvas or on a photograph. Tina, on the other hand, is very much alive and expects social advantages through her relationship with Nedelin: she requests Yelena's jewels and dresses, and – provoking Nedelin further – she removes the tresses from their glass box and dons them as a boa. At this moment, Nedelin strangles her: a woman is the victim at the film's end. *Dreams* explores Nedelin's psyche and his obsession with his wife as he fails to realize that appearance alone (images, photos, similarities) do not make a character. His dream-vision of Yelena makes clear that the woman he loves was docile and submissive, unlike the active and independent Tina. Bauer uses this vision to explain Nedelin's obsession, which is further rendered through a home overburdened with images and objects that bear evidence of her presence, or rather absence. The doors at the back of Nedelin's room are on medieval hinges that make the apartment look like a fortress: Nedelin is secluded, sealed off from the outside world and cannot cope with reality.

Bauer's women do not always advance on their own initiative, but their men are always victims. In *Children of the Age* (Deti veka, dir. Bauer, 1915) Vera Kholodnaya, who would become the 'queen of the silver screen', appeared in the role of Maria Nikolaevna, while Glinskaya played Lidia Verkhovskaya, and Bibikov (who had appeared in *The Brigand Brothers*, as father-in-law in *The Daughter-in-Law's Lover* and the tyrant Dymov) was the rich suitor, Lebedev. Maria lives a simple life (the sewing machine in the living room speaks not of luxury) with her husband and baby son. She is a caring and loving wife and parent who spends money on some clothing for the baby rather than on herself. Window-shopping in the Upper Trading Rows (the modern GUM, built in the 1890s) she meets her old friend and socialite Lidia. Here, a rare moment of lateral tracking occurs when the camera moves along with the two women across a bridge in the trade rows. Maria is invited to Lidia's and enjoys moving in those social circles, which are entertained with gypsy music and boating, whilst her husband, a lowly bank clerk, is not at ease. The influential Lebedev pursues Maria and makes advances in open or visible spaces: the garden, a glass conservatory, a park, and a car. Lebedev uses his influence at the bank to have Maria's husband sacked, without her knowing. Eventually Maria surrenders, and – ashamed and guilt-stricken – she leaves her husband, who is offered money from Lebedev to let Maria and the child go; outraged, he refuses and kills himself. Here Bauer juxtaposed interior and exterior spaces and inverted their traditional function: the open space is turned into a place for private encounters. The interiors are oppressive: the small space of Maria's home with the sewing machine in the living room and the baby sleeping in the parental bed is just as oppressive as the cluttered office where the husband is blackmailed (Bauer redeployed the set of Nedelin's room with medieval hinges and heavy doors), and the office in the bank which the husband shares with several other clerks. The heroine, Maria, is here not the one who aspires to a different life but who is the victim of Lebedev's intrigues: he deprives the breadwinner of his employment and seduces Maria despite her resistance. The class conflict is further enhanced by the perception of society as a place where money can buy everything – even wives and children.

Bauer's best-known film is *A Life for a Life* (Zhizn' za zhizn', dir. Bauer, 1916),[24] starring Kholodnaya alongside the Moscow Art Theatre actress Lidia Koreneva. The millionaire's widow Khromova (Olga Rakhmanova) has two daughters: Musia (Koreneva) and the adopted Nata (Kholodnaya). Nata is in love with Prince Bartinsky (Polonsky), but the wealthy Zhurov (Ivan Perestiani, 1870–1959) also loves Nata. Bartinsky is a gambler who has lost substantial sums and needs to marry a rich girl.

Figure 1.5 Vera Kholodnaya.

Zhurov suggests he should marry Musia, while Zhurov himself will marry Nata. Despite Khromova's reservations about Bartinsky, the double wedding goes ahead. Musia and Bartinsky leave on a honeymoon, but after their return he rekindles his affair with Nata, who tells Khromova the truth. However, Nata sees her love for Bartinsky as fate: in a flight of fancy that underlines the permanence of their love, Nata and Bartinsky feature as lovers in an ancient Roman setting, a cinematic device that places them on the same level as the statues that decorate the interior of their homes. Meanwhile, Musia gives Bartinsky all her money, which he loses at the races and the gambling table. As a mother, Khromova has failed: she has spoilt her child and cannot convince Musia that Bartinsky is not the best match. Zhurov catches Bartinsky in a tête-à-tête with his wife, but is incapable of killing him: he is another one of Bauer's weak men. Moreover, Zhurov is unable to push through with his allegations of forgery and have Bartinsky arrested. When Khromova finds herself alone with Bartinsky, she suggests: 'Be a man for once in your life' – implying he should kill himself and take responsibility for the disgrace he has brought upon himself and her family. But Bartinsky is a different kind of man: he only laughs and leaves the act of murder (disguised as suicide) to the strong woman. The decadent lifestyle (partying, tango, gypsy dances and courtesans) featured in most melodramas of the period in connection with nobility: Prince Bartinsky is a gambler; Prince Dolsky abandons his wife because she has been a victim of rape; the millionaires Dymov and Lebedev are tyrants. Khromova is a matriarch, capable of taking action and making decisions.

Kholodnaya was relegated to the secondary role of the adopted daughter Nata (rather than Musia), because she was not an actress by training. She had married a lawyer in 1910 and showed an interest in the arts. She was spotted in a crowd scene and cast by Bauer, who found a successful way of working with her: unequipped with the psychological acting methods of the Moscow Art Theatre and Russian theatre schools of the time, Kholodnaya did not play, but merely existed in front of the camera. This skill had to be deployed carefully and Bauer therefore often cast Kholodnaya in roles that were suited for such an approach rather than in the main part. A contemporary critic commented astutely on Kholodnaya's talent:

> The acting of L. M. Koreneva would be followed attentively it moved and touched but you would remember another character of another heroine, who did not act but who lived on the screen ... However beautiful L. M. Koreneva may have been in *Life for a Life*, her stage manners, the calculated dramatism of expression, and the habit of formulae of reflexive and accurate acting could be felt. V. Kholodnaya did not create. She remained herself ... (V. Turkin, 1918)[25]

In 1916 she parted with Khanzhonkov and joined Kharitonov's studio, travelling with the company to Odessa in 1918 at a time when she was leaving her husband and breaking up with her screen partner Maximov. Kholodnaya died of Spanish influenza in Odessa in 1918, although legends about her death persisted: according to rumours that circulated among a population refusing to believe in her so tragically ordinary death, she was the victim of an assassination as a result of her espionage for either the Reds or the Whites.

The women in Bauer's melodramas tended to be powerful and decisive, taking action when their male counterparts failed to do so. But often they had to pay a price. *Nelli Raintseva* (Bauer, 1916) tells Nelli's (Zoya Barantsevich) story as a flashback, based on her diary that her maid Tanya finds after her death. Like *Dreams*, the film begins with Nelli in her coffin. Nelli had been neglected by her parents and tried to find her calling in the arts: playing the piano, writing, or mingling with the hussars. She accompanies Tanya to a servants' party, where she is inebriated and is raped by her father's postman. When she finds she is pregnant, she kills herself. The film makes interesting use of the flashback, presenting the entire story as an explanation for the image of Nelli in her coffin. Nelli is a woman who is bored, and because she has no scope for activity in her provincial home, she is asphyxiated by the world that surrounds her.

Figure 1.6 Bauer's *The Dying Swan*: Vera Karalli.

Bauer's films after Kholodnaya's departure from the studio continue the thematic and cinematic searches of his earlier films. *The Dying Swan* (Umiraiushchii lebed', 1916) starred the former ballerina Karalli in the role of the mute Giselle. The young Viktor (Polonsky) courts her under the watchful eye of her father. When she sees him with a young woman, she is jealous and asks her father to take her away and let her dance on stage. Giselle makes a stage career and her performance is seen by the painter Valeri Glinsky, who then attempts to capture 'death' on canvas. Seeing her as dying swan in the ballet – a dance choreographed originally by Marius Petipa for the prima ballerina Anna Pavlova – he asks her to sit for him so he can paint her in the final lifeless pose of her dance. When Viktor finds Giselle and explains the misunderstanding, they decide to marry. The energy in her expression hampers Glinsky in his necrophile portrait: he kills Giselle so that he can complete the portrait. The theme of eroticism and death (Glinsky loves Giselle but needs her dead) is a further development of the desire to see women as static, frozen objects rather than moving characters. The theme also reflects the artistic decadence of the period.

One of Bauer's last films is *For Happiness* (Za schast'em, dir. Bauer, 1917), which portrayed another overpowering woman who destroys her own happiness for the sake of her child. Zoya Berenskaya (Koreneva), a wealthy widow, is in love with the lawyer Gzhatsky. However, she is over-protective of her daughter Li and postpones the marriage as she is afraid of upsetting her child, who has problems with her eyes. On a sojourn in the Crimea, a young man, Enrico (the first screen appearance of Lev Kuleshov), proposes to Li, who rejects him because she is secretly in love with Gzhatsky. Berenskaya overhears the conversation and implores Gzhatsky to marry Li. Gzhatsky refuses and when he tells Li that he loves her mother, the girl goes blind. The symbolic blindness follows the over-protectiveness of a woman who never thinks of her own happiness, thus making genuine happiness impossible for her child.

Bauer's melodramas explore the sentiments of people who inhabit an exquisite and tasteful world – a world that was slipping away during the First World War and would disappear forever with the Revolution. Unlike their Western counterpart, 'Russian melodramas ... did not restore order, accordingly had "unhappy" endings'.[26] The conflict that leads to these unhappy endings (death or blindness, suicide or murder) represents a clash between male and female worlds, between classes of 'noble decadence and bourgeois morality',[27] between ancient and modern culture.

In early Russian cinema, women appear largely as objects of contemplation for men: as moral values crumbled, men preferred to fetishize women rather than engage with them on an equal footing. When women try to break free from that role, the men fail to cope with them. In the early Bauer films, women who gain independence cause their men to die; later women become victims of violent deaths (*Dreams*, *Dying Swan*) or murderers (*A Life for a Life*). Thus, social change appears as undesirable and dangerous. Overwhelming and overpowering maternal love (Berenskaya in *For Happiness*, Khromova in *A Life for a Life*) is as detrimental as its absence (Raintseva). Fathers are largely absent, but when present they too always keep a watchful eye on their children (*Dying Swan*).

Women are usually sensitive and emotional; they have visions, dreams and flights of fancy. Men are more pragmatic and rely instead on rules and norms, such as the legal system (Bartinsky, Lebedev) and social convention (Dolsky). However, both men and women have sensibilities: Viktor may well be in love with Mary-Mania; Maria's husband genuinely loves his wife; Dolsky suffers from emotional distress when Vera rejects him; and Pavel loves Ellen although she betrays him. They are all afraid of the decadence that surrounds them and encroaches on their domestic safety (as in *Children of the Age* or *Silent Witnesses*), and that turns their wives into mistresses, courtesans and frivolous dancers – worst of all of the tango.

The genre of the melodrama explored the lives of individuals within the context of social circumstance, thus laying the blame or responsibility for personal unhappiness (which abounded in Russian cinema) at the feet of society. By dwelling on emotions and their repression through social or personal mechanisms, the melodrama echoed the current interest in the exploration of the human psyche. The concern with emotions made the genre of melodrama especially appealing for women: 'Women supposedly flocked to movies in order to retreat into a melodramatic fantasy world, a deceptive celluloid paradise that lulled them into a false sense of security about their place in patriarchal society'.[28] McReynolds suggests that films offered opportunities for escapism from a reality that was doomed with defeatism and overdue the social, political and economic change that had been demanded in the revolutionary movement.

The Revolution and its Aftermath, 1917–19

After the February Revolution of 1917 and the abdication of the tsar, many revolutionaries returned from their exile, including Vladimir Lenin. Newsreels and films touching on themes that had formerly been outlawed by censorship (the tsar and the clergy, notably) were popular with the new regime. As had most branches of the industry, film producers and distributors also formed trade unions, which began to organize strikes to strengthen demands for better pay.

Khanzhonkov, Ermoliev, Libken and Vengerov, as well as the companies Era (formerly Thiemann & Reinhardt) and Rus still had studios in Russia. Khanzhonkov and Ermoliev were working in Yalta, Kharitonov in Odessa. However, the nationalization of the industry was on the cards as the staff of studios and film exchanges (rental offices) refused to work for private proprietors; those in turn packed up their equipment and moved south. On 4 March 1918, the closure of cinemas was prohibited in order to stop the disappearance of equipment. Film stock in particular had become rare since all trade relations with Western countries had been interrupted. It was largely the government's inability to find a way of ensuring the support and collaboration of private enterprises that led to the ultimate nationalization of the film industry. The Skobelev Committee, originally set up as a charity, had engaged in film production in 1914 and produced films with a political agenda since the beginning of the First World War, and had been the only non-private film producer in the pre-Revolutionary era. It now shed responsibility for film production to the Committee for Education, but finally a Cinema Committee was put in charge of the industry. In a unique move that led to one of the greatest scandals in Soviet film history, the state placed one million US dollars into an account for Cibrario de Goden, an Italian film agent who promised to purchase film stock and equipment for the Soviet government in the US. Instead of proceeding with the purchase, de Goden pocketed the money and disappeared. The film stock crisis continued until the Treaty of Rapallo was signed in 1922, allowing trade with Germany to resume.

Cinema visits became a luxury, and many cinemas closed; film stock became a deficit; and numerous film artists and producers moved to the studios in the Crimea (Odessa and Yalta). But in the south, too, the political situation changed constantly as the Reds advanced even into the last strongholds of the White army. Khanzhonkov experienced one episode of military reality infringing on cinematic life, when, during the filming of a ball scene in a pavilion, Red officers charged on to the set, ready to arrest the 'bourgeois enemy'. The atmosphere of this time is beautifully captured in Nikita Mikhalkov's *Slave of Love* (Raba liubvi, 1975), which enacts a similar scene. As the Red Army advanced, Ermoliev and his crew fled, on 10 February 1920, from Yalta via Constantinople to Paris, where they arrived in the late summer of 1920. In France, the vogue for Russian art had swept across the country since Diaghilev's Ballets Russes (1909) and continued now with an interest in Russian films and stars that drew audiences in the early 1920s. Ermolieff (as he now spelt his name) created his own studio, which was later taken over by Alexander Kamenka's Albatros. Fedor Otsep (1895–1949), co-writer of Yakov Protazanov's *Aelita*, worked in Germany and France before emigrating to North America in the 1930s. Protazanov himself had also left Soviet Russia after the Revolution and made several films in Berlin and Paris before returning to the USSR in 1923; his influence has been acknowledged by important directors in French cinema, such as René Clair. Protazanov's assistant Alexander Volkov (Volkoff) gained international reputation with *Kean* (1924, starring Mosjoukine, as he now spelt his name, and Lisenko) and *Casanova* (1927, with Mosjoukine), developing the decorative style that had characterized early Russian cinema. By 1925 the attraction of the Russian colonies abroad had faded and Russian actors, directors and producers found it difficult to integrate into the national cinemas, from the point of view of acting style and language as well as demand. Jay Leyda astutely comments that the Americans preferred their own actors even for Russian parts – a comment that holds still true today.[29]

Many artists had remained in Moscow, declared capital in 1918, and expressed their loyalty to the new regime. Mayakovsky offered his film scripts; and the Latvian cameraman Eduard Tisse came to Russia to film the May Day parades on Red Square. Agit-trains were dispatched across the country to show newsreels to the (largely illiterate) peasant population. Tisse joined one of the agit-trains, while the young David (Denis) Kaufman (later known as Dziga Vertov) was in charge of the developing process in a laboratory in Moscow. The *agitka* – the political skit – became a popular form.

Despite the lack of film stock in post-Revolutionary Russia, Lev Kuleshov began his career as a filmmaker. Kuleshov had worked as production designer with Bauer, and made his first film in the year of the Revolution. Kuleshov asserted that the narrative of film lay in the selection of shots. As filmmaking became a distinct art form, the skill of the filmmaker consisted in the use (or manipulation) of images to tell a story.

> The essence of cinema art lies in the creativity of the director and the artist: everything is based on composition. To make a picture the director must compose the separate filmed fragments, disordered and disjointed, into a single whole and juxtapose these separate moments into a more advantageous, integral and rhythmical sequence. (Kuleshov 1917)[30]

Kuleshov's first experiences in film are contained in *The Project of Engineer Prite* (Proekt inzhinera Praita, dir. Lev Kuleshov, Khanzhonkov 1918): it tells the story of the engineer Prite, who has invented a hydro-turbine and is sabotaged by capitalists who want to control the production of electricity. Prite's new electric station prevents them from holding on to their monopoly. Prite is in love with a girl, who happens to be the daughter of the company director behind the sabotage. The film painted a portrayal of capitalist exploitation that does not refrain from sabotage and created the image of the new engineer, who drinks and shakes hands with the workers in a genuinely socialist manner. The love plot with the daughter of the capitalist enemy culminates in a happy ending, which also sees the saboteurs caught and the electric station run by a workers' collective, where the engineer is on a par with the workers.[31] Kuleshov shot most of his film in the open air rather than in studios (mostly dysfunctional at the time). Moreover, in the absence of suitable locations he had to resort to the principles of editing and montage he would develop in the early 1920s: to overlap two frames to create the image of electric masts in the countryside.

A complex film that is symptomatic more of the melodrama period is *Be Still, Sadness, Be Still* (Molchi, grust', molchi, dir. Chardynin, Kharitonov 1918). Pola (Kholodnaya) is a circus artist whose husband Loria (Chardynin) has a drink problem and has an accident during a performance that leaves him crippled. Pola attracts the attention of men (Polonsky, Maximov and Osip Runich), and when she and Loria are busking in the streets, they are invited to play for a gentlemen's party. Pola is spoilt with jewellery and courted by the men, and moves in with the artist Volynstev (Maximov) when she can no longer survive on the money she and Loria make busking. Volyntsev, however, soon takes possession of her and tries to sell her to Terepnev, but Pola makes her own choice and goes to live with a gambler who loses his money. He then devises a plan to rob Terepnev while Pola distracts the host and the other guests with a song. However, he sets off an alarm, and shoots himself in horror at the disgrace. The complicated plot does not serve the film well, but the story of a woman seeking improvement in her life is typical of early Russian melodrama. Pola's rise in society is reflected by her increasingly luxurious dresses and shawls, which replace her circus costume. Chardynin's film was a huge success, as it brought together the leading stars of pre-Revolutionary cinema.

The films of the period 1917–19 represent the end of the melodramatic tradition that was characteristic of early Russian cinema. It brings to the foreground themes that are of concern for the new regime, such as scathing portrayals of the clergy,

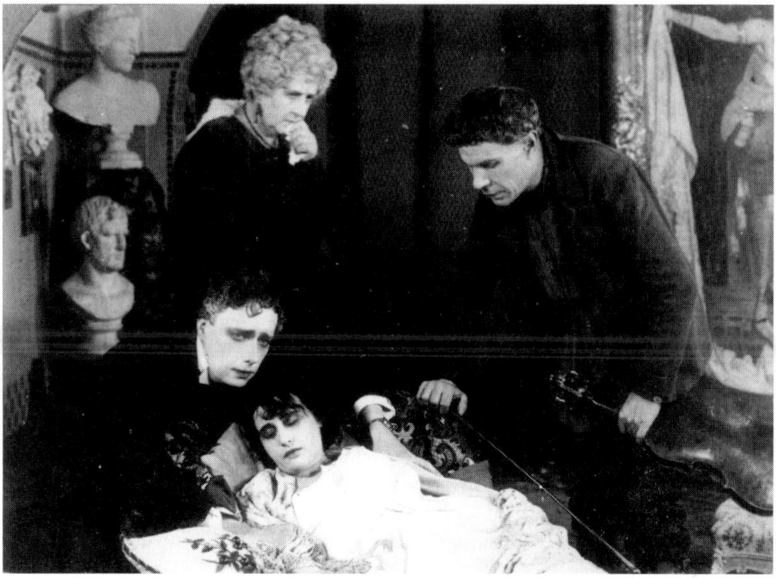

Figure 1.7 Scene from Chardynin's *Be Still, Sadness, Be Still.*

sabotage of workers' collectives, the ethos of construction and progress. Moreover, the working class – in the form of engineers and workers – features more prominently in positive roles in films such as Kuleshov's *Prite*, but also Bauer's last films *The Revolutionary* (Revoliutsioner, 1918) and *Alarm* (Nabat, 1918). The first years of the Soviet era would, however, see film production hampered and stalled due to nationalization, reorganization and – very basically – lack of film stock.

In the films made between the two Revolutions and immediately after the October Revolution, there is a striking concern with evil and the satanic, themes that had been banned by censorship before 1917. The melodramas gave way to the doom and gloom that followed the Revolution which brought, in the first instance, chaos and upheaval, and in the second instance led to a civil war. Protazanov's *Satan Triumphant* (Satana likuiushchii, Ermoliev 1917) was set in a remote and foreign country to distance the action. In the first part of the film Pastor Talnoks (Mozzhukhin) holds a tight grip on the morality of his family: he forbids his sister-in-law Esfir any pleasure – from playing the piano to sex with her husband. The Devil sees a malleable target in Talnoks and introduces himself to the house, playing the 'Hymn Triumphant' on the piano. The Devil triggers a chain of events, culminating in Talnoks' committing adultery with Esfir, an act that is punished by the church collapsing and killing him. In the second part, Esfir's and Talnoks's son Sandro has become a talented pianist and finds the score of the 'Hymn'. When he plays it, the Devil possesses him. The film attacked the hypocrisy of the clergy, and alluded also to the harmful influence of clergy (the monk Rasputin) on women (the tsarina). Tapping into the interest in madness, insanity and the dark forces that would become typical of German expressionism, this film became a blockbuster, enhanced by the fact that it touched upon a topic previously forbidden by the tsar's censors. *Father Sergius* (Otets Sergii, dir. Protazanov, Ermoliev 1917) was based on Tolstoy's story, which could not have been adapted for the screen earlier as the representation of the tsar – here Nicholas I is seen as a seducer – would not have passed the censor. The Countess Marie Orlova attracts the attention of a prince (Mozzhukhin), who proposes to her. On the eve of the wedding she confesses that she is the tsar's mistress. Horrified, the prince enters a convent to purge himself of sexual attraction and becomes Father Sergius. He suffers from his erotic dreams of Marie and often cannot resist temptation, which leads to self-mutilation. Ultimately he is arrested and perishes. The film comments on the hypocrisy of society and the imperial court, while accusing the clergy of forming a refuge for psychopaths to cure their problems rather than practise faith.

Protazanov's *Little Ellie* (Maliutka Elli, Ermoliev, 1918) was based on Maupassant's *La Petite Roque* and is also set in an unnamed Nordic country to distance the events. Here the mayor, Norton (Mozzhukhin), is engaged to Clara (Lisenko), whose little sister Ellie has been murdered. Norton, who is identified as murderer to the viewer by his torn shirt and elbow injury, is plagued by guilt: he eventually confesses and kills himself. The film does not adopt a linear psychological narrative, but instead shows through visions and flashbacks how the murder happened, thus dwelling on the psychological impact it has on the protagonist. Both sexual deviation (the rape) and confession lead to destruction: no new order is offered at the end of the film, nor is change on the cards, echoing the collapse of values of the period with no new authority in place.

Protazanov established himself as an able director who made films wanted by the audiences whilst using interesting stylistic devices. Protazanov excelled at portraying the evil and demonic in his characters, thus showing his penchant for German expressionism, which undoubtedly equipped him well for working abroad, where his success continued until 1923 when he returned to Russia.

On 27 August 1919, the film industry was nationalized. Few foreign films found their way to Moscow during the Revolution and the ensuing Civil War (1918–21); likewise, few new films were made. The Studio Rus produced *Polikushka* (1919, dir. Alexander Sanin) with the cast of the Moscow Art Theatre, filmed under appalling conditions, without heat or means of transport and largely relying on the enthusiasm of the ensemble with Ivan Moskvin in the role of Polikei (Polikushka), which marked his debut on the screen. The film remained the only new Russian release of a fiction film for several years after the nationalization of the industry. It deals with a servant, who is a drunkard but avoids the army draft with a promise to improve. He is sent to collect a debt for his mistress, but despite staying sober he loses the money. Having failed in his mission, Polikushka returns home and hangs himself; as his wife Akulina rushes to the scene, she forgets her baby in the bathtub and the infant drowns. Akulina goes mad. Another servant later finds the money by the roadside, reinstating Polikushka's honour. The film typically stressed the suffering and endurance of the people, echoing the dire situation in a country in the grip of two wars.

At the same time, the Bolsheviks quickly realized the power of the cinema, both documentary and live-action, to reach the masses.

> Generally speaking, every art, as Tolstoy once remarked, is above all a means of instilling the artist's emotions into the masses. Education in the wider sense of the word consists in the dissemination of ideas among minds that would otherwise remain a stranger to them. Cinema can accomplish both these things with particular force: it constitutes, on the one hand, a visual clarion for the dissemination of ideas and, on the other hand, if we introduce elements of the refined, the poetic, the pathetic etc., it is capable of touching the emotions and thus becomes an apparatus of agitation. (Lunacharsky 1919)[32]

In the first of the two decades covered in this chapter, the new medium of cinema conquered Russia as an imported innovation. In the second decade the exotic, imported *films d'art* gradually lost their grip on Russian audiences as imports were hindered by the First World War and Russian production rose. The 1910s saw the emergence of Bauer's art films, but also of the popular films by Protazanov and Chardynin, as well as the discovery of puppet animation by Starewicz – a tradition disrupted until after the Second World War. After the Revolution, the Bolshevik and later Soviet regime would gradually assume control over cinema, but first followed a period of proliferation of methods, genres and styles in the most exciting time for Russia cinema: the 1920s.

–2–

Revolutionary Cinema, or Cinema for the Masses (1919–29)

> Of all arts, cinema for us is the most important.
>
> Lenin, 1922

> Cinema is an overrated little machine that damages your eyesight – and nothing more.
>
> Proletkino, 1923[1]

The role of the cinema in the new socialist state of Soviet Russia as described in these two statements could not be more disparate. The first attributes a hitherto unknown power to a medium that filmmakers thought they could use to strengthen cinema's role, but that would ultimately replace their artistic freedom with the shackles of ideology; the second underplays the role of cinema by classifying it as a pure mechanical attraction. Oscillating between those concepts of a vanguard art form and a cheap fairground attraction, cinema steered its way through the decade. The 1920s are probably not only the most interesting and diverse, but also the most celebrated period in Russian and Soviet film history. Experiments in all the arts, not only the cinema, dominated the period. In theatre, Meyerhold opposed Stanislavsky's traditional approach to the actor's psychological motivation for his role by employing devices from popular theatre – *commedia dell'arte* and circus – and developed the method of 'biomechanics', whereby the actor's body movement expresses a character's psychological state. In the visual arts, the realist practice of the nineteenth century had moved through cubism and futurism towards constructivism, fragmenting reality into geometrical forms and laying bare devices and structures. This is evident in architecture projects such as the constructivist plans by Vladimir Tatlin for the Monument to the Third International in 1919. These developments also informed costume design, which relied on geometrical shapes that made the human body look like a construct or machine, such as the costumes by El Lissitsky and Kazimir Malevich for the futurist opera *Victory over the Sun* in 1913. Varvara Stepanova and Liubov Popova designed *prozodezhda* (production clothing), which combined a machine-like appearance with functionality, to dress the new proletarian class in the 1920s. In literature, Mayakovsky described the composition of poetry in terms of 'building blocks'. All these tendencies echo the concern for mechanization and industrialization that would appear high on the political agenda by the end of the 1920s. Moreover, the futurists and constructivists actively supported the Revolution when they formed the Left Front of Art (LEF), arguing that art should reveal the production process, lay bare means and unmask psychological realism. The collection of essays on cinema, *The Poetics of Cinema* (*Poetika kino*), which appeared in 1927 and was edited by Boris Eikhenbaum, provided the context for the debates in the 1920s on acting in film and on the importance of fictional and documentary film.

It is indeed this Soviet avant-garde that is best known in cultural history. Cinema allowed the assemblage of images to construct a new world. Those who created films were among the cultural elite that supported both the Revolutionary cause and the new regime. However, cinema also remained a popular art form for the broad masses who wanted to be entertained rather than confronted with obtuse artistic experiments. This popular side of Soviet cinema has only recently moved back into the focus of academic study,[2] and has been an often forgotten or obliterated part of Soviet history because of its (alleged) bourgeois origins in the 1910s. The dual role of cinema as high art and popular entertainment informed not so much the artistic, but the ideological debates on cinema towards the end of the 1920s. When discussing the cinema of the 1920s in this chapter, it is important to discern between experiment and entertainment (in a similar way as we would today differentiate between art-house and commercial cinema), especially in the light of the ideological constraints placed on film production in the 1930s: to what extent were realist narrative forms imposed by Socialist Realism, and to what extent had they developed throughout the revolutionary 1920s?[3]

This chapter situates Soviet cinema in its historical context, looking at the practical implications that the Revolution and Civil War had on the industry. It then looks in detail at some of the early Soviet films that provided entertainment and instruction, before covering in depth the work of the montage filmmakers Pudovkin, Kuleshov and Eisenstein; the poetic cinema of Dovzhenko; comedies and adventure films; the documentary montage cinema of Vertov; and animation. The chapter closes with a look at some films made at the height of the Cultural Revolution, which led to a streaming of the arts.

After the October Revolution, the country was in turmoil and shaken by the Civil War. The period after 1919 was characterized by the building of a multinational (union) state: the Bolshevik regime expanded its influence, as a result of which the Union of Socialist Soviet Republics (USSR) was formed in 1922. At the same time, the first dissonances arose within the Communist Party, notably between Lenin and Stalin; when Lenin died in January 1924 he left a so-called 'testament', in which he warned of Stalin. Stalin advocated the policy of 'socialism in one country', realizing that revolutions in other European countries were more and more unlikely. Moreover, Soviet Russia found itself in international isolation, because the new regime had not yet been recognized by Western nations, and in the aftermath of the First World War, trade embargoes were still in place; foreign interventions in support of the Whites as they opposed the Bolshevik regime were continuing. A famine made practical action necessary: the New Economic Policy (NEP 1921–28) was introduced to alleviate the dismal economic situation by allowing private trade, and with it foreign trade, on the Soviet market.

A period of economic growth through NEP, which encouraged foreign investment, gave way in 1928 to the First Five-Year Plan (1928–32), which envisaged rapid industrialization and agricultural reform. NEP had made it possible for film exchanges to open, and for commercial concessions to be granted to foreigners so that the ruined infrastructure could be revived through foreign investment. The films of Abel Gance, Ernst Lubitsch, Fritz Murnau, Fritz Lang, and D. W. Griffith were amongst the most popular imports.

In this economic atmosphere, the nationalization of the industry took shape slowly. Goskino (Central State Film and Photo Enterprise [Tsentral'noe gosudarstvennoe kinofotopredpriiatie]) was established in December 1922 with the remit to distribute films, but was replaced in 1924 by Sovkino (All-Russian Photo-Cinematic Stock Company [Vserossiiskoe fotokinematograficheskoe aktsionernoe obshchestvo]).[4] The production company Mezhrabpom was merged with the Rus Studio in 1923, and continued to receive support from the German 'Internationale Arbeiterhilfe' (International Workers' Relief). In 1919 a film school was established (GTK, State Film Technicum), headed by veteran director Vladimir Gardin. With the cinemas in a shambles, film-trains and a film-boat (*Red Star*) took newsreels to the countryside. However, whilst the regime was concerned with the new medium that could so attractively reach the largely illiterate rural population, filmmakers were debilitated by the absence of film stock: Lev Kuleshov 'filmed', or rehearsed, with no film in the camera. The production figures reflect the dismal situation of the early post-Revolutionary years, as well as the rise in film production towards the mid-1920s when film stock became available again (Table 2.1).[5]

The absence of material, especially film stock and projectors, but also foreign films and cinemas, could only be remedied through imports, which became possible once again after the signing of the Treaty of Rapallo in 1922. Film stock and cameras, both for filming and projection, were not produced in Soviet Russia, which relied on imports until well after 1928, when a factory in the Ukrainian town of Shostka began to produce the Soviet film stock *svema*; for art films, however, the industry continued to rely on imports from Agfa-Gevaert (Belgium) and Kodak (Germany). Foreign feature films, largely from Germany and America, provided entertainment for the cinema audiences and therefore dominated film distribution.

The 'Americanitis' of 1921–24

The term 'Americanitis' (*amerikanshchina*) was employed by Kuleshov in 1922 to describe the popularity of American films in pre- and post-Revolutionary Russia.

Table 2.1 Film Production by Year

Year	*No. Films Made*
1918	6
1919	57
1920	29
1921	12
1922	16
1923	28
1924	69
1925	80
1926	102
1927	118
1928	124
1929	92
1930	128

When analysing the reasons for their popularity, Kuleshov singled out the fast movement within the frame and the condensation of shots in the editing process.[6] Indeed, in 1924, 95 per cent of films in distribution were foreign (German, American, French). This is not surprising considering that from 1916 to 1922 there had been a ban on American imports, thus increasing the demand for westerns and serials; moreover, the production low of the Soviet industry meant that no new Soviet title had appeared since the 1918 *Polikushka* (discussed in Chapter 1).

Kuleshov ascertained that American films depend on action and conclude with a happy ending (a term alien to pre-Revolutionary cinema and translated into Russian as *kheppi end*). The US industry spent more money on script and design, whilst in Soviet Russia the bureaucracy devoured most of the budget with a 15:1 ratio of administrative to creative staff; moreover, Soviet films required a longer time for both shooting and editing, and had a low export rate. Foreign films composed two-thirds of the repertoire in the 1920s, a balance adjusted only in the last years of the 1920s.[7] Most popular were *The Thief of Baghdad* (dir. Raoul Walsh, 1924) and *The Mark of Zorro* (dir. Fred Niblo, US, 1920), starring Douglas Fairbanks in the role of the romantic thief and the champion of the people. The production of posters, postcards and brochures on foreign stars is a further testimony to their popularity.

Sovkino reviewed the profitability of Russian studios and ordered unprofitable studios to close by 1926. This left only Mezhrabpom-Rus working alongside the Moscow and Leningrad branches of Sovkino as national studios. Sovkino was guided in its policies by Lenin's missive for the 'cinefication' of the countryside (*kinofikatsiia strany*) in order for the medium with the potential to reach the largely illiterate masses to work effectively. Furthermore it was guided by the so-called 'Leninist proportion', stipulating the production of 75 per cent of entertainment to 25 per cent of propaganda films. Sovkino further understood that, given the need for cinema to be self-financing, films had to generate income; this could be achieved through the purchase and distribution of popular foreign films that catered for audience taste and would finance Soviet film production with the box office revenue generated through these imported features. Sovkino rightly assumed that gradually new Soviet films would be successful enough to sustain the industry. Sovkino's head, Ilya Trainin, was fully aware of the financial dependence on foreign film and considered the commercial orientation of Soviet cinema, both in production and distribution, as the only way to develop the industry. Trainin reverted to pre-Revolutionary principles to put the industry on its feet; at the same time, the ideological demands that were growing both among film critics and Party members contradicted the bourgeois diet that imported films provided for the Soviet viewer. In calling for the cinema to appeal to the masses, the Party bureaucrats forgot that the ticket prices were so high that only the middle class and the Party apparatus could afford cinema visits; the cheaper cinemas and film programmes at workers' clubs were usually of an unsatisfactory technical quality.

Many of the avant-garde directors who had supported the Revolution made experimental films that had little mass appeal because of their complexity; on the whole they were not profitable. The box office relied on popular entertainment as provided by the genres of crime, adventure and romantic comedy. Foreign films, which filled those gaps, peaked in Soviet distribution in the period from 1923 until 1926, when Soviet film production picked up. By 1927 the box office receipts of Soviet films were almost on a par with foreign films.[8]

In the first half of the 1920s, Soviet cinema slowly recovered. The economy was gradually restored and people had money to spend on tickets. The supervision of cinema matters came under the Commissar for Education (Narkompros),[9] with the playwright, literary critic and theorist Anatoli Lunacharsky (1875–1933) at its head, an office he held from 1917 to 1929. However, vociferous criticism was levelled at cinemas' management. The Association of Revolutionary Cinematographers (ARK, established 1924, renamed ARRK – Association of Revolutionary Workers of Cinematography in 1928) stated in 1924 that:

> The nationalized studios are either idle or working at less than 10 per cent of their capacity. The films released do not, in the overwhelming majority of cases, meet the ideological and artistic needs of the proletariat. There is no scientific or educational cinema. Our screens are packed with productions from the bourgeois West.[10]

In an editorial in July 1923, *Pravda* also voiced the opinion that the industry could do more.[11] It is arguable whether Lenin's statement on the role of cinema helped the art or exposed it to more scrutiny than the more established art forms. However, criticism of the level of productivity, of the kind of films and of the role of cinema in ideological propaganda, grew louder throughout the decade. Proletkult – originally established in October 1917 to promote amateur art of the proletariat through factory clubs – established a film section, Proletkino, in 1923, which was, amongst other things, in charge of the distribution of films to workers' clubs.

In fiction films, Revolutionary themes were prominent in the first years of Soviet film production: Viacheslav Viskovsky made films such as *Red Partisans* (Krasnye partizany, 1924) and *The Ninth of January* (Deviatoe ianvaria, Sevzapkino 1925). Vladimir Gardin made *Four and Five* (Chetyre i piat', aka as *Steel Wings*, [Stal'nye zhuravli], 1924), produced by Mezhrabpom-Rus, using elements of the American gangster film in a plot revolving around sabotage and combining this with the romantic tale of a Soviet hero and a simple peasant girl. Mitia Gai is the son of a worker and dreams of flying. For Soviet cinema, the dream is no longer a form of escapism from reality as it was in pre-Revolutionary films; instead, the inventor Mitia realizes his dream to become an aviator. Moreover, he develops a powerful lethal gas. The beautiful actress Ilona distracts him and he crashes, having missed the collective take-off with his team. It is the village girl Natasha who nurtures him back to health and helps him disclose the saboteurs and Ilona, who attempted to steal his invention. The sharp contrast between the muddy countryside and the beautiful embankments and parks of Moscow underlines the difference between town and country. The *kheppi end* brings Natasha to Mitia's house. The film combines the genre of melodrama with a love triangle between Mitia, the pretty but evil Ilona and the loyal Natasha, with the theme of sabotage of the new industrial power that the USSR represented (or wanted to represent).

Stalin attributed to cinema the same importance as to other arts, and in his function as Commissar for Nationalities he supported both national minorities programmes and the establishment in 1921 of a film production section in his native Georgia under Narkompros. In 1922 followed the foundation of the Ukrainian Film Studios VUFKU (Vse-Ukrainskoe Foto-Kino-Upravlenie). Produced in Georgia, Ivan Perestiani's *Red Imps* (Krasnye d'iavol'iata, 1923) was the first Soviet film that could compete with foreign films. It starred three circus performers, Pavel Esikovsky, Sofia Dzhoseffi and Kador Ben-Salim in the main parts. Set in Ukraine in the 1920s, it tells the story of two siblings, Misha and Duniasha, who lead a happy and peaceful life, spending their time reading adventure novels by James Fenimore Cooper and Ethel Voynich. As they read, the fictional world of the rebel-heroes is animated in imaginary sequences that illustrate the story, thus borrowing the device of dreams and visions deployed in pre-Revolutionary cinema. Soon, the fictional adventures of their heroes are to become reality – in their own fight for the Revolutionary cause. During an attack from the counter-Revolutionary and insurrectional army of 'Batko' Makhno (1888–1934, exile 1921), the children's father is murdered. Before his death he makes the children promise to fight for the Revolution. They flee and try to reach the Red Army; on their way they encounter the acrobat Tom Jackson, an ex-sailor from Sevastopol who entertains the public and is ripped off by local gangs. The siblings come to his aid and the three become inseparable. When they locate the Red Army, they also find a father-surrogate in the

Figure 2.1 Perestiani's *Red Imps*.

commander, Semen Budenny (1883–1973). In their pursuit of Makhno they run into a series of adventures: they are captured by the enemy and tortured – Duniasha is almost burnt at the stake and hanged; they employ guises, using stolen passports and false beards; and they fight one of Makhno's giants and triumph in the uneven fight by applying wit and agility, making the scene appear like a slapstick comedy. In the end, they capture Makhno and deliver him to Budenny during a parade. Perestiani's film impresses through the tension created by the series of adventures to which the protagonists are exposed. Moreover, he uses fast editing for his static camera shots, and composes his frames with effective use of shadows. One indication of the success of the film is the continuation of the adventure stories of the red imps.[12]

However, not only Gardin and Perestiani, who had both worked before the Revolution, proved capable of efficiently using genres to attract audiences. Studying American films, Kuleshov explored the use of expressive movement to render emotion; to this end, he relied on real persons rather than actors. Rejecting the psychological-theatrical approach, he argued that theatre schools offered unsatisfactory preparation for his requirements of the actor. He researched the effect of montage to manipulate, for example, city geographies by inserting close-ups of houses into streets of a different location; by combining the handshake of two actors with the face of another actor; or by showing a girl in a dressing room and juxtaposing these images with close-ups of the lips, eyes and a nose of a different actress. Kuleshov realized the possibility of creating space by filming people in Moscow and transposing the shots on to images of the White House. He thus determined that the content of a frame changes its meaning depending on the context: 'In the combination of the filmed fragments the important thing is the dependence (the relationship) of the first filmed fragments on the second and this dependence is the principal organizational element in the construction of a film.'[13] Kuleshov argued that the content of a single frame is not as important as joining two frames together: he juxtaposed a shot of Mozzhukhin expressing the pains of love with a frame showing a bowl of soup in a close-up – and the emotion in Mozzhukhin's face turned into hunger; when placed next to a coffin, his facial expression appeared to change to one of grief.

Kuleshov's *The Extraordinary Adventures of Mr West in the Land of the Bolsheviks* (Neobychainye prikliucheniia Mistera Vesta v strane bol'shevikov, Goskino 1924) drew on the western cowboy films for inspiration and employed circus stunts. Thus, the role of Jeddy was played by the boxer – and later filmmaker – Boris Barnet (1907–65). The American Mr West (Porfiri Podobed, 1886–1965), the president of the YMCA, decides to visit Soviet Russia to verify the stories about the barbaric Bolsheviks that he reads in the American press. He is accompanied by cowboy Jeddy as a bodyguard, but Jeddy cannot prevent the theft of Mr West's briefcase immediately after their arrival in Moscow. Jeddy chases the briefcase across Moscow, and in the course of this meets his old friend Ellie, who lives in the city. She takes him to the police who assure assistance. The portrayal of Jeddy, with his stunts on a tightrope that he uses to get from one house to another, with his chases across roofs and streets, with his manner of riding on a horse-drawn carriage in cowboy style – all these scenes serve to express through exaggerated movement the fear and panic of the visitors. The responses of the local population to the foreigners are equally exaggerated: a woman faints and glides down a lamppost as she watches Jeddy's dangerous driving. Jeddy is bailed out by Ellie, whom he had rescued once upon a time – an episode shown in flashbacks. Flashbacks are also deployed for the story that the bandit Zhban (Vsevolod Pudovkin) tells Mr West of how he found the case, which contradicts the real events that were shown only minutes before. The accelerated music in the style of American westerns assists the speed of the action, rendered through fast editing of images. The chase scenes are a clear attempt to emulate the pace of American cinema in order to appeal to the audiences 'in the cheaper seats', while drawing on a plot that promotes Soviet life over American capitalism.

> If we study American films and juxtapose our observations with the results of the unsuccessful attempts to achieve greater 'cinema specificity' and not a reproduction of 'theatricality' in films by using the well-known methods of our Russian directors, we cannot fail to appreciate the particularly strong impression left by films that are consciously composed of combinations of a series of rapidly changing scenes. (Kuleshov, 'Americanism', 1922)[14]

As the story unfolds, Zhban politely returns the lost briefcase and offers his services to protect Mr West from the barbarians. He convinces Mr West that he is in danger from the beastly Bolsheviks pictured in his brochures. In order to extort the American's money, Zhban enlists the help of his friends, the 'Countess' (Alexandra Khokhlova, 1897–1985) and the Dandy (Leonid Obolensky, 1902–91), and the One-Eyed Man (Sergei Komarov, 1891–1957). Zhban has almost reached his goal when the police arrest him and the gang. The Soviet secret service officer then treats Mr West to a tour of the real Moscow, which prompts Mr West to wire his wife and

Figure 2.2 Kuleshov's *Mr West*.

instruct her to burn all the misleading American papers and hang a portrait of Lenin in his office. The success of *Mr West* is largely owed to the adventure genre, the stunts and the comic plot, which could captivate an audience. Comedy and laughter were liberating, and the use of clowns and circus elements in cinema echoes the successful mixture of high and low art.

Kuleshov continued his interest in the style of American cinema, although his undoubted success with *Mr West* was hardly repeated in his later films. *By the Law* (aka *Dura Lex*, Po zakonu, Goskino 1926) was based on Jack London's story 'The Unexpected', adapted for the screen by the literary critic and writer Viktor Shklovsky. A small group of gold-diggers find gold in the Klondike. One day Michael Dennen (Vladimir Fogel, 1902–29) shoots his all his fellow diggers except Hans Nelson (Komarov) and his wife Edith (Khokhlova). Edith seizes the gun to shoot him, but realizes that Dennen should be put on trial. However, there is no judge in this isolated place. So the Nelsons hold court, performing both the roles of witnesses and prosecution. Even in the Alaskan wilderness the couple do not surrender to chaos but create their own order. The theme of isolation can easily be transferred on to the USSR – for many years not recognized by Western countries, as well as the desire not to allow lawlessness triumph (civil war). The film thus carried topical overtones despite the distant setting, and addressed universal moral issues of the right to judge. Kuleshov explored the psychological drama whilst capturing the silhouettes of the characters shot against the light, creating harsh contrasts of the white snow and the darkness inside the hut. If the film relied on the adventure genre and therefore suited Sovkino's agenda for popular films, *Death Ray* (Luch smerti, Goskino 1925) fitted neatly into the espionage genre. Thomas Lann (Komarov), a worker at the Helium factory, is arrested but escapes to Russia, where he must warn the inventor of the 'death ray' (a device that ensures the success of the Revolution) that the fascists are infiltrating his enterprise to steal the invention. The plot repeats many of the thematic moves of Kuleshov's debut film, *Engineer Prite's Project*. However, the threat that emanates from fascist Germany is articulated, but annihilated when Lann uncovers the plot and later puts an end to the exploitation of the Helium workers. Kuleshov's use of the camera lens, reducing it to the size of a spying glass, enhances the sense of being looked upon and represents an original device in this film, one that had been seen earlier in Bauer's reduction of the lens to a keyhole in *The 1,002nd Ruse*. Kuleshov remained within conventional narrative strategies and relied on a combination of montage and expressive acting to achieve his results.

The Politics of Soviet Cinema, 1925–28

The mid-1920s were a period that saw some of the most remarkable montage films and the height of the Soviet experiments in art, but it was also a time when political attention was focused on the consolidation of power by the country's new leader,

Iosif Stalin. Having adopted a policy of 'socialism in one country', the USSR became increasingly isolated in the world. The growing opposition to Stalin created considerable backlashes, evident in particular in Lev Trotsky's internal exile in 1929 and his subsequent deportation from Soviet Russia. A bad harvest in 1928 brought agriculture again to the forefront of attention and led to the first phase of (voluntary) collectivization, beginning in 1929.

Against this backdrop of Soviet isolation from world politics and a concern with internal policies, the heads of Sovkino, Ilya Trainin and Konstantin Shvedchikov, continued to implement a policy of increasing the imports of foreign film in order to raise income for the production of Soviet films. Sovkino would have to produce more films that could attract audiences and make a profit, and at the same time its heads were asked to produce films about the workers and for the workers, who were the new heroes. During this period the concern about the balance of cinema between entertainment and education was growing, and this was reflected in heated theoretical debates. Cinema became a plaything between political rivals, from the proletarian associations such as ARK to the Society of Friends of Soviet Cinema (Obshchestvo druzei sovetskogo kino, ODSK), established in 1925 (and disbanded in 1934) under the OGPU[15] and chaired by Cheka founder Felix Dzerzhinsky. Cinema was called a 'weapon for the cultural influence of the masses'.[16]

By 1927 the revenue from the release of Soviet and foreign films had been balanced.[17] However, cinema's popularity relied on foreign stars, partly because the heroes of Soviet cinema were not individualized enough to allow identification, and partly because directors were seeking different qualities in actors from those they could find in stage actors. Eisenstein relied in his films on 'typage', where the type or face was more important than the acting, while Kuleshov termed his actors 'models' (*naturshchiki*), and was interested in faces as well as physical action and training (as he found in Khokhlova and Fogel). Only the old guard of directors continued to cast theatre actors. Moreover, the new Soviet cinema relied on the stark and usually class-based contrast between the villain or enemy (bourgeois, NEP man, kulak, priest, officer, counter-revolutionary) and the (working-class) hero, who is part of a larger social group that gives him support. Workers therefore tended to be strong and muscular, peasants happy and smiling, thus providing dull and monotonous stereotypes instead of deep and fascinating human characters. This stereotypical approach to roles continued well into the 1930s and 1940s, when it led to films that appear rather conventional with increasingly ideological plots.

This lack of stars in Soviet cinema of the 1920s (by contrast both with the pre-Revolutionary period and the 1930s) explains the hype around American and foreign stars, as demonstrated when Mary Pickford and Douglas Fairbanks visited Moscow in 1926. They were filmed by Kuleshov's actor Sergei Komarov, who edited the footage into a spoof entitled *Mary Pickford's Kiss* (Potselui Meri Pikford, Mezhrabpom-Rus): the movie house usher Goga Palkin (played by Igor Ilinsky, 1901–87, the great comic actor from Meyerhold's theatre) receives a kiss from

Mary. He now has a crowd of female admirers, but ultimately he gets his girl. The film mocks the stardom of Pickford and Fairbanks by contrasting it with the true happiness of the simple people.

Vertov: Animation and the Documentary, 1922–29

Documentaries were among the earliest films made by the Lumières, so it is arguably the oldest cinematic genre. Many of the early films had documented Russian life and history. In Soviet Russia Dziga Vertov (real name David [Denis] Kaufman, 1895–1954) had worked in newsreel editing and campaigned against fiction (or acted) film, asserting that documentary film could help create a more perfect reality. Vertov's idea of the composition of reality led to films that lacked a linear plot – unlike the mass spectacles, such as Nikolai Yevreinov's *The Storming of the Winter Palace* in 1920, re-enacting the events with more participants than were actually involved. Film, both documentaries and montage films of historical events, constructed history and created myths. According to Roland Barthes, myth is neither lie nor truth, but a compromise. The concept of myth-making is particularly important for the 1920s in the context of rewriting history and assimilating practices in the context of the integration of territories into the new Soviet empire, rather than colonizing the distant republics (which is, however, what effectively happened with the imposition of Russian culture and language on the Soviet republics).

Perhaps the most important aspect of cinema of the 1920s therefore was the development of the documentary film. Newsreels were of crucial importance to inform and educate the illiterate masses. Film-trains were dispatched to document life in the country and to show newsreels to the people. The footage shot outside the capital – some of it filmed by Eduard Tisse (1897–1961), a cameraman of dual (Swedish-Russian) parentage who had come to Russia from Latvia and worked for the Skobelev Committee – was sent back from the film-trains to be edited and developed in Moscow by Dziga Vertov with his wife Yelizaveta Svilova (1900–75). Vertov then created newsreels in the form of *Kino-Pravda* (1922–25) and began to formulate a theory on the montage of documentary footage. He declared the camera to be more perfect than the human eye, because it lives and moves in space and time: his group was therefore called *kinoki*, the 'cine-eyes'. The fast movement of the camera does not copy the human eye. As a mechanical device, the camera is perfect: it is agile and mobile. The cine-eye creates the perfect reality and the perfect man, subjecting both perception and representation to the process of industrialization and mechanization. In this approach Vertov was not unlike Meyerhold, who saw the actor's body as a perfect mechanism for the execution of movement to express emotion when defining his 'biomechanics'. Vertov attacked fiction (acted) film and claimed that the documentary was superior: 'The film drama is the opium of the people. The film drama and religion are a fatal weapon in the hands of the capitalists.

Figure 2.3 Dziga Vertov with his camera.

The screenplay is a fairy tale thought out by literature for us ... Down with bourgeois screenplay fairy tales! Long live life as it is.'[18] Dwelling on the perfect eye of the camera Vertov did not, however, reject the editing process. His longer documentaries, such as *Man with the Movie Camera* (Chelovek s kinoapparatom, VUFKU Odessa 1929) contained innovative editing techniques, which reveal the hand of a director or editor who organizes the seemingly objective reality.

Vertov also made *agitki* – short sketches that would incite social improvement, agitating the population by presenting scenes in a dynamic and fast pace. *Agitki* illustrated the tasks of the workers and warned against mistakes in a humorous and educational manner. Alexander Medvedkin made a number of such sketches on the film-train in the early 1930s (see Chapter 3). Vertov also developed drawn animation for political cartoons as early as 1924 with *Soviet Toys* (Sovetskie igrushki, dir. Vertov, credited as 'Denis Kaufman'), which caricatures the NEP men, priests and high-society ladies by juxtaposing them with workers, peasants and soldiers – the citizens of the new Russia. Subsequently, cartoons would be used for propaganda purposes, such as *China in Flames* (Kitai v ogne, dir. Komissarenko, Merkulov, Khodataev, 1925) a spoof against the American attempt to turn China towards capitalism.

During the last years of the 1920s, the art of the drawn cartoon for non-political purposes was rediscovered. Having started his career in pre-Revolutionary film, Yuri Zheliabuzhsky completed only a few feature films in the early 1920s before turning to animation and popular science films. His drawn black-and-white animation *The Ice Rink* (Katok, 1927) was the first cartoon for children. Its technique resembles the simplicity of a child's drawing, using black and white lines. The cartoon follows a boy in a snowy city as he tries to get into the ice rink: he cannot pay the entrance fee and watches through a gap in the fence. On the ice a fat skater slips and a young, pirouette-spinning girl helps him up; they dance off into the distance. Assisted by a sailor, the boy climbs over the fence and crashes into the couple. While the fat man chases the boy with a bat, the audience watches two speed skaters. The boy on the run wins the race and is tossed into the air by the crowd. The story is truly entertaining and politically correct for the NEP era: the boy does not behave according to social rules (he gate-crashes the rink), but the crowd cheers him and not the fat, capitalist NEP man. The boy is mischievous and streetwise, which accounts for his popularity with the masses: he is a little rebel who – by breaking the rules – conquers the ice and the hearts of the people.

The Samoyed Boy (Samoedskii mal'chik, 1928), based on a northern folk tale, was created by Olga and Nikolai Khodataev with assistance from the Brumberg sisters (Valentina and Zinaida). A sledge is travelling through the snow when a polar bear snatches a little Inuit boy. The boy kills the bear and thus procures meat and fur for his family. However, the evil and greedy shaman (the healer-cum-witch of oriental folklore) snatches the provisions and expels the boy from the community. He is dumped into the icy sea, but a trawler rescues him and takes him to Leningrad, where he studies at the university, the 'rabfak' (Workers' School), and forgets about his home. His recollections are embedded in strong Soviet symbols: images of Lenin and Marx decorate the reading room in the school, and only rarely can images of his simple life on the Arctic Circle take root. The boy is an intelligent, new Soviet man: he sees through the shaman's tricks, thus discrediting folk belief and superstition. The boy is a model Soviet citizen who replaces his backward life and family with civilization and the larger Soviet family (with fathers Marx and Lenin). The drawings in thick pencil strokes make the images stout and immobile, resembling traditional woodcuts in their coarseness.

The Leningrad book illustrator Mikhail Tsekhanovsky (1889–1965) made the cartoon *The Post* (Pochta, Sovkino Leningrad 1929), based on a story by the Soviet children's writer Samuil Marshak (1887–1964). The film consisted of detailed black-and-white drawings and used sound technology with music specially composed by Vladimir Deshevov.[19] A boy is writing a letter to Boris Prutkov. The cartoon follows the journey of this letter from Rostov to Leningrad, where Prutkov has just left for Berlin; when the letter arrives in Berlin, Prutkov has just departed for London; as the letter arrives in London, Prutkov is already on a steamboat to Brazil; and once the letter is delivered by the postman Don Basilio, Prutkov is already on his way back to Leningrad – where the letter, having followed Prutkov around the world, finally reaches him. The film sings a song of praise to the global postal services and to the reliability of the postmen, but it also tells the story of a journey around the world, returning once more to the former capital: Leningrad.

The postmen in each country are endowed with rich local colour: the Leningrad postman is efficient and agile, climbing the stairs with no trouble; the German postman is fat and plump, proud of his uniform; the English postman shows no sign of emotion; the Brazilian postman takes a stroll through the jungle to deliver his post. The transportation of the letter is poignantly illustrated: the journey from Leningrad to Berlin is on a train that goes through a tunnel, visually turning into a vortex that echoes the motion of the train's wheels. Prutkov himself travels by air – with the plane offering a superior, aerial view on to the world. The sea passage to Brazil sees the steamship in turbulent waters. The return to Leningrad is by plane and zeppelin, as both travel around a globe displayed as a round ball with the letters 'USSR' usurping half of the round, an image Alexandrov would repeat in *The Circus*. These early cartoons for children laid the foundation for the Soviet animation studio Soyuzmultfilm, which was set up in 1936 and will be discussed in the next chapter.

In terms of the documentary genre, Vertov continued to develop this art. Vertov's *Man with the Movie Camera* is probably the best documentary of the 1920s, and Vertov's masterpiece. The film contains no inter-titles, relying exclusively on the images to form a narrative. *Man with the Movie Camera* operates on two levels: on the one hand, the film captures scenes from a day in the life of a city: a woman wakes up, the city bustles with life, workers rush to their offices, telephone exchanges are busy, trams run along the streets – where an accident happens which brings to the scene the ambulance and a cameraman. The film joins images of the life in a Soviet city in a fast-paced montage, whilst also cutting to other sites that offer an extension of time and space: for example, the film cuts to miners who provide the raw material for the electricity that is supplied to the city; or to the beach and the club that offer relaxation after a long day's work. The location moves from Moscow, where Vertov filmed in 1924–5, to Odessa and Kiev, where the footage for the film was shot in 1929, thus undermining spatial continuity. Moreover, Vertov incorporates scenes of a birth and a funeral, of a marriage and a divorce, of an accident and of leisure time activities, to cover the full breadth of human life. All these activities are captured by the camera, which itself plays an active role in the film and generates a second layer for interpretation. At the beginning of the film a woman, the editor, is working on a reel; then a film awaits its screening in a cinema. The camera and the cameraman, as well as the scrutinizing eye of the editor, appear again and again throughout the film, thus commenting on the role of the filmmaker in this modern, fast-paced world. As Jeremy Hicks has pointed out, the film shows 'how to make film, as well as how to think about it'.[20] The camera eye captures and selects, singles out and makes connections, impressing life on film without using a single word, and thereby genuinely transcends the language barrier. The camera towering as the all-seeing, objective eye above the cityscape in one sequence is an emblematic shot of Vertov's film, created through the superimposition of frames. The sequence where he splices frames to collapse Moscow's Bolshoi Theatre, the fortress of tradition, demonstrates powerfully the potential of the cinematic image.

The edited newsreel footage of Dziga Vertov, as well as the films of his colleague Esfir Shub (1894–1959), brought forth a documentary style that would characterize Soviet documentaries in the 1920s. Their use – by necessity – of mobile and hand-held cameras (when the newsreel footage had to be filmed from moving trains and cars) was an incentive for fiction films to explore the tracking shot. This influence was brought out most clearly in the work of the greatest Soviet director, Sergei Eisenstein.

Soviet Montage Cinema: Eisenstein and Pudovkin, 1925–28

Born in Riga, Eisenstein had studied engineering in Petrograd and joined the Red Army after the 1917 Revolution. From 1920 he worked as set designer in Meyerhold's theatre, where he made his first short film (*Glumov's Diary*) to illustrate the main character's motives in Ostrovsky's *The Wise Man* (1923). On the basis of his theatrical experience he developed his ideas on the montage of attractions, influenced by the way in which Meyerhold devised his productions of classical plays, fragmenting them into a series of episodes. Meyerhold used constructivist sets, which turned the actor into a cog in the wheel of larger machinery that represented reality. He perceived theatre as having a social and political function and closely monitored audience responses in order to heighten the comical and agitational elements in his productions; thus, he would shower audiences with leaflets, or record the moments when the spectators laughed. His actors were trained in 'biomechanics' (body movement to express states of mind and emotions) and movements on stage were choreographed rather than motivated by psychological identification of the actor with his role, thus bringing man closer to a perfect, machine-like state. Therefore Meyerhold required a completely different set of skills from his actors than the Moscow Art Theatre, where Stanislavsky expected the actor to develop a role from an event that triggered a certain emotional and psychological state, of which movement was a result. Both the textual fragmentation and choreographed movement were important for Eisenstein's work in the cinema.

Vertov and Kuleshov had already made significant discoveries about montage. In fiction films, montage could be used to compose the story rather than illustrate well-known literary scenarios or narrate, as most films had done before the Revolution. Both Kuleshov and his pupil Pudovkin used editing essentially to create a coherent narrative, whilst Eisenstein, inspired by the fragmentation used in Meyerhold's theatre, aimed in his use of montage at the collision of images that would not only tell a story but lead to a new understanding – emotional or intellectual.

In 1924, Proletkult commissioned Eisenstein's first film, *The Strike* (Stachka, Goskino and Proletkult, 1925). Dwelling on the principles of 'typage', where the facial expression and demeanour were more important than acting, *The Strike* presented the masses as the main hero and refrained from using trained actors. Eisenstein, working with the experienced cameraman Tisse, used a documentary approach, showing the strike movement in such a way that it touched the audiences although they could not identify with a single hero. Real workers were juxtaposed with the grotesquely drawn capitalist exploiters: the factory bosses puff cigars, boast of wealth and display their fat bellies; the police detectives are characterized as sly, cunning, devious or contriving through inserted non-diegetic images of animals – monkeys, owls, and bulldogs – displaying in an exaggerated fashion the appropriate quality: agile, watchful, and guarding. By similar method, Eisenstein compared the command to crush the workers' march with slaughtering an animal by intercutting a butcher ramming his knife into a table, thus underscoring the force and brutality of the event. Eisenstein's so-called intellectual montage relied on the Marxist principle of thesis and antithesis to create a new concept: 'Any two frames juxtaposed inevitably combine into a new concept…' (Eisenstein, 1926).[21] *The Strike* was constructed like a symphony, moving from oppression to protest and the eventual crushing of the workers. This carefully composed movement created an emotional response to the predicament of the workers and led to a sense of solidarity with the working class. Although Social Democrat agitators had peered into the factory in an attempt to raise awareness of the workers' exploitation, the workers took no action at this stage. It is the suicide of one of the workers that leads to unrest and strike. Thus, the strike is not a result of agitation but of injustice – as would also be the case for the mutiny on the battleship *Potemkin* in Eisenstein's next film. Moreover, the strike brings physical hardship to the workers' families, who suffer from the loss of pay and have to pawn their possessions in order to survive. The strikers are neither manipulated by the political activists, nor are they fooled by the police, who try to provoke aggression. The demonstration remains peaceful, and when the police charge into the crowd, causing a massacre of unarmed workers, the viewers' compassion has been shifted fully to the workers' cause.

After the success of *The Strike*, Eisenstein was assigned to a film that would commemorate the 1905 Revolution (see Chapter 1): *The Battleship Potemkin* (Bronenosets Potemkin, Goskino 1925). Eisenstein embarked on the project of 'The Year 1905' in Leningrad – a film covering several events leading up to 1905, but weather conditions made it impossible to continue filming. The film crew moved to Odessa to shoot what was intended to be a minor episode in the film: the mutiny on the battleship *Prince Potemkin*. This minor sequence turned into an entire film, which was shot to a modified screenplay over three months in Odessa, partly on the *Potemkin*'s sister ship *Twelve Apostles* (the *Potemkin* had been dismantled).[22]

The film presents the discontented sailors on board the battleship *Potemkin* protesting only when they are given rotten meat. When they are threatened with execution, the brave cry of the sailor Vakulinchuk makes the firing squad realize that they are about to shoot at their 'brothers'. This heroic deed costs Vakulinchuk his life: while the sailors seize control over the ship, he is shot by the senior officer, Giliarovsky. His body is taken to the port of Odessa, where the citizens mourn him and send supplies to the battleship. The tsarist troops try to control the crowds and, advancing from the top of the Odessa steps, shoot at the citizens. The battleship's guns fire at the general staff headquarters (the theatre) to defend the people of Odessa. The next day, the other ships of the fleet refrain from attacking the rebellious battleship.

Eisenstein stops his version of events at this convenient and advantageous point: he conflates historical events and neglects several historical facts. The entire action moves from the individual to the masses, from the part to the whole. The relationship between man and the crowd therefore stands at the centre of Eisenstein's film.

> We must look for the essence of cinema not in the shots but in the relationship between the shots, just as in history we look not at individuals but at the relationships between individuals, classes, etc. (Eisenstein, 1926)[23]

For Eisenstein, the emphasis lay in the juxtaposition of different movements within one frame or within sequences, on choreography and (arranged) chaos, on the lines and circles of movement. In his famous sequence of the Odessa Steps, the linear movement of the soldiers is juxtaposed with the unorganized, chaotic and elemental movement of the people who are 'bouncing down the steps like cherry stones',[24] and is further broken by the wheels of the pram rolling down the steps. In order to capture the movement on the Odessa steps from different angles, Eisenstein had camera trolleys built along the steps, and a circus-trained artist with a hand-camera strapped to his body ran with the people so that he could film the crowd movement.[25]

Eisenstein needed types, faces and physiognomies. His assistant Grigori Alexandrov played Giliarovsky, while the doctor – who with his pince-nez seems to be almost modelled on Anton Chekhov – was played by a stoker, and a gardener performed as the priest. Villains are mostly portrayed with a touch of the grotesque (the priest pretends to be dead when he falls down the stairs yet he winks in the following shot), while the sailors are shown in a realistic fashion, muscular and strong. Eisenstein relied on the masses as the hero: the crew, the battleship, the fleet. The mutiny on the ship served as a microcosm of the events that would spread

Figure 2.4 Eisenstein's *Battleship Potemkin*: The Odessa Steps.

across Russia, symbolically rendered through the fleet greeting and supporting the battleship in the end. Vakulinchuk merely serves as spokesman, asserting the temporary need for such a role as assumed by Lenin during the Revolution as a leader for the masses; but Vakulinchuk is also a martyr. *Potemkin* underlines that the Revolution was started by the unjustly exploited and oppressed people rather than by agitators. The shots fired by the battleship at the Odessa Theatre (the general staff headquarters) reveal the tsarist regime's impotence and infertility, contrasted with the energy and force of the sailors' potency, which are suggested in the imagery of the battleship's guns filmed from below to bring out their threatening position and phallic shape.

While *The Strike* was in three acts (oppression, protest and crushing), for *Potemkin* Eisenstein relied on the structure of classical tragedy: the film consists of five parts, complete with exposition, peripetia, and denouement. Each of the five 'acts' contains a change of mood: from quiet suffering (passivity) to declared dissatisfaction (active resistance); from the fear of execution (submissiveness) to mutiny (aggression); from mourning over the dead sailor (passive) to anger at the injustice (active); from sending boats to demonstrate solidarity with the sailors on the ship (building bridges) to the slaughter on the Odessa steps (destruction) that triggers the gunfire from the battleship (action); and from anxiety over the fleet's response (passive, subdued, insecure) to triumph (safety, active response, red flag). Each part thus moves from passive to active, from subdued to triumphant, from submissive to aggressive, exposing opposite principles (thesis/antithesis) and leading to the dialectical conclusion in the synthesis: progress.

Eisenstein's understanding of montage was based on the collision of images in terms of opposite or contradictory content (unified mass and lonely individual), movement (chaotic and organized), direction (upwards and downwards), or colour (dark and light). Montage can produce both movement and meaning, as in the three shots of the lions – sleeping, waking, rising – which create the illusion that the lion rises, symbolically. Eisenstein later differentiated between several types of montage: Metric montage determines the absolute length of a piece and refers to the rhythm or pace of a sequence (the number of shots per minute increases/decreases). Rhythmic montage refers to the movement within the frame (motionless, walking, pacing, running). Tonal montage refers to the choice of tone (light or gloom) within a frame. Intellectual montage implies the juxtaposition or comparison of one situation to another (non-diegetic images to create a metaphor).

Eisenstein's treatment of history, ending on a victory that the vessel never scored in reality, shows the extent to which cinema could manipulate reality through editing techniques. At a time where the objective reality was far from ideal – the country was shaken by the First World War and the Civil War – cinema supported the socialist cause by representing history in an idealized way. Films of the mid-1920s thus create a subjective reality: they construct rather than tell the truth. Cinema lent itself to the portrayal of a reality that had not yet taken shape and – looking ahead at the 1930s – made itself vulnerable to the principles of Socialist Realism, requiring the portrayal of history 'in its revolutionary development': showing in a realistic way the people of today having (almost) reached a perfect society, a concept that would be stringently required from works of art in the next decade.

Vsevolod Pudovkin (1893–1953) had studied chemistry before working in the cinema with Gardin, but later joined Kuleshov's workshop to develop as a filmmaker. Pudovkin took a different approach not only to montage, but also to acting: where Eisenstein rejected actors, Pudovkin worked with the Moscow Art Theatre actors; where Eisenstein used montage to collide images, Pudovkin used them to build and extend the storyline. For Pudovkin, montage facilitated the flow of the narrative and enriched it by removing 'insignificances' – things that were not relevant for the plot or the atmosphere. In a continuation of the polemic with Kuleshov and Eisenstein, Pudovkin posited his understanding of montage thus:

> Two shots cannot be joined together if one of them in some manner or aspect does not continue the other . . . joining two or more shots in a continuous development of a higher idea. (Pudovkin, 'O montazhe', 1945)[26]

In 1925, he undertook a project for Mezhrabpom that was extremely suited to a man who had trained as scientist: *The Mechanics of the Brain* (Mekhanika golovnogo mozga, Mezhrabpom-Rus 1925), which was designed to popularize Ivan Pavlov's (1849–1936) theory of reflexology, which represented a development of Vladimir Bekhterev's study of physiological stimuli and behaviour. Pudovkin linked the theory of montage to Pavlov's work on reflexes. In the same year he made *Chess Fever* (Shakhmatnaia goriachka, Mezhrabpom-Rus 1925), using documentary

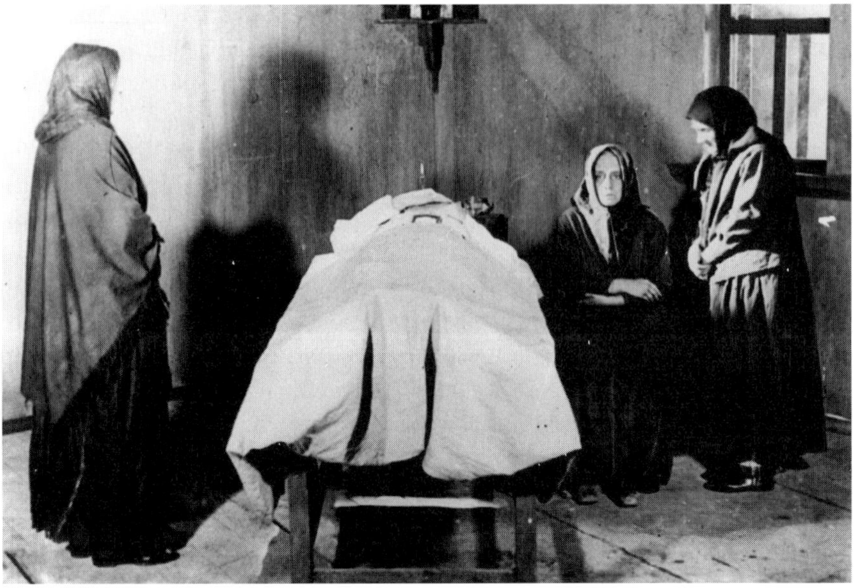

Figure 2.5 Pudovkin's *Mother*: the father's funeral.

footage taken during the 1925 world chess tournament in Moscow and newsreel shots of the world chess champion José Capablanca (1888–1942), and combining them with actors' hands and other objects and figures to tell the story of a fanatical chess player (Fogel) whose girlfriend is driven to despair by his obsession with chess.

Pudovkin's greatest and best-known film of the 1920s is without doubt *The Mother* (Mat', Mezhrabpom-Rus 1926), adapted by Natan Zarkhi from Maxim Gorky's novel: Pelageya Nilovna joins the revolutionary movement when her son Pavel is arrested and imprisoned, thus giving her life a meaning by continuing his cause. Albeit containing an apparently 'unhappy ending', the novel unfolds in great psychological detail the growing revolutionary consciousness of a simple woman. The film project therefore depended on a strong lead actress, whom Pudovkin (or rather his assistant Mikhail Doller, 1889–1952) found in the Moscow Art Theatre actress Vera Baranovskaya (1885–1935), who played Nilovna, and who was joined by Nikolai Batalov (1899–1937) as Pavel. The film script developed the role of the father in comparison with the novel: this expansion underscored on the one hand the mother's oppression by her husband (who physically towers over her with his shadow), whilst the negative portrayal of Vlasov's drunken lifestyle reflected the campaign against alcoholism of the 1920s and earmarked him as a villain from early on in the film. Nilovna is passive and almost immobile in his presence; she moves and acts only after his death, when she takes more responsibility and joins the revolutionary cause. The film's imagery created parallels between Pavel's self-denial and Christ-like martyrdom,[27] but it also portrayed the mother in an almost iconic manner, visually replacing the religious icons of the Madonna with her image of a revolutionary, independent and strong woman.

Nature imagery expressed the emotional states of the characters: the juxtaposition of characters and images such as the singing of birds, the breaking of the ice, or the playing of children translated symbolically Pavel's joy and happiness. The ice floes on the Volga and the ice breaking visually signal change. Such images of nature that continue or extend the characters' psychology illustrate well Pudovkin's use of montage as opposed to that of Eisenstein. Pudovkin's invaluable assistant, Doller, actually performed the stunt of jumping along the ice floes as both the actor and the stuntman refused. Pudovkin and Doller also devised novel devices for steering the crowd by running amidst the people in order to lead them in a particular direction. The camerawork of Pudovkin's permanent collaborator, Anatoli Golovnia (1900–82), a student of Kuleshov, captured effectively the downtrodden life of the workers from high camera angles, whilst the masses are heroicized with low-angled shots, a technique that would be used for decades to come.

In order to mark the tenth anniversary of the Revolution, a number of films were commissioned for 1927. Eisenstein had started a film on collectivization (*The General Line*, later *The Old and the New*), but suspended the project to make *October* (Oktiabr', Sovkino 1928) for the anniversary. Eisenstein's project was gigantic and he was under considerable time pressure, but it was nevertheless released in March 1928, only several months after the anniversary celebrations. *October* was an unwieldy film that used the principles of montage, which Eisenstein had so successfully deployed in his earlier films. Nevertheless, with a running time of almost three hours, *October* lacks the structural density and compositional rigour of his earlier films. It covers the events from the February to the October Revolution with meticulous authenticity, whilst neglecting the dramatic structure. However, *October* contains powerful symbolic images of the fall of the old world order, as for example the horse dangling from the raised bridge or the dismantling of the monument to the tsar.

Pudovkin's contribution to the anniversary was *The End of St Petersburg* (Konets Sankt-Peterburga, Mezhrabpom-Rus 1927), about a man from the countryside who comes to St Petersburg to find work in a factory. However, he has to cross a strike-line to earn money. Later, he denounces the very same worker who granted him shelter and help in the famine-stricken city. Gradually, he understands the strikers' hate for the old world and joins the Revolutionary movement. For the same occasion Esfir Shub made a documentary film, *The Fall of the Romanov Dynasty* (Padenie dinastii Romanovykh, Sovkino 1927), unearthing and editing rare archival footage. Grigori Kozintsev and Leonid Trauberg contributed *S.V.D.* (Soiuz velikogo dela, Sovkino Leningrad 1927) about the Decembrist revolt of 1825.

Comedies and Entertainment in the 1920s: From FEKS to KEM

An entirely different kind of cinema to Eisenstein's montage, one based on eccentricity, circus-like acting and stunts, was created elsewhere in Soviet Russia: the Factory of the Eccentric Actor (FEKS) was formed in 1921 as a theatre company staging comedies and in 1924 it became a film section of Sevzapkino, the film studio in Leningrad. FEKS was headed by Grigori Kozintsev (1905–73) and Leonid Trauberg (1902–90), and was made up of the actors Yelena Kuzmina (1909–79), Sergei Gerasimov (1906–85), Andrei Kostrichkin (1901–73), Yanina Zheimo (1909–87), Liudmila Semenova (1899–1990), and Petr Sobolevsky (1904–77), as well as the set designer Yevgeni Yenei (1890–1971), who had been influenced by expressionist art during his studies in Budapest and Vienna, and the photographer Andrei Moskvin (1901–61).

Their first film, *The Adventures of Oktiabrina* (Pokhozhdeniia Oktiabriny, Sevzapkino 1924), was political buffoonery: Oktiabrina is a young *komsomolka* working for the tax office and fighting a NEP entrepreneur and his business partner with the spoof name of Coolidge Curzonovich Poincaré[28] (allowing a satirical swipe at the US, Britain and France all in one), who try to recover the tsarist regime's debts from the Bolsheviks, although the new government had annulled all debts. The film uses inter-titles to parody the action of the capitalists shown on screen, such as a scene containing an attempted suicide that fails because the braces snap – followed by the inter-title 'Buy from state and not from private businesses'. Oktiabrina's chases on a motorcycle add to the adventure style of the group. The FEKS actors relied on expressive movement and circus tricks for their acting, and the editing was accomplished with an acute sense of pace and rhythm to make this comedy develop with the speed of Kuleshov's *Mr West*.

The Devil's Wheel (Chertovo koleso, Leningradkino 1926) was about gangsters in Petrograd during the Civil War, mixing historical facts with eccentric events revolving around a romantic encounter. The sailor Vania Shorin (Sobolevsky) meets Valia (Semenova) in an amusement park and, engaged in romantic pursuits, he misses the departure of his vessel. The two fall into the hands of a gang who force them to participate in their exploits until Shorin escapes and ensures the gang is arrested. The theme of the subversion of the good sailor and his girl through thieves and ruffians, of the sabotage both of the new regime's pride (the navy) and personal happiness, is turned here into an entertaining and amusing comedy with public appeal.

Gogol's *The Overcoat*, an absurd and grotesque story about a tragicomic character, provided ideal material for FEKS. *The Overcoat* (Shinel', Leningradkino 1926) interwove Gogol's depiction of St Petersburg as provided in his story 'Nevsky Prospect' with the tale of the poor clerk Akaki Akakievich Bashmachkin, who saves money to purchase a new overcoat – his entire pride. But Bashmachkin is a victim of the gloomy city: when the overcoat is stolen, he goes mad and dies. The film's Bashmachkin (Kostrichkin) is at first downtrodden and has given up, but once he

Figure 2.6 Protazanov's *Aelita*: on Mars.

dons his overcoat, his comportment changes and he appears in the frame like a hero, filmed at a low angle to make him rise in stature.

One of the most promising directors of pre-Revolutionary cinema, Yakov Protazanov had returned to Soviet Russia in 1923 to work at Mezhrabpom-Rus (later Mezhrabpomfilm). He not only understood audiences and their tastes, but also worked competently with actors and was incredibly prolific. His first Soviet film was *Aelita* (1924) based on Alexei Tolstoy's novel about a Soviet engineer, Los (Nikolai Tsereteli), who dreams of building a spaceship. Los seeks to escape from the world through his flight to Mars rather than discover a new planet. In this world, however, he suspects that his wife Natasha has betrayed him and shoots her. Los is followed in his pursuits by two men: Kravtsov, in the performance of Ilinsky, who gave a brilliant parody of the detective character in cinema; and the adventure-thirsty Red Army officer Gusev (Batalov). They accompany Los to Mars where they organize an uprising of the Martian slaves, which Princess Aelita (Yulia Solntseva, 1901–89), with whom Los has fallen in love, betrays. Los wakes up – on a Moscow railway station: his space flight was only a dream – neither has he killed his wife, nor has she betrayed him. The film had fine performances by actors who contrasted Earth and Mars by changing from a realistic and comic to a declamatory and serious style. The set and costumes for the Martian scenes were designed by the constructivist artist Alexandra Ekster, thus creating a sharp contrast between the decorativeness of the bourgeois lifestyle on Earth and the beautiful and geometrical shapes on Mars. The film also combined a story about science and conquest with a romantic adventure story, ensuring the film's popular success, whilst its critics continued to attack its non-real setting. Protazanov had turned the science fiction journey into Los's dream, a figment of his imagination, thus ridiculing the idea of a conquest of other planets. He was accused of a lack of ideological principles and of mocking Soviet life. The doyenne of Soviet film criticism, Neya Zorkaya, has argued that the film's eclecticism, or lack of a concept, reflects so well the chaos of life in the early 1920s, where Protazanov captures the surrounding reality in an unusually concise manner, which contributed to his popularity. She points out that Protazanov's choice of actors draws on a range of talents, creating less an ensemble (as did Kuleshov, for example), but a concert of disparate voices.[29]

Protazanov's *His Call* (Ego prizyv, Mezhrabpom-Rus 1925) reached the top ten films in popularity with an adventure plot in which an industrialist and his son Vladimir (Anatolii Ktorov) leave for Paris during the Revolution. When their money is up, Vladimir returns to retrieve the casket with the fortune that they left behind in what is now a communal flat. In order to gain access to the treasure, he seduces Katia, who now lives in the room in question, and even kills her grandmother (the grand old lady of the stage, Maria Bliumental-Tamarina). After these horrors Katia hears the call to join the Party, but at first she is too ashamed to follow. Then she accepts the call as a way of redeeming her sins. Protazanov made further successful comedies for Mezhrabpom-Rus, exposing the flaws of the Soviet bureaucracy, such as *The Tailor of Torzhok* (Zakroishchik iz Torzhka, 1925) which offers a critique of the housing system, or *Don Diego and Pelageya* (Mezhrabpomfilm 1928), which attacked the narrow-mindedness of Soviet bureaucrats: the old Pelageya is illiterate and crosses a railway line where there is a sign not to do so. Don Diego witnesses this 'crime' and arrests her, but the almighty power of the Party comes to Pelageya's rescue, establishing justice.

The Forty-First (Sorok pervyi, Mezhrabpom-Rus 1927; remake by Grigori Chukhrai, 1956) was based on Boris Lavrenev's play and set during the Civil War in Turkestan, thus using an exotic setting. The Red Army is crossing the Karakum Desert when a White officer is spotted; however, the sharpshooter Mariutka misses her forty-first target. Thus Lieutenant Govorukha is captured and Mariutka has to take him to headquarters across the Aral Sea. During a storm the two are stranded on an island, and they fall in love. When an enemy ship approaches, Mariutka shoots Govorukha, remembering that her duty to the army comes before love. The romantic story, with the unhappy ending that places political over personal, manifested the value of the collective (army) as worth more than bourgeois values represented by

Mariutka's love for the lieutenant. However, Protazanov underlines Mariutka's loss of her human values rather than her victory as a Bolshevik.[30]

Protazanov also used foreign settings for his anti-bourgeois comedies, such as *The Three Millions Case* (Protsess o trekh millionakh, 1926), where a banker sells his house to speculate on the food market and is outwitted by his wife and a thief, who in turn are tricked by another thief, ultimately leaving the two thieves with the money, the wife without her lover, and the husband bankrupt. The film contains a romantic melodrama and passes a judgement on the banker who speculates with other people's poverty; and there is adventure and slapstick in two thieves at one crime scene. In *St Jorgen's Feast Day* (Prazdnik sviatogo Iorgena, Mezhrabpomfilm 1930) Protazanov exposed the exploitation of a town by the Church during an annual festival now run by two thieves who extort money from the townspeople. Protazanov's films thus combine popular elements (adventures and espionage) with plots that are ideologically sound and which occasionally satirize the ridiculous bureaucracy of the system.

A conventional, but highly successful film of the 1920s was *The Bear's Wedding* (Medvezh'ia svad'ba, dir. Konstantin Eggert [1883–1955] with Vladimir Gardin, Mezhrabpom-Rus 1925), based on Prosper Merimée's 1869 horror story *Lokis*, adapted for the screen by Lunacharsky, the Commissar for Enlightenment. The film's success can largely be explained by its genre: a vampire story. Count Shemet (Eggert), who suffers from seizures that turn him into a bear, falls in love with an innocent girl and marries her. During the wedding night he is consumed by passion and mutilates her body. The girl's sister-in-law avenges the murder and kills him. With all the ingredients of romance and passion, the goriness of ghosts and vampires, and with a rigid black-and-white division between good and evil, the film attracted record figures. Similarly, Yuri Zheliabuzhsky's (1888–1955) *The Cigarette Girl from Mosselprom* (Papirosnitsa ot Mossel'proma, Mezhrabpom-Rus 1924) was a popular romantic comedy: the accountant Mitiushin (Ilinsky) loves the cigarette vendor Zina Vesenina (Solntseva), but Zina declines Mitiushin's proposal because she loves the projectionist Latugin (Tsereteli). When she visits the film studio, she meets the American businessman MacBride – with a grotesquely fat belly that marks him as a capitalist – who is also in love with her and invites her to be an extra; Zina, however, refuses. After having overcome a series of obstacles, Zina and Lagutin are united in a *kheppi end*. The film contained fine acting and stylized, expressive performances by the actors, especially the comic actor Igor Ilinsky.

One of the best-known melodramas of the period was created by Abram Room (1894–1976), who had come to the cinema from a medical background, having intermittently worked in amateur theatres before the Revolution and later assisted Meyerhold at the Theatre of the Revolution. After making several shorts and documentaries, he made *Death Bay* (Bukhta smerti, Goskino 1926) followed by *Bed and Sofa* (Tret'ia Meshchanskaia [literal translation: Third Meshchanskaya Street], Sovkino 1927), a film set in contemporary Moscow, which picked upon the issue of the housing shortage. The stonemason Kolia (Batalov) lives with his wife Liuda (Semenova) in a one-room apartment on Third Meshchanskaya Street (hence the title). He meets the print worker Volodia (Fogel), with whom he had fought in the war and who has come from the provinces to work in Moscow, but has nowhere to stay. He is offered a sofa in the apartment. When Kolia goes away for a few days, Liuda and Volodia start an affair: Volodia showers Liuda with gifts and attention, and even takes her on an aeroplane over Moscow. Upon his return, Kolia discovers the affair and moves out, but – unable to find alternative quarters – returns to the sofa. Now Volodia changes his demeanour vis-à-vis Liuda, paying less attention to her, bonding instead with his old friend Kolia, and Liuda returns to her husband. When Liuda discovers that she is pregnant (not knowing who the father is), both men demand an abortion, but Liuda decides to have the child, leaving the two men and Moscow.

Like the heroines of pre-Revolutionary cinema, Liuda is an object – not of male pride or possession (she is never 'displayed'), but of male convenience. She completes her domestic chores and ventures outside only with Volodia to walk around the city centre and take a flight above Moscow, which offers her an overview that her semi-basement flat denies her. She has no consciousness of herself as woman, and, in true socialist fashion, this is what she gains at the film's end. However, the remainder of the story hardly conformed to socialist ideas: in her 'liberation', Liuda makes

Figure 2.7 Room's *Bed and Sofa*: Kolia (Batalov) in bed, watched by Liuda (Semenova).

no contribution to society, not does she stay in the centre, the destination of most heroes in 1920s and 1930s narratives; instead she runs away and leaves Moscow on a train.

Liuda's visit to the abortion clinic (abortions were legal from 1920–36 and again after 1955) is revealing, as Julian Graffy has pointed out: it shows Liuda looking out of the window, from above, on to the street where she sees a boy nursing a doll and later a child in a pram. Her idealized vision of having a child does not fit either into the crammed flat, nor into the real-life scene that the nurse observes a few moments later: a pram with two infants and an empty bottle, echoing visually not only the crisis in relationships and role of women in a new society, but also housing and food problems.[31]

The film outraged audiences and critics alike for its amoral portrayal of life. It comically illustrated marital life and the affair by shifting characters from bed to sofa and vice versa. Moreover, it offers no traditional happy ending – Liuda leaves Moscow alone, without a job and without a husband. For a genuinely emancipated Soviet woman this would be a possible turn of events, but Liuda is a wife/housewife with no other role in society: she lives, albeit in Soviet conditions, a petty bourgeois lifestyle, enjoying gifts and entertainment from men without making her contribution to the construction of the new country. Her address is indicative of this: it is the 'Third Bourgeois' Street where she lives. She leaves the centre for the periphery and rejects the male-dominated patriarchal society of the city.

Boris Barnet had had a star performance in *Mr West* as the cowboy Jeddy, but he was a professional boxer and returned to film permanently only in 1926 when he made *Miss Mend* (Mezhrabpom-Rus 1926) with Fedor Otsep, based on Marietta Shaganian's popular adventure story written for a feuilleton. *Miss Mend* is a spy series about American bandits who plan biological warfare in Russia. Miss Mend is a stenographer for an American factory boss whose son (whom she educates) is abducted. The police refuse to help and the bandits kill the boy. Miss Mend goes to the USSR to avenge the murder and stop the gangsters from accomplishing their evil ploy of spreading the plague bacillus in Leningrad. Assisted by the Soviet police, they get rid of the bandits and Miss Mend returns to the US. The serial shows how the American police betray the citizens, but not so the Soviet police. Spun over several series, *Miss Mend* was immensely popular in the 1920s.

In *The Girl with a Hat Box* (Devushka s korobkoi, Mezhrabpom-Rus 1927) the milliner Natasha Korosteleva (Anna Sten, 1908–93) is in possession of a precious Moscow residence permit while living in a village with her grandfather. She lets her Moscow room to Madame Irena (played by the Moscow Art Theatre actress Serafima Birman, 1890–1976), who owns a hat shop and uses the extra room for her lazy husband. On the way to town, Natasha meets and takes pity on the peasant Ilya Snegirev (Ivan Koval-Samborsky, 1893–1962) who has – not unlike Volodia in *Bed and Sofa* – nowhere to stay, but has found work in Moscow. Through a fictitious marriage, Ilya obtains the right to stay in Natasha's room at Madame Irena's, to the landlady's dismay. Madame Irena fires Natasha, giving her the last wage in the form of a lottery ticket that wins 25,000 roubles. Now that she is free from external pressures, Natasha falls in love with Ilya, and their marriage becomes a real one. The film was exposed to vitriolic attacks for its immorality in the same way as *Bed and Sofa*.

Barnet's *The House on Trubnaya Square* (Dom na Trubnoi, Mezhrabpom-Rus 1928) was one of the last satirical comedies about the NEP. It was scripted by the imaginist writers and poets Anatoli Mariengof and Vadim Shershenevich, the satirist Nikolai Erdman, and the formalist Viktor Shklovsky. The film concerns the occupants of the house on Trubnaya Sqaure, where the peasant girl Parasha Pitunova (Vera Maretskaya, 1906–78, an actress of the Vakhtangov School) has found work as a maid. The petit bourgeois Golikov (Fogel) makes Parasha work both at home and at his hairdresser's shop – until a note arrives to tell her that she has been elected to the city council. All this is a mix-up, but for the moment, Parasha is fired and chased from the house with nowhere to go. The trade union defends her and condemns Golikov, thus establishing justice and creating a happy ending for the comedy of mistaken identity. Barnet's funny and ironic portrayal of the peasant girl in the city and her encounters with an alien culture made the film appealing.

Following the model of FEKS, Friedrich Ermler set up KEM (Kino-Experimental'naia Masterskaia) in 1924 with his secret service comrade Eduard Ioganson (1894–1942, died during the Leningrad siege) and the theatre actor Fedor Nikitin (1900–88), who was nicknamed the 'Russian Prince Myshkin' for his interpretation of intellectual characters. Friedrich Ermler is the German name that Vladimir Breslav adopted when he was engaged in espionage for the Red Army during the war. He kept this name, as well as his allegiance to the army and probably also the secret service. *Katka's Reinette Apples* (Kat'ka bumazhnyi ranet, Len-Sovkino 1926 with Ioganson and Nikitin) tells of a girl, Katka (Veronika Buzhinskaya, 1895–1983), who comes to Leningrad and sells apples. Seduced by underworld tsar Semka Zhgut (Valeri Solovtsov, 1904–77) she gets pregnant, but leaves him. In her attempt to lead an honest life apart from Zhgut, who is ultimately arrested, she is helped by the worker Vadka (Nikitin). In *Katka*, Ermler rewarded the heroine who had chosen the right path, and condemned the criminals. The film also contains a romantic story, which was well performed by two of the leading actors of the time and stirred audiences. In *The Parisian Cobbler* (Parizhskii sapozhnik, Len-Sovkino 1927), Ermler uses a similar constellation for the forces of good and evil, with the same actors. The heroine is once again a pregnant woman, Katia (Buzhinskaya), who is rejected both by her father – for living with a man outside wedlock in their small village, and by her lover Andrei (Solovtsov), who feels that having children is too bourgeois for a Komsomol (Communist Union of Youth) member. The deaf-mute Parisian cobbler Kirik (Nikitin), living by pre-Revolutionary values, supports Katia and defends her when Andrei plots to have her raped so as to bring about a miscarriage. Ermler stresses the presence of humanism as a separate issue from Party membership, making not all Party members good people by definition, although the film's end shows the Party confirming right over wrong by excluding Andrei from the Komsomol. Ermler mixes the genres of melodrama, adventure and slapstick. In *Fragment of the Empire* (Oblomok imperii, Len-Sovkino 1929), Ermler portrays the watchman of a small railway station, Filimonov (Nikitin), who has lost his memory due to injuries sustained in the First World War. Ten years later, seeing his wife through the window of a passing train, his memory returns. He travels to Leningrad to find this wife, who is now married to a bourgeois NEP man and is unwilling to abandon her present lifestyle. Filimonov finds a job at a factory, which is run by a collective, whilst his old employer is now penniless, but can still spare a coin for him to relive for a moment his old glory and stature. Ermler's films contain linear narratives and combine conventional photography with fine acting, telling stories with a sound moral message: that Party membership is no synonym for goodness, that bourgeois values have not yet been eradicated, but that poor workers can be trusted most – those roles in which he cast Fedor Nikitin.

Dovzhenko and Poetic Cinema, 1927–30

Alexander Dovzhenko (Oleksandr Dovzhenka 1894–1956) came to cinema in 1926 from a career as science teacher, diplomat with secret service connections and painter, having lived and studied in Berlin and Munich. His work in the 1920s was largely based at Ukraine's VUFKU in Odessa, where he made several films that established him as the doyen of Ukrainian cinema, determining its poetic style for decades to come. Dovzhenko created sequences, often beginning with static compositions that become animated, which defined the relationship between man and nature. *Zvenigora* (VUFKU 1927) told the story of an old man raising his two grandsons: Pavlo, an idle boy blowing soap bubbles and representing bourgeois nationalism; and Timoshka (Semen Svashenko, 1904–69, an actor of the famous Ukrainian theatre director Les Kurbas), a hard-working boy who represents Soviet values. The grandfather teaches the boys the stories of the mountain steppe Zvenigora, where the Tartars fought the Poles, and the legend about Scythian treasures hidden in the burial sites of Zvenigora. Pavlo remains oblivious to the Revolution, turning into a bandit and adventurer who leaves the country and dupes audiences in Paris, only to return with the money to the Ukraine to support the counter-revolutionaries. When Pavlo tries to draw his grandfather into his destructive plans, the Revolutionary hero Timoshka and his comrades take the grandfather with them on a train. Flowingly mixing myth and modern life, Dovzhenko created a poetic cinema style, where nature epitomizes stability and tranquillity, harbours the past and flexes towards the future. While the grandfather searches for a meaning in the past, Timoshka finds it in the Revolution. *Arsenal* (VUFKU Odessa 1929) continues the story of Timosh, now a socialist worker at the Arsenal factory. The conflicting forces of war and revolution, Ukrainian nationalists and workers have devastated the country, which suffers further due to a famine. In the opening scene, an invalid peasant beats his feeble horse as he despairs at the sight of a field with empty wheat ears. A mother beats her children who are crying from hunger, as she too is desperate for food. Two sequences that need no inter-titles powerfully express the desperation of the people. Soldiers are fighting; Timosh is among those who defend the factory against the Ukrainian Cossacks in an uneven fight, culminating in the massacre of the Revolutionaries that leaves only Timosh steadfast and invincible. The painterly arrangements of frames and the slow editing with little camera movement by the director of photography Daniil Demutsky (1893–1954), created poetic sequences that mourn the losses and sing praises to the heroes, whilst also standing in contrast to the fast editing and montage used by Kuleshov and Eisenstein.

Earth (Zemlia, VUFKU Kiev 1930) draws its title from the rich Ukrainian soil. In a village there is a conflict between the families of the Trubenkos and the Bilokins,

Figure 2.8 Vasyl in Dovzhenko's *Earth*.

and between generations of grandfathers, fathers and sons. The film opens with the death of the Trubenko grandfather and ends with that of his grandson Vasyl, as both frames capture the majestic and unchangeable cycle of nature with its sunflowers, apples and trees. Father Trubenko opposes collectivization, while his son Vasyl rejoices in working the land with the new tractors. The kulak Khoma Bilokin, who despises technology, kills Vasyl because he perceives technology as a threat and because he is angry at Vasyl's joy. This murder is a crass warning: driving the tractor to plough the fields elevates Vasyl to the master of the soil, breaching the peasants' view of man's role in relation to nature. Therefore the man-master of the soil has to be annihilated. Dovzhenko portrays Vasyl's murder as a ritual sacrifice, but Vasyl's legacy lives on when the peasants adopt his methods. *Earth* contains an ambivalent message about the use of technology to exploit nature. The use of folk motives and myths had to be shortened, and the implication of the ritual sacrifice removed, before the film could be released: by 1930 the first signs of ideological control became apparent and hampered production. Thematically, Dovzhenko's film anticipates the treatment of the theme of peasant superstition versus modernization that Kozintsev and Trauberg chose for their first sound film, *Alone*, discussed in the next chapter.

The Cultural Revolution

By 1928 the box office receipts for Soviet films had overtaken those of foreign films in distribution,[32] eradicating the dependence on imported films. In March 1928 the All-Union Party Conference on Cinema Affairs took place, where Party officials and critics of the proletarian organizations demanded that films should be intelligible to the millions. In 1928 the country had 9,000 cinemas, a figure that would double by 1930 and climbed to almost 30,000 by 1933.[33] However, Party officials ignored the fact that cinema tickets were expensive, and workers could see films cheaply only in factory clubs, which were equipped with old and often defunct projectors. Cinema audiences in the big houses in the city centre consisted mainly of the NEP bourgeoisie, *apparatchiki* and their children. The cinema for the workers had no market, and the cinemas that could return a profit needed to cater for audiences with bourgeois tastes.

Since cinema was, according to speeches at the conference, not fulfilling its role of catering for the masses, but spending instead huge sums of money on production, the industry was exposed to vitriolic attacks and serious criticism. The Party officials ignored the lack of equipment and film stock (still not produced in Soviet Russia in the desirable quality – fiction films continued to be made on imported film stock). The ramshackle cinemas and defective projectors, the cameras that were brought back by cameramen from trips abroad and the reliance on imported film stock betrayed the industry's lack of a reliable infrastructure. However, the blame for the huge budget required for Sovkino was placed at the filmmakers' feet.

In January 1929, a decree 'on the strengthening of cinema cadres' highlighted some of the consequences of the 1928 conference. It effectively envisaged a purge in film studios, in cinema associations and in the industry. In June 1929 the purges of the film administration and of ARRK began: they affected those who did not make 'films for the millions' and who were 'bourgeois reactionaries'. Formalism was targeted as it sought to narrate through structure and 'typage' rather than psychology and acting, and because its rejection of plot meant that films were complex in style and form. In the light of the fact that Trotsky had praised formalism, artists were drawn once again into political battles: in the anti-Trotskyite climate of late 1920s, attacks were levelled at the formalist critics Viktor Shklovsky, Boris Eikhenbaum and others.

The purges of the Association of Revolutionary Workers of Cinematography (ARRK, renamed in 1928 from ARK to offer proletarian credentials – the equivalent in literature was RAPP, the Russian Association of Proletarian Writers, which had succeeded its all-union equivalent VAPP in 1928) started in 1930, because this organization was easier to purge than the more complex film studios. In 1929 arrests of the association's members were made, from stokers and firemen to administrators and consultants, directors and artists. Film journalists, including the critic and scriptwriter Viktor Shklovsky, Khrisanf Khersonsky and Ippolit Sokolov, were excluded from the Association in order to put them under ideological pressure. Vladimir Nilsen, cameraman for Eisenstein and Alexandrov, was arrested and subsequently released, but he was arrested again and executed during the Great Purges – a fate he shared with many others (see Chapter 3).[34]

In 1927, filmmakers and industry staff were accused of economic crimes, i.e. squandering money, and put on trial. Bearing in mind the proportion of bureaucrats to creative staff, the regime largely had itself to blame for the structural flaws in the production system that prevented proper functioning. It appears that Soviet cinema achieved what it did during the 1920s largely thanks to the clever policies of Shvedchikov and Trainin, under whose management foreign films brought in 85 per cent of Sovkino's revenue on only 33 per cent of the released film titles. However, continuous accusations of making harmful films and wasting money plagued Sovkino. According to the Party leadership and the Political Enlightenment Section (Glavpolitprosvet), Sovkino should make educational films and films with revolutionary and ideological content, which could be understood by the millions. As a result of the allegations raised at the 1928 conference, Sovkino was purged in May 1930; it was abolished and replaced by Soyuzkino on 13 February 1930. Boris Shumiatsky became chairman of Soyuzkino in October 1930. Gradually, foreign films were removed from circulation or exposed to vituperative criticism. In the years following the abolishment of Sovkino (1930–33), film production dropped to thirty-five films per year compared to an average of 120 in the last half of the 1920s. From 1928 to 1932, the film industry was almost entirely destroyed – after it had just been rebuilt through the circulation of popular foreign films and Soviet films relying on bourgeois values and tastes, made by the old guard of the pre-Revolutionary generation of filmmakers, including Protazanov, Sabinsky, Chardynin, Gardin and Perestiani, who had been so much more productive and successful with audiences than Kuleshov, Vertov, Eisenstein and Pudovkin.[35] At the end of the decade, high and low culture were far apart and, although cinema could technically reach the masses, it did not cater for the peasants or workers, who may, indeed, not have constituted the majority of cinema-goers at the time.

> The cinema culture of the 1920s was a multifaceted one, but one based on 'bourgeois' entertainment films of foreign and Soviet origins. It was the profits from these films which funded the work of the avant-garde.[36]

Following the so-called Cultural Revolution, which placed the workers' concerns high on the thematic agenda and applied a 'value and ideology for money' policy to cultural production, filmmaking continued along the lines of narrative films with simple plots and realistic characters. However, many films were banned between 1929 and 1933 (some at the pre-production stage), others were cut (such as *Earth*) or had restricted releases (*The Old and the New*); others ran into censorship problems not because they were anti-Revolutionary, but because they contained comic and satirical elements. The films of the Cultural Revolution thus mark a stylistic turning point for their directors.

Pudovkin was assigned to film *Storm over Asia* (Potomok Chingiz Khana, Mezhrabpomfilm 1928) in Mongolia. The film told a Civil War story set in 1918 during the British occupation of Mongolia, when the Mongol herdsman Bair (played by Valeri Inkizhinov, 1893–1973, a Buryat actor at the Moscow Art Theatre who emigrated in 1930) tries to sell a rare silver fox fur on the market. He is cheated by an English trader and escapes after a brawl. He joins the Red partisans in their fight against the occupiers. Their commitment is powerfully expressed in a scene that shows a woman partisan suckling her baby, successfully combining personal life with political devotion. When the partisan leader dies – with a vision of a sunset over Moscow's Kremlin in the background – he encourages the others not to abandon the fight. Bair's tribe is threatened by the requisitioning of cattle, and Bair, trying to come to its aid, is captured. When the occupiers discover an amulet that suggests Bair is a descendant of Genghis Khan, they place him on the throne to establish a Mongolian puppet regime. However, the Mongolian army sweeps across the land – creating literally a storm over Asia that wipes the British from the map. The film offers a fine portrayal of Mongolian life and rituals, largely thanks to Inkizhinov's fine acting, but also through the near-documentary footage of a ritual at the lamasery, filmed by Pudovkin after the Lama had consented to bring forward an annual ceremony to allow for the filming. The story is captured through the exotic imagery of the Mongolian steppe, while the events fulfil the requirements of an adventure film, but there is also blunt propaganda supporting the cause of the Red Army (such as the image of the Kremlin).

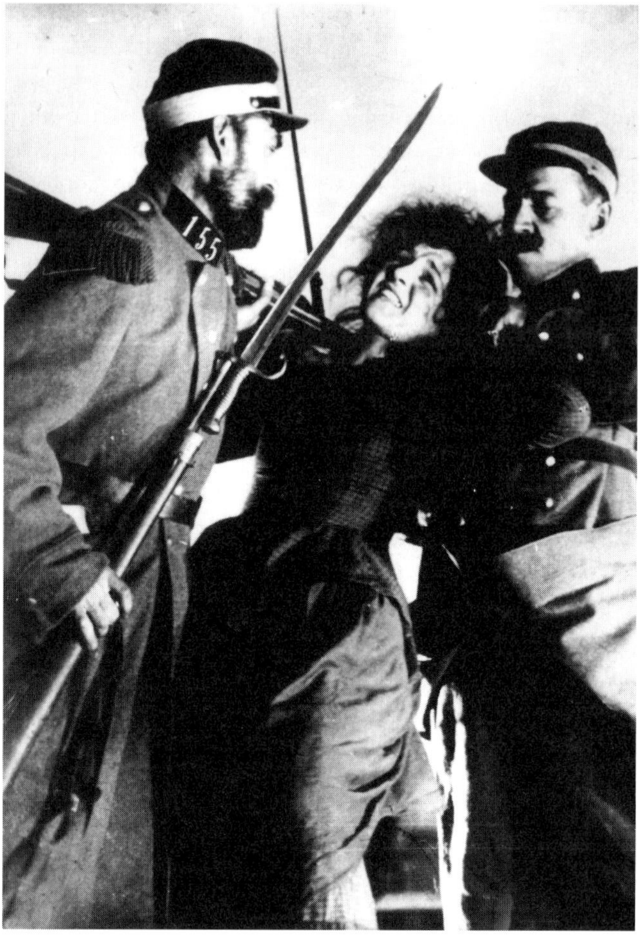

Figure 2.9 Kozintsev and Trauberg's *New Babylon*: Louise is arrested.

Kozintsev and Trauberg's *New Babylon* (Novyi Vavilon, Sovkino Leningrad 1929) combined the eccentric acting style of their previous films with a historical plot. *New Babylon* draws on the insurrection against the French government in 1871, when, in the wake of the Franco-Prussian War and France's defeat under Napoleon III, the proletariat opposed the capitalists and formed the Commune, which was dispersed in the 'bloody week' when governmental troops crushed the communards. The events hardened the opposition between the bourgeoisie and the workers. The film begins in a department store on rue de Babylone, where Louise (Kuzmina) serves rich customers. As the German army advances, the rich capitulate while the workers, among them Louise, resist. Louise joins the Commune, and the dreary everyday work suddenly becomes meaningful and joyful. The score by the young composer Dmitri Shostakovich underlined the mood changes in the Commune. Louise's beloved, the soldier Jean, joins the government army at Versailles after returning from the war, although Louise begs him not to do so. When Jean learns that those who stayed in the Commune will be killed, he has visions of Louise that reveal his plagued conscience.

New Babylon often plays with situational absurdities, which is a characteristic feature of FEKS films. Thus, for example, the verbal and visual often provide ironic contrasts. The inter-title 'For sale' (*prodaetsia*) appears when Louise is selling goods in the store – and is invited out by her floor manager. In the same way as visual montage could create different meaning by juxtaposing images, here the title could refer to Louise or to the goods – what is for sale? Similarly, the final sequence of the film inverts the hope that the earlier titles and images contained: the slogan 'Vive la Commune' stands next to a raised hand – of a dead body; the slogan 'Order' precedes a scene showing the dead bodies of the communards.

In numerous ways, *New Babylon* conformed to the genre of the melodrama – Louise separated from her beloved who helplessly witnesses her death – and this was a melodrama with the unhappy ending so characteristic of pre-Revolutionary Russian cinema. In terms of the historical context, the film provides a parallel to the fight of the workers reaching back into the last century but also concerning another country, France, thereby creating the illusion of the possibility of an international workers' revolution – a correct statement to make at the time and one that would fit politically into the Party agenda.

Eisenstein's *The Old and the New* (Staroe i novoe, made as General'naia liniia, Sovkino 1929) tried to conform to the political agenda by addressing the theme of farming, supporting the drive for collectivization. However, having begun the film in 1926, Eisenstein had based the script on the notion of cooperative work that was advocated at the time; when he returned to the project after completing *October*, the 'general line' had changed and collectivization was on the agenda instead of cooperation. Political circumstances had changed, and thereby the film had become controversial. Marfa Lapkina, played by a non-professional actress, is an illiterate peasant woman who heads a milking brigade. When collective work is introduced and the *artel* 'October's Ray' acquires a cream separator, the farm's production rises. The mechanical, perfect movement of the machine spinning is celebrated with visual montage showing the wheels and cogs turning at different speed and in different size, until the cream splashes over Lapkina's face. At the end of the film, tractors arrive to assist the peasants in ploughing the fields, and a dozen tractors perform dance-like movements in the fields in a visual celebration of technology. The film praises the introduction of mechanical devices into the countryside and agricultural modernization, but it contained no conflict that characters had to overcome, nothing that justified the triumph of the tractors, thus depriving it of a dramatic structure. At the end of the 1920s, Eisenstein left for Hollywood and Mexico, where he spent the height of the Cultural Revolution, from 1929 until 1932.

A few documentary educational films (*kul'turfil'm*) were made in the late 1920s, such as Viktor Turin's *Turksib* (1929) about the Siberian railway line that had just opened, and Mikhail Kalatozov's *Salt of Svanetia* (Sol' Svanetii, 1930) about life in the mountain region and its ethnic population in the Caucasus, and their isolated life until the Bolsheviks build a road that connects them to the world. Kalatozov's debut as filmmaker is characterized by a proximity of the filmmaker to nature, using staged scenes to enhance the impact of the documentary footage. Vladimir Yerofeev (1898–1940) and his travel films also reveal the attraction of the other and the Soviet Union's concern with assimilation of the periphery.

In 1930, Soyuzkino took over film production under the control of Boris Shumiatsky, who – until his arrest in 1938 – would coin the 'cinema for the millions' in Stalin's Russia, epitomized in the cult film *Chapaev* (1934) and the musical *Circus* (Tsirk, dir. Alexandrov, 1934), discussed in the next chapter.

–3–

The Purges, the Second World War and the Cold War, or How Stalin Entertained the People (1930–53)

We were born to make fairy tales come true.

'Aviators' March'

This chapter embraces almost the entire Stalin era, from the Cultural Revolution that consolidated State and Party control over culture to Stalin's death, covering the Purges of the 1930s, the Second World War, the 'cosmopolitan campaign' and the Cold War. In a number of ways, the Second World War interrupted Stalin's drive to rid the country of potential rivals and make the Soviet Union one of the most progressive countries in the world. The hatred of enemies – 'of the people' and of the USSR during the war – led to a vilification of foreign elements that unifies this period, and the vilification of external and internal enemies continued in the post-war period in the campaigns against Jews and medics, and in the animosity towards America and the West in the Cold War. Moreover, the period is united by a realist mode allowing little experimentation with form or structure, and concerned with building heroic images on the screen. The chapter divides the development of the era into three stages, with the third segment continuing the paranoia evident in the 1930s.

The 1930s were marked by terror and fear, arrests and executions. By 1932, the Cultural Revolution that had begun in 1929 had led to all artistic movements being streamlined into monolithic artistic unions (writers, filmmakers, artists, composers, etc.) that would ultimately implement the Party's ideology rather than defend their members from political interference in art, as stipulated in a Party Decree of 1932. Between 1932–34 the (forced) collectivization of the countryside was completed through a programme of 'dekulakization', involving campaigns, arrests and murders of kulaks for undermining the creation of collective farms (*kolkhozes*), where work and equipment was shared by a collective that delivered all but a small proportion of the produce to the state. Having streamlined culture and the economy, and the Party leadership, the political sphere came under further scrutiny. The purges of the Central Committee began, externally visible with the assassination of Stalin's rival, the popular Leningrad Party chairman Sergei Kirov, on 1 December 1934. A series of show trials were held between 1935 and 1938 against high-ranking Party members who were accused of espionage, sabotage and conspiracy; their cases were based on fraud allegations, as was demonstrated by the Dewey Commission in 1937.[1] During this period Nikolai Yezhov headed the NKVD, but he was succeeded by Lavrenti Beriya immediately after the trials. The repercussions of the Purges could be felt also in the arts: in 1938 the Meyerhold Theatre was closed, Meyerhold arrested and then murdered in 1940.

Whilst Stalin was internally cleansing the Party apparatus of any potential rivals to his absolute power, there were also signs that the Soviet Union was isolating itself internationally and consolidating its control over the constituent socialist republics. On 5 December 1936 the new Constitution (that would remain valid until 1977) came into force, redesigning government structures and guaranteeing its citizens the right to work, healthcare and social services. Historians have argued that this constitution was a pure propaganda document. The 1930s also saw other visible achievements: work on the construction of the Moscow metro began; in the Don Basin the miner Alexei Stakhanov extracted 102 tons of coals in six hours, setting a record and triggering the call for Stakhanovite performances of workers, so-called shock-workers; the pilot Valeri Chkalov (1906–38) flew non-stop from Moscow to Portland (Washington) in 1937.

Many foreigners visited the Soviet Union, partly to see communism in action and to support the new regime. The Soviet Union encouraged such visits, seeking international approval in such visitors as André Malraux, who spoke at the Writers' Congress in 1934; Romain Rolland, an ardent Stalin supporter and personal friend of Gorky; or Leon Feuchtwanger, who approved of the show trials when he visited in 1937; H. G. Wells and G. B. Shaw also visited in the period, and Erwin Piscator was one of many German artists to seek refuge in the Soviet Union when Hitler came to power in 1933, making the film *The Revolt of the Fishermen* (Vosstanie rybakov, Mezhrabpom 1932–34). In that year the United States recognized the Soviet Union, and both in 1939 and 1942 Stalin was named 'Man of the Year' by *Time* magazine. Moreover, some foreigners were attracted to Moscow to assist with the ambitious industrialization projects in the country, and subsequently stayed. A reminder of the strong foreign presence in the Moscow of that time is *Moscow News*, an English-language weekly newspaper established in 1930 by Anna Louise Strong to cater for the foreign community.[2] Despite its apparent internationalism, the Soviet Union became increasingly xenophobic: foreigners were asked to leave the country or assume Soviet citizenship in 1936, and the rise of fascism in Germany scared both the government and the people. More surprising was the signing of the non-aggression pact (Molotov-Ribbentrop Pact) in 1939, forming an alliance between communist Russia and fascist Germany. This alliance was a tacit approval of Hitler's subsequent invasion of Poland, whose territory was to be divided between the Soviet Union and Germany. The Red Army was involved in a war with Finland, suffering huge losses in Karelia, and ending in a treaty with Finland in 1940. In the same year the Soviet Union annexed the Baltic states (Lithuania, Latvia and Estonia), which it had invaded a year earlier. During the 1930s foreign film imports fell to almost zero and only private screenings in the Kremlin showed foreign films for Stalin and his close friends. Another effect of the xenophobia was the liquidation in 1936 of Mezhrabpom – funded by the German International Workers' Relief. The children's film studio Soyuzdetfilm (renamed Gorky Film Studio in 1948) set up base on the premises of Mezhrabpom; headed by Sergei Yutkevich, Soyuzdetfilm began making films for children: Mark Donskoy turned Maxim Gorky's autobiographical trilogy into film (1938–39) just after the writer's death in 1936.

The shift towards realism that followed the Writers' Union Congress in 1934 accounted also for the development of live-action children's and fairy-tale films – rather than cartoons, which were largely demoted to a political function in the 1930s whilst Walt Disney, with much more efficient production methods, took the lead in this art form internationally. Alexander Ptushko (1900–73) and Alexander Rou (1906–73) made numerous films for children, based on adventure stories and fairy tales.[3] Ptushko's *New Gulliver* (Novyi Gulliver, Mosfilm 1935), based on Jonathan Swift's adventure tale, is one such film that enjoyed great popularity thanks to the original use of puppet animation to render the discrepancy in size between the giant and the Lilliputians. Other popular children's films include *Captain Grant's Children* (Deti kapitana Granta, dir. Vainshtok and Ptushko, Mosfilm 1936) adapted from Jules Verne with the part of adventurer Jacques Paganel played by the versatile actor Nikolai Cherkasov (1903–66), who later played Ivan the Terrible. The film was the first adaptation of Verne's novel, and Isaak Dunaevsky's score with Vasili Lebedev-Kumach's lyrics made it tremendously successful. The production of children's films was seen as a priority, leading to the creation of a children's film studio. A pioneer, often forgotten in the history of Soviet cinema, was Margarita Barskaya-Chardynina, an actress and the wife of the director Petr Chardynin. Her film *Torn Shoes* (Rvanie bashmachki, Mezhrabpomfilm 1933) was one of the first children's films, about children and for children. Her second feature, *Father and Son* (Otets i syn, Soyuzdetfilm 1936) was banned because she was a friend of Karl Radek (committed in one of the show trials), and she committed suicide in 1937.

In cinema organization, the 1930s saw further streamlining of the administration. The cartoon industry was reorganized with the formation of Soyuzmultfilm in 1936. In order to cope with growing demand from Sovkino, Soyuzmultfilm had to recruit new staff, and train designers in-house by giving trainees figures to animate. Demands to adopt the methods of Disney (especially the use of the cel) for efficiency hampered the development of animation in the 1930s. In 1930 Soyuzkino (Union Cinema) was established as the sole body to produce and control films. In 1931 the Moscow film studio, Mosfilm, took over the premises of the Ermoliev and Khanzhonkov studios. In September 1932 the Film Institute established directors' courses, which were run by Sergei Eisenstein, who had returned from Hollywood; in 1934 the State Film Technikum (GTK) became the Film Institute (VGIK, Vsesoiuznyi gosudarstvennyi institut kinematografii). In February 1933 the Main Directorate of Cinema (GUK) was placed in charge of cinema matters instead of the Committee of Enlightenment (Narkompros). In 1934 the USSR participated in the Venice Film Festival and Moscow hosted its first international film festival in spring 1935:[4] Soviet films were validated on the national and international stage. In August 1934 the first Congress of the Writers' Union, founded in 1932, resolved that Socialist Realism was the only acceptable method for artistic work: works should display the socialist idea (*ideinost'*), national character (*narodnost'*) and Party loyalty (*partiinost'*). Art should aim to show 'reality in its revolutionary development' (Zhdanov), thus presenting history teleologically, leading towards the communist future. The principal tenets of Socialist Realism (a term allegedly coined by Stalin and Gorky) were developed fully in the speeches of the Party ideologue Andrei Zhdanov and Maxim Gorky at the Congress. The All-Union Creative Conference on Cinema Affairs in 1935 basically adopted the principles of Socialist Realism as set out for literature. In order to show the development of history, art would thus present the (bright) future as present, creating essentially utopian narratives ('fairy tales'). The line from a popular song ('Aviators' March'), 'We are born to make the fairy tale come true',[5] fitted the artistic aesthetics of the 1930s. The positive hero had to reveal his growing consciousness of the socialist cause, which led him to identify with the collective and thus achieve great feats in the name of socialism. Revolutionary leaders, Party officials and historical figures thus lent themselves to reinterpretation, whilst contemporary man could prove his commitment to socialism through superhuman acts in the name of the Party.

The Soviet Republics were 'cinefied' properly only in the 1930s, while the first national films were created largely after the Second World War. During the 1940s, newsreels were made at the Kyrgyz studio, which produced its first Kyrgyz feature in 1955. The Kazakh studio was established in 1928 and completed its first Kazakh feature in 1954. Uzbekfilm was founded in 1924, and the first Uzbek films appeared in the 1930s; the Tajik and Turkmen studios were set up in the late 1920s and early 1930s.[6] During the war, the studios in Alma-Ata, Tashkent, Samarkand, Ashkhabad and Dushanbe served as placed of evacuation.

In December 1931 the film-train (*kino-poezd*) – under Alexander Medvedkin – was launched. The train travelled across the country and Medvedkin made (often on location) short, satirical sketches and skits on the harmful behaviour of workers and peasants, such as on the themes of theft or alcoholism. These films would be developed and edited, and shown to the local people in order to educate them and raise their awareness of areas in need of social improvement. Thus, Medvedkin would travel to mining regions or agricultural areas to expose inefficiency and improve productivity, underlining with an intrusive camera and satirical inter-titles the flaws and weaknesses at the location.[7]

Short, agitational sketches as produced on the film-train and in the newsreels of Vertov's *Kino-Pravda* did not, however, endanger the significance of the documentary form itself in the 1930s. Apart from Vertov's documentary films that were set to sound, documentaries continued to focus their attention on the traditions of the Soviet nationalities as well as on expeditions into remote areas of the empire. The Arctic expedition of the icebreaker *Cheliuskin* was filmed in the polar region by the director Vladimir Shneiderov (1900–73), who had been part of the air expedition to Mongolia and China in the late 1920s, and made numerous adventure-expedition films, drawing attention to and exploring the expanses of the Soviet Union. The exploration of the Arctic also stood at the centre of feature films, such the Sergei Gerasimov's *Brave Seven* (Semero smelykh, Lenfilm 1936) where the Soviet expedition members learn from the native Chukcha population as well as helping them, thus strengthening the multi-ethnic socialist narrative. A curious experiment was the film *A Day of the New World* (Den' novogo mira, Tsentral'naia studio kinokhroniki 1941) editing footage that was shot on 24 August 1940 at a range of different locations in the Soviet Union and collated by cinematographer Boris Tseitlin, who had previously worked with Vertov.

Sound Film, 1929–34

With the establishment of Soyuzkino, the all-union organization in charge of production and distribution, the film industry entered a new era; but it also did so because of the arrival of sound, which meant that new equipment had to be installed, forcing an overhaul of the industry. Warner Brothers had introduced sound in 1926 (Vitaphone, recording sound separately), and Fox launched the Movietone sound system in 1927. In Moscow, Pavel Tager (1903–71) was working on sound systems at Mezhrabpom when Alexander Shorin (1890–1941) equipped Leningrad's Sovkino with sound. However, sound was slow to be adopted both by filmmakers and the industry, where additional problems were encountered at the level of distribution. In 1932 there had been plans for eighty-five silent films and forty sound films, but the Soviet Union had only 200 sound projectors compared to 32,000 silent ones; by 1936 the production of sound films had risen to 100 per cent, although not all cinemas were equipped.[8]

The different aesthetic principles for silent and sound film had worried filmmakers since the late 1920s. In 1928 Pudovkin, Eisenstein and his assistant Grigori Alexandrov had issued a manifesto on sound, advocating sound not to provide a realistic acoustic narrative, but to use music, words and sounds to counterpoint the images, thus complementing the visual montage with a sound montage. They contended that the montage of sound should run parallel to a montage of images, making sound essentially a-synchronous in a work of vertical montage (sound on top of image or vice versa).[9] A fine example is *Alexander Nevsky*, discussed later in this chapter.

Sound was used in documentaries, such as Abram Room's *The Plan for Great Works* (Plan velikikh rabot [Piatiletka], Soyuzkino 1929/30), a film about the Five-Year Plan, which also contained animated sequences. Documentary film adapted to sound easily and successfully. Vertov's *Enthusiasm – The Donbass Symphony* (Simfoniia Donbassa – Entuziazm, VUFKU 1930) combined sound montage with edited documentary footage in an experimental and original manner. *Three Songs of Lenin* (Tri pesni o Lenine, Moskinokhronika 1934) used Central Asian folk music to accompany documentary footage. The film narrated three stories about Lenin: first, 'My face was in a dark prison' is set in Central Asia, showing the liberation and emancipation through the Soviet Revolution of veiled women who have become educated (images of schools, universities, books) as new ways of life coexist with the old: an image of a camel stands next to the image of a bicycle. The loss of Lenin, reported on radio and visualized through the empty bench in front of his dacha, frames this episode, which shows the people's grief for their leader. The second episode, set to the song 'We love him', combines footage from Lenin's funeral and from examples of his achievements. The third section, 'In the great stone city', sees the future of Lenin's legacy with the Dneprostroi project, a sequence containing live interviews with workers. At the conclusion stands the victory of socialism. Vertov's film is interesting in the use of music to set counterpoints to the visual narrative and create, for the first time in his documentary work, an emotionally appealing film.

The earliest fiction films with sound were Yuli Raizman's (1903–94) *The Earth Thirsts* (Zemlia zhazhdet, Vostokkino 1931) about a multi-ethnic group of engineers who build an irrigation system in a Turkmen village. Whilst the local *bai* (representing the old regime) opposes the innovation, the engineers find support among the villagers. The film relies on the plot to show the linear development of the local people from an unenlightened mass to a conscious collective, as well as the rapid industrialization of the countryside and the integration of the socialist republics of Central Asia.

Kozintsev's and Trauberg's *Alone* (Odna, Soyuzkino Leningrad 1931) contained fragments of dialogue, but the most prominent sound effects were those of new machines. With the skilful use of alarm clocks and telephones – as signs of new technology – permeating the narrative, as well as the radio providing a guiding commentary on the action, Kozintsev and Trauberg accompanied the reluctant move of the novice teacher Yelena Kuzmina (played by the FEKS actress Kuzmina) from Leningrad to a remote area in Altai where she has been assigned her first job. The cultural contrast between the technologically developed city and the Altai region, still under the spell of shamanism, could hardly be greater. Kuzmina struggles against the village elders in their reluctance to accept progress, until she is seriously injured and airlifted – leaving behind a village that begins to accept the values she has tried to instil in them and echoing the ideological message of Raizman's film.

By 1934 films provided a realistic narrative through dialogue, such as Nikolai Ekk's (1902–76) *The Path to Life* (Putevka v zhizn', Mezhrabpomfilm 1931, with

Tagephon sound, i.e. using Tager's sound system), which also uses folk music. It tells the story of the commissar Nikolai Sergeev (Nikolai Batalov), who reforms a gang of orphans living in an open camp. The appearance on screen of *besprizorniki* (homeless orphans) reminded the viewer of the great number of children left without parents after the turmoil of a world war and a civil war. The orphans were portrayed through their use of language, each speaking in a different manner: Kolka with his communist ideals, or Dandy Mustafa Fert (played by the poet and actor Iyvan Kyrla [Kirill Ivanov] born in Mari El 1909, and purged in 1937; died 1943), with his eccentric ways. Sergeev engages them through common work on a railway line leading to the camp, highlighting the construction theme typical of Soviet culture of the time, but also the railway that will connect the camp with the outside world. The gang of Zhigan (Mikhail Zharov, 1900–81, the notorious 'baddie') undermines Sergeev's efforts, and kills Mustafa during a sabotage attempt. Ekk's *Grunia Kornakova* (also *The Little Nightingale*, Mezhrabpomfilm 1936) was the first Soviet colour film and is set in pre-Revolutionary Russia, where Grunia's father works as caretaker at a porcelain factory. The film follows Grunia from her duties at home to her role as a Revolutionary leader in the uprising of the exploited workforce at the factory. The film is set on Christmas Eve, but there is no carnival spirit and no relaxation of class divisions commonly associated with the holiday:[10] the happy seclusion of the Kornakov family is a mere illusion of peace that crumbles away when a fire destroys the factory, thus enabling the proprietor, drawing on insurance funds, to replace the wooden building with a new brick wing – at the cost of thirty-nine lives, among them Grunia's father. The film points up the backwardness of folk beliefs and their danger to Revolutionary energy: if Grunia had not been torn away from her Christmas tree by the events, she would never have become a Revolutionary and fought for the workers' social cause. The blame for the lack of social progress is laid at the feet of bourgeois traditions that have no room in Stalin's Russia: Christmas. As such, *Grunia Kornakova* is very much a film of the 1930s, made at the beginning of the Purges.

As Socialist Realism gripped literature, Boris Shumiatsky (in charge of Soyuzkino) hoped to create a cinema for the millions and entertain the masses. He wanted filmmakers to appeal to the consciousness of people with an engaging plot and do what the Aviators' March had articulated: 'to turn a fairy tale into reality'. They should create films that were fairy tales rooted in Soviet reality – of workers achieving their dreams, since the main principle of happiness according to Soviet ideology lay in hard physical labour (which is therefore choreographed and executed in light, ballet-like movements). Cinderella stories of weavers coming to Moscow to 'play' on the machines in the textile industry, of peasants rejoicing in the working of the fields and happily riding on tractors, all beautifully and neatly dressed, with smiles that reveal their immaculate white teeth and red cheeks as a sign of health, were the staple diet of the 1930s. The culmination of personal happiness often lay in meeting a nice man (or woman) and – infallibly, an encounter with Stalin, direct or indirect, that allowed them to understand the meaning of communism. Such were the dream plots of Socialist Realist musicals. Since films were supposed to show reality developing towards a bright future, the present – if it features at all – is a mere transition phase, an accident or a bump on the road that leads to higher realms. One may infer here a parallel between Orthodoxy, where believers expect a reward for earthly sufferings in the other world, and communism, adopting religious concepts to exploit folk rituals and faith for its own ends, as is also evident in the replacement of religious icons through portraits of the leaders.

Soviet Musicals, 1934–41

The first musical, *Accordion* (Garmon', Igor Savchenko, Mezhrabpomfilm 1934) is one such film: Timofei Dudin is the best worker on the *kolkhoz* and the most talented accordionist. When he advances to Komsomol member and joins the village council, he becomes ashamed of his accordion and packs it away. After a group of kulaks wreak havoc on the *kolkhoz* and undermine the working morale with their entertainment, a musical warfare starts: Timofei unwraps his accordion, wins over the kulaks and marries his girl. The most prominent exponents of the musical comedy were without doubt Ivan Pyriev (1901–68) and Grigori Alexandrov (1903–83). Whilst Pyriev chose largely rural settings and *kolkhozes* for his plots, Alexandrov's musicals are set in provincial or urban locations. Both directors use pre-recorded music for their musical interludes, and both consistently work with the team of composer Isaak Dunaevsky (1900–55) and lyricist Vasili Lebedev-Kumach (1898–1949). Both directors' respective wives were the stars of their musical comedies: Pyriev's wife Marina Ladynina (1908–2003) and Alexandrov's wife Liubov Orlova (1902–75) – a practice that would come under attack after the war. The plots tend to revolve around the imperfections of the hero, which are overcome with the collective's support. Meeting places for the couples are parades, celebrations, or the All-Union Exhibition of Agriculture that started in 1935 and opened its gates in a purpose-built space in 1939.[11] Thus the emphasis is – in line with the goal-rather-than-road ethos of Socialist Realism – on achievement rather than hard work. The Soviet musical thus adapts the conventions of Hollywood musicals: to devise a plot where two characters of opposite values or lifestyles are confronted and where these oppositions can be overcome through music.

Grigori Alexandrov's musical debut came with *Jolly Fellows* (Veselye rebiata, aka *Happy Guys*, Moskinokombinat 1934), scripted by Alexandrov with the satirists Vladimir Mass and Nikolai Erdman, the latter the author of the great satires *The Suicide* and *The Mandate*. The film titles announce: 'This film does not star Buster Keaton, Harry Lloyd and Charlie Chaplin.' Soviet cinema no longer relies on imports, but has its own star: Leonid Utesov (1895–1982). Utesov, as well as Alexander Tsfasman (1906–71), was one of the most famous jazzmen of the 1930s and 1940s, who produced an equivalent of big-band swing for dancing. Dunaevsky's composition is here clearly inspired by jazz music. *Jolly Fellows* is about the musically talented shepherd Kostia Potekhin (Utesov), who plays the 'March of the Happy Guys' on his whistle, which attracts a range of followers as he walks through the fields. The maid Aniuta (Orlova) admires Kostia and falls in love with him: she sings while doing her chores at the inn where she works. Following the pattern of conventional comedy, Kostia is mistaken for the foreign conductor Frasquini by the attractive Lena, one of the bourgeois tourists visiting the countryside. Thus he accidentally ends up in Moscow, where he replaces Frasquini in conducting a music hall orchestra before running away to form his own band. In the meantime both Lena and Aniuta compete in an audition at the Bolshoi Theatre, where, after a series of slapstick situations and adventures, the band arrives and Kostia is united with the woman he loves: Aniuta. The film confirms that amateur singers and musicians can easily move from the countryside to the city and create genuine art. Moreover, it exposes as excessive the taste of the bourgeoisie, which is caricatured in a scene where Kostia's herd, responding to a tune he plays on his flute, storms into the restaurant where Aniuta has set the opulent tables for the guests' dinner – and wreaks havoc. The film touches upon another sensitive issue: the bridge between high and low, the high aspirations that Soviet art has whilst wanting to remain accessible to the people. This potential conflict is happily resolved in *Jolly Fellows*. The film is also noteworthy for Vladimir Nilsen's photography, deploying composite shots and filming and editing footage in such a manner that the viewer is led to believe that he is marching along with the band.[12]

Alexandrov's best-known musical is *The Circus* (Tsirk, Mosfilm 1936), based on a script by satirists Ilya Ilf (1897–1937) and Yevgeni Petrov (1903–42, real name Kataev) and the latter's brother, Valentin Kataev (1897–1986). Both *The Circus* and *Jolly Fellows* were thus the literary product of a group of satirists, signalling that comedy cannot be rooted in realistic depictions but requires a grotesque, absurd plot. Whilst Alexandrov's comedies adhere to the ideological requirements of the time, they also expose reality as varnished or artificial. As would the Christmas setting for Riazanov's *Carnival Night* in the 1950s, the choice of the circus setting removes the film from reality. *The Circus* explores the journey of the circus artiste Marion Dixon (Orlova) from America to Soviet Russia; from capitalist exploitation to communist happiness. Dixon boards a train in the remote American town of Sunnyville to escape from a crowd that chases her because she has a mixed-race child out of wedlock, and to do so is socially unacceptable. On the train she meets von Kneischitz (modelled on Hitler with his moustache and stern look, obsessed with racial issues and a clear representative of German fascism), who becomes her manager, but who exploits and beats her. As the train moves, its plate turns into a ball that in turn becomes a globe with the letters 'CCCP' (USSR) written across it – and this spinning ball transports Marion to Russia as it reappears on the nose of a seal juggling the ball in the Moscow circus. Alexandrov's films are full of curious

Figure 3.1 Alexandrov's *Circus*: Marion (Orlova) with Martynov and Jimmy.

turns and slapstick. In *Circus*, slapstick is primarily associated with Skameikin, the fiancé of the circus director's daughter, Raika. He accidentally fires at the engineer Martynov, he fails to present a bouquet of flowers to his fiancée, he enters a lion's cage, he mixes up letters, and he believes that Marion's black child Jimmy is so dark because he has got dirt on his face.

The love intrigue unfolds at work, in the circus. Marion's circus number consists of a 'flight to the moon': she is catapulted by a canon on to a swinging sickle of the moon under the big top; much of her act depends on luck and on the skilful use of props. By contrast, the new number prepared by Soviet engineer Ivan Martynov (Sergei Stoliarov, 1911–69) is called 'flight into the stratosphere': conquering space rather than planets is the Soviet ambition, evidently reflecting the research into space travel undertaken by the mathematician, theorist and inventor of the concept of a multistage rocket, Konstantin Tsiolkovsky (1857–1935), at the time. Historical scientific achievements made the material for other films also, such as *The Cosmic Voyage* (Kosmicheskii reis, Mosfilm 1935), which celebrated the flight of the inventor Sedykh and two assistants to the moon, landing on the other side, and thus marking the Soviet conquest of other planets. Tsiolkovsky even acted as a consultant to the film.

Martynov's number relies on technology and engineering skills, with the collective performing disciplined choreographed movements to celebrate the act. While Marion's is an individual number, Martynov's is created and supported by the collective. When Marion performs the premiere instead of Raika, who has been held up by Kneischitz in a sabotage attempt, she becomes part of that large collective of performers and audience. Indeed, the audience becomes her new family that 'adopts' her child, cradling Jimmy – who is exposed as the product of her racial crime to the circus audience by Kneischitz – while singing a lullaby in different languages of the USSR, including Russian, Ukrainian, Georgian, and Yiddish. The large Soviet family comprises all colours and nationalities: there is more than tragic irony in the scene where Solomon Mikhoels (1890–1948), the great actor of the Yiddish Theatre in Moscow, sings the lullaby in Yiddish: he was murdered during the 'cosmopolitan campaign' against Jews in 1948.

The contrast between light and dark crudely draws the line between good and bad characters: Kneischitz is dark-haired, Martynov blond and (presumably) blue-eyed. Marion changes from dark hair to blonde as she falls in love with Martynov. She changes her clothes too and slips into the white outfit of the Soviet collective when she marches across Red Square for the May Day Parade, where she sees Stalin – and she 'understands' (communism). Richard Taylor has highlighted that 'the religious nature of the experience is underlined by the fact that her eyes clearly light up when she sees Stalin off-screen on the podium'.[13] Masha, as she now calls herself, sings the 'Song of the Motherland' that Martynov had taught her on the piano: this song became the unofficial anthem of the USSR. Composed by Dunaevsky, who took his inspiration for this film from marching music, the song praises the freedom of Soviet man, amply documented in the new Constitution: 'I don't know of any other country where a man can breathe a freer air!'[14]

The Circus signals several political concerns of the 1930s: in 1936 foreigners were asked to leave the country or adopt Soviet citizenship – Marion makes the 'right' choice. The film also shows the Soviet Union's opposition to fascism and consequently a hatred of Nazi Germans. Finally, it offers intriguing views of the new Moscow created by Stalin's grand plan, which began with the demolition of the Cathedral of Christ the Saviour in 1931, supposedly to make room for the new Palace of Soviets (designed by Boris Iofan, 1934), towering over the city and reaching into the skies, with a statue of Lenin on top. The film also shows scenes on the roof of the Hotel Moscow on Manege Square, at the time of filming only partly completed, which has a curious architectural history: the architect Alexei Shchusev (1873–1949) had submitted two versions of the façade on one draft, which was approved and signed by Stalin, who did not realize that there were two proposals there. Thus, legend has it, the hotel had to be built with an asymmetrical façade.

Alexandrov's *Volga-Volga* (Mosfilm 1938), scripted by Erdman with satirist Mikhail Volpin (1903–88), is set in a village full of natural musical talents and with two amateur musical collectives. The film exposed to laughter the comic figure of the Soviet bureaucrat Ivan Byvalov (Ilinsky, the comic actor who had played such roles as the hapless Lovelace Mitiushin in *The Cigarette Girl …* in the 1920s), dreaming of a job in Moscow. He considers no one in the village worthy of participating in a Moscow amateur competition, where he wants to take Alesha Trubyshkin to conduct a symphony orchestra. The local post girl Dunia Petrova, nicknamed 'Strelka' (The Arrow), played by Orlova, meanwhile entertains everybody with her songs and also travels to Moscow. As Byvalov's steam boat *Sevriuga* (North-South) races against Strelka's sailing ship *Lesorub* (Woodcutter) on the Volga, the singing competition on the river becomes a prelude to the actual competition, which Strelka wins, conquering the capital with music loved by the masses: low culture triumphs over the high art of the symphony orchestra, and natural talent over the bureaucrat. The use of boats as means of transportation emphasized another achievement of the Stalin era: the construction of canals, such as the Belomor Canal and the Volga-Don Canal.

The Radiant Path (Svetlyi put', Mosfilm 1940) is a Cinderella story of the simple country girl Tania Morozova (Orlova). who comes to work in an urban textile factory (periphery to city) and becomes the best worker. She falls in love with the engineer Lebedev, repeating the conflation of peasant and worker, country and urban culture as expressed in Vera Mukhina's (1889–1953) Paris Exhibition sculpture *Worker and Collective Farmer* (Rabotnik i kolkhoznitsa, 1937), which stood at the entrance of the All-Union Agriculture Exhibition during the Soviet era and later became the emblem of Mosfilm. Tania advances to a shock-worker, studies and is elected deputy to the Supreme Council. In the finale, she takes a magic drive in a black limousine above the clouds and across the Soviet territory, symbolically reflecting her conquest of the spacious Soviet land, looking back at the exhibition space, itself a fantasy microcosm of the Soviet future.

That broad and wide Soviet land, the fields and open spaces, stood at the centre of Ivan Pyriev's films. Pyriev had first made feature films: his *Party Card* (Partiinyi billet, Mosfilm 1936) was supported by Stalin, but in the aftermath of the film's release Pyriev was suspended from work at Mosfilm for two years and went to work in Kiev.[15] *Party Card* had explored the love of a conscientious worker, Anna, who falls in love with a new worker. When it turns out that he is a spy and enemy of the people, she exposes his activity. *Rich Bride* (Bogataia nevesta, Ukrainfilm 1937) was made in Kiev, but subsequently shelved until Shumiatsky's demise; it received a successful release under the new Soyuzkino head, Semen Dukelsky.[16] Marina

Figure 3.2 Pyriev's *The Tractor Drivers.*

Kukash (Ladynina) works on a collective farm, and the accountant Alexei wants to marry her. He manipulates the statistics to make Pavlo, a fellow tractor driver with whom she is in love, look like a bad worker unworthy of marriage. His deceit is revealed: the Party uncovers the falsified statistics and love ultimately triumphs. The plot resembles that of *Bed and Sofa* and those of pre-Revolutionary melodrama: a woman between two men, both too weak to conquer her, but she – fortunately – is strong enough to make a decision and choose between them. In *Tractor Drivers* (Traktoristy, Kiev Studio 1939), Klim Yarko (literally: the bright; played by Nikolai Kriuchkov, 1911–94) is demobilized and returns to the Ukrainian *kolkhoz* where Mariana Bazhan (Ladynina) works. He has seen her photograph in *Pravda*, where she featured as a leading tractor driver and shock-worker. Again, in a similar ploy to pre-Revolutionary films, the woman is apprehended as an object for desire – not because of her beauty, though, but because of her achievement. In order to fend off her many suitors and admirers, Mariana pretends to be engaged to the lazy Nazar. When Klim becomes aware of this, the upright gentleman that he is, he decides to leave. However, the collective brings him back and he is able to conquer Mariana's heart through hard work and with the support of the collective. Once again the strong woman is decisive as she stands between two men.

In *The Swineherd and the Shepherd* (Svinarka i pastukh, Mosfilm 1941) Glasha Novikova (Ladynina) and the idle Kuzma travel from Vologda to the All-Union Agriculture Exhibition in Moscow. Kuzma (Kriuchkov) is fond of Glasha, but Glasha – a true Soviet model worker – is more interested in new farming methods. As she roams around the exhibition she meets Musaib, a Dagestani shock-shepherd, and they agree to meet again a year later. Back home, a letter from Musaib is deliberately mistranslated through Kuzma's intervention, while others remain undelivered. Kuzma thus makes Glasha believe that Musaib is married and she accepts Kuzma's proposal. Upon his return to Moscow, Musaib looks for Glasha and learns of the deceit and the impending marriage: he saddles his horse and rides from Moscow to Vologda to be reunited with his love – to the performance of the 'Song of Moscow', with the refrain 'I will never forget a friend I met in Moscow'. Once again, a woman between two men is deceived, the evil man undergoes betterment (Nazar, Kuzma) and is taught a lesson, while the shock-worker (Klim, Musaib) is rewarded. The singing that accompanies the hard work in the fields contributes to making physical work look easy and enjoyable, spreading happiness all around. Dunaevsky's music contained elements of folk tunes and even entire folk songs, as well as specially written lyrics commenting subtly or broadly on the love intrigue. Happiness is only possible when duty, vis-à-vis the collective and work, is fulfilled.

Pyriev continued in the *kolkhoz* musical genre after the war, as for example *The Kuban Cossacks* (Kubanskie kazaki, colour, Mosfilm 1949), a love story of the chairman and chairwoman of rival *kolkhozes*. In the opening scene of the film the tractors appear to dance in the fields as the celebration of the harvest is announced: again, not work but achievement are central. Galina Peresvetova (Ladynina) and Gordei Voron are in love, but his Cossack pride prevents him from courting her. If in earlier musicals the woman had a strong role and her male counterparts had no problem in accepting that, here the emancipated Galina has to let Gordei win a race so that his male pride remains undamaged. It is through the Party leader that he learns of her love – the Party once again takes on the role of the deus ex machina, only in personal matters – and they are united in a *kheppi end*. The space of Soviet territory, knowing no limits or borders, is captured by the camera through images of blue skies and yellow fields (by 1949 in colour), which would be confined in the 1940s by borders and guards as the fear of attack grew: the border guard, watching over the territory, became a leitmotif.

Peasant and Worker Heroes, 1934–38

Peasants and workers appeared to remain relatively safe terrain for filmmakers. They became not only the heroes of Party narratives, recipients of medals and awards, but also subjects of art and popular culture: they were depicted in the paintings of Alexander Deineka (1899–1969), showing textile workers at work (*Tekstilshchitsy*, 1927), with the shapes and colours of the women in harmony with the machines. His later painting *The Tractor Driver* (*Traktorist*, 1956) shows a young man, forward-looking and painted from below to enlarge his stature (repeating the device of heroic portrayal through low camera angles in film), with a small farm and toy-sized cattle in the background: man is larger than nature. If Deineka's painting were part of the official trend to monumentalize the new Soviet man and the everyday world, then Party leaders were glorified in Socialist Realist art in Isaak Brodsky's (1884–1939) paintings of Stalin and Lenin. In popular culture, Soviet heroes replaced folk heroes, as for example on the traditional Palekh boxes,[17] whose motifs were traditionally derived from fairy tales. In the Soviet period they often reflected themes of work and industry: *Fame to the Miners* (Alexei Kovalev, 1949) is one example. Likewise, Gzhel porcelain figures were created to praise the new Soviet man, as in the figurine *Kolkhoz Maid* (Natalia Danko, 1936). Across high and low, the worker and the peasant occupied the same rank as Party leaders: they were all heroes. In a division of the world into communists and capitalists, into hero-workers and enemies of the people, there were not many grey shades for psychological portrayals on the silver screen. Characters tended to be drawn in black-and-white, goodies against baddies, with little scope for change. Heroes were heroes and would only need a foil to demonstrate their heroism so it could appear more starkly. A typical plot explored in the musicals was that of the excellent worker rewarded for his or her achievements with personal happiness, which spurs him or her to an even better work performance.

The theme of collectivization and the happiness that it brings was important in Pyriev's musicals, but was also treated seriously in Ermler's *Peasants* (Krest'iane, Lenfilm 1934), which explores the communist rationale behind the 'dekulakization'. During the collectivization, an unexpected rise in the number of piglets has led to a crisis in food supply. Gerasim Platonovich decides to divide the piglets into small herds and have them fed by individual households, effectively introducing a small kulak venture. Gerasim's wife, Varvara, tries to gather the pigs when the political section leader Nikolai Mironovich arrives for an inspection. Gerasim has sworn to ruin the *kolkhoz*, because he is a former kulak whose family was disowned. It is with disgust that he listens to his wife praising the bright communist future of their child; this dream was originally rendered in the film in an animated sequence showing Varvara with the child and Stalin, but this had to be deleted as it was not deemed suiable for the leader to appear in animated form.[18] When Varvara realizes that Gerasim tries to sabotage the *kolkhoz*, she runs, in Pavlik Morozov style, to denounce him. Gerasim kills her brutally, disguising her death as suicide, but Gerasim's murder is unmasked and justice done. Ermler's film showed the struggle of the régime to convince peasants of the advantages of the system, but it also hints at Stalin as the ideal father of Varvara's unborn child in the animated dream sequence.

A more subtle and nuanced, but much less realistic, portrayal of the countryside pervades the films of Alexander Medvedkin (1900–89). *Happiness* (Schast'e, Mosfilm 1934) is made in the farcical style of a *lubok*: Khmyr is sent by his wife

Anna to find happiness. Right away, the search is presented as unreal: to find an abstract concept is impossible, but 'happiness' is found by the roadside, where Khmyr spots a purse. He buys a horse and all the objects of wealth that he has seen at his neighbour's. But this chance happiness does not bring Khmyr joy: the kulak, the landowner and the priest take the harvest away from him. The police authorities order him to be flogged and send him to the war. Returning after the Revolution, Khmyr refuses to believe in a better life to be had by participating in the collective, but after he prevents sabotage he becomes a motivated collective worker. The character of Khmyr is tragicomic in the two-dimensional spaces that are reminiscent of cartoons. The soldiers lack psychological depth and are grotesquely reduced through paper masks, while the stealing nun and the avid priest are caricatured. In *The Miracle Worker* (Chudesnitsa, Mosfilm 1936), Zinka dreams of becoming the best milkmaid. She is invited to Moscow to speak and meet Stalin when her collective is awarded a prize. The shepherd Ivan does not share Zinka's humble attitude to work but is boisterous; nevertheless he rescues the cattle. The two are united when they realize that they both serve the state. Medvedkin's films expose, in a comic cartoon-style manner, the weaknesses of characters who will eventually become good Soviet citizens. This style is in many ways an extension of Medvedkin's short films on the film-trains, which were designed to re-educate the population and raise awareness of new work methods and warn of corruption.

Alexander Medvedkin's *New Moscow* (Novaia Moskva, Mosfilm 1938) was banned. The film concerns the engineer Alesha, who travels to Moscow to show a model of the New Moscow he has built with his friends after the announcement of the plan for reconstruction. On the journey he meets Zoya, who travels to visit her friend Fedia, a painter. On the same train is the swineherd Olga with a rebellious, but prize-winning, piglet (Heinrich) – whom she will display at the All-Union Agriculture Exhibition. The new Moscow features in all is aspects: Olga's piglet fits only with difficulty into the settings of escalators and metro carriages; Fedia cannot capture the city on canvas as houses disappear or move all the time; Alesha has built a 'live' model of Moscow, showing its evolution under the great reconstruction plans, to present to an audience of specialists at the exhibition. However, Alesha is delayed for his presentation and Zoya switches on the projector, but the pictures move backwards. Instead of the developing and burgeoning new Moscow, the audience sees the city revert back to its medieval look. Alesha arrives just in time to adjust the projection, and he is reunited with Zoya who – in another strange digression from cultural paradigms of the 1930s – follows him to his village and thus inverts the hero's movement from periphery to centre. Like many of Alexandrov's and Pyriev's comedies, *New Moscow* too has a meeting of the lovers in the carnivalesque atmosphere of the popular Gorky Park (Park kul'tury i otdykha imeni Gor'kogo), another novelty in Stalin's Moscow.

Several major Soviet industrial projects featured in films and turned workers into heroes: Dneprostroi, the hydro-electric complex on the Dnepr and one of the most gigantic power station projects of Soviet Russia in the period of industrialization; the Five-Year Plans; or the construction of industrial cities such as Komsomolsk or Aerograd. Alexander Macheret (1896–1979) made his debut with *Man and Jobs* (Dela i liudi, Soyuzkino Moscow 1932), filmed in a realistic manner with authentic-sounding dialogue as the Dneprostroi worker Zakharov and the American engineer Clines clash when the latter suggests applying different work methods: Zakharov's methods are, of course, better. Echoing the slogan of the 1930s, to 'overtake and surpass America', the worker wins over his capitalist counterpart.

The 'conflictlessness' (*beskonfliktnost'*) of a plot where a good man becomes even better, which would become a guiding principle in the 1940s, deprived films and plays of an essential ingredient: the clash that led to development of the plot. Instead, the 'conflictless' films tended to present snapshots of a 'great society'. Ermler's *Counterplan* (Vstrechnyi, Rosfilm Leningrad 1932) dealt with the first Five-Year Plan (1928–32) and the project of a powerful new turbine, revealing a new attitude to work. As in *Peasants*, Ermler observed workers and relationships minutely to create a realistic portrayal. The theme song 'Song of the Counterplan' by Dmitri Shostakovich, with the upbeat lyrics of Boris Kornilov (arrested in 1937 and executed in 1938), became the anthem for the United Nations in 1945. Dovzhenko's *Ivan* (1932) follows the pattern of good to betterment for the hero: Ivan is a collective farm worker who arrives at Dneprostroi, where he works hard; he decides to study and join the Party. Pudovkin's *Deserter* was first intended as a co-production with Germany, but when Hitler came to power the film was made solely in Russia. The German communist Karl Renn, a dockworker in Hamburg, abandons his comrades during a strike in 1932 to accept an invitation to the USSR, where he now works. Hearing of the death of his socialist comrade Zeile, he realizes that he deserted his comrades and returns to Germany. Another good communist, albeit foreign, becomes even better. The attractiveness of the Soviet Union is also emphasized in films featuring the return of those who had left the country before the Revolution, such as the character Lev Gorizont in Kuleshov's *Gorizont* (Mezhrabpomfilm 1932), who comes to Russia with the American army and sides with the Reds.

The new cities too become heroes of films: Dovzhenko's *Aerograd* (Mosfilm and Ukrainfilm 1935) was set in the early 1930s: the hunter Stepan Glushak chases Japanese infiltrators in the taiga as he guards the border to Manchuria and kills one spy while another escapes. When he visits his old friend Khudiakov, he notices that he is hiding the saboteur and collaborating with the Japanese. Glushkov kills Khudiakov and the Japanese saboteur. The border-guard theme, becoming increasingly important for Soviet Russia both in the east and the west, features here as well as in *Volochaev Days* (Volochaevskie dni, Vasiliev Brothers, Lenfilm 1937) about the fight against Japanese intervention during the Civil War. Similarly, *Dzhulbars* (dir. Vladimir Shneiderov, Mezhrabpomfilm 1935) deals with the life of border guards and the loyal dog that protects the Soviet territory.

Sergei Gerasimov's *Komsomolsk* (Lenfilm 1938) dealt with the new industrial city projected to be built on the River Amur in 1932, and the potential sabotage of this project. On a train from Lake Baikal, the Komsomol leader Chekalov is murdered and the saboteur steals his identity. The Chekalov imposter forces those workers who have been reprimanded to help him start a fire in a store room, and then kills them when they try to report the sabotage.

These films highlight threats from within and from outside that are designed to bring the new regime to a downfall, implicitly laying the blame for failures at the feet of the 'enemy' and thus creating a justification for the Purges. Despite the theme of sabotage, which brings tension to the plot, these films are not appealing because they use stereotypical role models of the good worker and the villain, or, in the worse case, there is no villain to overcome at all.

Political and Historical Heroes, 1933–39

Apart from workers and peasants, individuals who had supported the regime during the Revolution or the Civil War attained heroic status. Films were made about historical rebels, such as Stenka Razin, but it was the monumental hero rather than the popular folk hero who inspired cinematic narratives.

Barnet's *Outskirts* (Okraina, Mezhrabpomfilm 1933) is a tragicomedy set in 1914 on the outskirts of a remote village that is under German attack. It is one of the few films to choose as its setting the First World War (rather than the Civil War). The tragicomic effect is achieved through grotesque and exaggerated acting: for example when a drunkard tries to embrace a lady with a little dog and is rebuked, but manages to achieve his goal in the turmoil of the announcement of the war, making use of the common shock. As he walks off with the lady in his embrace, he turns round to blink at the camera.

The film tells of the events of the First World War, leading up to the October Revolution. The owner of a shoe factory, Greshin (Sergei Komarov, who had acted in 1920s comedies), supplies the army with boots. He is friendly with his German neighbour, Robert Karlovich, who turns into an 'enemy' when Germany declares war on Russia. The cobbler Kadkin's two sons, Nikolai and Senka, join the army. The reality of the war quickly destroys their illusions, when Senka is killed by enemy fire. Later, when the army brings German prisoners of war into the town, Greshin's daughter Manka (the FEKS actress Yelena Kuzmina) discovers her feelings for the POW Müller. Her father persists with his anti-German feelings, while Kadkin offers Müller work as cobbler. Greshin is almost caricatured when he smashes the framed pictures of one idol after another: first Robert Karlovich, later the tsar. Despite the dramatic plot, Barnet uses situational comedy: Greshin may lend his cap to Robert Karlovich (played by Robert Erdman, the playwright Nikolai Erdman's father), but he takes it back when the war commences and Greshin's old chess partner turns into the enemy. Similarly, Nikolai often laughs and plays tricks on his fellow soldiers, once pretending that he has been hit as they lie in a trench.

The free Russian land that belongs to the people is shown in panning shots of trees and rivers, yet this is but a dream before the attack. Nikolai is executed for fraternizing with the enemy, just as the news breaks of the storming of the Winter Palace, reaching the fellow soldier who sits by the dying Nikolai. This frame makes way for the finale of people marching towards the camera: they have made their dream come true. Barnet showed the repercussions of changes in the centre on the periphery, causing rippling waves rather than creating upheavals. He orchestrated this early sound film with musical scores, sounds of explosions and shots, whistles and sirens, as well as dialogue. He captured the reality of life in a small town, with political agendas remaining on one level and life on another.

The Baltic Deputy (Deputat Baltiki, Lenfilm 1936, dir. Alexander Zarkhi and Iosif Kheifits) with Nikolai Cherkasov (1903–66; he would later perform in Eisenstein's films) as Polezhaev, is set in Petrograd in 1917, where the Reds combat fraud and speculation. Based on the biography of the botanist Kliment Timiriazev (1843–1920), Professor Polezhaev writes a newspaper article to support the workers' cause, which appals the intelligentsia and the students alike. Rejected by his own social class, he becomes a deputy under the new regime. Polezhaev's counterpart is Alexandra Sokolova (Vera Maretskaya) in *Member of the Government* (Chlen pravitel'stva, Zarkhi and Kheifits, Lenfilm 1940), who becomes chairwoman of a *kolkhoz*, coping well with her new role, to the dismay of her husband Yefim who cannot live with an active and successful wife. She leaves him in order to become a deputy of the Supreme Council, where she thanks the Kremlin in an address. Both films show the tendency to place the political above personal and everyday commitments.

Many other films of the late 1930s deal with the strength of Revolutionary heroes: *We Are From Kronstadt* (My iz Kronshtadta, dir. Yefim Dzigan, Mosfilm 1936) is set in October 1919, when Petrograd was threatened by the Whites, and the communists, supported by the sailors from Kronstadt, scored a victory. The sailor Artem Balashov turns from an adventurer into a conscious fighter for the Revolutionary cause, providing meaning in life. *A Man with a Gun* (Chelovek s ruzh'em, dir. Sergei Yutkevich, Lenfilm 1938) deals with the support at the front line of the Civil War in 1917. Lev Arnshtam's *Girl Friends* (Podrugi, Lenfilm 1935) tells of three girls who meet with secret Revolutionaries. During the war they are nurses at the front line; after the Revolution the girls return, but are attacked by the Whites, and one girl is fatally injured. Mikhail Romm's *Thirteen* (Trinadtsat', Mosfilm 1936) transposes the Revolutionary battle into an exotic setting: ten Reds, a geologist and a couple cross the Karakum Desert. They are desperate for water and find a small well, but an army of 200 Basmachi rebels[19] arrive and claim it all for themselves. The Reds die, but only after having slain the Basmachis. The readiness for sacrifice for the political cause becomes clear in these films.

Figure 3.3 Boris Babochkin as Chapaev (right), explaining military strategy with potatoes.

The most popular films of its time, which has since become a cult film, was no doubt *Chapaev* (Lenfilm, 1934). Released on the seventeenth anniversary of the Revolution, it was watched by millions: 'The whole country will be watching Chapaev' read the headline of *Pravda* on 21 November 1934.[20] Directed by the Vasiliev 'Brothers' (Georgi and Sergei Vasiliev, who had met while re-editing foreign films during the 1920s), the film is set in 1919 and based on Commissar Dmitri Furmanov's novel. Chapaev's anarchic crowd merges forces with the detachment of the political commander Furmanov, and they score a victory over the Whites. A little later Chapaev is killed, but his army continues the fight. This film was the most successful portrait of a military commander, largely thanks to Boris Babochkin (1904–75), creating Chapaev as a man from the simple people (Chapaev had been illiterate until the Revolution) who explains battle strategy with the help of potatoes. The psychological attack of the White Army approaching in three black columns from the distance across the steppe, a faceless, amorphous mass, while their disinterested officer smokes a cigarette as if he cannot be bothered to even engage in the fight, is countered by a strategic plan that confronts and surprises the enemy. Drums beat as one column falls and the next moves in, underlining the fearlessness of the thin lines of Chapaev's men, where the young sniper Anka handles the only machine gun, helped by Chapaev's orderly, Petka. Chapaev is driven by his character (rather than action): he is a charismatic figure, especially in comparison to the fatherly guidance provided by Furmanov, thus emphasizing the harmony between intellectual and simple man. The directors used long sequences rather than fragmenting views, thus showing the battle from Chapaev's perspective, from whence it seemed to extend in time. The film was shown at the Paris Exhibition in 1937 and in the Moscow International Film Festival of 1935.

Chapaev was so popular that quotations from the film are almost as frequent in everyday speech as the jokes about Chapaev. The remark 'Yes, a merry discussion this!' often refers to a situation that is taking a bad turn. 'Quiet, people, Chapaev is thinking' (in the film accompanied by Petka firing a gun) is an ironic comment asking for silence while mocking Chapaev's talent as a 'thinker' (which he was not). However, the phrase 'Are you mocking Chapaev?' is used to eliminate any doubt about the person in question: Chapaev may not be a thinker, but his support for the cause (the Revolution) is beyond doubt.

In terms of the attempt to create a national hero, the Ukrainian equivalent of *Chapaev* was *Shchors* (dir. Solntseva and Dovzhenko, Kiev Studio 1939), even if it was not as popular by a long way. It was a very different film, although the hero was as close to the people as Chapaev and also perished in battle. It was infused with personal memory and images of death and devastation. The historical situation of

Figure 3.4 Dovzhenko's *Shchors*.

1919 saw the Ukrainians push back the Germans; Kiev was controlled by Petliura's nationalist bourgeois army. Mykola Shchors (Yevgeni Samoilov, 1912–2006, a Meyerhold actor) entered Kiev while the fatherly Batko Vasyl Bozhenko liberated Vinitsa and other towns. In the summer 1919, Polish attacks followed and Bozhenko was killed; Shchors suffered losses but new commanders continued the fight. The film captures the German intervention of 1918, the Polish invasion of 1919 and Petliura's Ukrainian nationalist army during the Civil War, thus confronting the hero with a more complex political situation than that faced by Chapaev, who was fighting a clearly defined enemy.

The film follows, broadly speaking, the historical events, but whilst Shchors died in battle on 30 August 1919, Dovzhenko's Shchors still inspects the Red Army troops twenty years later. Shchors had actually been a rather forgotten historical figure, whose myth was evoked in *Pravda* in 1935, shortly before Stalin suggested to Dovzhenko that he should make a film about Shchors, knowing full well that Dovzhenko had been in Petliura's army and had been tried in 1919. Whether Stalin wanted to trip up Dovzhenko or enable him to redeem himself during the height of the Purges remains a mystery, but circumstances took a turn for the worse. In 1938 the former deputy of Shchors's division, Dubovy, was arrested and executed after a forced confession, saying that he had shot Shchors in order to take control of the army. Dovzhenko had wanted Shchors to die in battle, but had to change the ending in the light of Dubovy's confession: with his temporal jump of twenty years he neither defended nor attacked Dubovy, but immortalized Shchors.

Even if *Chapaev* and *Shchors* were popularized, because they dealt with popular heroes, numerous films were made about Lenin, as well as other historical figures, who – despite the hardship they had endured – led the country forward. Maxim Straukh (1900–74) and Boris Shchukin (1894–1939) were the two actors who were traditionally cast for the part of Lenin, while Mikhail Gelovani (1893–1956) appeared in the role of Stalin. Romm's *Lenin in October* (Lenin v oktiabre, Mosfilm 1937) dealt with the October events and Lenin's subsequent criticism of Trotsky, Zinoviev and Kamenev – using the disagreement to suggest that Lenin would have been supportive of the show trials. *Lenin in 1918* (Lenin v 1918g., Mosfilm 1939) covers the role of the secret service, which prevented attacks on Lenin. Such a threat was real, as was clear from the shots that Fanny Kaplan had fired at the leader in August 1918. Shchukin's Lenin was an agitated and mobile figure, while in later films Straukh would make him more immobile, as he was represented in the portraits by Isaak Brodsky. Both Shchukin and Straukh were of small stature, as was Lenin. Although Mikhail Gelovani was much taller than Stalin, he displayed the calm and quiet demeanour of the leader. Ermler's *Great Citizen* (Velikii grazhdanin, Lenfilm 1938–9) also sought to support the show trials. It drew on more contemporary political events by exploring the murder of Leningrad Party chairman Sergei Kirov, in the film featuring as the character of Shakhov, whose murder – according to the film version – particularly worried Stalin. Part I was set in 1925 and showed the progress of industrialization, outlining the danger of foreign contacts as well as disagreements within the Party; Part II was set in 1934, when foreigners had become enemies as they threatened the new regime with sabotage. Ermler, as in most of his films, could venture farther into politics and exposure of plots due to his (albeit alleged) secret service background.

In the mid-1930s, Kozintsev and Trauberg worked on the Maxim trilogy: *The Youth of Maxim* (Iunost' Maksima, Lenfilm 1934) set in the Stolypin era, when the communist Polivanov and the teacher Natasha are in hiding. The workers Andrei, Dima and Maxim see Natasha distribute leaflets at the factory and cover for her. Andrei dies in a work accident, and Dima and Maxim become engaged in Natasha's Revolutionary groups until they are discovered by the police. When another worker dies at the factory, protests follow, during which Dima and Maxim are arrested. In prison they meet Polivanov; Dima is executed and Maxim joins the secret Revolutionary organization. In *The Return of Maxim* (Vozvrashchenie Maksima, Lenfilm 1937), set in 1914, the ever more bold and daring Maxim, with growing confidence, supports the strikers at a factory, discloses intrigues designed to undermine their cause, and is injured by the gambler Platon Dymba (Mikhail Zharov, the actor who traditionally played the villain). In *The Vyborg Side* (Vyborgskaia storona, Lenfilm 1938) Maxim is entrusted with work for the state bank and manages to avert sabotage from the Black Hundreds under Dymba. He also prevents an attempt on Lenin's life – à la Fritz Platten, the Swiss communist who had shielded Lenin in a previous attempt on his life. Maxim then joins the fight against the Germans who threaten the new republic. The trilogy chronicles the growing Revolutionary consciousness and the political commitment of Maxim, thus offering a perfect Socialist Realist narrative.

Many films of the late 1930s praised and glorified the achievements of historical figures, such as Vladimir Petrov's *Peter the First* (Petr Pervyi, Lenfilm 1937–8), underlining the political necessity for unusual action; Pudovkin and Doller's *Suvorov* (Mosfilm 1940), about Russia's 'Generalissimo' (1727–1800); Igor Savchenko's *Bogdan Khmelnitsky* (Kiev Studio 1941), on the Ukrainian struggle against Polish occupation in 1648; Sergei Yutkevich's *Yakov Sverdlov* (Soyuzdetfilm 1940), set in 1914 when Sverdlov engaged in agitprop in the Urals, was arrested and exiled, but nevertheless continued to support the Revolution; and Pudovkin's *Minin and Pozharsky* (Mosfilm 1939), about the men who had liberated Moscow from the Poles in 1612. These films were made in an attempt to use historical references to justify and compare Stalin's dictatorship with other historical periods.

Another film that follows, superficially, the call for historical narratives was Eisenstein's *Alexander Nevsky* (Mosfilm 1938), set in thirteenth-century Russia at a time when it had come under attack from the Teutonic knights. After the fall of Pskov, where Russians were burnt alive, and the threat to Novgorod, Nevsky aroused the peasants and the *druzhina* (the prince's [*kniaz*] bodyguards) to fight the Teutonic knights on Lake Peipus (also known as Lake Chudskoe) and scored a victory. The film's tripartite structure follows, like *Battleship Potemkin* had done before, that of classical tragedy: the introduction of the threat is followed by a climax, in the battle, and ends with a triumphant resolution. Drawing on an event that was little documented in historical records, Eisenstein was free to use his imagination. Since the city of Novgorod preserved few buildings of the period, most of the filming took place in a studio; even the frozen lake was created artificially for the battle scene. The music, composed by Sergei Prokofiev, had symphonic quality and provided the counterpoints to the action that Eisenstein had sought to define in his 1928 statement on sound.

For the 'Battle on the Ice' Prokofiev used the concept of audio-visual counterpoint in vertical montage. Together with Eisenstein, he made a drawing of the rhythm and its movement, which he replicated in the score. The music thus matches exactly the composition of the shots. As Eisenstein stated in a lecture in 1947, 'Prokofiev had a striking talent for creating images in music'.[21]

The film displayed the determination of the secular leader in fighting the Christian army, confirming the stance adopted by Stalin vis-à-vis religion, with the destruction of churches in the early 1930s. The Teutonic knights feature as faceless aggressors, predecessors of the fascists that were threatening Russia at the time of the film's shooting and thus enhancing the contemporary significance of the plot.

> The theme of patriotism and national defence against the aggressor is the subject that suffuses our film ... We want our film not only to mobilize even more those who are in the very thick of the worldwide struggle against Fascism, but to bring spirit, courage and confidence to those parts of the world where Fascism seems as indestructible as the Order of the Knights appeared in the thirteenth century.[22]

The film thus projects present troubles (the fear of invasion) on to the past, seeking energy and justification for the resistance at a time when Germany was the Soviet Union's enemy – a situation that changed when the non-aggression pact was signed in August 1939, at which point the film was removed from repertoires until the German invasion in 1941, when once again it suited the political agenda. This constantly changing situation, both ideologically and politically, reflects the shifting politics in which filmmakers had to work: in the quicksand they could appear to be ardent supporters today and subversive elements tomorrow, depending on politics.

At a time when political demands and expectations changed so rapidly, the classics provided relatively safe ground for filmmakers: Alexander Ostrovsky's *The Storm* (Groza, dir. Vladimir Petrov, Soyuzfilm Leningrad 1933) and *Without a Dowry* (Bespridannitsa, dir. Protazanov, Rot-Front 1936); Saltykov-Shchedrin's *Golovlev* (Iudushka Golovlev, dir. Alexander Ivanovsky, Soyuzfilm Leningrad 1933) or *Petersburg Night* (Peterburgskaia noch', Soyuzfilm 1934, dir. Grigori Roshal, Vera Stroeva), based on Dostoevsky's 'White Nights' and 'Netochka Nezvanova', as well as *Dubrovsky* (Lenfilm 1935, dir. Ivanovsky), based on Pushkin's story, are some examples.

The Purges in the Cinema, 1937–39

Censorship interventions increased in the late 1930s, but more importantly, purges of the industry led to a depletion of creative forces. The 1929 purges had touched the film industry, but the Great Purges would affect it profoundly. Vladimir Nilsen, cameraman to Eisenstein and Alexandrov, had been arrested in 1929 and released; he was again arrested at the height of the Purges and executed in 1938. The director Konstantin Eggert was arrested; he was released and rehabilitated in the 1950s. The Meyerhold actor Ivan Koval-Samborsky was repressed because he had been abroad from 1927–32. Shumiatsky was arrested in 1938. The Purges affected studio heads, artists, consultants, technicians – especially those with foreign connections, who were seen as potential enemies of the people.

At the All-Union Creative Conference on Cinema Matters in January 1935, Eisenstein was subjected to severe criticism for not having produced any new films since his return to the USSR. His arch enemy, Shumiatsky, in charge of cinema matters, had expressed on numerous occasions his desire to see filmmakers make films 'for the millions', a phrase he also chose as title for his 1935 book on the industry. He suggested the genres of musical and historical drama as particularly suitable, and rejected the complex montage that provided no coherent plot.

> We need genres that are infused with optimism, with mobilizing emotions, *joie de vivre* and laughter. Genres that provide us with the maximum opportunity to demonstrate the best Bolshevik traditions: an implacable attitude to opportunism, with tenacity, skill and a Bolshevik scale of work.[23]

Under Shumiatsky, Soyuzkino maintained the Party's presence in studios to increase control during the entire production process, ensuring that the right balance between commerce and ideology was struck. Despite – or because of – that control, numerous films were stopped during production or banned.[24] In 1936, Shumiatsky advanced to the chair of the Committee of Arts Affairs, overseeing not only film production, but the entire arts sector. Shumiatsky had grand plans for a Soviet Hollywood on the Black Sea, which were hampered by reality: in 1935 he had delivered merely forty-three of the 120 films planned, followed by a further drop in production, which led *Pravda* to accuse him of wasting money (9 January 1938). Shumiatsky had indeed used a large slice of the state budget and had not delivered the number of films promised; moreover, he had put his foot wrong with his handling of Eisenstein's *Bezhin Meadow*. In the same year, the Committee of Cinema Affairs was split from the Committee for Arts and received ministerial status, signalling the importance of the industry as a separate branch. Its new head, Semen Dukelsky, remained in that post until June 1939, when Ivan Bolshakov took over.

Eisenstein had been in Hollywood from 1929 until 1932, when his contract with Paramount was cancelled because of differences in opinion. Eisenstein had travelled to Mexico to make a film when he was recalled to Soviet Russia by a telegram from Stalin; he had to leave most of the unedited film footage behind. From 1933 onwards he taught at the Film Institute. Back in Soviet Russia, Eisenstein first applied to make a film based on a comedy script entitled *MMM* (Maxim Maximovich Maximov), a project he abandoned. A project for a film about Moscow was also dropped. When *Thunder over Mexico* was released in Hollywood by MGM in 1933, Eisenstein realized that his footage had not only been lost, but it had been appropriated and reused, since the Mexican footage had been sold to Hollywood, an act that was partly encouraged by Shumiatsky who did not want it back in the USSR. In 1935 Eisenstein began working on *Bezhin Meadow* (Bezhin lug, Mosfilm 1935–7), which was loosely based on Turgenev's *Huntsman's Sketches*, comparing old and new ways of peasant life. Stepok, the main character, was modelled on Pavlik Morozov, the legendary pioneer boy who denounced his parents for hoarding grain and who was murdered by his relatives.[25] *Bezhin Meadow* showed an iconic image of Stepok, making him a martyr (indeed, as Pavlik was turned into a saint in Soviet hagiography). The disturbing theme of both the Morozov legend and the film is that of betraying parental links for the sake of Party loyalty. Moreover, there is a scene when the peasants enter the church where the kulaks have been hiding, destroying the interior, which reflected Stalin's anti-religious campaigns that had culminated in the destruction of the Cathedral of Christ the Saviour in 1931. Whilst the workers had biblical features, the scene extended its religious meaning by suggesting that Stalin was a (pagan) god, who dominated Soviet culture in the 1930s – as is visible in the iconic positioning of portraits of Stalin on the walls of houses, offices and banners. *Bezhin Meadow* was halted in March 1937 by Shumiatsky, although two million roubles had been spent on production. Eisenstein had to write about his 'errors' in the film in 1937 and publicly repent.

Amidst growing fear of ideological errors, Purges and repressions, and in a climate where alliances changed within weeks (Germany was an arch enemy until 1939, then a friend, and became an enemy again in 1941 after the invasion), political circumstance often changed before films were completed (see the case of *Shchors*, for example). The style of films in the latter half of the 1930s became dull and non-experimental, relying on traditional linear narratives, at best infused with a little humour. The acting became stale, reminding Jay Leyda of the style of old fashioned performances: 'tug-of-war ... between the theatre of the past and the cinema of the future'.[26]

The Great Patriotic War (Second World War), 1941–45

On 22 June 1941 Hitler invaded the USSR, breaking the non-aggression pact by sending three million troops along three front lines under code name 'Operation Barbarossa'. The advancing army was stopped, short of Moscow, by the cold weather of December 1941. Deportations of the German settlers on the Volga testify to Stalin's fear of foreigners within the Soviet Union. The Siege of Leningrad (the 'blockade') lasted 900 days (8 September 1941–27 January 1944), costing over one million lives as the population was isolated from supplies and had no heating, no water, and no food. Sergei Loznitsa's documentary *The Blockade* (Blokada, 2005) shows harrowing archival footage of the time and presents a powerful testimony. On 8 May 1945, Germany capitulated as the Red Army entered Berlin. In June, Soviet soldiers were demobilized and returned to Moscow to a triumphant Victory Parade.

In the autumn of 1941, Lenfilm and Mosfilm were hurriedly evacuated to Central Asia: they were dispatched to Alma-Ata where the Central United Film Studios, or TsOKS (*Tsentral'naia ob"edinennaia kinostudiia*) operated. During 1941–45, the directors and staff of TsOKS made war chronicles and worked on feature films.[27] The Ukrainian studio was evacuated to Tashkent, Soyuzdetfilm to Stalinabad (now Dushanbe), and Soyuzmultfilm to Samarkand. In evacuation, filmmakers in Tashkent – without production facilities – started the 'Theatre for the Film Actor' to entertain the population and make their contribution to the war; this theatre became stationary on its permanent base on Povarskaya Street (Soviet name: Vorovsky Street) in Moscow after the war.

Filmmakers concentrated on making agitational skits, the 'Fighting Film Albums', to support the army at the front; they also made short films to boost morale – such as 'Chapaev is with us' (Chapaev s nami); 'Meeting with Maxim' (Vstrecha s Maksimom); 'Girl Friends to the Front' (Podrugi, na front) – facilitating encounters of the soldiers with the heroes of the silver screen. However, these sketches were made in the immediate response to the German invasion, and they were discontinued in the summer of 1942 as the war continued and calamities grew. Filmmakers continued to devote their creative energy to boosting people's morale. The *Film Concert* (Fil'm-kontsert) provided entertainment at the front, where artists could not travel; it contained appearances of Klavdiya Shulzhenko with her song 'The Blue Kerchief' (Sinii platochek) and of the great comedian Arkadi Raikin. For the secret service (NKVD), an ensemble was put together to entertain the officers: this NKVD Ensemble of Song and Dance curiously united the most controversial artists of the 1930s: the *enfant terrible*, composer Dmitri Shostakovich, the filmmaker Sergei Yutkevich, the actor Yuri Liubimov, the satirist and former exile Nikolai Erdman, and the designer Boris Messerer.

Feature films vilified the enemy in bleak and evil colours, while the Russians suffered but were victorious in the end: Leonid Lukov's *Alexander Parkhomenko* (Kiev, 1942) told of a Lugansk worker who helped expel the Germans from Ukraine in 1919. As Denise Youngblood has argued in her ground-breaking study of what she terms the 'historiophoty' of war in Russian cinema, neither the combat film nor the woman-staying-at-home scenario were suitable themes for Russian cinema, since in the early years of the war the front lines saw huge losses, while women and families were evacuated or suffered the hardship of occupation.[28]

The highly popular film by Mark Donskoy, *The Rainbow* (Raduga, Kiev/Ashkhabad, 1943), portrayed women partisans: Olessia Kostiukh returns to her village to give birth, but she is brutally killed by the Nazis. Her child is murdered in a shed, just before Christmas; another boy falls into barbed wire that forms a crown around his head, so that the film is permeated with religious imagery that underlines the theme of sacrifice. She is juxtaposed with the despicable character of Pusia, the wife of a partisan, who betrays her husband with a German officer. When the village is liberated, Pusia's husband returns and shoots her. The praise of Olessia's loyalty is visually rendered through a rainbow extending over the village after the liberation.

Yuli Raizman's *Mashenka* (TsOKS 1942) is set in the Winter War. Masha Stepanova works at a telegraph exchange and attends evening classes to become a nurse. She meets the cab driver Alexei Soloviev and encourages him to prepare for the entrance exam for technical college because she is fond of him – until she sees him with another girl. During the Winter War, Alexei is injured and is brought into Mashenka's care in a field hospital. Inspired by her sense of duty, he returns to the front. *Mashenka* is a more engaging film thematically, which nevertheless brings home two points: the need to learn and advance oneself; and the need to place social interests above private ones. Ermler's *She Defends the Motherland* (Ona zashchishala rodinu, TsOKS, 1943), with Maretskaya as Praskovia (Pasha) Lukianovna, was an equally engaging film: Pasha is a happy woman before the fascists mortally wound her husband and hurl her son under a tank. Full of anger she organizes resistance, dispels the false news of Moscow's fall and raises the people to fight. When the Germans capture Pasha, the partisans liberate her. Whereas earlier in the war, films tended to show the suffering, towards 1943 films became more assertive: Pasha's resistance is ultimately successful. Barnet's *Secret Agent* (Podvig razvedchika, Kiev Studio 1947) explored the mission of Russian agent Fedotov (Pavel Kadochnikov 1915–88), who infiltrates Nazi Germany during the war. Other war films showed the betrayal and moral compromise faced by those who helped partisans (Barnet, *A Priceless Head* [Bestsennaia golova], TsOKS 1942) or who took a risk by hiding Soviet soldiers (Barnet, *Dark is the Night* [Odnazhdy noch'iu], Yerevan Studio 1945). Lev Arnshtam's *Zoya* (Soyuzdetfilm 1944) enshrined on the screen the myth of Zoya Kosmodemianskaya (1923–41), the legendary partisan spy engaged in sabotage of the Nazis on Soviet territory. Zoya did not betray her comrades and was hanged by the Nazi invaders.

Alexander Stolper's *Wait for Me* (Zhdi menia, TsOKS, 1943) advocated the necessity for hope and loyalty through the story of a soldier, Yermolov, who takes with him his apartment keys when leaving for the front. His wife Liza waits, never giving up hope, even when he goes missing. Her devotion and faith are contrasted with that of her friend Sonya, who abandons hope and arranges her life with a prosperous lover; her husband dies during the war. The film showed the task of Soviet women: Believe in the victory and thus assist its realization. Leonid Lukov's *Two Soldiers* (Dva boitsa, Tashkent Studio 1943), about the friendship of the soldiers

Arkadi and Sasha, offered an inspiring portrait of the soldier, especially since Arkadi was played by the actor-singer Mark Bernes (1911–69), who performed 'The Dark Night' (*Temnaia noch'*), a ballad about a soldier in battle who is addressing his wife and child: they should not give up hope, and as long as they think of him he will be spared. Most of the films made during the war end with the return of soldiers: this holds true for Pyriev's *At 6 p.m. after the War* (V 6 chasov vechera posle voiny, Mosfilm 1944), about a meeting of two lovers on Red Square. Two lieutenants, Vasili and Pavel, had met the attractive Varia (Ladynina) in Moscow. Vasia falls in love with her and they vow to meet in Moscow at 6 p.m. after the war. Vasia falters when he loses a leg, but Varia finds him in the turmoil of the war and reassures him of her love. The theme of hope that is rewarded and of happy reunions reflects the growing sense of desperation in a war that continued so much longer than expected in 1941, but they also instil faith in the possibility of victory. Showing the end of the war before it actually happened made this film a key example of Socialist Realism: to anticipate the bright future. The film reached 26 million viewers, an extraordinary number for the time.

In Semen Timoshenko's *Celestial Sloth* (Nebesnyi tikhokhod, Lenfilm 1945), three bachelor pilots vow not to fall in love until the war is over, yet one after the other they break their vow when they meet women pilots. The women are, however, not portrayed as devout Soviet soldiers, but as flirtatious and pretty, guided by these strong men. The film was a box office success after is release in 1946, bringing an upbeat note to Soviet life. In Abram Room's *The Invasion* (Nashestvie, TsOKS 1944), the support of the Soviet campaign extends to the ex-prisoner Fedor Talanov, who had served a sentence – unjustly. He wants to fight, but is not trusted. Only when he kills a German officer and subsequently goes to the gallows to save the partisan chief who had rejected him earlier can he redeem himself and profess his true love for the fatherland. The film caused controversy when the authorities refused to believe that soldiers would be rejected, arguing that Soviet men were never sentenced unjustly. All these films draw compassionate and appealing portrayals of the heroes and heroines who sacrifice their lives for the fatherland or are unjustly treated. The notion of sacrifice of life for the country carried within it religious overtones, further enhanced by the sudden return of church officials to the public arena at the height of the war.

The single most important film during the war is without doubt *Ivan the Terrible* (Ivan groznyi, Mosfilm), made in two parts and comparing the leadership of the sixteenth-century tsar with Stalin. Stalin had commissioned Eisenstein to make a film about Ivan the Terrible, wanting to have comparisons drawn between his own strong leadership and that of Ivan, who had unified Russia in the sixteenth century.

In the first part Eisenstein showed Ivan's coronation and his plans for a Russian state, which are opposed by his close friends Kurbsky and Kolychev. Ivan (in a stunning performance by Cherkasov) wins the support of Maliuta Skuratov, who would become his most faithful servant. Kazan is freed from the Tartar yoke and a

Figure 3.5 Eisenstein's *Ivan the Terrible*.

new ally, Basmanov, warns Ivan of the boyars. Ivan marries Anastasia and is grief-stricken when she is poisoned by Yefrosinia, who, in a plot with the boyars, tries to place her son Vladimir on the throne. When Basmanov suggests the formation of an army of *oprichniki* (the tsar's private guard), the tsar agrees, but retires to the convent Alexandrova Sloboda and will only return at the people's request. The people approach the monastery, forming an impressively long line in the snow-covered fields, confirming to Ivan that he is loved by the people, the assertion he sought. Ivan forms a towering figure against the white walls of the monastery in the final frame, as he rises to the challenge. The first part satisfied Stalin: it revealed parallels both in personal and political life, such as the theme of betrayal through friends, which reflected Stalin's increasing suspicion after the Purges; Stalin's grief after the loss of his wife Nadia, allegedly killed by his enemies (she actually committed suicide); and the need for a private guard (Stalin's NKVD). All these parallels served to justify Ivan's actions, sanctioning them through the final scene, which expressed the people's approval. Having united the people behind him and sidelined the boyars, the film depicts a strong Ivan.

The second part revisited Ivan's old friends: Kurbsky conspires with the Polish king, while Kolychev has become the monk Filipp, whose family is executed at Ivan's order by his 'henchman': old friends have become traitors. Ivan is full of fears and doubts, and his hatred of the boyars is explained through flashbacks to his childhood: Ivan will rule without the boyars. Filipp tries to shame Ivan into repentance by performing *The Fiery Furnace* – a play about the murder of innocent children by the *oprichniki*. This development in the plot is reminiscent of the play Hamlet had performed for Claudius and the Queen. Yefrosinia and the boyars plot to kill the tsar, but during a banquet (filmed in colour) Ivan changes roles with Vladimir, who is killed instead.

There are parallels not only with Ivan's skilful military leadership (and Stalin's as head of the Red Army – now at war), but also with personal isolation: the loss of his wife, the increasing isolation in the Party, the desire to be loved by the people, and the need for the NKVD to protect him, with Beriya/Maliuta at its head. Part II was banned, as Stalin did not approve of the comparisons suggested in the film. In a discussion at the Kremlin he expressed criticism, in particular of the *oprichniki* being portrayed as a hooded army reminiscent of the Ku Klux Klan. According to Stalin, Ivan shows lack of confidence and remorse – he is plagued by flashbacks that give personal motives for his hatred of the boyars. Ivan's isolation makes him a lonely man who loses his friends. His self-reflexivity and doubt reminded Stalin of Hamlet, whom he saw as a weak-willed man unable to avenge his father's murder. Stalin commented:

> Your tsar is irresolute like Hamlet ... Ivan the Terrible was very ruthless. One can show that he was ruthless. But you must show why IT WAS NECESSARY TO BE RUTHLESS. One of Ivan the Terrible's errors was that he failed to knife through five large feudal families. Had he wiped out these five families, there would have been no Time of Troubles. But Ivan the Terrible executed someone and then he felt sorry and prayed for a long time. God hindered him in this matter. Tsar Ivan should have been more resolute.[29]

There is something else in the references to Hamlet that must have disturbed Stalin: if Hamlet tries to tease a confession from Claudius by the performance, it cannot be excluded that Stalin suspected Eisenstein of doing the same to him, with his film, regarding the Purges.

The first part of *Ivan the Terrible* received the Stalin Prize; the second part was banned and released only after Stalin's death. Eisenstein once again fell victim to policy changes. Part I was completed during the war and Stalin compared his campaigns to those of Ivan: a campaign for a great Russia. Part II was completed after the victory, with a strong Stalin who saw himself reflected in a crooked mirror in an Ivan who knows fear and remorse. As with *The General Line*, completed after a change in the agricultural policy, or *Nevsky*, released during a period when Germany stood as enemy and withdrawn from distribution a year later, *Ivan the Terrible* is a victim of circumstance: the characterization of Ivan in parts one and two has fundamentally not changed.

Even with the end of the war, films about heroic acts continued to appear on the screens and enjoyed great popularity. Sergei Gerasimov's *Young Guard* (Molodaia

Figure 3.6 Stolper's *Tale of a Real Man*: Meresiev (Kadochnikov).

gvardiia, Gorky Studio 1948) was based on Alexander Fadeev's novel and set in 1942 in the coal-mining town of Krasnodon, which was abandoned by the Red Army. The film drew controversial comments, claiming that the Red Army never 'abandoned' a town. It shows a group of young people defending the town and assisting the Red Army; however, they are arrested by the Gestapo and executed just before Red Army can liberate the city. The films made after the end of the war show that suffering and loss have been sustained, but that the sacrifices were offered by heroes and that suffering is rewarded. Alexander Stolper's *Tale of a Real Man* (Povest' o nastoiashchem cheloveke, Mosfilm 1948), set in 1942, followed the pilot Alexei Meresiev (Kadochnikov), whose aircraft is shot down. Although he is injured (and later loses both legs) he crawls to the front line to join his army. He is allowed to fly again: the fatherland provides a meaning in life. Meresiev is not abandoned but integrated back into Soviet aviation. The objections levelled at these films show an increasing concern with historical facts treated, allegedly, not as they really happened. The critics and officials appeared to forget that these were fiction films, treating them as documentaries whilst expecting events to be varnished and the course of history to be rectified.

The 'Film Famine' after the War, 1946–53

Immediately after the war, in March 1946, the Directorate of Cinema acquired ministerial status (called Ministry of Cinema) and Ivan Bolshakov was appointed to its head. A second important cinematic event was the establishment, in 1948, of Gosfilmofond: located in Belye Stolby, a small town to the south of Moscow, this is one of the most important facilities for research, with a rich film archive.

The cultural diversity to which the soldiers returning from the western front had been exposed appeared as a threat to the regime. Xenophobia soon reigned in a similar fashion to the pre-war fear of 'enemies of the people', those who had been exposed to Western influences, potential saboteurs and spies. Paradoxically, in this climate the films that the Soviet Army had brought back from Babelsberg's UFA studios outside Berlin – known as 'trophy films' and consisting of German, American, British and Italian films – were partly released in the USSR despite the fact that they had been made by the Nazi enemy for propaganda and entertainment.[30] The American films were largely used for closed screenings only.

Andrei Zhdanov's 'cosmopolitan campaign' of 1946–48 was a result of this return to xenophobia: Zhdanov (1896–1948) was put in charge of culture and ideology in 1946 and launched attacks on the new editorial board of the literary journals *Zvezda* [Star] and *Leningrad* for publishing 'ideologically harmful works' – by the poet Anna Akhmatova and the writer Mikhail Zoshchenko, who were subsequently excluded from the Writers' Union. He then criticized theatre repertoires for showing Soviet people as 'ugly caricatures' 'lacking cultural education', while villains appeared as strong and powerful in new plays (Central Committee Resolution, 26 August 1946). Jazz music came in the firing line of ideology when it was classified as hysterical and cacophonous. Zhdanov ordered the arrest of jazz musicians, such as Eddie Rosner and Leonid Piatigorsky, but also the 'arrest' of saxophones. On 4 September followed a Resolution on cinema, attacking Lukov's *Great Life* (Part II, Soyuzdetfilm 1946), *Ivan the Terrible* (Part II, Mosfilm 1946), Pudovkin's *Admiral Nakhimov* and Kozintsev and Trauberg's *Simple People* (Prostye liudi, Lenfilm 1945). The period is therefore usually referred to as *zhdanovshchina*. Pudovkin was accused of distorting historic truth by dwelling on Nakhimov's attendance at balls and dances instead of considering the military achievements, while Eisenstein's film was discussed in full by Stalin and Molotov in a meeting in the Kremlin on 25 February 1947. Lukov's second part of *Great Life* was about a former saboteur, who now finds the support and trust of the collective of miners in the Donbass region, having redeemed his sins of the past. Zhdanov alleged that the film did not reflect fully the role of the Party, paying instead too much attention to private, everyday life. It appeared, he alleged, that the workers had no support in the reconstruction of the industry after the war, encountering opposition from within the Soviet system. The film's content therefore did not correspond to the title and mocked Soviet reality. Furthermore, the impression was created that manpower and not technology achieved outstanding results: 'Such a representation of links between state organizations and worker collectives is false and erroneous', claimed the Resolution. The attack on *The Young Guard* reverberates from a distance: the Red Army would never have abandoned Krasnodon. *The Young Guard* was made with students of the Film School, thus embracing generational change and offering fresh views on communism: Sergei Bondarchuk (1920–94), Inna Makarova (b. 1928), Nonna Mordiukova (b. 1925), and Viacheslav Tikhonov (b. 1928) appeared in the film. Sergei Yutkevich's *Light over Russia* (Svet nad Rossiei, Mosfilm 1947) was banned although it was based on a Soviet classic, Nikolai Pogodin's *The Kremlin Chimes* (Kremlevskie kuranty, 1940), dealing with electrification. In 1947 Mikhail Suslov (1902–82) was elected to the Central Committee, where he would be in charge of ideology for the rest of his life. Film narratives were consistently treated by bureaucrats and Party officials as representations of reality. As *Potemkin* had replaced the actual events of 1905, so films were considered to supersede events and provide the historic narrative of the future. In this context the realistic manner of cinema of the period assists that illusion, but also makes the films dull and stale.

In 1948, a campaign targeting Jews began: the 'cosmopolitan campaign' attacked Jewish writers and art critics, leading to expulsions, arrests and the murder of Solomon Mikhoels. This xenophobic climate resulted partly from a fear of the enemy, partly from the increased alienation among the allied forces after the victory. Stalin's sense that the US and the UK had let down the Soviet Union by their refusal to intervene in the war earlier and attack Germany, led to his claims at the Yalta conference that allowed him to control significant parts of Eastern Europe, thus preparing what would become known as the Cold War.

The term 'Cold War' was introduced as the USSR remained suspicious of US policies, whilst the American government (Roosevelt and Truman) was wary of the Soviet non-aggression pact and feared a change to the policies agreed in Yalta and Potsdam. On 5 March 1946, Churchill employed the term 'iron curtain' for the first time, in his Fulton speech. Gradually, divisions were marked externally, and the USSR was increasingly isolated.

Films of the late 1940s and early 1950s reflected the new division of the world: more anti-American films followed, in the same way as America would produce films that cast the Soviet Union in a negative light.[31] Alexandrov's *The Meeting on the Elbe* (Vstrecha na El'be, Mosfilm 1949) depicted the Americans cooperating with former Nazis to plunder the occupied Germany's industry. Romm's *The Russian Question* (Russkii vopros, Mosfilm 1948) was about an American journalist who refuses to allege that the Russians had wanted the war: having written about the Soviet Union's peaceful disposition, he is sacked. *The Secret Mission* (Sekretnaia missiia, Mosfilm 1950) was about the American allies leading separate negotiations with Germany during the war, trying to prevent further advances of the Soviet army into Europe. Kalatozov's *The Conspiracy of the Doomed* (Zagovor obrechennykh, Mosfilm

1950) was based on a script by the playwright Nikolai Virta, about a plot against communism in some Eastern European country, sponsored by the Americans in a coalition government, which is dismantled by the Soviet Union. Mikhail Chiaureli's *The Unforgettable Year 1919* (Nezabyvaemyi 1919g., Mosfilm 1951), based on a play by Vsevolod Vishnevsky, sees the city of Petrograd under the threat of a foreign intervention as young Stalin is dispatched to the front to avert the invasion. Room's *Silvery Dust* (Serebristaia pyl', Mosfilm 1953) told of secret laboratories in the US where American scientists, together with former Nazis, develop radioactive weapons and perform experiments on black Americans. Dovzhenko's incomplete *Farewell America* (Proshchai, Amerika, Mosfilm 1951, reconstructed 1996) dealt with an honest American girl who cannot live in the espionage den of the American embassy in Moscow and breaks off with America, becoming a Soviet citizen. These films represented the Cold War sentiment that pervaded Soviet cultural politics, but they also give an indication of the political agendas that informed the medium of film, making it extremely difficult to find 'safe' plots. Biopics about heroic leaders abounded: about the scientist Michurin (Dovzhenko, 1948); about the composers Musorgsky (Roshal, 1950), Glinka (Arnshtam, 1952) and Rimsky-Korsakov (Kazansky and Roshal, 1952); about literary figures such as Zhukovsky (Pudovkin, 1950); Shevchenko (Savchenko, 1951); Belinsky (Kozintsev, 1951), Dzhambul (Dzigan, 1952) and Przhevalsky (Yutkevich 1951).

The post-war period consequently saw a drop in production (alongside the bans on films), which led to a film famine (anaemia), the so-called *malokartin'e*, in the late 1940s.[32] If in the 1930s production had been around fifty feature films per year, then after the war production did not rise – on the contrary, it dropped radically to an all-time low of under ten (Table 3.1).[33]

Table 3.1 Post-War Production Figures

Year	*No. Films Produced*
1945	19
1946	23
1947	24
1948	18
1949	16
1950	13
1951	9

It was not until after Stalin's death on 5 March 1953 that these figures recovered; the 'famine' also spread to other creative spheres. In the theatre, the playwrights Nikolai Virta and Boris Lavrenev had challenged the traditional dramatic structure, claiming that a conflict between good and evil (especially in the light of Zhdanov's resolution about more interesting villains than positive characters) should be abolished: drama did not need a conflict – of course, an essential ingredient. They conceded that a conflict between 'good' and 'better' might be acceptable. Consequently, plays were of such poor quality that only a few theatres staged them.

Stalin on Screen, 1946–50

Films about Stalin, the leader who had taken responsibility, who had become isolated from the people, who lived at a distance from the masses – a distance that had to be overcome, also marked the era. Chiaureli's *The Vow* (Kliatva, Tblisi Studio 1946), about Stalin's oath to Lenin, confirming Stalin as Lenin's contemporary embodiment, was followed by *The Fall of Berlin* (Padenie Berlina, Mosfilm 1949), a semi-fictional and semi-documentary two-part film completed for Stalin's seventieth birthday. It justified the post-war division of Europe and the Cold War by revealing the sources for the Soviet leadership's mistrust of the UK–US alliance. The film was shot in colour (on Agfa film stock, brought back from Babelsberg) and had a score composed by Shostakovich. Following the classical love plot between country and city, peasant and worker, the film evolves from the story about Alesha, a shock-worker at a steel factory, who is awarded the order of Lenin for his outstanding work, and Natasha, a highly cultured and educated schoolteacher in the local *kolkhoz*. Alesha, somewhat embarrassed by his lack of understanding of Pushkin and the opera which Natasha so enjoys, is invited to Moscow to receive his award from Stalin. Stalin offers fatherly advice on his relationship with Natasha. Soon after declaring their love for each other, Natasha and Alesha's village is bombed by German planes. Alesha's mother is killed, Alesha wounded, and Natasha seized by the Germans. When Alesha has recovered, he joins the Red Army in their defence of Stalingrad before they take Berlin. He ascends the Reichstag to complete the conquest, placing the Soviet flag on top.[34] Alesha and Natasha are reunited by comrade Stalin as he is met by the people on an airfield in Berlin. It is through looking at him that Alesha recognizes Natasha and vice versa. Their union is blessed by Stalin, whom Natasha kisses like an icon. If there had been hardly any appearance of Stalin on screen during the war, although he remained in Moscow throughout, then he resurfaced on screen in the late 1940s. The historical figures in the film (featuring the Yalta conference and Berlin) all serve merely to inflate Stalin's image as a caring, just and capable leader of the people and father of the nation, thus boosting the personality cult.

Most of these films are stylistically conventional and illustrate narratives about heroes or set models for behaviour. They are of enormous interest to the historian in illustrating the changing myths of the country's leadership, but of little interest for cinematic history. It would seem that for this reason many films of the 1930s and 1940s remain unavailable to Western audiences, with the exceptions of some musicals and Eisenstein's films. The films paint a bright picture of life, which varnishes reality and leads people into the illusion of a happy life in the present rather than the future. With its remit of showing history in its development, Socialist Realism had led artists to show not the here-and-now, opening the present to criticism that could lead to improvement, as was done in Medvedkin's sketches on the film-train and as audiences would call for in the Thaw: to expose corruption in order to improve society. Instead, Stalin-era films showed the perfect communist ideals as if they had already been achieved and the war as if it had already been won – and contributed, in Khrushchev's opinion, to the possibility of Stalin's personality cult. In his Secret Speech in February 1956, he blamed the cultivation of the personality cult on cinema, with filmmakers establishing and maintaining the image of the leader and varnishing reality in the glorified portrayal of industry and agriculture.[35] An entirely new generation of filmmakers was needed to revive cinema as an art form, and many of these artists were waiting in the wings: Grigori Chukhrai and Marlen Khutsiev, Tengiz Abuladze and Sergo Parajanov.

–4–

The Thaw – New Beginnings, New Lives (1954–66)

My vam pokazhem Kuz'kinu mat' (We will teach you a lesson)

N. S. Khrushchev

The so-called Thaw (*ottepel'*) is a period full of ambiguities and complexities, just like the above phrase by Khrushchev, which he pronounced during a visit to the United States in 1959 – leaving his interpreter in a huge dilemma: 'We will show you Kuzma's mother' is the literal translation of this phrase, whose etymology remains obscure (it means to teach somebody a lesson). Referring with a folksy phrase to Soviet superiority at an international level, it became clear a few years later what Khrushchev meant by 'Kuzma's mother': on 30 October 1961 a hydrogen bomb (*tsar'-bomba*) was tested in the polygon of Novaya Zemlya.

As complex as it is to define the beginning of the period called the Thaw – by choosing between Stalin's death, Khrushchev's Secret Speech in 1956, and the publication of Ilya Erenburg's (1891–1967) novel *The Thaw* (Ottepel') in 1954 as markers – it becomes almost impossible to find consensus on the date that would 'close' the period: Khrushchev's deposition on 14 October 1964, the Soviet invasion of Czechoslovakia in August 1968, or the arrest and trial of Andrei Siniavsky (1925–97) and Yuli Daniel (1925–88) for the publication of 'anti-Soviet' works abroad under the pseudonyms of Abram Terts and Nikolai Arzhak in 1966, leading to sentences of seven and five years in labour camps. The last of these three dates seems a good cut-off point for a history of cinema, because from that moment onwards the clampdown in culture that had occasionally flared up before became consistent, obvious and widespread, especially since the year 1967 marked the fiftieth anniversary of the October Revolution and led to a further tightening of control as national and international delegations visited the capital Moscow.

The Thaw in Politics and Culture

The Thaw revived the Soviet film industry: comedies could be made once again, and films could turn the hero back into an individual human being, placing humanist values before ideological concerns. The films of this period concerned the simple man and ordinary lives rather than leaders, heroes and shock-workers. The period is, however, very hard to define or divide into phases. When Stalin died in March 1953, he had accumulated the offices of the General of the Army, Chairman of the Council of Ministers (Head of State), and First Secretary of the Communist Party. Stalin's 'henchman' Lavrenti Beriya, head of the NKVD, was arrested and executed in December 1953. Khrushchev was elected First Secretary of the CPSU in September 1953, and Head of State in March 1958, having survived a political crisis in 1957 when opponents blamed the unrest in Hungary and Poland on his Secret Speech, which he delivered at the Twentieth Party Congress on 25 February 1956, and where he disclosed the crimes of the Stalin era. After the Secret Speech a period of liberalization set in, both in political and cultural terms. The denunciation of Stalin's personality cult was formally sealed with the renaming of Stalingrad as Volgograd, the removal of Stalin's body from the mausoleum in 1961, and the rehabilitation of many people arrested during the Purges. It was thus not until 1958 that Khrushchev had consolidated political power, and even then his political agenda remained unstable in economical and agricultural terms, in foreign and cultural politics.

The Thaw had a number of positive effects on cultural life: the publication of works which were critical of Soviet society, such as the appearance in 1962 of Alexander Solzhenitsyn's *A Day in the Life of Ivan Denisovich* (Odin den' Ivana Denisovicha), about life in a prison camp, on the pages of *Novy Mir*, the most influential of the literary journals of the Thaw; the opening of new theatres, such as the Oleg Yefremov's Sovremennik (Contemporary) Theatre in 1956 and Yuri Liubimov's Taganka Theatre in 1964; the move away from the glorification of collective Soviet heroism towards an appraisal of individual sacrifice in films such as Mikhail Kalatozov's *The Cranes Are Flying* (Letiat zhuravli, Mosfilm 1957), or Grigori Chukhrai's *Ballad of a Soldier* (Ballada o soldate, Mosfilm 1959); the opening of modern art exhibitions, such as the Picasso exhibition of 1956; and the celebration of the International Youth Festival in Moscow in 1957. During the 1950s, the *stiliagi* (style hunters) appeared: people who imitated Western dress and style, copying the dandy look and concerned with the consumer culture of the West, thus rebelling against the stifled dress habits in the Soviet Union.

The works and voices of new writers resounded in the literary journals; young poets gathered to recite their poetry near the new Mayakovsky statue erected in 1958. Vladimir Mayakovsky's satires of the 1920s, which had been banned from the theatre repertoires, were revived under Valentin Pluchek at the Satire Theatre in Moscow; and the year 1958 saw the release of Eisenstein's *Ivan the Terrible (Part II)*. The Second Congress of the Writers' Union was held, twenty years after the first, in 1954. The works of Ivan Bunin (1870–1953), who had emigrated in 1919 and been awarded the Nobel Prize in 1933, were published. A good deal of Western literature became available in translation and cultural exchanges took place, such as foreign film programmes, exhibitions and tours. The village prose movement began: writers shifted the setting of their novels to villages, allowing them to portray simple life and folk traditions rather than shock-workers and industry heroes. Leisure and social facilities expanded, as did the cinema network. In 1958 the largest open-air swimming pool opened – ironically built on the site of the Cathedral of Christ the Saviour destroyed in 1931. Better housing was built, with Khrushchev's campaign of five-storey apartment buildings on the outskirts of Moscow, referred to as *khrushcheby* in popular parlance; the production of consumer goods increased rapidly and social reforms were introduced in 1960, such as the eight-hour day, the right to change employment, and minimal wages, as well as a school reform (ten compulsory years) in 1958. All these changes showed a concern for living standards and placed the individual before industrial progress – a concern reflected in the cinema of the Thaw. In the countryside, Khrushchev initiated agricultural reforms by launching the Virgin Lands programme in Kazakhstan and Siberia in an attempt to increase the harvests.

Between these positive and encouraging impulses, Khrushchev's home and foreign politics were erratic, reflecting the limitations imposed by the hardliners in Central Committee and the Politburo. The crushing of the reformist uprising in Hungary in 1956 and deposition of the anti-Soviet government of Imre Nagy is one example of Soviet intrusion into foreign politics in order to assert its control and dominance. In line with these ambitions of a superpower, during the late 1950s the Soviet Union boasted its achievements in military and industrial power: thus, in 1957 a *sputnik* (satellite) transported the dog Laika into space, followed by a successful space flight by Yuri Gagarin (1934–68) on 13 April 1961.

Despite Khrushchev having advocated peaceful coexistence between East and West in 1955, the formation of NATO and the Warsaw pact as military alliances of East and West spoke of the opposite. In 1959 Khrushchev visited the US for the first time, followed by a second visit in 1960 to the United Nations assembly, where he famously banged his shoe on the table. In August 1961, American vessels landed at The Bay of Pigs (Bahia de Cochinos) on Cuba, beginning an invasion designed to overthrow Fidel Castro, who had come to power in 1959. The Soviet Union supported the Cuban defence against the US by stationing missiles on the island. When these were located by US reconnaissance, the American government levelled allegations at the Soviet Union: Khrushchev agreed to dismantle the base, thus preventing further escalation of the so-called 'Cuban missile crisis'.

Soviet foreign policies thus veered between rapprochement and military dominance, reflecting the insecurity of Khrushchev's power. In the cultural sphere, too, the increasing dominance of hardliners over reformers within the Party can be seen in the refusal to let Boris Pasternak accept the Nobel Prize for his novel *Doctor Zhivago* in 1958; the defection of ballet dancer Rudolf Nureev (1938–93) in 1961, fearing arrest in the Soviet Union on the grounds of homosexuality; the arrest, trial and internal exile of the poet Joseph Brodsky (1940–96) in February 1964 for 'parasitism' (not having a job); the clampdown in the early 1960s on public performances of the bard-poets Bulat Okudzhava (1924–97), Vladimir Vysotsky

(1938–80), and Alexander Galich (1918–77). The most notorious of these events was the scandalous Manege exhibition of 1 December 1962, when Khrushchev labelled the Soviet abstract paintings in the exhibition as 'shit' and their painters 'sodomites' – in the company of a whole delegation of ideologues of the Central Committee. In the aftermath of this event, filmmakers and artists were constantly warned not to copy or imitate Western art. In meetings with artists and the intelligentsia, Khrushchev criticized writers, warning them that cultural liberalism could bring about a similar situation to the crushing of the Nagy government in Hungary: in other words – beware.

The tension in the Central Committee of the Communist Party climaxed with the removal of Khrushchev from office on 14 October 1964. Leonid Brezhnev (1906–82) became First Secretary of the Party, while Alexei Kosygin (1904–80) succeeded Khrushchev as President of the Council of Ministers. The period that followed is commonly called the Stagnation, as it consolidated communist rule through pragmatic policies rather than opening an ideological debate about the adaptation of communism to contemporary society. This political and cultural climate sent contradictory signals to artists and filmmakers: although they could never be sure of the boundaries of the permissible, film politics largely benefited from the chaotic policies of the Thaw.

Film Politics

For the film industry, the Thaw boosted production. The sixth Five-Year Plan (1956–60) foresaw investment in cinema infrastructure, studios and cinemas in the context of Khrushchev's emphasis on improving leisure facilities. Above all, the cinema network expanded with new cinemas and better production facilities. As a consequence, ticket sales rose. Feature film production also started in the republican studios.

Ivan Pyriev became head of Mosfilm in 1954, using his influence to support young filmmakers who had just graduated from the Institute. Mosfilm, as well as other studios, had an artistic council that vetted all scripts and films, and 'creative units' to decentralize control of and responsibility for production. Pyriev started working towards the establishment of a professional union in a meeting on 23 November 1957, when he resigned as head of Mosfilm to devote himself to this task. The Union of Filmmakers (or Filmmakers' Union, FU) held its constituent congress in November 1965, after a long drawn-out dispute between the authorities and the FU Organizing Committee as to its necessity. The Union drew its subsidies partly from membership fees, partly from the glossy bi-monthly *Soviet Screen* (Sovetskii ekran) and the sale of posters and cards. Its members were provided with medical and social support, and had at their disposal the facilities of a veteran's residence in Matveevskoe, sanatoria in Bolshevo and Krasnaya Pakhra, and other recreational and leisure services.

On the administrative level, the former textile worker and first female member of the Politburo, Yekaterina Furtseva (1910–76) was put in charge of ideology at the Central Committee from 1956 to 60 and became Minister of Culture from 1960 to 74. Furtseva's policies were, like most of the Thaw, a mixture between repression and benefaction. Her lack of formal education often left her at sea in official meetings, when she would be unsure of how to behave. In 1953 the Main Directorate for Cinema (GUK) became part of the newly established Ministry of Culture, but by 1963 its independent ministerial status was restored as Goskino, presided over by Alexei Romanov from 1963 to 1972.[1] Goskino classified films, determined the number of copies of each new release and thus established whether a film would get wide or limited release.

Most important, in 1959 the Moscow International Film Festival was revived: it took place bi-annually, alternating with Karlovy Vary. However, Soviet films consistently won the main awards, sometimes in a tie with other films, which in turn were frequently from a socialist country. There were two exceptions in the Soviet era: in 1963 Fellini's *8½* (Otto e mezzo) received the main award in a decision of jury president Grigori Chukhrai, despite the fact that Khrushchev had slept through the entire film. In 1987 Fellini's *Interview* (Intervista) won the Golden Prize – but this was already in the glasnost era. Indeed, the pattern of wanting to award Russian films the main prizes seems to carry on at the Moscow Film Festival to the present day (see Appendix 1).

The style of films changed as critics and bureaucrats were debating what audiences wanted. Instead of presenting a varnished reality in musicals or historical hagiography, films should portray everyday, ordinary life; however, this proved a complex task. Filmmakers strove for verisimilitude (*dostovernost'*), trying to demonstrate that their images and plots were true to life by following the developments they had seen in the *cinéma-verité* or the neo-realism of the French and Italian films that were shown to avid audiences in Moscow during the late 1950s. Therefore, human characters and emotions were no longer rendered as crass, black-and-white portrayals, but became more differentiated. The communist, worker and pioneer became simply a 'man', and children and adolescents moved into the focus of attention. Filmmakers began to explore the genre of comedy, which was a potential minefield because it was difficult to gauge what could be exposed to laughter. Therefore, a variety of thematic branches developed simultaneously during the Thaw: the war was revisited, with the emphasis now on the individual's contribution and the problems of return to ordinary life; other films showed the everyday life of families and of the younger generation; and the genres of science fiction and comedy were developed in the period. This range of concerns and themes reflects the variegation of taste, and with it the fragmentation of society from a monolithic mass (of the Stalin era) into smaller groups with different interests and concerns. First and foremost, however, the 1950s were concerned with the experience of the Second World War – a theme that would never lose its grip on Soviet and post-Soviet audiences, as Denise Youngblood has clearly demonstrated with her study of war films.

The War Revisited

During the war, filmmakers showed unconditional support for the military cause. Often, though, facts were hushed up: for example, that released prisoners of war were arrested because they had had contact with the enemy and to prevent them from telling stories. Handicapped or even crippled veterans were taken to the far north to efface traces of the war action, and Stalin even abolished Victory Day in 1947 (reinstated under Brezhnev for the twentieth anniversary in 1965). The Thaw cinema showed images of invalids and presented heroic acts not in terms of the glorious defence of the fatherland, but as personal achievements. Individuals were once again normal people acting courageously and heroically in an exceptional and unique situation, one that could not be easily transferred on to others and thereby generalized to a universal level. In this sense, the cinema of the Thaw shows most clearly the shift from a social narrative to the individual and his fate. Films addressed problems of loss and returned the victory to the people rather than to politics. The individual, not the collective, stood therefore in the forefront of cinematic narratives about the war. Moreover, historical myths could be challenged, as in Alexander Stolper's *The Living and Dead* (Zhivye i mertvye, Mosfilm 1963), which alluded to the diminished numbers of army officers as a result of the Purges, leading to huge losses in early phase of the war as a result of poor military strategies and lack of battle experience. Alexander Alov (1923–83) and Vladimir Naumov's (b. 1927) *Peace to Him Who Enters* (Mir vkhodiashchemu, Mosfilm 1961) told about three Russian soldiers and a pregnant German woman, who misleads them deliberately while they try to be humane. In the midst of a devastated country she gives birth – a pointer to a peaceful future. Zakhar Agranenko and Eduard Tisse's *Immortal Garrison* (Bessmertnyi garnizon, Mosfilm 1956) for the first time showed on screen Soviet soldiers in captivity and dying in agony. Even the Civil War hero became part of the myth of individual suffering and sacrifice for the victory and the country: Alov and Naumov's *Pavel Korchagin* (Kiev Studio, 1956), based on Nikolai Ostrovsky's *How the Steel was Tempered* (1942), unfolded the hero's sacrifices for the sake of the Revolution as a flashback of the paralysed and dying hero.

Pudovkin's *The Return of Vasili Bortnikov* (Vozvrashchenie Vasiliia Bortnikova, Mosfilm 1952) was one of the first films to show a war veteran returning to ordinary life and encountering difficulties in adapting. Bortnikov (played by the student of the Vakhtangov Theatre's Shchukin School, Vasili Lanovoy, b. 1934), a former *kolkhoz* chairman, was believed dead and his wife Avdotia has not waited for him, but lives with another man, who leaves the house shortly after. The neutral treatment of the unfaithful wife was a novelty for Soviet war films, which had previously condemned women for disloyalty. Bortnikov is once again elected *kolkhoz* chairman and finds fulfilment in his work. In this ending Pudovkin's film remains within the Socialist Realist requirement, with an emphasis on work and collective, but the betrayal of the wife and Bortnikov's difficulties with adapting to a life in peacetime were an indication of a change in tone, making it possible for such problems to be addressed.

Revising the myth of the war started with a re-visioning of the Civil War through a remake of a silent film: Grigori Chukhrai's (1921–2001) *The Forty-First* (Sorok pervyi, Mosfilm 1956) was a remake of Protazanov's 1926 film. The teacher and director Mikhail Romm had come to Chukhrai's rescue when the latter was fired from the Kiev studio for criticizing a script; Romm agreed with Chukhrai's criticism and brought him to Moscow, where Pyriev set him to work with cameraman Sergei Urusevsky (1908–74). Chukhrai and Urusevsky created timeless images of the landscape, the desert and the island, which form a perfect harmony with man. Although for Mariutka (Izolda Izvitskaya, 1932–71) faith in the fatherland and the Revolution is ultimately stronger than love, the personal and political are not that easy to divide: Mariutka cares for the enemy, the White officer in her captivity, Govorukha Otrok (Oleg Strizhenov, b. 1929), and shows compassion when he is sick. She kills the officer at the end when support from the Whites is on its way, but she cradles in her arms the man she has come to love. Chukhrai planned to cast the actors Strizhenov and Izvitskaya in *Ballad of a Soldier*, which was delayed due to an accident that necessitated a change of the cast, replacing the professional actors with two students, Zhanna Prokhorenko (b. 1940) of the Moscow Art Theatre School and Vladimir Ivashov (1939–95) of the Film Institute.

However, before *Ballad of a Soldier*, another film caused a stir in the film world, both on a national and international level. Mikhail Kalatozov's (1903–73) *The Cranes Are Flying* (Letiat zhuravli, Mosfilm 1957) was based on Viktor Rozov's (1913–2004) play *Forever Alive* (Vechno zhivye), which had opened the Sovremennik (Contemporary) Theatre in 1956. The Sovremennik was founded by young students of the Moscow Art Theatre school, who wanted to implement in their productions a new performance style and engage with the audience, sharing their feelings. The collective of Oleg Yefremov sought to stage modern plays – and decided to begin with two plays: Rozov's *Forever Alive*, and Alexander Galich's *Matrosskaia Tishina* (often wrongly translated as *Seaman's Silence*: this is actually a street name in Moscow). The latter play – which has recently (in 2004) been turned into a film, *Papa*, directed by Vladimir Mashkov – led to the intervention of the censors and to a ban on the production. The history of this ban is documented with a distanced and cynical touch by Alexander Galich in his novel *The Final Dress Rehearsal*.[2] The play, set during and after the war, showed a Jewish pianist making his sacrifice for the country. A central argument of the officials was that the Jews may have fought in the war, but their contribution to the Soviet victory could not be shown on Soviet stage. It is an incident that illustrates well the oscillating cultural policies of the early

Figure 4.1 Kalatozov's *The Cranes Are Flying*: Boris (Batalov) prepares to leave for the war.

Thaw, where arguments of the Central Committee officials still echoed the slogans of the 'cosmopolitan campaign' of the late 1940s.

The Cranes Are Flying is set in Moscow, with its embankments, parks and the Kremlin in the frame of the camera. Boris Borozdin volunteers for the front and, aware of the risk, he wants his bride Veronika to be free. Veronika does not manage to say a personal farewell, as her voice is lost in the general farewell of many others when the individual dissolves in the mass acoustically, while the camera keeps track of individual faces. The troops leave to the 'Slav Woman's Farewell' (Proshchanie slavianki), a march composed during the First Balkan War (1912–13) by Vasili Agapkin, which has become a standard accompaniment for departures of battalions for the front. While Boris keeps Veronika's photograph, she receives no letters from him. Veronika's parents die in a raid and she moves in with the Borozdins. During a further air raid, Boris's cousin Mark takes advantage of Veronika – a rape that is shown through a montage sequence of the flashing lights of explosions and curtains stirred by the wind as the windows have fallen out. The film cuts to Boris and his detachment in a swamp, surrounded by dead trees. Before a reconnaissance mission, Boris loses hope and gives Veronika's photo to the soldier Stepan. Boris's fellow soldier is injured and Boris carries him through the bog; while resting under a tree, Boris is hit by a sniper. He collapses, looks into the sky and sees the birch trees, which begin to spin. As the crown of the tree swirls in front of his eyes, the image turns into the staircase of Veronika's house, which spirals upwards; the doors at the top open and bridegroom Boris and bride Veronika step on to the staircase in their wedding robes. With the hand camera in constant motion, Kalatozov's cameraman Sergei Urusevsky captures the dream that Boris has before his death, which visualizes the life and the future he has lost. The scene of Boris's death is one of the most innovative in cinema of the time: filmed without cuts and edits, but with a mobile camera, it creates not a series of images that pass before the eyes of the dying man, but a single continuous vision of a happy life. The energy of the camera betrays the life that seeps out of Boris's body.

The film echoes a new approach in thematic terms as well: no judgement is passed on Veronika for 'betraying' Boris, even though Mark raped her and even though that rape is immediately followed by Boris's death, implying a connection between the two events. The cause-effect chain that accounted for the linear structure of the Socialist-Realist master plot no longer applies: Veronika may feel guilty, but is not responsible for Boris's death. The cranes that fly to the south return in the spring – Boris does not. However, the cranes also hint at another interpretation with the legend of Ibycus, the sixth-century Greek poet who was attacked by robbers and left for dead. Ibycus called to a flock of cranes, which followed the murderer and hovered above him until, stricken with guilt, he confessed to the crime. The cranes are a constant reminder of the guilt that will run through Veronika's life: whether it is expressed through the patient in the hospital whose wife betrayed him, mirroring Veronika's betrayal, or the little boy Boria who brings back meaning to Veronika's life, or the silent look of Irina Borozdina, the doctor's daughter, or the squirrel that Boris gave her for her birthday. It is not Boris, but Veronika who is the heroine: she has to live with the scars of loss.

The performances of the Moscow Art Theatre's actor Alexei Batalov (b. 1928) as Boris and the ballet student and actress Tatiana Samoilova (b. 1934) as Veronika were astonishing: Samoilova was not beautiful but expressed both the naivety and innocence of a young girl, the suffering of the war and the guilt caused by her acts. Batalov, young, energetic, and attractive through a quiet confidence that needed no boasting or arrogance, became a hero of the Soviet screen, and still holds the attention of spectators when he makes one of his public appearances today. Samoilova was subsequently cast for Giuseppe de Santis's *Attack and Retreat* (Italiani brava gente, 1965) about Italy's unsuccessful attempt to attack the USSR during the war, playing alongside Zhanna Prokhorenko, the actress who played Shura in *Ballad of a Soldier*. *The Cranes Are Flying* remains to date the only Russian or Soviet film to have garnered the prestigious Golden Palm at the Cannes International Film Festival. *The Cranes Are Flying* was one of the first Soviet films to gain international renown, impressing both with innovative film language and the way it radically changes the view of war, seeing it not as a collective triumph but a personal nightmare.

Grigori Chukhrai's *Ballad of a Soldier* also dismantles the concept of heroism. The film, scripted by Valentin Yezhov, who had himself served at the front, is entirely narrated as a flashback of Alesha's mother. It opens with a woman waiting on a road for her son to return, knowing that he is dead: she is dressed in black, wearing a kerchief, and is filmed in an angle that makes her resemble the Madonna, referring to the eternal suffering of the mother figure. Alesha is a soldier: in battle he knocks out two tanks because he is scared. The camera tilts upside down to create the impression of Alesha's vision as he lies in the trench, trying to run away, as instructed by the commander, but unable to do so. The general – a figure who is designed to represent the army as a family, with the commander to replace a real father (that Alesha does not have) – suggests a decoration, but Alesha asks to go home to fix the roof. On the way Alesha meets a number of people whom he helps, and in these acts lies his real heroism: the invalid Vasili who wants to spare his wife the shame of an invalid husband and whom he encourages to brave the meeting, missing his train; the greedy soldier on the train, to whom he concedes a tin of food but who is eventually punished; the scared Shura, for whom he misses the train while fetching water; or Pavlov's wife, who is having an affair and whom he denies the soap her husband has sent to her. Alesha delivers the luxury product instead to Pavlov's father. Alesha is a hero without arrogance, but with an acute sense of justice and honesty. His mother is not at home, and he meets her on the road when it is already time to go back. In this sense, Alesha's experience and manifestations of kind human gestures on the

Figure 4.2 Chukhrai's *Ballad of a Soldier*: Shura and Alesha say farewell.

road (a road movie could be a genre usefully applied here) reveal an interest more in the everyday rather than the battlefield: in the question of how to be heroic in everyday life. *Ballad* was also shown in Cannes but, two years after *Cranes*, it stood in competition alongside films that belonged to a new wave of European and world cinema that was looking into different directions: artistic experimentation, a quality that *Ballad* lacked.

Chukhrai's next film, *Clear Sky* (Chistoe nebo, Mosfilm 1961) interweaves two stories through a flashback, stretching from the war to the post-war period. Before the war there is a romance between the pilot Alexei Astakhov (Yevgeni Urbansky, 1932–65, who had played the invalid Vasili in *Ballad*) and the girl Sasha, who adores him. Later she receives his posthumous decoration: he is thought to have died in the war. The legend, however, is one thing and real life another: Alexei returns. Unlike Vasili Bortnikov's wife, Sasha has not betrayed him, but he returns with an injury that marks him for life: a scar across his face. Moreover, he is not allowed to fly or to join the Party, because he is suspected of collaboration with the enemy after serving time as a German POW. He despairs and takes to drink, feeling worthless. In an argument with Sasha's younger brother Serezha (the young theatre actor Oleg Tabakov, b. 1935), who had not fought in the war – but is a Party member, Serezha fails to explain why this is so. Likewise, Sasha trusts Alexei, but never challenges the system that suspects him of being an 'enemy of the people'. The quiet indifference of people is unbroken – until the ice literally breaks in a montage sequence after Stalin has died. Alexei's Party membership is restored and he is rehabilitated. It is, however, only from above that a change can be effectuated: people remain a helpless and essentially passive mass, victims of the system.

Other films, too, dealt with the aftermath of the war rather than the war itself. Gerasimov's students Lev Kulidzhanov (1924–2002) and Yakov Segel (1923–95) made *The House Where I Live* (Dom, v kotorom ia zhivu, Gorky Studio 1957), which foregrounds the relationships of people in a house in pre-war Moscow before the war disrupts their lives. It was the first time that some class difference was acknowledged, presented in the film through slices of life: in 1935 people live in a new apartment building with modern music, stylish clothes and nice accessories in their new habitat. The geologist Dmitri Kashirin (the outstanding stage and film actor Mikhail Ulianov, 1927–2007) is married to Lida, but they have no children, because Lida is selfish and wants to enjoy life: she has an affair with the neighbour Kostia while her husband is away on an expedition. During the war people perish: Dmitri is presumed dead, leaving behind his estranged wife, who eventually marries Kostia, who has come back from the war as an invalid. The neighbour's son, Serezha, becomes a geologist and continues Dmitri's exploits: even though Dmitri has no children, continuity is created through the younger generation. The rigidly vertical structure of the Stalinist family is broken, and the young Serezha chooses his ideological father. The absence of real fathers (the death of Stalin as father figure and the loss of so many family men during the war) leaves a gap that is filled by society. Alexander Prokhorov has argued that the link to the father figure in several Thaw films is represented through shots that position the protagonist against the sky, alluding to the place where the dead father is presumed to be: 'The vertically structured ideology is not suspended completely: instead, it acquires a metaphysical dimension. Serezha maintains a spiritual rather than physical link with his former neighbour.'[3] In Khutsiev's *I am Twenty* (see below), the link is even visually illustrated with the appearance of the father's ghost – unable to provide the required guidance. *The House Where I Live* showed a new approach to film narrative: it has no coherent plot or development, but echoes, with its loose composition, the fragmentation of life in a similar way as *Cranes* had broken the causal chain.

Marlen Khutsiev (b. 1925) had graduated from the Film Institute in 1952, and his *Two Fedors* (Dva Fedora, Odessa 1958) sees Fedor (Vasili Shukshin, 1929–74) returning on a train from the front when he observes an orphan, little Fedor, stealing food. He takes him on the train and back to his home. The mature Fedor proves much less practical than the boy in everyday life, and the two form a comic duo. When Fedor marries Natasha, the jealous boy cuts Natasha's braid and runs away, but is found and integrated into the home, thus making a happy ending for a film with a rounded plot, which assembles a new family for the orphaned boy.

Figure 4.3 Kulidhzanov's *The House Where I Live*.

Gerasimov's student Sergei Bondarchuk (1920–94), who had graduated in 1948, made his directorial debut with *The Fate of a Man* (Sud'ba cheloveka, Mosfilm 1959), based on Mikhail Sholokhov's short story. The film touched on the theme of Nazi captivity and is intriguing both visually and thematically. Andrei Sokolov (Bondarchuk) escapes from a prison camp and waits for a ferry, telling his story to a fellow passenger: how he left for the war, how his family (wife and two children) had perished and how devastated he is. Sokolov had fought for family and homeland, and with their death he has lost the meaning in life. On the last day of the war, he learns that his eldest son has also been killed. Sokolov shows endurance and reflects the suffering of the entire country. As he narrates his story, he remembers – through flashbacks – a happy life, refreshes his memory and expresses the pain of loss. The lopsided camera angles and slipped perspectives echo the hero's psychological dislocation. On the site of his Voronezh house he finds only a crater. He leaves the town with the orphan Vania. After his performance in the film, Bondarchuk was cast as Fedor Nazukov in Roberto Rossellini's *Blackout in Rome* (Era notte a Roma, 1960) appearing in the same outfit, improvising from his earlier part, but – although he became one of the Soviet Union's highly recognized artists – never again did he create such a profound performance of the tragedy of loss as in *The Fate of a Man*.

Mikhail Romm's student Andrei Tarkovsky (1932–86) made his debut with *Ivan's Childhood* (Ivanovo detstvo, Mosfilm 1962). Tarkovsky and his fellow student Andrei (Mikhalkov-)Konchalovsky (b. 1937) were asked to rewrite a script based on a story by Yuri Bogomolov that had already been approved for production, about the 12-year-old Ivan (played by Nikolai Burliaev), who volunteers to spy on the enemy army after his parents have been killed. Ivan returns from one of his reconnaissance missions at the beginning of the film, and perishes in his next mission. Tarkovsky explained his fascination with the character of Ivan:

> [The boy] immediately struck me as a character that had been destroyed, shifted off its axis by the war. Something incalculable, indeed, all the attributes of childhood, had gone irretrievably out of his life. And the thing he had acquired, like an evil gift from the war, in place of what had been his own, was concentrated and heightened within him.[4]

Ivan is orphaned, but he is devoured by feelings of hatred and vengeance. His report to Lt. Galtsev on troop strength is that of an adult, yet he is frail, emaciated and stutters, all external signs of his emotional scars. He is neither the ideologically obsessed partisan Zoya Kosmodemianskaya, nor the little girl from *Once Upon a Time There Lived a Girl* (Zhila-byla devushka, dir. Viktor Eysimont, Soyuzdetfilm 1944), a film which portrayed the life of the little girl Katia during the Leningrad siege and shows her playing with dolls and building bomb shelters for her doll as she tries to master reality. Ivan's personality has been destroyed, eradicated by the horror he has seen – he is already dead and comes alive as a human being only in the dream sequences.

Figure 4.4 Tarkovsky's *Ivan's Childhood.*

The narrative is framed by images of peace, before and after the war: the time that Ivan no longer experiences. Time plays a vital role in Tarkovsky's films: he perceived the role of the filmmaker as one of 'sculpting in time'. As time is both historical and individual, memory plays an important part.

> Cinema, like no other art, widens, enhances and concentrates a person's experience – and not only enhances it but makes it longer, significantly longer … What is the essence of the director's work? We could define it as sculpting in time … The film-maker, from a 'lump of time' made up of an enormous, solid cluster of living facts, cuts off and discards whatever he does not need, leaving only what is to be an element of the finished film, what will prove to be integral to the cinematic image.[5]

Tarkovsky incorporated dreams into *Ivan's Childhood*, for which his cameraman Vadim Yusov (b. 1929) often reversed the camera point to look on objects or figures from above or below, while insides turn into outsides, and closed spaces open up and close again. Thus, the vision of Ivan as a happy child on a sandy riverbank by a tree flips to the image of the boy in a bleak landscape. In another dream sequence, Ivan sees himself at the bottom of a well while in reality sitting in a bathtub, exhausted: the image of the water in the bathtub is thus extended into the dream sequence. The surface of the water reflects the image of Ivan and his mother leaning over the well at the top. As the mother shows the child a star inside the well, Ivan plunges back into the depths and sees from below how the mother drops her bucket: she is killed by the Germans. The sequence illustrates the importance of water – as a surface for reflection and a lens that offers an insight – in all of Tarkovsky's films. Moreover, Tarkovsky uses changing camera angles to switch from dream to reality and back. The dream sequences make reality appear like a nightmare, bleak and deprived of colour and life, and the dream sequences contain a time in flow. The film blurs the line between dark reality and bright dreams: the destroyed houses could just as well be a nightmare, and the swamp with its dead trees looks so unlike reality.

An epilogue seals Ivan's fate: he is captured, tortured and killed by the fascists, as Galtsev finds out when he discovers Ivan's dossier after the Red Army has seized Berlin. This is complemented by documentary footage of Goebbels's dead children: the death of any child prevents the flow of time, as the child is a sign of the future. All that remains of Ivan and the dead children are frozen, static pictures that can no longer partake in the flow of time.

The film was attacked as bourgeois in the Soviet press (a euphemism for the non-linear structure of the film) and defended by the French philosopher Jean-Paul Sartre after its screening in the Venice Film Festival, where it won the main award: Sartre argued that the child was turned into a monster by the horrors he had seen, and this experience explains the mix of reality and hallucination used in the film.[6] Tarkovsky's pessimistic view of the predicament of mankind (who has lost all values and sense of humanism through the atrocities of the war), as well as his poetic approach to the medium of cinema, failing to provide narratives but creating meaning through images alone, had an impact on his later oeuvre and would lead to controversies with the authorities.

A different perspective on the war is offered in *Wings* (Kryl'ia, Mosfilm 1966), scripted by Valentin Yezhov and directed by Larisa Shepitko (1938–79), wife of Elem Klimov, who had studied with Dovzhenko and Romm. Her first film, *Heat* (Znoi, Kirgizfilm 1963), was shot in Kyrgyzstan and contrasted different attitudes to socialism: the young Kemal works on the virgin soils while Abakir, a socialist superman, is fanatic in the worse sense: he is motivated by money and becomes heartless and arrogant, thus subverting the moral ideals of the socialist worker. Ultimately he leaves the brigade, while Kemal scores the moral victory. In *Wings*, Shepitko explored the role of women during and after the war. Nadezhda Petrukhina (the relatively unknown actress Maya Bulgakova, 1932–94) was a fighter pilot in the war; in the present she is an honest but very strict head teacher who finds it difficult to get on with people. She is successful neither as mother to her adopted daughter nor as teacher. With her authoritarian behaviour she appears like a relic of an era that has passed, and she fails to adapt to the new life. Petrukhina is a war hero, and heroism and military discipline have deformed the individual and the woman who is now out of sync with everyday life, where such superhuman acts are no longer required. Instead, heroes are listed and displayed in museums: the war hero has survived physically, but is given no opportunity to live up to that image in peacetime. Doubt is cast over Petrukhina's femininity, as she is endowed with a masculine appearance.

Figure 4.5 Shepitko's *Wings*.

The opening scene captures this dilemma between male and female: she is measured by a tailor to have a suit made, because she fits into no standard size. Petrukhina is non-standard: too large for the everyday and too small for a hero in peacetime. She is lonely and emancipated, refusing the cliché of a housewife. It is she who proposes to Pasha, who replies aptly: 'The director of the museum marries his exhibit.' Flashbacks show Petrukhina's role in the war, and her love of a man with whom she was on a par, but who was shot down. She longs to return to her past role and take off in an aeroplane – to be away from the world with its petty everyday problems, as she feels aloof and literally above them. Petrukhina flies off into the clouds in the final scene of the film, leaving the ending open as to whether she returns to the airfield or kills herself. The latter seems more consistent with her growing realization that a former hero has no place in the modern world, but such a negative ending had to be veiled in ambiguity in order to pass the censors.

Shepitko also addresses the issue of the role of women in society: during the Revolution women were placed on an equal footing with men; during the war they took on extra responsibilities, often fighting with the partisans; after the war, domestic life took priority in cultural and political terms, the state engaged in a military race, while women were dumped from the social agenda and deposed from their roles.

The emancipated woman is, for the cinema of the Thaw, a new phenomenon: single mothers, women who adopt children, former heroines – all these types of women will find their full screen representation in a film that garnered Soviet Russia an Oscar: *Moscow Does Not Believe in Tears* (1979), which is discussed in the next chapter.

All these films of the war are fragmented. The flashback in silent cinema had been used for dreams or visions; in the 1920s the past could appear in montage sequences to explain cause and event or to juxtapose; Socialist Realism made filmic narratives linear and chronological, while the Thaw began to use the flashback to explain action and indulge in the psychological realism of the Moscow Art Theatre, where a basic event triggers the action of the character in the present. This explains the conflation of theatre and film actors in the Thaw, as cinema moved away from external portrayals (types) to fine psychological acting. In this process many new talents were discovered, most frequently theatre actors of the Moscow Art Theatre, among them Alexei Batalov, Oleg Yefremov and Oleg Tabakov. Innokenti Smoktunovsky (1925–94) had trained as a stage actor in Siberia and gained a reputation at the Leningrad Bolshoi Drama Theatre under Georgi Tovstonogov, and later worked at the Maly Theatre and Moscow Art Theatre. Andrei Mironov (1941–87) is probably best known for his role of Johnny First in Alla Surikova's western spoof *The Man from the Boulevard des Capucines* (Chelovek s bul'vara Kaputsinov, Mosfilm 1987). Mironov was a graduate of the Shchukin School and later an actor at the Satire Theatre, but was known also for his roles in popular comedies of the 1960s, such as the part of Ostap Bender in a television film of the satire *Twelve Chairs* (Dvenadtsat' stul'ev, dir. Mark Zakharov, Ekran 1977). Most actresses of the period, curiously, were graduates of the Film Institute (Nonna Mordiukova, Maya Bulgakova, Liudmila Gurchenko) – with few exceptions. This may serve to highlight the emphasis on male roles in plots where women were used as a backdrop for reactions and discoveries.

Ordinary Life

Numerous films of the period showed the immediate effect of the Thaw on the present and focused on family life. Filmmakers were encouraged to be truthful and authentic, and to avoid the glossy portrayal and falsification of the Stalin era film. Natural or *cinéma-verité* style dominated also in other European cinema schools, such as neo-realism in Italy or *cinéma-verité* in France. Filmmakers employed long shots that created the sense of duration, emphasizing the flow of life in the frame rather than creating motion and movement through montage. They fragmented the narrative with flashbacks. The music was usually simple rather than orchestral, and black-and-white was the preferred film stock while Kodak colour film remained rare and the 'trophy' film stock from Babelsberg was exhausted.

Documentarism and *cinéma-verité* harked back to Vertov's ideas on the camera as the observing eye. One of the most significant works of the era was Romm's *Ordinary Fascism* (Obyknovennyi fashizm, Mosfilm 1965), scripted by the critics Maya Turovskaya and Yuri Khaniutin. Fascism is shown through archival footage of Nazi propaganda material, offering close-ups and enlargements on those film sequences and still photography that showed the simple people, highlighting the faces of those who were betrayed by those very propaganda images. The film, premiered in Leipzig, was shelved in the USSR in 1967, because of the possible associations of German totalitarianism with the contemporary Soviet Russia. Gerasimov made several semi-documentaries with his cameraman Vladimir Rapoport, such as *Men and Beasts* (Liudi i zveri, 1962, Gorky Studio with DEFA, GDR), about a Soviet officer in captivity during the Second World War, and later *The Journalist* (Zhurnalist, Gorky Studio 1967), about a journalist travelling to investigate a complaint letter, or *By the Lake* (U ozera, Gorky Studio 1969), about the ecological problems surrounding Lake Baikal.

The observation of the everyday thus played an important and new role in Thaw cinema. The family stood in the centre, and work was no longer driven by shock-workers and competition between the good and the better: the theory of non-conflict receded. The more experienced directors tackled this new theme after having been relegated to making biopics or politically motivated films in the 1930s and 1940s. They relished this opportunity: Iosif Kheifits (1905–95), who had worked with Alexander Zarkhi as assistant director for a long time, made his own debut with *The Great Family* (Bol'shaia sem'ia, Lenfilm 1955), an epic about the Zhurbin family over three generations. Here, women leave their husbands because of neglect, but more important is the introduction of the single mother who appears as a suitable wife for Zhurbin's son, the worker Alesha (Batalov). Mistakes are made and corrected without Party intervention in its deus ex machina role; and no one is to blame for the breakdown of relationships. The film shows rather than condemns, while conforming to the style of authenticity and verisimilitude.

The Rumiantsev Case (Delo Rumiantseva, Lenfilm 1955), based on a story by prose writer Yuri Gherman (1910–67), saw Alexei Batalov in the role of Sasha Rumiantsev. For the first time, characters were not divided rigidly into good policemen and bad criminals, but human qualities were spread across professions: there is an incompetent policeman and a sharp prosecutor, a corrupt trucker and an honest driver. The schematic black-and-white characterization is broken up, and shades begin to appear. The boss of a truck depot uses Rumiantsev to transport stolen goods. When Rumiantsev is arrested and imprisoned, the boss, together with his accomplices, sets up a case against him in order to evade prosecution. The chief of police cannot get to the bottom of the matter, but when a general looks into Rumiantsev's case, justice is done. Although shading in grey tones, the film still has the good triumph at the end, when Rumiantsev is rewarded with personal happiness. There may be corruption in the system, but the need for trust in the individual is highlighted through a man from the very top of the hierarchy, as is also clear in *A Person is Born*, where the 'system' guaranteed the single mother Nadia the shift that she had been denied by her manager. The Party does not intervene, but it is there to see that justice is done, still playing an active role in people's lives.

Yuli Raizman's *Lesson of Life* (Urok zhizni, Mosfilm 1955) looks at the marriage of Natasha and Sergei Romashko. Sergei is a committed worker, whose zeal has led him to develop brutish and egoistic traits that are unmasked in a newspaper article. However, his wife is supportive and she selflessly gives up her teaching job and follows Sergei to a remote construction project – an example of female devotion. While the Party still condemns and intervenes in the lack of work discipline and morale, it has no influence on the family. The correlation between career and private life is defined in no uncertain terms: 'As Sergei's career prospers, his morals deteriorate. Power, in other words, corrupts'.[7] Careerism is condemned along with corruption and the desire for social advancement as a motif for work: private and public lives have to harmonize.

Ermler's *Unfinished Tale* (Neokonchennaia povest', Lenfilm 1955) shows the devotion of a doctor, Yelizaveta Maximovna (Elina Bystritskaya, b. 1928), to her patients and contrasts it with the coldness of her colleague Aganin (Yevgeni Samoilov, who had played Shchors). By casting Bystritskaya, an established theatre actress who had served as a nurse during the war, Ermler added an element of verisimilitude to the film. Yelizaveta Maximovna's efforts and care help the paralysed teacher Yershov (Bondarchuk) get better; finally, Yelizaveta Maximovna, a single woman, finds happiness with him. In care-giving jobs, professional devotion may still be rewarded with personal happiness, offering a way out of loneliness in the early years of the Thaw. Ermler uses the genre of melodrama to instil hope for the rebuilding of families – many of which were broken, and many women widowed, as a consequence of the war.

The theme of single women led to another issue: of single mothers. Vasili Ordynsky (1923–85) had graduated from Gerasimov's class at the Film Institute in 1954 and his debut *A Person is Born* (Chelovek rodilsia, Mosfilm 1956) shows a different approach to contemporary life. His film offers neither a happy ending, nor a solution to the problems it investigates in the narrative. The country girl Nadia is first seen in a Moscow maternity clinic where everybody receives visitors, except her: she is alone. Flashbacks reveal the reason: she failed her exams, fell for the layabout Vitali, whom she dropped and will not take back even though he picks her up from the clinic. Nadia is a strong woman who will manage on her own. The student Gleb finds her a room; she works night shifts as a bus conductor and manages to cope with job and child. When she asks for a day shift she is at first denied it, but later the system helps (bureaucrats may be mean, but the system is good). She is an everyday heroine, a simple single mother. She moves from the countryside to the city, and although she lives literally and socially on the periphery, she works and procreates.

Before his war film *Two Fedors*, Marlen Khutsiev made, as was custom for young directors in the 1950s, his debut film together with another director, Felix Mironer (1927–80); both had studied under Savchenko. *Spring on Zarechnaya Street* (Vesna na Zarechnoi ulitse, Odessa Studio 1956) echoes one of the plotlines of *The Fall of Berlin*: it is about a foundry worker and a teacher who – without Stalin – do not find each other in a clear-cut way. Tatiana Levchenko is posted to a provincial school for adult workers; Sasha Savchenko (Nikolai Rybnikov, 1930–90) is the best worker in the foundry, but he drops out of her classes. Tania begins to reflect and pay more attention to her students and their needs (she previously ignored the pregnancy of one student, and the sleepless nights of a new father). And Sasha begins to pay attention to his shallow life when observing Tania, who is elated by a concert on the radio. Gradually the barrier that Tania establishes between herself as an urban intellectual and the provincial workers begins to collapse: she learns from the workers. At the end, a fresh spring breeze sweeps through an open window, symbolic of new views on life. The film was set in a provincial town, with the typical uniform Soviet architecture, but Khutsiev showed untidy and bleak streets, and interiors of apartments were cluttered with accessories that indicated a more individual touch typical of the Thaw. The film alludes for the first time to a potential class conflict between aloof and arrogant intellectuals and the working class, which would become an important concern for Stagnation films. The young directors reveal a fresh approach in their treatment of everyday life: they show its episodic structure rather than teleology. They also use flashbacks to frame the narrative: what they present in their films is an explanation for the reasons why people are the way they are and how they cope with the present – as best as they can.

Life in the provinces and migration from the city to the countryside and vice versa, as seen in these films by Ordinsky and Khutsiev, led to a re-visioning of the countryside. Eisenstein's student Mikhail Shveitser (1920–2000) had only co-directed two films before making *Alien Kin* (Chuzhaia rodnia, Lenfilm 1955), which showed the countryside in very long takes to enhance the authenticity of the setting. Fedor Soloveikov (Rybnikov) marries into a peasant family, the Riashkins, who dislike innovation and still hoard material possessions. Eventually his wife Stesha (Nonna Mordiukova) moves with him into a dormitory. The ideal socialist lifestyle wins over old life. The film's conventional narrative presents an ending that resolves, in an abrupt manner, the clash between old and new.

Almost ten years later, *The Chairman* (Predsedatel', dir. Saltykov, Mosfilm 1964) offered a different and even more complex outlook on the experience of socialism and the war. Yegor Trubnikov (Ulianov) is a peasant with a vision for the collective and the will to reform the hard work of the soil, whilst his brother Semen holds values of the past and guards his material possessions and personal welfare in the first instance. The confrontation between individual and collective is, however, complicated: it is no longer a straightforward solution for the collective, but one that makes transparent Trubnikov's character flaws, which border on self-destruction, with his obsession to make the world a better one. This obsession with socialist ideals, which is far from making characters heroes, but which shows the negative effects of a stubborn pursuit of ideals, is a novelty in the Thaw films, which also affected the debut films of Larisa Shepitko and Andrei Konchalovsky.

The main contribution to a radical review of life in the country was offered by the writer and filmmaker, Vasili Shukshin. If life in the city was diffuse and seemed to lead nowhere, signalling the entropy that would later characterize the Stagnation period, then rural areas were affected similarly. Shukshin explored rural life in his debut film *A Lad Like That* (Zhivet takoi paren', Gorky Studio 1964), about the truck driver Pavel Kolokolnikov, who drives along the highway and across the countryside. Uncultured and uneducated, he looks for change without finding any inspiration in the urban lifestyle he sees. *Your Son and Brother* (Vash syn i brat, Gorky Studio 1965) canvassed the fate of the children of a large family: Stepan escapes from prison back to his village. His brother Maxim goes to Moscow and is at a loss in the big city whereas his brother Ignat, a wrestler, has settled there by marrying a woman without much taste. Vasili and the deaf-mute Vera find support in the village community. Shukshin sketches scenes from rural life without seeing the city as an alternative – neither in the style of his films nor for his characters.

The Thaw period also brought forth science fiction films, which became extremely popular: *The Amphibious Man* (G. Kazansky and V. Chebotarev, Chelovek-Amfibiia, Lenfilm 1962) was a box office hit. The story concerns a father, Dr Salvator, and his son, who has been turned into the amphibious Ikhtiander. Dr Salvator is a scientist who dreams of an underwater society and has implanted shark's gills into his son during a childhood illness. Now Ikhtiander rescues the drowning girl Gutierra and follows her into the world, where she marries Zurita in order to save her father from debt. Zurita, the evil man with dark shadows, is played by the heartbreaker Mikhail Kozakov, thus endowing Zurita with a positive trait. Ikhtiander has no sense of material values, and is an innocent and exploited child whose life is spoilt: '*The Amphibious Man* ... comes down squarely on the side of the children who are paying for the dream and desires of their fathers'.[8] The obsessed scientist father exploited Ikhtiander, while the circus now uses him as attraction. The ambivalence of nuclear experiments of *Nine Days* resounds here in the blind belief in science, thus making a rather subversive statement at a time when physicists were protesting against the use of nuclear energy for weapon production.

> He came from the ocean. And now, full of love for mankind, he suddenly leaves them for the ocean, this time forever. What had Ikhtiander come for? – you wonder ... He came to remind those who live on the earth that man can and should be happy only on earth. (S. Grigoriev, 14 March 1962)[9]

The doyen filmmaker Mikhail Romm touched this controversial theme in his film *Nine Days of a Year* (Deviat' dnei odnogo goda, Mosfilm 1961), where scientists

Gusev (Batalov) and Kulikov (Smoktunovsky) experiment in a nuclear physics laboratory. The theme itself was highly topical at the time, when the H-bomb was tested on Novaya Zemlya. The Soviet Union was striving for nuclear dominance, and science was geared to assist in this ambition: Akademgorodok was founded outside Novosibirsk in the 1950s as a research centre with privileged access to consumer goods and to research facilities. A project of a proton accelerator, which had been begun in 1949 in Dubna, had led to the construction of a nuclear research lab there, which opened in 1956. Nuclear experiments were the backdrop for the melodrama of *Nine Days*, where the scientists are both friends and rivals in love. They are polar opposites in their attitudes to science: Gusev sacrifices everything for the job, keen to advance science; Kulikov wants to enjoy life and keeps an ironic distance from innovation. Gusev is a practitioner, Kulikov a theorist. Lelia lives with Gusev but decides to marry Kulikov when she is bored with his lack of devotion to her. At this point Gusev makes a ground-breaking discovery, but is exposed to radioactivity and falls ill; Lelia marries him out of pity. The film consists of nine episodes, underlining the fragmented nature of life. However, the ideas as expressed in the dialogue remain central to the film and are illustrated. Batalov's Gusev, with the predisposition of the actor, came across as positive: ready to sacrifice, he aroused compassion – not only in Lelia. However, Smoktunovsky's Kulikov, with his scepticism about nuclear experimentation, made him an ambiguous character, especially in the context of Andrei Sakharov's warnings about nuclear armament in the late 1960s.

The Younger Generation and Children

Although children appear prominently in this period, as Josephine Woll has shown in her seminal study of the cinema of this period,[10] adolescents and young people are the real protagonists of Thaw cinema, emphasizing the youthfulness of the era. This period also saw a rise in films for children and in the animation industry, which produced cartoons and puppet animation. Mikhail Kalik's *Man Follows the Sun* (Chelovek idet za solntsem, Moldova Film 1961) looks at the world through the eyes of the child, Sandu, whose magic glasses change the colour and the reality of the world around him. Tarkovsky's diploma film *The Steamroller and the Violin* (Katok i skripka, Mosfilm 1961) also explored the relationship between the 7-year-old Sasha, who plays the violin, and the young steamroller operator: both benefit from the other's specialized knowledge and view of the world.

Georgi Daneliya (b. 1930) was a graduate of the Higher Courses for Directors and Screenwriters (Vysshie kursy) that Pyriev had established at Mosfilm. The young filmmaker of Georgian descent would become a very popular figure in the 1970s. Together with the theatre director Igor Talankin (b. 1927), who had also completed the Higher Courses, he made the debut film *Serezha* (Mosfilm 1960) about a fatherless boy whose mother remarries the kind and engaging Korostylev

(Bondarchuk). Serezha loves his new father, but is not impressed with the arrival of a little brother. When Korostylev gets a new posting, he decides to leave the sick Serezha behind temporarily, but changes his mind at the last moment. The film shows the adult comprehension of the child's world, and demonstrates that the adult perception of the world has become much more sensitive since *Two Fedors*. The film adopts the view of the child, placing the 5-year-old Serezha in the centre of the world and showing events from the boy's perspective: 'the child's fresh point of view, conveying Serezha's wonder at the universe he discovers around him by keeping ... the camera at Serezha's eye-level for much of the film'.[11] The film was genuinely innovative in its camera angles, but also for placing the child in the centre: it might seem conventional, but this child has the right to a world of his own rather than a politically charged world of the Pavlik Morozovs of the 1930s.

Next, Daneliya created a popular film about the younger generation with *I Walk Around Moscow* (Ia shagaiu po Moskve, Mosfilm 1963). The hero, Kolka (short form of Nikolai, played by Nikita Mikhalkov, b. 1945, in his debut on screen), is a young metro construction worker who makes the acquaintance of a visitor, the technician and young writer Yermakov, on the metro. He accompanies the visitor around the capital and directs him to the address he is looking for. Having worked a night shift, Kolka manages to get some sleep before he is woken by his friend Sasha, who wants Kolka to help him get his army draft deferred by a few days so that he can get married. With charm, Kolka manages to get the deferral for Sasha, who now doubts the commitment of his fiancée. However, the wedding goes ahead, but when the bride learns of Sasha's immediate departure, she is upset. Kolka saves the situation by selflessly taking the blame and bringing the two sides together for their wedding night. Then he facilitates a happy encounter between the record-seller Alena and Yermakov, before the latter leaves for his construction work in the provinces with a promise that Alena will visit. Kolka is a catalyst for meetings with happy endings. As a metro construction worker he is glorified as a builder of the new Moscow, yet he remains alone: he is at one with the metro and the city, and this harmonious union is ultimately more stable and long-lasting than personal relationships where the men are torn away from their women. The final image of the film represents this bond, as Kolka leaves the metro station 'University' on an escalator, singing the title song to the lyrics of the writer Gennadi Shpalikov (1937–74). Happiness lies in contributing to the great construction work of the metro, and it is this experience that Kolka will one day take with him when he sets out to explore the vastness of the Soviet land. Kolka is a carefree contemporary child of the post-war period, who looks into the future rather than being crippled by the horrors of the Second World War and the Purges of the 1930s.

A similar take on the new generation is offered in the work of Marlen Khutsiev. His *Ilyich Gates* (Zastava Il'icha; later released as *I am Twenty* [Mne dvadtsat' let], Gorky Studio 1964) was based on a script by Gennadi Shpalikov about three friends in Moscow: Sergei, who returns from the army and falls in love with Ania;

the construction worker Slava (the theatre actor Stanislav Liubshin, b. 1933), who is married with a child; and Kolia (film actor Nikolai Gubenko, b. 1941), the carefree engineer who resists an attempt to make him an informer. The film accurately imprints the parades, music and meetings of the time. It compares dreams and aspirations to reality: Sergei consults with his dead father, who cannot offer advice on what is best to do. This scene in particular was criticized, among many other comments on the lack of meaning in the lives of the three protagonists, and the film was re-edited in 1965. It shows a younger generation that has no ideals, drifting in life, making it one of the most controversial films of the Thaw period and linking it to the theme of absurdity of life sensed by many European playwrights and writers during the same period. Similarly, in *July Rain* (Iul'skii dozhd', Mosfilm 1966), co-written with Anatoli Grebnev (1923–2002), Khutsiev explores the discrepancy between ideals and reality. The 27-year-old Lena is an engineer at a printing house, and her lover Volodia lives in affluence. The relationship is passionless and disaffected. Lena is more alive through a phone affair with Zhenia, a recent visitor to the capital who once lent her his raincoat during a shower in the July rain. Lena rejects Volodia's proposal as she realizes she is not in love. In general, adolescents and young people in Thaw films are pursuing personal, not social goals – and personal happiness has nothing to do with work.

Alexander Mitta's (b. 1933) *Answer the Doorbell* (Zvoniat, otkroite dver', Mosfilm 1965) was based on a play by Alexander Volodin (1919–2001) and shows the estrangement between children and parents. Tania is alone, because her mother has joined her father on an expedition. Her friend Gena is also neglected. They try to engage with the pioneer organization, but the leader slams the door on them. Gena's stepfather Pavel Kolpakov (Rolan Bykov, 1929–98) explains the pioneer movement to Tania and Gena and sets a role model for them. This film anticipates in many ways the concerns of animation, where the figures of Cheburashka and Uncle Fedor (see Chapter 5) are also rejected by the pioneers, isolated from the other children, from their parents and from the adult world.

Children's films echoe the divide between intellectual and worker, mocking the intellectual's inability to cope with life, as in *Aibolit 66* (dir. Bykov, Mosfilm 1966) based on the famous children's writer Kornei Chukovsky's (1882–1969) story of the same title and starring Oleg Yefremov as Doctor Aibolit, who goes to Africa to heal animals. There he is trapped by gangsters, but despite all odds and his intellectual helplessness, he overcomes the enemy and gets the job done. Aibolit is, on the one hand, like the bookish Shurik of *Operation Y*, with his black-rimmed thick glasses, who is also helpless and hapless. Yet the setting in the exotic world provides ample scope for colour in this film. Edmond Keosayan (1936–95) made *The Elusive Avengers* (Neulovimye mstiteli, Mosfilm 1966), a remake of *Red Imps* that was also turned into a series with *New Adventures of the Elusives* (Novye prikliucheniia neulovimykh, 1968), about four teenagers fighting anarchists and Cossacks. Most popular was the film *Republic SHKID* (Respublika ShkID, Lenfilm

1966) by Gennadi Poloka (b. 1930), about life in the 1920s in a Leningrad boarding school for former homeless children, the *besprizorniki*. The orphans are collected from the streets by the Dostoevsky School (Shkola imeni Dostoevskogo, in short ShkID) and are educated by a team of fine teachers and the director Viknixor (played by the well-known stage actor Sergei Yursky, b. 1935, then the star of the Bolshoi Drama Theatre in Leningrad), who turn them into real citizens. Viknixor organizes the school as a republic, thus endowing the children with responsibility and trust, rather than treating them as rascals in need of re-education. The film was not only a parable for the need to give man more responsibility under socialism, which essentially took responsibility away from the individual and instead transferred it on to the collective with its hierarchy of administrators, but it also pleased children and adolescents.

Comedy: Riazanov, Gaidai and Klimov

The exposure of flaws in the system had become possible during the Thaw, when it seemed acceptable to mock obstructive bureaucrats by ridiculing them – as long as they were removed them from their everyday setting into a special environment to allow for a carnivalesque atmosphere that created a comic, ironic or satirical touch. Laughter may be liberating, but it discomfited officials, who were not sure how to control it. Such a light satire on bureaucracy is superbly achieved in a film set on New Year's Eve, an ideal setting that allowed extraordinary and exceptional things to happen, starring Igor Ilinsky, who had successfully played Byvalov in *Volga-Volga*. Eldar Riazanov's (b. 1927) *Carnival Night* (Karnaval'naia noch', Mosfilm 1956) is a musical comedy with the debut performance of Liudmila Gurchenko (b. 1935) in the role of Lena Krylova, probably the best-known and most celebrated of all new year films still shown today on television on 31 December.

Lena Krylova is in charge of a New Year's party at a House of Culture in Moscow; the director is on leave and has left Seraphim Ogurtsov in control. Grisha Koltsov, who is also preparing the show, is in love with Lena. In fact, the names already give away the story: Seraphim (the angel) Ogurtsov (*ogurets* means gherkin) makes a fool of himself, while the 'winged' Krylova (*kryl'ia* are wings) rescues the show and receives a proposal (symbolically a ring) from the 'ringed' Koltsov (*kol'tso* means ring).

Lena is devoted to the organization of the ball, but Ogurtsov prefers to conceive the event as a serious and official ceremony, especially since he is expecting a Soviet official. Consequently he dismantles Lena's plans: a Soviet man should not hide behind a mask, so no masks were to be worn; the ballerina performing *Swan Lake* should cover up her legs to avoid indecency; the jazz music performed by a quartet should be performed by a 'mass quartet' – a plain contradiction in terms; the orchestra which, in his view, played inappropriate music should be replaced by the orchestra

Figure 4.6 Riazanov's *Carnival Night*: Lena and Grisha.

from the neighbouring Veterans' Club; the librarian could play the piano and sing (but add to the line 'I am alone, all on my own' the words 'with my collective'), and the accountant could recite a fable he has not rehearsed since he finished school forty years ago. Ogurtsov's ideas echo the silly and incomprehensible requests Party and state bureaucrats would often make regarding any cultural or artistic activity. The enemy (the bureaucrat) is parodied, something that is possible thanks to the setting of the film on the night in which everything is inverted, permissible and carnivalized.

Carnival Night is a classic of Soviet cinema on the theme of the new year, both because of the songs (the most popular being 'Five Minutes') and the atmosphere of carnival, but also for its implied parody of Soviet bureaucracy and officialdom that wants to see everything going according to plan even on the one night of the year when carnival should reign. New Year's Eve is also the most suitable time for declarations of love and proposals: the declaration of feelings at the conclusion of a year instils hope for the future and for the new relationship (or a fresh start) in the next year. Grisha's proposal to Lena is made in public, since feelings were not part of the private sphere in Soviet society of the 1950s. In fact, Grisha records his declaration of love on a record, which Lena accidentally plays on the transmission system for the entire House of Culture during the rehearsal. This is also an indication of the lack of privacy, especially for young people, at a time when many families were living in communal apartments and sharing facilities (such as bath and kitchen) with other families.

Riazanov's work in the comedy genre continued in the almanac *Absolutely Serious* (Sovershenno ser'ezno, 1961)[12] containing five novellas. Riazanov's novella, 'How Robinson was Created' (Kak sozdavalsia Robinzon) was a satire on the attempt to pep up a children's magazine – and thus a sweeping parody on the entire cultural policies of the Thaw. His comedy *The Complaint Book* (Daite zhalobnuiu knigu, Mosfilm 1964) was set in the Dandelion restaurant, whose inefficient management Riazanov has exposed to laugher. After the restaurant's service has been mocked in the press, the management tries to implement reorganization, but it faces difficulties in motivating its staff. *Beware of the Car* (Beregis' avtomobilia, Mosfilm 1966) featured Yuri Detochkin (Innokenti Smoktunovsky), an insurance agent who steals cars, sells them and redistributes the profit to orphanages. He is a Robin Hood of the modern city. Riazanov here parodies the detective genre by having both thief and detective (Oleg Yefremov, 1927–2000) play in an amateur performance of *Hamlet* alongside a star-studded cast with Andrei Mironov, Georgi Zhzhenov (1915–2005), Yevgeni Yevstigneev (1926–92), and Donatas Banionis (b.1924). Riazanov creates situational comedy, placing his characters in extraordinary situations that may, however, occur in real life and which he uses to mock the social and political agendas of the time.

Leonid Gaidai (1923–93) used a more physical kind of comedy: for the almanac *Absolutely Serious* he produced 'Dog Barbos and the Unusual Race' (Pes Barbos i neobychainyi kross), which introduced the trio of Georgi Vitsin (1918–2001), Yevgeni Morgunov (1927–99), and the clown (and later director) of Moscow's circus, Yuri Nikulin (1921–97) – in short, ViNiMor – who captured Soviet audiences as a stock slapstick trio. Morgunov was Byvaly (the Experienced), Nikulin was Balbes (Dumb Ass), and Vitsin was Trus (Coward). Their characters combined the flatness of folk characters with streetwise behaviour, making them immensely popular on screen. Gaidai's *Operation Y and Shurik's Other Adventures* (Operatsiia Y i drugie prikliucheniia Shurika, Mosfilm 1965) was composed of three short episodes about Shurik, a young intellectual marked out with thick glasses, who is completely unfit for reality. Shurik is a 'modern version of Ivan-the-Fool … incapable of any transformation until he is assisted by miraculous coincidence and modern versions of magic helpers'.[13] The first episode shows Shurik in a fight as he defends the right

Figure 4.7 Klimov's *Welcome, or No Trespassing*: Kostia Inochkin.

of a pregnant woman to sit on a bus; in the second he prepares for an exam looking over somebody's shoulder for the whole day; and in the last, 'Operation Y', Shurik prevents a simulated robbery where the crooks are played by ViNiMor. In the sequel, *The Prisoner of the Caucasus* (Kavkazskaia plennitsa, ili novye prikliucheniia Shurika, Mosfilm 1966), Shurik travels to the Caucasus to study folk legends, and falls in love with a girl who is supposed to marry a high-ranking bureaucrat. Gaidai's films employ physical slapstick and rely on circus elements and gags, and this work would culminate in *The Diamond Arm* discussed in the next chapter.

Elem Klimov (1933–2003) came to film through the comedy genre too. *Welcome or No Trespassing* (Dobro pozhalovat' ili postoronnym vkhod zapreshchen, Mosfilm 1964) was set in a holiday camp for children. Its director, Dynin – derived from the word *dynia*, melon – (Yevstigneev) is an old-style bureaucrat resistant to innovation. Kostia Inochkin breaks the rules by swimming to an island; he is expelled from the camp but he dares not go back to his grandmother. Instead, he hides under a rostrum and is supported by the children, who conspire against the director: they pretend to be affected by an epidemic (after jumping into nettles) in order to cancel the Parents' Day and prevent Kostia's grandmother from discovering the disgrace. Kostia's fantasies give the film a particularly comic edge: he imagines how his grandmother would say that he is 'driving her to the grave' with his behaviour, and visualizes her funeral; or he imagines how Dynin might fall ill and require a blood transfusion which only Kostia could give. Kostia is a child who vies for attention and love, and lives through flights of fancy that offer fairy-tale escapes from the squabbles in the camp and the endless prohibitions. The staff in the camp are portrayed in grotesque fashion, as they are shot like one-dimensional cartoon figures with exaggerated proportions, or in close-ups that enlarge ears and eyes to visualize the child's perception of control and supervision everywhere. Klimov also uses the device of fast-forwarding the film to create a sense of topsy-turvy adventures. On Parents' Day it is not the niece of a high Party official who gets the prize for the most stunning costume, as Dynin had planned, but Kostia peeling out of the figure of the Corn Queen (an allusion to Khrushchev's agricultural policies), thus destroying the director's scheme to rig the results and leaving the Party official outraged. Kostia leaves with his grandmother in a fanciful imagined flight to the island. Klimov exposes the bureaucracy in similar ways to Riazanov, choosing an extraordinary setting and the vision of a child to deform objects and people in the holiday camp.

Adventures of a Dentist (Pokhozhdeniia zubnogo vracha, Mosfilm 1965) is narrated through a commentator who occasionally disrupts the narrative. The dentist Chesnokov works with a magic touch: he can extract teeth without pain. However, such skills are not required by society and he is ostracized by his colleagues and patients for his special skill, because he alienates himself from the collective by elevating himself above them. Soviet society needs no individualism. Chesnokov's magic touch disappears and is transferred to a new student who suffers the same isolation: the collective allows no special talents to develop but wants standard performances. The film caused controversy for its subversive view of the collective and socialism. Klimov would make no more comedies: his films in the 1970s and 1980s are of a more serious nature, although they would elicit equal controversy.

Comedy may have been a popular genre – most of the comedies were box office hits, but it left authorities at a loss, because the laughter comedy caused was one of those 'uncontrollable reactions' that they could not predict and which were feared because they could potentially instil a rebellious feeling. *Carnival Night* brought in 50 million viewers, *Operation Y* had 70 million spectators, and *Prisoner of the Caucasus* was seen by 75 million.[14]

Thaw or Freeze?

The Thaw saw some interesting work from the republics, although the real boost of productivity there would be in the Stagnation period, when the distance from Moscow allowed a little more laxness in the republican film studios than for filmmakers at Mosfilm.

In *Someone Else's Children* (Skhvisi Shvilebi [Chuzhie deti], 1958), Tengiz Abuladze (1924–94) told about a woman who marries a widower to raise his children, and then does not abandon them when he leaves her. Abuladze and Rezo Chkheidze (b. 1926) made *Magdana's Donkey* (Lurdzha Magdany, Georgian title: Magdanas Lurja, 1955), a short film about a donkey that is adopted by a mother and her children during hard times, which helps with the transportation of goods once it has recovered. After the war the donkey's owner returns and claims it back, and has his claim confirmed by the courts. Abuladze here created a parable for the difference between law and justice, something that would remain an important theme for his glasnost film, *Repentance*.

Sergo Parajanov's (1924–90) *Shadows of Forgotten Ancestors* (Ukrainian title: Tini zabutykh predkiv, Ukraine, 1964) tells a legend about Ivanko and Marichka, who live in the Hutsul community in the highlands of the Carpathian mountains. They are in love, but their families are feuding. Ivanko has to tend sheep in the mountains, and Marichka follows him; she drowns when she tries to rescue a sheep. Ivanko marries Palagna, who cheats on him with the shaman Yuri, whom Ivanko kills. There is a biblical allegory here to John the Baptist (Ivanko), with Maria drowning in the water used for baptism in an attempt to save a lost sheep. The painter Parajanov splashes colour across the screen: red paint flows to symbolize death. Parajanov uses the frame as a canvas and paints scenes inspired by primitive and folk art. He collates on the screen an array of colours, shapes, ornaments and decorative objects that create pictures of the uttermost beauty. His attention to detail, to authentic fabrics and garments, gives the overburdened frames an artificiality that contradicts authenticity. Parajanov's *Kiev Frescoes* (1965) was blocked for its 'mystical representation' of the Great Patriotic War (Second World War). The footage was confiscated and destroyed and only twenty minutes survive.[15] The censorship that would clamp down on individual artistic expression in the Stagnation era began to reveal itself. Here the suspicion about the talented artist began; he would face prosecution for homosexuality in the 1970s, leading to a four-year prison sentence from 1973–78. Homosexuality was unlawful under the Soviet legislation, although evidence in court cases was often fabricated, as was the case in Parajanov's trial, or that of the Leningrad theatre director Zinovi Korogodsky (1926–2004), who spent several years in prison. In 1961, Rudolf Nureev probably suspected rightly that he would be arrested upon his return from Paris – and so he defected.

Andrei Konchalovsky made his directorial debut at the Kyrgyz studio in Frunze (now Bishkek) with *The First Teacher* (Pervyi uchitel', Kirgizfilm and Mosfilm 1965), which was based on Chingiz Aitmatov (1928–2008), one of Kyrgyzstan's greatest writers. After the Civil War, the Red officer Diuishen (Bolot Bejshenaliev) is dispatched to a village to set up a school during the Soviet campaign against illiteracy. Barely educated himself, but a committed Bolshevik, Diuishen enthusiastically and arrogantly builds a school. Diuishen belongs to the group of over-committed socialists who, in blind pursuit of their ideals, fail to see reality. The villagers take little interest, but the wealthy *bai* Nodyrbek is suspicious of all innovation. Nodyrbek marries Altynai (Natalia Arinbasarova) and consummates his marriage during the wedding night against Altynai's will, a fact conveyed by sounds rather than images. Diuishen interferes: he sends Altynai to town to study. When he returns to the village, he finds that the school has been burnt down. He begins to build a new school and starts by axing the sacred poplar tree in the village, an act of revenge that visually captures the destruction of tradition for the sake of innovation. The film shows the confrontation between the centre and the periphery, between Bolshevism and the traditional values of Central Asia, where customs are different. Konchalovsky touches upon a delicate theme: the relationship of Moscow to the republics and their culture. The film won Konchalovsky's wife, Arinbasarova, an award as best actress at the Venice Film Festival.

The Thaw also saw developments in the representation of history and literature. The Revolution celebrated its fiftieth anniversary in 1967 and on that occasion numerous films were banned (see next chapter). Of the ones that celebrated the event, few made an impact in a film world that had produced, in the preceding decade, more interesting films on human and everyday problems and comedies. There were films about Lenin for the centenary of his birth: Sergei Yutkevich's *Stories About Lenin* (Rasskazy o Lenine, 1957) with Straukh as Lenin; Donskoy's *A Mother's Heart* (Serdtse materi, 1965) and *A Mother's Devotion* (Vernost' materi, 1966) about Lenin's mother, with Rodion Nakhapetov in the role of the young Lenin; Yutkevich's *Lenin in Poland* (Lenin v Pol'she, 1965) and *Lenin in Paris* (Lenin v Parizhe, 1981), de-heroicizing the leader and showing the private life of a normal man.

Literary adaptations remained a safe ground for films: it was easier to gain approval for a text that had already been published, because it would already have passed Glavlit, the literary censorship board. Thus adaptations had an advantage over new contemporary scripts. Examples of the period include world classics, such as Yutkevich's *Othello* (1955) and Kozintsev's *Don Quixote* (1957) alongside the Soviet classic, *And Quiet Flows the Don* (Tikhii Don, 1958) by Sergei Gerasimov. Kozintsev's *Hamlet* (1964) interpreted the Shakespearean text in a modern manner: the state of Denmark is at fault for Hamlet's dilemma, as the state is based on a lie. Smoktunovsky's Hamlet is a strong and decisive individual who blames Claudius for having turned Denmark into such a prison. Ophelia (Anastasia Vertinskaya, b. 1944) is a victim of that state. The reading of the play echoes blatantly the political agenda of the Thaw: the denunciation of the state and the 'false' king, Claudius-Stalin, who has turned the country into a prison and made Ophelia a victim. Shveitser's adaptation of Tolstoy, *Resurrection* (Voskresen'e, 1960–61) and Zarkhi's *Anna Karenina* (1967); Pyriev's adaptations of Dostoevsky with *The Idiot* (1958), *White Nights* (Belye nochi, 1959) and *The Brothers Karamazov* (Brat'ia Karamazovy, 1968) concerned the Russian classics of the nineteenth century. Samson Samsonov's version of Chekhov's story, *The Cricket* (Poprygunia, 1955), with Bondarchuk and the popular actress Liudmila Tselikovskaya (1919–92), had stimulated interest internationally. *The Lady with a Lapdog* (Dama s sobachkoi, 1960) was directed by Kheifits, starring Iya Savvina (b. 1936) as Anna Sergeevna and Alexei Batalov as

Gurov. Bondarchuk's *War and Peace* (Voina i mir, four series, 1965–67) was not only the Soviet Union's most expensive film, but it also garnered the first Oscar and led to Dino de Laurentiis inviting Bondarchuk to direct *Waterloo* (1970, Italian-Soviet co-production) with Rod Steiger as Napoleon; Bondarchuk later made two series of *Red Bells* (Mexico, Italy, USSR, 1982–83). *War and Peace* impressed by its ambitions on a Hollywood scale, observing minor detail in the creation of the set, down to borrowing museum exhibits, and the large organized battle scenes.

At the end of the Thaw, the interference that Khutsiev and Klimov, among others, had experienced earlier in the decade seemed like a casual intervention in comparison to what was to come: numerous scripts were censored and rejected. Alov and Naumov's *The Nasty Tale* (Skvernyi anekdot, Mosfilm 1966), based on Dostoevsky's stories, mocked the concept of democracy. When a government official drops in on a lowly clerk's wedding, the mixing of classes does not work because people have no experience of democracy. The visions of the general and the nightmarish orgy of the wedding feast blur the lines between reality and horror, rather than expose social difference, as Chekhov had done in his satirical sketches of the 1880s. The film vanished without even a sign of an official ban. The Experimental Studio at Mosfilm produced the almanac film *The Beginning of an Unknown Era* (Nachalo nevedomogo veka, 1967), consisting of three novellas of which only two are preserved; both were banned and the experimental unit was closed. Shepitko's *Homeland of Electricity* (Rodina elektrichestva) was based on Andrei Platonov and set in the aftermath of the Civil War, when a young Komsomol saves an entire village during the famine. The portrayal of the hero as a saviour bringing 'light' carried messianic overtones that would be more evident in Shepitko's *Ascent*, but were unacceptable in conjunction with a Komsomol. Andrei Smirnov's *Angel* was based on a story by Yuri Olesha and associated the Revolution with violence: after the destruction of the railroad a motley group of people are ambushed by a criminal gang, and after the confrontation of the Red commissar with the gang leader 'Angel', the commissar is brutally executed, battered to death with a hammer.

An extraordinary case was that of Konchalovsky's *Asya's Happiness* (Asino schast'e)[16] made in 1965–66 in the village of Bezvodnoe, without professional actors, thus following the documentary approach; only Iya Savvina was cast for the main part. In the film poor peasants with scarred faces and bodies, living in a simple and muddy environment, told their stories: a hunchback peasant, a war veteran and an old farmer with a term spent in prison camp. This setting disgusted the officials, who constantly demanded cuts. What made matters worse, though, was that despite the traumas and histories, these people got on with life and their positive, life-enhancing attitude stood in sharp contrast with the mood of resignation that made itself known in Soviet Russia with the onset of Stagnation. Konchalovsky seemed to send the message that repression and prison sentences cannot shake or break human nature.

Asya's Happiness was based on a script by Yuri Klepikov (b. 1935) and tells of the peasant woman Asya, a lame cook who refuses a townsman's proposal because

Figure 4.8 Konchalovsky's *Asya's Happiness*.

she does not love him. Instead she loves and expects a child from Stepan. She gives birth on the roadside, but has no intention of marrying Stepan because he is unreliable and often drunk. The authorities were appalled by the theme of single motherhood (unlike the response to *A Person is Born*) and the absence of a father figure (the *bezottsovshchina*), as well as the indifference to work and the sadness of people's lives. They wanted an upbeat assurance that Asya and Stepan would stay together – something that even Konchalovsky's sequel, *Riaba Ma Poule* (Kurochka Riaba, Russia/France 1994), would firmly reject. The film was granted a license in March 1967, but when it was shown to the district committees, it was rejected. There were, in the view of the officials, still too many invalids in the film and it was 'too realistic'. KGB officer Bobkov called it a 'lie' that showed 'Soviet people in an ugly and slovenly manner'.[17] The realism of the 1930s, glossing over reality, seemed to have returned to the cultural and political agenda by 1967, the fiftieth anniversary of the Revolution, when the theatre repertoires in Moscow were purged of controversial productions, such as Tvardovsky's *Terkin in the Other World* and Mozhaev's village prose adaptation about a *kolkhoz* worker, *From the Life of Fedor Kuzkin*, staged and banned at the Taganka Theatre.

With his next film after the successful debut *Ivan's Childhood*, Tarkovsky turned to a historical period that had been little documented, so that he could use his imagination to invent a biography of the mediaeval icon painter in *Andrei Rublev* (1967–71). The script had been completed and published in 1964, and approved in April 1965; the film's first cut was ready by July 1966. However, the Artistic Council at Mosfilm, and later Goskino, requested changes and cuts, to shorten the 200-minute film and to remove some of the violence and cruelty. In 1967 the film was invited to the Cannes Film Festival, but the Soviet Union sent Bondarchuk's epic *War and Peace* instead; it was shown in Cannes out of competition in 1969 and awarded the Critics' Prize. In 1969 the foreign rights were sold, yet the film was still not released in the USSR, where it opened in December 1971. This delay – a nerve-wracking period for any director – was one method used by the authorities to force artists to revoke their individual artistic style and conform with 'Soviet' art.

The film begins with Rublev leaving the monastery together with the painters Daniil and Kirill, and walking the Russian land to paint icons in churches and on commission. Unlike his teacher Theophanes, Rublev does not see man as sinful, and this does not change when he experiences the cruelty of both Tartars and Russians. The Grand Prince has the artists who decorated his church blinded so they cannot repeat their work, but Rublev also observes the brutality and violence of the people: the torture of the fool; the prosecution of the pagans; the burning of Vladimir by the Tartars. Russia's brutal history is an experience that leads to endurance rather than revolt, which essentially contradicts the possibility of glorifying warfare – and would worry the censors, who were also outraged by the graphic depiction of violence. Yet each act of violence is followed by a symbolic gesture, abstracting violence from the incident and turning it into a universal statement. Rublev (Anatoli Solonitsyn, 1934–82) is first and foremost an artist: never superior or closer to God, he is humble and suffers with the people. This acceptance of suffering enables him to find the truth: 'For us the story of Rublyov is really the story of a "taught" or imposed concept, which burns up in the atmosphere of living reality to arise again from the ashes as a fresh and newly discovered truth.'[18] Artistic creation is seen not as a God-given impulse, but as a task that requires both hardship and sacrifice, as is also evident in the figure of Boriska (Nikolai Burliaev, who had played Ivan), who casts a magnificent bell although he has not learnt this art. The artist's responsibility towards the people is central to Tarkovsky's work, not only in this film. Artistic truth can only be found in harmony with the people and not in separation.

The black-and-white film moves to colour only for the panning shots of icons at the end, capturing the products of Rublev's artistic creativity that function like the icon painting: they open the view on the absolute.

The cases of *Rublev* and *Asya* show the impossibility for artists of developing their cinematic language without interference from the authorities. Both Konchalovsky and Tarkovsky pursued their paths during the Stagnation, but ultimately emigrated in the 1980s. The next chapter explores further the intervention of the Party authorities in the creative process, which weighed in particular on the late 1960s.

–5–

The Stagnation: Mainstream and *Auteur* Cinema (1967–82)

> The wolf hunt is on, the hunt is on!
> . . . Why, pack leader, answer us,
> Do we turn toward the shots as if doped,
> And never try to go beyond the prohibitions?
>
> 'The Wolf Hunt' (Okhota na volkov), Vladimir Vysotsky

Illusions and hopes raised during the Thaw – for a socialist system that took account of the individual and his aspirations, which was genuinely interested in exposing (often to laughter) mismanagement and over-zealous bureaucrats – were gradually shattered in the years after Khrushchev was ousted. The ban on Klimov's *Adventures of a Dentist*, with its emphasis on individual skills, and Konchalovsky's *Asya's Happiness*, placing individual interests above collective needs and social expectations (to marry and have a family), in a documentary style, showed that the official attitude to individual initiative, exposure to laugher and to documentary style was negative, thus pointing at a reversal of the politics of the Thaw. These films were singled out and criticized after completion: from 1967 onwards the control would get even tighter at the level of passing scripts for production. The last hopes for a liberalization of cultural politics were shattered with the trial of Andrei Siniavsky and Yuli Daniel, surrounded by massive protests and international campaigns that represented the first step towards the formation of a dissident underground movement, splitting society into 'conformist' and 'dissident'. The dissident voices in art adopted themes and styles that did not form part of mass culture, and rejected linearity in favour of structural experiments. Thus, a divide came about between *auteur* cinema, largely created by filmmakers who were classified as 'difficult' or openly 'dissident', and 'movies for the masses', made by talented filmmakers using more conventional narratives (although often tackling controversial issues as well). This divide led to international interest in and recognition of the 'difficult' filmmakers, who paradoxically came to represent Soviet cinema abroad. Moreover, due to a drop in cinema visits by almost half in the 1970s, there was an increased need for commercially viable films to compensate for the industry's loss in box office revenue; this, in turn, led to a surge in entertainment films, notably comedies and adventure films, often with exotic settings.[1]

This chapter outlines first the cultural and political context of the Stagnation era, before looking closely at some of the shelved films. Then it proceeds in a broad chronological order, while singling out the two prominent filmmakers, Tarkovsky and Mikhalkov. Towards the end of the 1970s films began to criticize the predominant passivity and inertia, while films for children highlighted the child's isolation in society. The chapter concludes with a brief look at the blockbusters of the period, including the Oscar-winning *Moscow Does Not Believe in Tears*.

Political and Cultural Stagnation

During the so-called period of Stagnation (*zastoi*) – formally starting with the ousting of Khrushchev in 1964, but setting in gradually, and ending with the change in leadership after Brezhnev's death in 1982 – the Soviet Union continued the Cold War struggle for military superiority. Competition between the two superpowers, the Soviet Union and America, heightened with the 'conquest' of the moon when Apollo 11 landed on 20 July 1969, giving the Americans a lead in the international space race. However, the space stations Saliut and Mir put the Soviet Union ahead in terms of the conquest of space, the 'cosmos'. At the same time, the space race led to negotiations on limitations of a strategic arms race (SALT) between 1969 and 1972, when an agreement was signed between the two superpowers. A further rapprochement between East and West was signalled by the Treaty of Moscow (1970), which recognized the GDR and thus eased the relationship between the Federal Republic of Germany and the Soviet Union. In 1975, the USSR signed the Helsinki Security Agreement, which granted support from Western countries for Eastern European economies to cover the chronic consumer goods deficit; in return the USSR agreed to honour human rights. Although production of consumer goods for the first time exceeded industrial output, there were constant 'deficits', leading to the formation of black markets and a shadow economy, illegally producing or importing from abroad goods that were in high demand (for example Western-made jeans, leather coats produced 'on the side' by textile workers, etc.) and sold by the *fartsovshchiki* or the *spekulanty*.

The Soviet intervention in Afghanistan in 1979 led to an international outcry, culminating in an embargo of grain imports and the boycott by sixty-four countries of the 1980 Olympics in Moscow. In the same year the United States stationed medium-range missiles in West Germany, adding to the tension between East and West. Thus, the Stagnation period brought about no relaxation in terms of economics or foreign politics. Effectively, nothing shook the balance of power during the 1970s, internally or externally; only Brezhnev consolidated his power as head of Party, state and army by the late 1970s.

The 1960s saw a series of trials of dissidents and human rights activists, ending mostly with prison sentences or sequestration into psychiatric clinics, the so-called *psikhushki*. One such prominent incident was the demonstration on Red Square in August 1968, protesting against the Soviet invasion of Czechoslovakia, led by Larisa Bogoraz (1929–2005), then the wife of Yuli Daniel, together with the poet Natalia Gorbanevskaya (b. 1936) and five others. They were all arrested; Gorbanevskaya was admitted to a psychiatric clinic. Another was the formation and suppression of the Helsinki Group, founded in 1976 to oversee the implementation of the Helsinki Final Agreement of 1975, thus adopting a similar role to that of Charter 77 in Czechoslovakia.[2] In the following year most of its members were arrested, and by 1982 the group had disbanded.

In cultural politics, matters looked worse. Alexander Solzhenitsyn, who had been excluded from the Writers' Union in 1970, was arrested and deported from the USSR in February 1974; the Leningrad poet Joseph Brodsky was expelled from the Soviet Union; the liberal editor of the leading liberal literary journal *Novy Mir* was sacked in 1970. In the visual and performing arts, repressions and exiles followed suit: in 1974 an open-air exhibition of modern art in the Moscow suburb Beliaevo was knocked down by bulldozers (the so-called 'Bulldozer Exhibition'). In the same year, the cellist Mstislav Rostropovich (1927–2007) and his wife, the soprano Galina Vishnevskaya (b. 1926), left the country and were later stripped of their citizenship, because they had, among other things, sheltered Solzhenitsyn.

As many writers could not publish their works, they resorted instead to the so-called *samizdat* (self-publishing typescripts with carbon paper – in the absence of photocopiers). A major underground publication was the almanac *Metropol*, which collated works that had not been accepted for publication in the Soviet Union. The gloom and doom of the late 1970s was offset, however, by the beginning of activities in the underground, including studio and amateur theatre and 'private' art exhibitions (the so-called *kvartirnye vystavki*) of conceptualist art. The songs of the bard Vladimir Vysotsky (1938–80) voiced opposition to the system by addressing taboo issues such as alcoholism and drugs, as did some semi-legal rock bands. There was a revival of jazz groups: the 'Ganelin Trio' (1971–86), with Viacheslav Ganelin, Vladimir Chekasin and Vladimir Tarasov, was one of the most respected jazz bands of the 1970s, playing avant-garde jazz that fused different styles and presented theatrical performances. The authorities fought back and hampered performances. Films, of course, had no underground outlet because the medium required technological backup and could not be made without the state's finances. However, this stagnation of innovation, experiment and search for new paths that dominated the 1970s led to an atmosphere of resignation, fear and entropy. Comedies were treading very careful ground – and lost their comic appeal; satires became impossible – and if attempted, they were banned; problems of human existence were tolerated – as long as they did not imply that unhappiness was a result of something that could remotely be connected to the Party. In the republics, far away from Moscow, an Aesopian style sometimes allowed hidden references to man's predicament in Soviet society to pass or slip the (less experienced) censor's attention.

The Stagnation led to a dearth of activity in Soviet cultural life. Many artists and intellectuals emigrated in the first half of the 1970s, ripping a large hole in artistic circles. Several filmmakers emigrated, staying abroad after making films, notably in Italy and France: Andrei Tarkovsky, Andrei Konchalovksy and Otar Ioseliani. Kira Muratova and Alexei Gherman were largely barred from filmmaking during the 1970s.

While the 1960s were governed by clampdowns, censorship and bans, the 1970s saw deportations, exile and house arrests. The atmosphere of rebellion changed to one of resignation as the dissidents' fight within the Soviet Union was superseded by the state's attempt to eliminate any opposition. Therefore, feelings of despair often characterize the films of the 1970s. The issue of the individual's conscience in the face of a choice between active protest and passive resignation preoccupied artists and filmmakers in their search for answers to this moral dilemma. Such answers were often sought through the protagonists' spiritual journeys and through obscure references to the acceptance of suffering that underlies Orthodox faith.

In the film industry there were debates on the role of cinema between commerce and *auteur* cinema, but few administrative or managerial changes took place. Under the management of Nikolai Sizov, a system of a partly autonomous budget (*khozraschet*) was introduced at Mosfilm, allowing supply and demand to stimulate production so that the income generated from profitable films could be channelled into *auteur* cinema.[3] The divide between popular and *auteur* cinema widened, and most of the profit was used to cover losses in the republics' studios. The 1970s also saw a decrease in the number of cinemas and audiences, largely due to the emergence and rise of television.

In 1972, Filipp Yermash (1923–2002) was appointed head of Goskino, succeeding Alexei Romanov; Yermash would hold this position until 1986. Goskino supervised export (Sovexport), co-production (Sovinfilm) and festival organization (Sovinterfest), as well as the analytical journals *Iskusstvo kino* (*Film Art*) with a print run of ca. 50,000, and the bi-monthly glossy magazine *Soviet Screen* (Sovetskii ekran), with a print run of two million. The Film Institute (VGIK), a technical institute, and the research institute VNIIK (founded in 1973), as well as Gosfilmofond, an orchestra, the Theatre of the Film Actor, and the 'Higher Courses for Scriptwriters and Directors' (*Vysshie kursy stsenaristov i rezhisserov*), were all overseen by Goskino. Thus the film industry was a fully fledged branch of the Soviet economic and administrative system.

Television (Gosteleradio, GTR) became a rival for cinema not only in commercial terms as a new medium, but also in terms of film production. Thus, the television serials based on the crime and spy novels of Yulian Semenov, *Seventeen Moments of Spring* (Semnadtsat' mgnovenii vesny, dir. Tatiana Lioznova, Gorky Studio for GTR, 1973), a twelve-part series on the role of the Soviet spy Stirlitz (Viacheslav Tikhonov, b. 1928) in the Hitler administration, and *TASS is Authorized to Declare* (TASS upolnomochen zaiavit', dir. Vladimir Fokin, Gorky Studio for GTR, 1984), were very popular. The same is true for the monumental war epic *Liberation* (Osvobozhdenie, dir. Yuri Ozerov, Mosfilm with DEFA, Polish Television and Dino de Laurentiis, 1969), showing for the first time since the Thaw the image of Stalin on screen, or for the spy thriller *Shield and Sword* (Shchit i mech, dir. Vladimir Basov, Mosfilm 1968), starring Stanislav Liubshin as agent Alexander Belov, also known as Johann Weiss. *The Meeting Place Must Not Be Changed* (Mesto vstrechi izmenit' nel'zia, Odessa Studio for GTR, 1979) by Stanislav Govorukhin was another popular television serial about a police department in Moscow fighting a criminal gang called Black Cat (*Chernaia Koshka*), and starring Vladimir Vysotsky. However, as television and film production aimed at mass audiences to break even on the state's investment, drawing on the popular genres of adventure films, spy thrillers and detective stories, other filmmakers experienced further and major problems with the authorities, often afraid to pass anything that could even remotely displease the Central Committee, let alone the General Secretary.

The Shelving of Films, 1967–71

Alexander Askoldov's *The Commissar* (Kommissar, Gorky Studio 1967, released by Mosfilm 1987) had an extraordinary history of censorship, but the biographical background of the filmmaker is also unusual. Askoldov's parents had been arrested in 1937 when he was five years old. A Jewish family in Kiev sheltered him from the NKVD before sending him to his grandmother in Moscow. This experience impacted on the portrayal of the Magazannik family in the film. The mature Askoldov worked in the Directorate for Theatre Censorship, where he helped the actor and theatre director Rolan Bykov get a theatre production in Leningrad passed, before making his first – and last – film. After *The Commissar*, Askoldov was barred from filmmaking (for reasons of 'non-professionalism') and expelled from the Party and the Filmmakers' Union, thus deprived of the right to work even as assistant director. When the Filmmakers' Union began to remove films from the shelves in 1986, *The Commissar* was not among them. On the contrary, on 28 November 1986, Goskino confirmed the ban on *The Commissar*. In a press conference during the Moscow International Film Festival in 1987, the chairman of the Filmmakers' Union, Elem Klimov, charged with the release of previously banned films, was asked about the progress of unshelving banned films – and allowed Askoldov to answer the question. Upon hearing that his film was still shelved, Gorbachev allegedly intervened.[4] On 22 July 1987, Goskino determined that 'in the given situation the film … is to be released', and Askoldov was invited to the San Francisco Film Festival by its director Peter Scarlet, giving *The Commissar* immediate international publicity. *The Commissar* has never participated in a Russian film festival.

The film was banned not for a scene, a theme, or a tune; it was banned because of its profoundly pacifist message, condemning all warfare, whatever the cause. Even the ideal of Bolshevism does not merit the loss that Vavilova suffers when her lover

Figure 5.1 Askoldov's *The Commissar*: Vavilova (Mordiukova) is measured by Maria.

dies, nor her loss of femininity and motherhood when she rejoins the Red Army after having given birth.

The film opens with the image of a Madonna with child in the open Russian landscape. This peaceful scene is disturbed by an infantry passing by. Vavilova (Nonna Mordiukova, who had played Stesha in *Alien Kin*, 1955) is not a woman, but a commissar: she detests her pregnancy and resents that she has to abandon the army to give birth. She is accommodated with a Jewish family, the Magazanniks, where mother and father lovingly care for their numerous children and emulate the ideal of family. Vavilova has a room to herself while the family are cramped in the only other room.

Yet this family is predestined to perish. A sequence where Efim anticipates the Holocaust visualized the impossibility of that peaceful, harmonious life and annihilated the possibility for hope in the future. Moreover, the children imitate in their play and with their dolls the violence that surrounds them, leading to a disturbing scene when the smallest girl is tortured and beaten up by the others. War generates aggression, and only peace can change this perpetuation of violence.

Efim (Bykov), however, has a positive outlook on life, which is evident from his singing and humming while he works; he also plays with and feeds the children. Vavilova's child will never have such a father and the logical conclusion, namely that the Jewish father is better than the Revolutionary (who is not there because he sacrificed his life for an idea) could not be lost on the censors. It is, interestingly, Efim who makes a dress for Vavilova after his wife Maria has taken the measurements, and he prepares the cradle and clothes for the baby that Maria delivers with her mother.

The birth scene allows Askoldov to create a human dimension for Vavilova: she has visions, in the form of flashbacks, related in sensation to the different stages of her contractions and reviewing the relationship that led to her pregnancy. Vavilova recollects soldiers pushing a cannon through the sand of the desert, with a vision of water in the distance, a mirage that is turned upside down in the frame. The second vision shows Vavilova with the leather-clad commissar in the desert as a sandstorm rages. The military power of the cannon is visually confused with the (male) commissar's sexual power. The third vision accompanies the birth of the child and sees the cavalry crossing a bridge as the commissar is shot, leaving his riderless horse as a marker of death. The birth of the child is thus associated with death: the child has no future, at least not with Vavilova as mother.

Vavilova ultimately abandons her child, having seen the Magazanniks' family life and realizing that she will never have a happy family, because womanhood and family are incompatible with her commitment to the Bolshevik cause. The fact that the Magazanniks are a Jewish family did not help the fate of the film: images of the Holocaust were feared to cause undesirable associations with the Jewish question and issues of anti-Semitism in the USSR, such as the 1949 'cosmopolitan campaign' or the tragedy of Baby Yar in September 1941, passed off in Soviet historiography as a crime against the Soviet people rather than an atrocity committed against the Jews. The Jewish theme is likely to have been a major reason for the film's ban.[5] *The Commissar* is one of the most important films on Soviet history and its relationship to the individual citizen.

Other films touching upon history were also subjected to scrutiny and banned. Alexei Gherman's (b. 1938) debut film concerned the juxtaposition of historical and personal memory. *Trial on the Road* (Proverka na dorogakh, Lenfilm 1971, released 1986) dealt with the Red Army officer Lazarev, who has been captured by Germans and is seized by a group of partisans as they stop a German car by a roadblock (hence the film's title). The partisans do not trust Lazarev, although he procures important documents. Major Petushkov (Solonitsyn) is a fanatical ideologue, who does not trust anyone, but Commander Lokotkov (Bykov) goes by basic instinct and trusts Lazarev. When a soldier is wounded in an ambush, Lazarev is implicated and attempts suicide. He is given another 'trial', or test to pass: he is charged with rerouting a German supply train. He dies as he accomplishes this mission. The camera dwells on the foggy location that limits visibility, physically and figuratively. The suggestion that Soviet soldiers may be wrong in their assessment while a former POW held by the Nazis has not compromised his values and is morally superior, caused the film to be banned for many years.

As late as 1975, Elem Klimov's *Rasputin* (Agoniia, Mosfilm 1975) was 'delayed' and premiered at the Moscow International Film Festival in 1981, starring Alexei Petrenko (b. 1938) as Rasputin. The film combined historical newsreel footage, such as images of the First World War revealing Russia's weakness, of the Khodynka fields and the events of Bloody Sunday, with images of an aristocracy in thrall to healers and mystics, taking a Tibetan breathing session from a Buryat doctor. The inability and unwillingness of those in power to take action is highlighted and contrasted with Count Yusupov's decisiveness when he murders Rasputin. Klimov creates a compassionate image of the tsar by surrounding him, essentially, with freaks, including the tsarina who believes that the Siberian *starets* Rasputin can cure the tsarevich's haemophilia. Documentary footage of riots and unrest further undermines the peace at the imperial court. Rasputin's abduction and robbery by a gang and his subsequent cure of the tsarina boost his influence, allowing him to meddle in political decisions while drawing his advice from his dreams and sexual desires. Klimov employs fast montage to render the feverish and hallucinatory qualities of Rasputin's visions. He focuses on detail to underline the absurd and sickening conduct of the aristocracy. *Rasputin* presents history as a theatrical performance. However, the portrayal of the tsar, who was not entirely an abject or despicable character, but more a victim of circumstance, led to the film's delay.

Some films were banned for their portrayal of contemporary life: this lay at the heart of the controversy around Kira Muratova's two films of the period. Muratova had studied at Moscow's Film Institute and returned to Odessa after divorcing her first husband, the filmmaker Alexander Muratov. She was consistently accused of bourgeois realism, a term that described her concern with small and insignificant people, and most of her films made during the Stagnation era were banned. *Brief Encounters* (Korotkie vstrechi, Odessa Studio 1967, released 1986) is about two women and one man: Valentina (Muratova) is an active and emancipated woman, but she yearns for personal happiness and fulfilment. She has to pay a high price for her independence, which strains her personal life. Not unlike Petrukhina from *Wings*, she also cannot come to terms with the household chores. Nadia (the Vakhtangov Theatre's new young talent Nina Ruslanova, b. 1945) is a simple and naive country girl. The man between them is Maxim (Vysotsky), a geologist whose figure is idealized as he is seen exclusively in flashbacks and through the reminiscences of the two women, but never in the present. Muratova here cleverly inverts the concept of the woman as an object in pre-Revolutionary cinema, making the man object of female recollection and imagination. Casting the bard Vladimir Vysotsky as the irresistible social outcast created additional controversy, but the role of Valentina, unmarried, childless and non-committal in her work also did not conform to the Party's image of the worker. In her succinct analysis of the film and the reasons for the ban, Anna Lawton underscores the anachronistic interior of Valentina's apartment, 'more fit for a Chekhovian anti-heroine than for a Party executive', and creating an image of the '*embourgeoisement* of the Party cadres'[6] that would

Figure 5.2 Muratova's *Brief Encounters*: Maxim (Vysotsky) and Valentina (Muratova).

certainly have displeased the authorities. Muratova's 'provincial melodramas', as Jane Taubman[7] calls her first two films in Odessa, did not fit in with great cinema required in the centre.

At the beginning of the film, Valentina composes a speech: she begins to record this, but does not get beyond the address as she has nothing to say. The power of language is further undermined when she uses the phrase 'to be or not to be' (*byt' ili ne byt'*) for 'to wash or not to wash' (*myt' ili ne myt'*), reducing Hamlet's existential issues to a banal everyday level. Valentina thus discloses the emptiness of official rhetoric and reveals her mechanical work attitude. It is also a mechanical device – telephone or recorder – that transmits Maxim's voice. Valentina's job at the municipal office concerns the inspection of new flats and their water supply. Water as the essence of life is what Valentina takes for granted whilst others wait to be connected to the supplies; she cannot even be bothered to wash up.

The film is structured in a series of flashbacks, which are not organized in chronological order. Nadia recalls meeting Maxim and fixing his jacket; then Valentina remembers sitting with Maxim on the patio and eating crayfish; Valentina remembers telling Maxim of her colleague's death and a quarrel with Maxim; Nadia recalls how she and her village friend Liuba left for town, how she dreamt of buying herself a pair of boots, how she stayed at the road restaurant to work, and how she met Maxim; Valentina remembers Maxim on her birthday. Effectively, the women remember a different man: the attractive geologist, the man from town with no home and no one who looks after him; and the man who wants no home and seeks to escape from conventional family life. Muratova's concern with misunderstandings – created through language and gestures – would remain an important theme in her later films.

Long Farewells (Dolgie provody, Odessa Studio 1971, released 1987) told of a divorced mother, Yevgenia Vasilievna (the Leningrad theatre actress Zinaida Sharko, b. 1929), who cannot let go of her son. The boy wants to live with his father, an archaeologist in Siberia, but he too is unable to change his life, echoing with his indecision the issue at the heart of the general stagnation. After the ban of both films, Muratova did not work until she was asked to adapt a classic for the screen and chose Lermontov's 'Princess Mary', which was stopped in production in 1976. She then made *Getting to Know the Big White World* (Poznavaia belyi svet, Lenfilm 1978), which positioned the plasterer Liuba (Ruslanova) between two men, one of whom she has to choose. The film marks a departure in the Muratova's work in its accentuated use of decorative elements to grotesquely exaggerate character features, something that would become a trademark for her films in the 1990s. *Among Grey Stones* (Sredi serykh kamnei, Odessa Studio 1983, released 1987) was edited by another director and Muratova removed her name from the credits.

Muratova's films of this period differ from her later work in some respects, but they share the provincial settings, the attention to decorative details to highlight character features, and her concern with language. For Muratova. language is an insufficient means of communication and therefore often incongruous with action and emotions.

Another shelved film was Gennadi Poloka's (b. 1930) eccentric comedy *The Intervention* (Interventsiia, Lenfilm 1968), which portrayed a foreign invasion during the Civil War, mockingly confronting armies of reds, whites and greens while the undercover Bolshevik Brodsky, who hides under the guise of the gallant teacher Mikhail Voronov (played by Vysotsky), takes under his tutelage the naive and stupid Zhenia (the Taganka Theatre's actor Valeri Zolotukhin, b. 1941), the son of a wealthy lady. The film was set in a decor that resembled a circus arena, with two-dimensional, cardboard-like flights of stairs for parades that were choreographed to dance music, thus mocking army parades and taking a flippant view of the Civil War. The 'Song about Wooden Costumes' (1967) performed by Vysotsky and written especially for the film, warned people not to wear stifling masks, giving a serious twist to the persiflage of the Civil War, which was shunned and banned by the authorities. The appearance of Vysotsky, whose songs were spreading underground through *magnitizdat* (the duplication of tapes), no doubt was a thorn in the flesh for the authorities, who were angered by each public appearance of the actor, who was frequently banned from the stage (because of bouts of alcoholic excess) and reprimanded for illegal concert activity. His songs, rendered with his rough voice, mocked in a dead-pan intonation the excesses of Soviet society, from prostitution to discipline. Vysotsky's 'Wolf Hunt', cited in the epigraph to this chapter, was a song that summarized the persecution of the artist by the state in a comparison to the lonely wolf chased by a crowd of hunters, and was one of the most popular songs of the 1970s.

The Soviet East and the Caucasus

On the periphery, the cinema of the republics thrived in the Stagnation period. Most studios had only launched fiction film production after the war, and although many filmmakers came to Moscow to study, staying at a distance from the tight control of the centre sometimes gave more liberty. Thus, by drawing on their own culture and traditions, the republics were able to inspire the centre, if only by restoring the power of the poetic image of all-powerful Mother Nature. Furthermore, their use of symbolic objects instead of character portrayal and the creation of metaphors through colour and texture went beyond the realist linear narratives that dominated mainstream cinema made in Moscow.

In the constant attempt of the Soviet empire to demonstrate the intrinsic and inseparable link with its republics, Kazakhfilm, which had hosted the Moscow and Leningrad studios during the war, made its first feature film in 1954 (*Poem About Love* [Poema o liubvi], dir. Aimanov). Shaken Aimanov's film, *Land of Our Fathers* (Zemlia otsov 1966), is a parable about the idea of 'homeland', explored through the tale of an old man and his grandson who set out to bury a Kazakh warrior on the land of his ancestors. During the 1960s and 1970s, Kazakhfilm played a most active role in the rewriting of early Soviet history, with the production of a trilogy about the involvement and determination of local heroes in establishing socialist rule. This trilogy consisted of *The End of the Ataman* (Konets atamana, 1970) – the last film directed by the legendary Shaken Aimanov, *Trans-Siberian Express* (Transsibirskii ekspress, dir. Eldar Urazbaev, 1977) and *The Manchurian Version* (Mandzhurskii variant, dir. Igor Vovnianko 1989). The three films tell the story of a secret agent: in 1921 the Red officer Chadiarov – himself a Chinese prince – has to kill Ataman Dutov, who collaborates with the Whites. During this mission he exposes a spy in the Red headquarters in his Kazakh hometown. The second film, *Trans-Siberian Express*, follows Chadiarov – now the secret agent Fan – to the Manchurian city of Harbin in 1927. Fan is forced into taking a train to Moscow, on which a gang plots to assassinate the Japanese businessman Saito, who wants to offer to the Soviet regime economic collaboration with his company. Fan debilitates the gang. Chadiarov's final task of ensuring safety during a secret summit after the war ultimately cost him his life in *The Manchurian Version.* The first and second parts of the epic about the Kazakh support of socialism were scripted by Andrei Konchalovsky and Nikita

Mikhalkov. The trilogy represents the Soviet version of a spy thriller, mixed with adventure and the chase elements of the western.

In Kyrgyzstan, the documentary filmmaker Vladimir Shneiderov had worked actively during the 1920s and 1930s. Kirgizfilm served as the basis for film chronicles during the Second World War, and produced its first feature film in 1955. In the early 1960s, Shepitko and Konchalovsky made their debut films here. However, the 'miracle of Kyrgyz cinema', as the film critic Gulnara Abikeyeva labelled the period,[8] began in 1967 with the work of Tolomush Okeev and Bolat Shamshiev. The latter made *The Red Poppies of Issyk Kul* (Alye maki Issyk-kulia, 1972) about Soviet power in Kyrgyzstan, and the lyrical *The White Ship* (Belyi parokhod, 1975) about the boy Nurgazy, raised by his grandfather while mother and father work in the city. Nurgazy invents stories to explain to himself the mountain world: thus he dreams of reaching out to the lake where he imagines his father on a white ship. Tolomush Okeev (1935–2001) made *The Sky of Our Childhood* (Nebo nashego detstva, 1967) about the collision of nomad life and new Soviet modern life. An old man lives with his youngest son, who should keep the herd; the elder sons have all left for the city. But the young man goes to town when a road is being built. The film was controversial because it pleaded for the preservation of Central Asian culture. *The Fierce One* (Liutyi, 1974) tells of a child, Kurmash, who takes in a wolf cub and domesticates the animal. When released, the wolf turns into a wild beast and when Kurmash runs away from home, the wolf kills him. The film is a social parable on the forced adaptation of Central Asian culture, a theme that preoccupied Okeev's later work, such as *The Descendant of the Snow Leopard* (Potomok belogo barsa, 1984) about a hunter who kills a snow leopard, threatening the lifestyle of the northern people who have hitherto lived harmoniously with the animals. Again Okeev speaks of the danger of destroying tradition. His films are visually powerful, capturing the beauty of his land.

During the war, Turkmenistan's capital Ashkhabad hosted the evacuated Kiev Studios. Turkmenfilm was created only in 1958 and three feature films were made in the 1960s. These were directed by Bulat Mansurov (b. 1937), whose *The Competition* (Sostiazanie, 1964) was the first Turkmen film, followed by his adaptations of Yuri Trifonov's *Quenching the Thirst* (Utolenie zhazhdy, 1967), dealing with the construction of the Karakum Canal, and *The Slave* (Rabynia, 1970), based on Andrei Platonov. Mansurov worked with director of photography Khodzhakuli Narliev (b. 1945), whose own film *The Daughter-in-Law* (Nevestka, 1972) placed Turkmen film on the map. Ogyulkeik (played by Narliev's wife, Maya Aimedova) lives with her old father-in-law as they both await the return of his son from the war. She cannot leave, because that would remove the hope that he will return. The film captures the life in the *yurt* and the beautiful steppe, but also the hardship of everyday life. With the failure of Ogyulkeik's fiancé to return from the war, the film emphasizes the republics' contribution to the Soviet cause as well as the hardship of life without men in the steppe.

Tadzhikfilm hosted a group of directors during the war, although its activity started properly in 1957 with the creation of a studio. Several Mosfilm directors went to make films there to use the locations, and the work of Boris Kimiagarov is worth mentioning. However, it was not until the 1980s that Tajik directors emerged in their full force, notably in the figure of Bakhtior Khudoinazarov (b. 1965) with his film *Kosh-ba-kosh* (1993), already in the post-Soviet era.

Tashkent also served as base for Russian studios during the evacuation. In Uzbekistan, the film industry began to work immediately after the war, and during the 1950s produced a number of films about Uzbek life before and after the Revolution, although it was with the films of Shukhrat Abbasov that Uzbek cinema established itself. Ali Khamraev created some fine films on Uzbek tradition, such as *The White Storks* (Belye, belye aisti, 1966) for which he turned to the Uzbek myth of a girl who is forced to marry, and becomes unhappy when she finds real love. His subsequent films gained huge popularity as Khamraev engaged in the genre of the 'eastern': *The Seventh Bullet* (Sed'maia pulia, Uzbekfilm 1972) was set in Central Asia of the 1920s, where – in their fight against Soviet rule – the Basmachi bring destruction to the local people, while the local militia leader Maksumov surrenders to the Basmachi in an attempt to convince his men of the right cause. The attacks of the 'wild' Basmachi lend themselves for chase scenes. *The Bodyguard* (Telokhranitel', Tadzhikfilm 1980) was another successful and popular eastern following the journey of the native Mirzo, who is charged to take the main Basmachi leader – who has been captured by the Soviet army in the 1920s – to Bukhara. Khamraev has remained a popular director, who went on to work at Mosfilm and for Russian television.

The popularity of remote settings and distant culture explains the success of the eastern as a new genre, replacing the western. A most successful adventure story with an exotic setting was *The White Sun of the Desert* (Beloe solntse pustyni, Mosfilm, Lenfilm 1970) by Vladimir Motyl, written by Valentin Yezhov and Rustam Ibragimbekov about the clash between traditional and new values, as was the case for many films set in Central Asia. However, Motyl turns the plot into an action film. The Soviet power has stripped the *bai* (landlord) Abdullah of everything; he seeks revenge and follows the Soviet officer Sukhov, who guards Abdullah's last and most precious possession – his harem of nine women. Sukhov, however, is an ethnic Russian and positive representative of Soviet power. He misses his wife, as is evident from dream sequences, and – although he is attracted by 'his' wives, he respects them and clumsily tries to instil in them Soviet values. However, he fails to understand the full meaning of local Muslim traditions, which gives rise to a series of amusing misunderstandings and funny situations.

In the Caucasus republics, the Georgian studio dominated production: Tengiz Abuladze here made *The Prayer* (Molba [Vedreba], 1967) about the destruction of the medieval myth of Georgia as paradise in modern times. In *The Tree of Desires* (Drevo zhelanii [Natvris Khe], 1976) Marita cannot bear her separation from her beloved. She is led on a donkey around the village to display her disgrace, and dies of shame. Traditions cripple emotions, unlike in the films of the Central Asian republics.

Otar Ioseliani debuted with *Falling Leaves* (Listopad [Giorgobistve], 1966), where the young Niko tries to introduce new methods in wine production, but confronts the traditions held by the older generation. *There Was a Singing Thrush* (Zhil pevshii drozd [Iko shahsvi mgalobeli], 1970) concisely captured the lack of meaning and direction that was typical for the films of the Stagnation era: the musician Giya Agladze makes no career as musician, fails to compose a song, searches for distractions among friends and women, and leads a life that lacks perspective and direction. One day he is killed in a road accident. Ioseliani here captures the futility and absurdity of human life when set against grand plans and ambitions.

Irakli Kvirikadze is known first and foremost as scriptwriter. He directed *The Swimmer* (Plovets [Motsurave], Gruziafilm 1981), a film about three generations of swimmers living under different regimes. In each period, Kvirikadze captures accurately the signs of the time, both visually and emotionally. All these outstanding individuals are outcasts that do not fit into society, just like Petrukhina fits into no standard suit size. The style of the film is reminiscent of Abuladze's arranged, stylized and artificial-looking characters, who seem to pose for the camera.

Figure 5.3 Ioseliani's *There Was a Singing Thrush*: Giya Agladze.

Sergo Parajanov spent most of the decade in prison, which explains the gap of fifteen years in his creative output. His *Colour of Pomegranates* (Sayat Nova [Nran Guyne], Armenfilm 1969) captured the life of the eighteenth-century Armenian troubadour, poet and monk Sayat Nova, and is composed of a series of tableaux. *The Legend of Suram Fortress* (Legenda o Suramskoi kreposti [Ambavi Suramis tsikhitsa], Gruziafilm 1984) illustrates a Georgian legend about a boy who has to be buried in the wall of a fortress to preserve the building for posterity. Parajanov created no narrative cinema, but a series of still lifes that occasionally moved, stirred or shifted. Like his collages, his frames abounded with objects and trinkets, details and accessories, fixating through texture and colour the folklores and traditions of different ethnic groups.

Mainstream Cinema Playing Safe, 1969–73

In the period following the frequent bans of films, many filmmakers stuck to potentially 'safe' material: either by adapting literature for the screen, or by continuing to exploit the popular genres of comedy, or by setting their films in the countryside, which had become increasingly popular with the 'village prose' movement.

After the ban on *Asya's Happiness*, Andrei Konchalovsky turned to the classics, too: he adapted Ivan Turgenev's novel *A Nest of Gentlefolk* (Dvorianskoe gnezdo, Mosfilm 1969) and Anton Chekhov's *Uncle Vania* (Mosfilm 1970). *Uncle Vania* begins with a series of documentary photographs of scenes from Russian life in the 1890s: the exploitation of the soil, foreboding the end of an era, the end of the Romanovs, the end of nature, the end of mankind. Konchalovsky uses these photos as a document of the real world that he contrasts with the artificial setting inside the house, thus emphasizing the frivolity of the everyday melodrama unfolding in the house. Konchalovsky confines the entire action to the inside to stress the characters' disaffection with the external world and with the historical events that happen around them. The characters remain entrapped both physically and emotionally in their little world, thus reflecting the general entropy at the turn of the century, which also carried a topical resonance to the contemporary world.

The comic genre that had flourished in the 1960s was adversely affected by the Stagnation. Filmmakers were uncertain of the permissible limits of laughter. Some operettas enjoyed great success, such as *Trembita* (Sverdlovsk Studio 1968) and *Wedding in Malinovka* (Svadba v Malinovke, dir. Tutyshkin, Lenfilm 1967). One of the most popular films of the period was Leonid Gaidai's *Diamond Arm* (Brilliantovaia ruka, Mosfilm 1968), which was probably the best comedy of the Stagnation period, including the physical slapstick of his earlier films, with pursuits, falls and fights, using the film techniques of silent cinema to expose physical disproportions to humorous effects. Semen Gorbunkov (Yuri Nikulin, 1921–97) is on a cruise in Istanbul and mistaken for a diamond smuggler when he slips, breaks

Figure 5.4 Gaidai's *Diamond Arm*: Gorbunkov (Nikulin).

his arm and has it cast in plaster (and diamonds). He returns to Soviet Russia and is now chased by the smugglers, while the police are after the smugglers. The plot of the film allows for chase scenes that are part of a genuine action movie, with numerous comic effects thanks to the physical agility of the clown Yuri Nikulin. After the tremendous success of *Diamond Arm*, Gaidai made a film version of Ilf and Petrov's satire, *Twelve Chairs* (Dvenadtsat' stul'ev, Mosfilm 1971), an adaptation of Gogol's comedy *The Government Inspector* (Revizor) as *Incognito from Petersburg* (Inkognito iz Piterburga, Mosfilm 1977), and *Ivan Vasilievich Changes Profession* (Ivan Vasilievich meniaet professiiu, Mosfilm 1973), based on Bulgakov's play.

Among the films set in the countryside, the work of Vasili Shukshin, who had come to filmmaking in the 1960s, signalled major innovation. His *Pots and Pans*

(Pechki-Lavochki, Gorky Studio 1972) told of the naive and yet alert peasant Ivan Rastorguev travelling with his wife on a train to a sanatorium on the Black Sea. He confronts the dangerous and busy Moscow before reaching his destination to find that there is no place for his wife in the sanatorium. The criminal world of the big city also posed a threat in *Red Guelderbush* (Kalina krasnaia, Mosfilm 1973), which was an extremely popular film about Yegor Prokudin (Shukshin), who returns from a prison sentence and is drawn into danger when he visits his old gang of Guboshlep. Liuba Baikalova (Lidia Fedoseeva-Shukshina, b. 1938) lives in a village and offers the prospect of a new life, leaving behind his criminal past by integrating him into the village community. Yet Yegor is ashamed of his past and betrays his mother, visiting her in a disguise with dark glasses. The past catches up with him when Guboshlep kills him just as he has decided to change his life. Yegor is restless and rootless. He has no clear-cut personality, as is evident from the various roles he adopts, from thief to peasant:

> Throughout the movie, Egor assumes various identities ... He changes costume and he changes his name. Now he is Gore the gang member in his black leather jacket and flaming red shirt, not the 'poor relative' Zhora in Liuba's husband's old underwear and shorts. On his visit to the city he is Georgi in his newly acquired loud tie, tweed jacket, beret and suede shoes. Ploughing the fields in his quilted peasant's jacket he is simply Egor.[9]

Yegor first tries to engage with the gang, then leaves for the countryside to make a new start, but returns to town and then goes back to Liuba. The departure from the countryside and the loss of roots associated with it, together with the dissatisfaction of the younger generation, give this film a fine and sensitive resonance. The sentimental images of trees and churches contrast with the world of crime, while folk songs echo emotions and harmonize with the tunes of prison songs that Yegor brings back. Shukshin portrays in his characters men who have lost a sense of direction, who are lost in society as much as they are lost in the open space that he captures in wide-angle shots and contrasts with interiors and close-ups. Shukshin presents a world in which change from criminal to honest citizen is not possible – not for psychological reasons, but because of social immobility, thus proffering a critical view of contemporary Soviet society. Shukshin's films enjoyed great popularity because of their setting in the countryside, with its authentic folk rites and rituals, and characters that did not protrude as artificial, and the fine acting of himself and his wife.

Gleb Panfilov (b. 1934) located his characters not in villages, but in the provinces, which allowed him to capture more accurately the psychology and mood of contemporary characters. Panfilov had worked in the Urals and studied under Leonid Trauberg at the Higher Courses in the 1960s, and made his debut with *No Path through Fire* (V ogne broda net, Lenfilm 1967) in which he created the finely

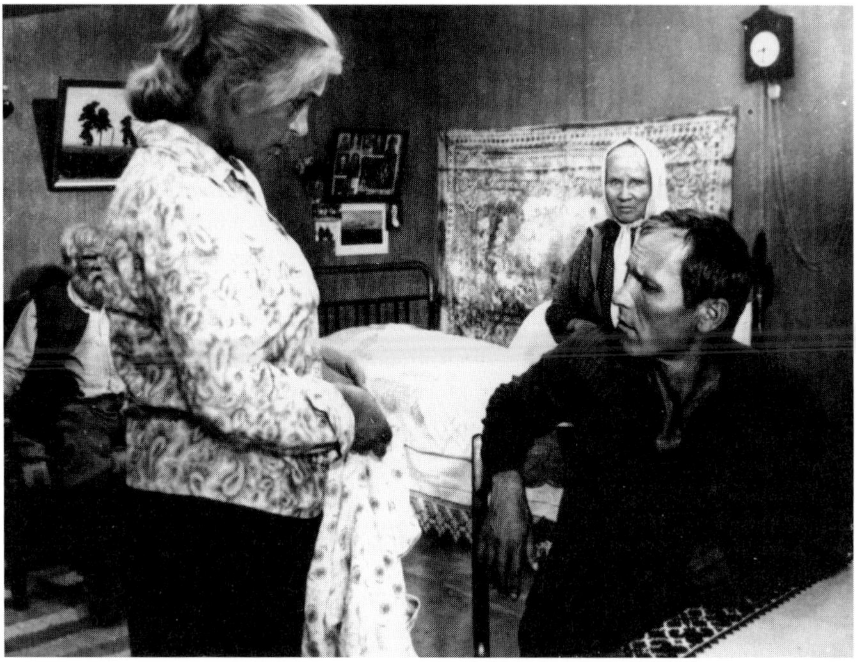

Figure 5.5 Shukshin's *Red Guelderbush.*

drawn character of Tania Tetkina, played by his wife Inna Churikova (b. 1943). Tetkina is a peasant woman and a talented painter. When she is captured by the Whites and sees her comrades perish, she loses the will to live. Churikova plays her and, in following roles, women with extraordinary talents, which are, however, not the most important features of the character. In *The Debut* (Nachalo, Lenfilm 1970) the working girl Pasha (Churikova) is spotted in an amateur theatre and cast for the role of Jeanne d'Arc. She gives a brilliant performance in that part, but is not tempted by stardom and returns to her village. Churikova's face was extraordinarily intriguing on the screen: not conventionally beautiful, she displayed loyalty and straightforwardness through her demeanour. In this sense, her roles contradict the clear-cut views on life required by the authorities. Yelizaveta Uvarova (Churikova) of *I Wish to Speak* (Proshu slova, Lenfilm 1975) is a town mayor and ex-sportswoman – an elegant, cultured and sophisticated woman. She has ideas and plans for a garden city. However, she cannot articulate her own thoughts, as she has no words of her own, relying on slogans, empty phrases and newspaper jargon. Her ambivalent character, displaying more affection for politics than for people, pointed at man's increasing alienation from his environment, which dominated the Stagnation period.

Literary adaptations always proved a way out, as they required no submission for script approval. Adaptations of the Stagnation era followed the model of Mikhalkov: to retreat to a pre-Revolutionary Russia as an idyllic state, where those emotions crippled in the stifling atmosphere of the 1970s could fully develop. Two popular screen adaptations were created by Emil Loteanu (1936–2003), a Moldovan director working at Mosfilm: Chekhov's *My Tender and Affectionate Beast* (Moi laskovyi i nezhnyi zver', 1978) and Gorky's *Queen of the Gypsies* (Tabor ukhodit v nebo, 1976). Other films were based on Tolstoy's *Father Sergius* (Otets Sergei, dir. Talankin, 1978), Pushkin's *Little Tragedies* (Malenkie tragedii, dir. Shveitser, Mosfilm for GTR 1979), and Ostrovsky's *Without a Dowry* (Bespridannitsa) under the title *A Cruel Romance* (Zhestokii romans, dir. Riazanov, Mosfilm 1984). Alov and Naumov adapted Bulgakov's *The Flight* (Beg, Mosfilm 1970), with the first part showing the evacuation of Sevastopol and the second highlighting the grotesque aspects of life in emigration. Historical pictures were made about the engineer Tsiolkovsky (*Take-Off* [Vzlet], dir. Kulish, Mosfilm 1979), Peter the Great (*Peter's Youth* [Yunost' Petra], dir. Gerasimov, Gorky Studio and DEFA 1980) and *Tchaikovsky* (dir. Talankin, Mosfilm 1969) with Innokenti Smoktunovsky.

Sergei Soloviev's *The Stationmaster* (Stantsionnyi smotritel', Mosfilm for GTR 1972) was based on Pushkin's *Tales of Belkin*. Captain Minsky stops at a station to change his horses and is taken by the stationmaster's daughter Dunia. Pretending to be ill, he stays and later elopes with Dunia to St Petersburg. The heartbroken stationmaster travels to the capital, but Minsky denies him access to the house. When Dunia returns for a visit to her father's home with her children, it is too late: he has died. Soloviev employs three narrative voices: that of Belkin for his first visit to the station; that of the stationmaster telling Belkin about Dunia's elopement on his second visit; and finally the voice of the new stationmaster's son, who briefs Belkin about the most recent events. The complexity of voices is juxtaposed with Dunia's silence, making her a victim of male discourse in a male-dominated society.

Some films presented not a costume version, but a modernized reading of the text, in line with the leading theatre productions of the time, which adopted a style of contemporary readings of the classics, especially in the absence of good contemporary plays. Gleb Panfilov adapted Gorky's *Vassa Zheleznova* (Vassa, Mosfilm 1983), which exposed the moral corruption of a family for the sake of the façade of their business. Konchalovksy's *Uncle Vania* has been discussed elsewhere in terms of its theme of disaffection with the modern world.

Andrei Tarkovsky's Films, 1974–82

Auteur cinema encountered difficulties in the 1960s and 1970s, partly because its poetic language remained inaccessible for the masses and made no considerable win at the box office, and partly because its symbolism was often feared to lead astray Soviet cinema's political agenda. Sometimes international pressure or support could mean that a film was released for international screenings, while it remained undistributed or in low distribution at home. This applies to most films of the leading *auteurs* of the period: Andrei Tarkovsky, whose *Andrei Rublev* was delayed for several years; Alexei Gherman, whose *Trial on the Roads* was banned; Alexander Sokurov, whose films were stopped during production (*Anaesthesia Dolorosa*); and Kira Muratova, who had two films banned and was prevented from working as director until the 1980s.

Auteur cinema, which emphasized the individual artistic impulse, stood in sharp contrast to the socialist principle and was condemned, even with hindsight, by Sergei Gerasimov in 1988: 'They [the *auteur* filmmakers] want to preach like a genius, a messiah. That is a position that is incompatible with our communist ethics.'[10] The filmmaker assumed the role of a preacher, as no moral guidance was provided by a state exclusively concerned with political and ideological matters. Assuming this function and associating it with 'high art' handicapped the development of cinema in the post-Soviet era, when filmmakers for a long time failed to define their relationship to the audience. The role of a preacher also exposed the filmmaker to criticism from the Party, which claimed that role for itself. However, this response highlights more the fear of the authorities of losing control, since filmmakers merely presented films that expressed their own spiritual search in the absence of any value system: 'Art is born and takes hold wherever there is a timeless, insatiable longing for the spiritual, for the ideal.'[11] Tarkovsky formulated his understanding of cinema quite concisely in 1972: 'For me, cinema is a moral occupation and not a professional one.'[12]

The Mirror (Zerkalo, Mosfilm 1974) is an autobiographical film that conflates personal and historical time and illustrates well Tarkovsky's notion of making films according to the notion of 'sculpting in time'. The film begins with footage of a boy with a stammer who is put under hypnosis by a doctor; at the end of the treatment he is able to speak fluently. The past (trauma) and the present (the stammer and its removal) are inextricably linked in personal histories. The scene is widely regarded as a parable for the artist unable to express himself who, through the mirror of past, cures his inability to speak. In this sense, *Mirror* is Tarkovsky's own hypnosis session.

A woman, Maria (Margarita Terekhova, b. 1942) is sitting on a fence outside a wooden house in the summer before the war. The image duplicates photographs of Tarkovsky's family album showing his mother in this pose near the family home, which was reconstructed for the film. The woman has two children, the boy Alexei and a girl. The father watches as the woman washes her hair in a bowl. Water runs down the walls and mirrors. The mother stands in front of a mirror and wipes the surface, clearing the image of herself as an old woman. In the present, the adult Alexei speaks to his mother on the phone as she enquires when certain things happened in the 1930s. She learns that her friend Liza has died; they had worked together before the war. The film switches to that time, the 1930s: Maria is running to the printing house where she works, frightened that she may have made a mistake, and she has an argument with Liza. In the present, Alexei and his ex-wife Natasha argue about their son Ignat; Natasha is reminded that she looks like Alexei's mother. Ignat stands between mother and father when documentary footage interrupts the scene with images of a bullfight, the Spanish Civil War, the May Day of 1939 and a balloon flight; then Ignat reads passages from texts about Russia's mission. His father (Alexei) tells him of his first love, a redhead girl, and a flashback shows them together, followed by documentary footage. A landscape similar to Brueghel's winter landscape with snow and sledges shows Alexei as a boy with other children, including the Leningrad orphan boy Asafiev. Later, the adult Alexei is ill in bed and releases from his fist the bird that the flashback had shown sitting on Asafiev's cap. In Alexei's past, a similar scene occurred: the children looked into the same volume of Leonardo da Vinci's drawings that Ignat has now, and they too argue. In the final scene, Alexei's mother Maria is observed by Natasha (also played by Terekhova) in a conflation of past and present in a single frame, for which Tarkovsky's cinematographer Georgi Rerberg (1937–99) used double exposure. The memory of a past that is shared, told, imagined and dreamt is the subject of this complex film. Memory consists of images that often do not move, or move slowly; thus the image prolongs actual time through long takes, contradicting the concept of development that was created by montage in Eisenstein's films. The technique is the ultimate reflection of entropy: to capture states of mind and memory, and intersect them with the present. Classical music contributes to the rhythm created by images.

> The cinema image comes into being during shooting, and exists *within* the frame ... Editing brings together shots which are already filled with time, and organizes the unified, living structure inherent in the film; and the time that pulsates through the blood vessels of the film, making it alive, is of varying rhythmic pressure. The idea of 'montage cinema' – that editing brings together two concepts and thus engenders a new, third one – again seems to me to be incompatible with the nature of cinema. Art can never have the interplay of concepts as its ultimate goal.[13]

Tarkovsky's approach to time is crucial to an understanding of his films: time as past and present, as personal and historical time, is the material for the filmmaker who trims the flow of time as captured in the frame. Cinematic images are capable of creating an intersection of different flows of time, different tempi, different kinds of time, and it is this quality that distinguishes Tarkovsky's films.

> The distinctive time running through the shots makes the rhythm of the picture; and rhythm is determined not by the length of the edited pieces, but by the pressure of the time that runs through them. Editing cannot determine rhythm ... indeed, time courses through the picture despite editing rather than because of it. The course of time, recorded in the frame, is what the director has to catch in the pieces laid out on the editing table.[14]

Tarkovsky's adaptation of a science fiction novel, *Solaris* (Mosfilm 1972), by the Polish writer Stanislav Lem, served as a basis for a journey into the outer space that symbolizes a journey into the self. The scientist Kelvin (Banionis) is called to an emergency on a spaceship as the scientists in space experience strange occurrences in connection with the 'ocean' that visualizes their memory, innermost dreams and fears. For Kelvin the ocean brings to life his wife Hari who had committed suicide – for which he feels responsible. For Tarkovsky, the ocean that offers a visual reflection of man's thoughts, dreams and ideas, is part of this world. Like human memory, it gets things wrong, for example when it creates Kelvin's past. Indeed, Tarkovsky's Kelvin maybe never leaves earth, as his journey leads him to a harmonious balance within his self, having explored his relationship with his wife: at the end of the film, Kelvin is still at his father's house, filing old papers – only the water runs down the windows inside the house rather than outside, signalling an inversion of interior and exterior. As often in Tarkovsky's films, water or rain, glass or mirrors serve to reflect not the exterior, but the inner world of a character – his past, his alter ego, his inner self. The ocean is part of man's earthly experience rather than an abstract cosmic mass. If Lem was concerned with the human insufficiency vis-à-vis cosmic space, Tarkovsky places the human being at the centre of the universe and makes the journey to the space station a mere figment of the imagination.

His next film, *Stalker* (Mosfilm 1979), was also based on a science fiction story, this time by the Strugatsky Brothers (Arkadi 1925–92; Boris b. 1933). A writer and a scientist decide to venture into a post-nuclear-disaster zone with a guide, the Stalker (Alexander Kaidanovsky, 1946–95), who is both a holy fool and a messiah: he knows the path to the inner chamber of the zone, where secret wishes unknown to man come true. When the men reach the chamber, however, no one enters. The desire for self-recognition and for an exploration of the innermost world that also stood at the centre of *Solaris* is disappointed as knowledge is denied, rejected, and feared. The life of the Stalker and his family features at the beginning and end of the film in sepia, while the majority of the film set in the zone is shot in colour, contrasting once again a dull reality with a rich imaginative world, a device used in Tarkovsky's first film, *Ivan's Childhood*. The final sequence of the film confirms that the zone has miraculous powers: the Stalker's invalid daughter has acquired the skill of telekinesis.

Nostalghia (RAI and Sovinfilm, 1982) deploys a similar approach to *Mirror* with regard to the time structure. Through spatial rather than temporal dislocation, it explores the journey of the writer Gorchakov (the Lenkom Theatre actor Oleg Yankovsky, b. 1944) to Italy, where he hopes to discover his self and his sense of home. Gorchakov researches the life of the composer Pavel Sosnovsky, who had never been free (but a serf) in Russia, yet he longed to go back. Nostalgia, the longing for home, is thus established as the theme.

The film begins with a flashback into the Russian countryside, accompanied by a folk song. Gorchakov, however, is in Italy. His interpreter Eugenia embodies the abstract concept of a beauty that lacks the spiritual qualities of his Russian wife. They visit the chapel of San Galgano, where Eugenia observes women venerating the Madonna of Childbirth. She remembers a story about a maid who burnt the house of her employers in northern Italy because it kept her away from her home in Calabria. Gorchakov remembers Sosnovsky's life and that he committed suicide upon his return to Russia. A parallel is drawn between the maid who kills to return home and the composer who kills himself after returning home. Gorchakov dreams of his wife Maria and Eugenia embracing, merging the world of here and there, Italy and Russia, carnal and spiritual love. When visiting the cloister in Bagno Vignoni, Gorchakov meets Domenico, who had kept his family locked up for years, awaiting the end of the world. Domenico asks Gorchakov to carry a candle across St Catherine's Baths for him: he mirrors Gorchakov, who sees Domenico in the mirror instead of his own reflection. While Domenico immolates himself near Michelangelo's statue of Marcus Aurelius to Beethoven's *Ode to Joy*, Gorchakov accomplishes his mission: he returns to the drained St Catherine's Baths, crosses the pool on his third attempt (a scene shot in real time), and collapses – dead. Gorchakov takes on Domenico's mission – crossing the water like Jesus crossed Lake Gethsemane – and shares his fate. The mission of artists, writers and poets also informs Tarkovsky's last film, *The Sacrifice* (Offret, Swedish Film Institute, Argos Film and Film Four, 1986), made in Sweden, where Alexander offers himself to God in order to save mankind from an impending disaster.

Nostalghia's final frame positions Gorchakov near his Russian dacha with its pond, which is located in the middle of Italian ruins, as the frame reveals when the camera slowly tracks backwards. Gorchakov longs for Russia and dies in Italy; Sosnovsky returns to Russia and kills himself; the maid destroys a house to return home: the sensation of longing for another space is never conflated with time, as in *Mirror*, but different time strands run separately. Tarkovsky uses a tracking camera with extremely long takes and slow motion to freeze time almost to a standstill. Looking forward to Sokurov's work, this principle is applied to its extreme and frozen images only very gently, slowly and reluctantly begin to move, as for example the opening sequence of *Mother and Son*. Tarkovsky juxtaposes the eternal values of Russia – maternity, family, home – with the decay, sickening beauty and masquerade of the West.

Alexander Sokurov found employment at Lenfilm thanks to the intervention of Tarkovsky, who called him one of his 'heirs' – the possible reasons have been mentioned above. Sokurov, a historian by training, placed history at the centre of his films, and it is through accurate historical depiction or documentary footage that he reflects the psychological states of the characters. He employs slow motion with a camera that lingers on objects, settings and surfaces, or even freezes movement, although in his later work the camera can also penetrate the surface of painterly works (for example in his documentaries on the Hermitage). Most of his work was completed after perestroika, but his emergence as filmmaker falls into the period of Stagnation.

At Lenfilm he created a series of documentaries, and the documentary style bears on his later work in fiction film. Among them were *Maria* (1978), about a peasant woman; *Sonata for Viola* (Al'tovaia sonata, with S. Aranovich, 1981), about Shostakovich; *Elegy* (Elegiia, 1985), about Fedor Shaliapin; *Moscow Elegy* (Moskovskaia elegiia, 1986), about Tarkovsky's absence from Russia after exile and death; *A Soviet Elegy* (Sovetskaia elegiia, 1989), about Boris Yeltsin; *And Nothing More* (I nichego bol'she, 1987), about the Second World War. His fiction feature film, *Lonely Voice of Man* (Odinokii golos cheloveka, 1978–87), was based on Andrei Platonov's story, 'Potudan River' (1937), about the Red Army officer Nikita who marries but is unable to consummate the marriage. For him the Civil War has created an upheaval of the social world order that affects him so profoundly that he is incapable of procreation. He seeks regeneration by experiencing another circle of hell: that of an NEP market, where vulgarity and filth abound. He returns to his wife when she attempts suicide. With inserts of old photos, Sokurov recreated the world lost in the Civil War, thus emphasizing his concern for the individual in the grip of historical change. *Anaesthesia Dolorosa* (Skorbnoe beschuvstvie, 1983, released 1987) was based on Bernard Shaw's *Heartbreak House* (1919) and used documentary footage of the writer who watches the characters enact his play, at the end of which the house literally breaks apart when Sokurov plays with deformational optical devices.

The films of Tarkovsky and Sokurov represent the other side of 'playing safe' for the mainstream cinemas. Towards the mid-1970s, more filmmakers tried to offer a critique of society, albeit largely through narrative devices.

Social Criticism, 1974–82

As the situation in the country stagnated with persistent and repeated crop failures, with arrests and exiles of dissidents, and with a continued demonstration of military superiority vis-à-vis the United States, filmmakers echoed this gloomy mood. However, they also began to criticize those areas that were clearly of concern for Soviet Russia, but stopped short just before an outspoken attack of Soviet ideology. Thus, filmmakers expressed concerns about ignored corruption and stifling bureaucracy; about the assessment of the war as to boost the country's heroic profile; and about the exploitation of nature, as is evident in such films as *Siberiade* and *Farewell*.

Konchalovsky's epic feature film *Siberiade* (Mosfilm 1978) stretches from the Revolutionary era to the present (1970s), showing life in a Siberian village. It intersperses documentary footage of historical events with generations of men who struggle against nature, trying to dominate it in order to achieve their dreams. Thus, for example, the village is threatened in its existence: if no oil is found, a hydroelectric station (GES) will be constructed and this will mean the disappearance of the entire village under water, in a scenario not unlike that of Elem Klimov's

Farewell. Alexei Ustiuzhanin (Mikhalkov), who returns to his native village on a steamer after army service and study, saves the village from its fate. He is marked as a stranger, but impresses everybody with his charm, from the old women to the workers. Yet he fails to recognize the love of his youth, the girl Taya (Gurchenko), whom he once taught the tango to the tunes of 'Utomlennoe solntse' (The Weary Sun), the tune that would reappear as a leitmotif in Mikhalkov's Oscar-winning *Burnt by the Sun* (1994). Alexei works on the site drilling for oil with his comrade Tofik. As Alexei is about to leave the village, the oil bursts from the drilling rig, causing an explosion that kills him. For Konchalovsky, exploitation of natural resources in Siberia is an issue, but he mainly focuses on the village community and the preservation of its values.

Farewell (Proshchanie s Materoi, Mosfilm 1982) was completed by Elem Klimov after the tragic death in an accident of his wife Larisa Shepitko (1938–79), who had started the project. The film caused some controversy because of its references to the condition of the Aral Sea and the Siberian river plans. It was based on the village prose of Valentin Rasputin and set old traditions against innovation. Klimov portrayed the harmony of nature and man – those villagers on the island of Matyora who live in communion with nature. The island has to be evacuated to make way for a hydroelectric power station (GES). At the centre of the film stands the Pinegin family: Daria lives on the island and refuses to leave, her son Pavel is the foreman in charge of the evacuation of the island, and Pavel's son Andrei meanwhile fixes the electrical gadgets that are a novel curiosity for the villagers. He has a utilitarian view of the power station that will last for a hundred years, arguing that at last the island will be good for something. Daria communes with nature: she prays in the woods, touching the moss and observing the sunset in a semi-pagan ritual. She washes the house in preparation for its 'burial' as if it were a human corpse, revealing the close bond of the islanders with their environment. Klimov includes other rituals also, such as the naked bathing in the river after jumping over a fire on the night of 7 July, marking the conflated Orthodox holiday of the Birth of John the Baptist with the pagan festival of Ivan Kupala. The folk ensemble of Dmitri Pokrovsky accompanies the villagers and contrasts acoustically with the songs of Vysotsky and pop star Alla Pugacheva that are heard from the radio and television. The wooden huts contrast with the blocks of concrete in the town, which are designed to accommodate the settlers – seeing it, even Pavel's conscience is troubled. Omens worsen the evacuation: the old tree cannot be felled by an axe or a saw: its growth and age are highlighted through a camera shot from below. Even the bulldozer cannot carry it away; instead, Andrei crashes his head into the windscreen when trying to ram the bulldozer into the tree.

The film opens with black-and-white footage – the camera moves towards the island that is no longer, an absence shrouded in fog. When the past is brought alive Klimov moves to colour. At the end of the film, a boat speeds towards the island to collect Daria. The boat loses direction when a siren sounds, personifying the island in the distance as if it were alive. However, the calls of the men on the boat cannot be heard: all sense of direction has been lost. The final image of the tree reassures us that the past is indestructible.

Another theme that was exposed to criticism was corruption, which had already been a concern during the Thaw era. Sergei Mikaelian's film *The Bonus* (Premiia, Lenfilm 1974) was based on a play by Alexander Gelman. The film is in no way remarkable as such, as it basically follows the format of a theatre production, but it touches on the theme of a workers' collective refusing a bonus, which covers up corruption at the top that damages production as a whole. The issue of corruption and black markets, of the shadow economy replacing the dysfunctional Soviet economy, became prominent in the mid- to late 1970s.

The social inertia was likewise exposed in cinema. Panfilov's film *The Theme* (Tema, Lenfilm 1979, released 1986) touched upon the creative crisis of a playwright, Kim Esenin (Ulianov), who travels to Suzdal for inspiration and meets the philologist Sasha Nikolaeva (Churikova). The writer's crisis is rooted in the discrepancy between the lie of his artistic work and his roots, creating fictional plots that are just as estranged from truth as he is alienated from the world. Sasha is parting with her lover Borodaty (Stanislav Liubshin), a dissident who is preparing to emigrate to Israel. She contends that a writer must not sever his roots, whereas Borodaty feels that he is not free. The treatment of the complex issue of separation through emigration and exile was superbly rendered in the acting, but the film was banned.

None of Churikova's heroines were allowed the scope for change: they all have to remain static and deal with their lives where they are and as they are. This inflexibility of society also extended to the possibility of social mobility. A fine example of a man who responds only and never takes the initiative is the professor Andrei Buzykin (the Leningrad Bolshoi Drama Theatre actor Oleg Basilashvili, b. 1934), in Daneliya's *Autumn Marathon* (Osennii marafon, Mosfilm 1980). The retired Abrikosov (Ulianov) in Yuli Raizman's *Private Life* (Chastnaia zhizn', Mosfilm 1982) is another example of a man who has lost touch with reality, having lived the secluded life of a privileged official. The film highlights the individual's alienation, but also the isolation of people from everyday life. An unsuccessful attempt to break free from the stifling world that alienates and reduces man to passivity is undertaken by Sergei Makarov (Yankovsky) in Roman Balayan's *Dream Flights* (Polety vo sne i naiavu, Dovzhenko Studio 1982), who stages his own suicide to express his 'death' in the modern world.

The genre of comedy underwent modifications that reduced the physical gags and heightened instead the exposure of the bureaucratic apparatus to laughter. Riazanov's *Irony of Fate, or Have a Good Sauna!* (Ironiia sud'by, ili s legkim parom, Mosfilm 1975) focuses on marriage proposals made on a New Year's Eve in Moscow and Leningrad: that of Zhenia to Galia (in Moscow) and Ippolit to Nadia (in Leningrad). The connection between the two proposals is the completely unusual story which can only and exclusively happen upon New Year's Eve, thus profiting from the exceptional situation necessary for a true comedy. Zhenia tells his old school friends that he is getting engaged to Galia when they are on their traditional New Year's Eve visit to the bathhouse; as is Russian custom, they drink to this event. They are inebriated when accompanying Pavel to the airport; here they have a few more drinks. Eventually, they are so drunk that they cannot remember who was supposed to travel to Leningrad, and put Zhenia on the plane instead of Pavel. Zhenia next finds himself in a taxi that takes him to his house: Flat 12, No. 25 Third Construction Street. He opens the door with his key (standard locks), and enters a flat that is furnished like his (standard furniture). Zhenia lies down to sleep off his hangover; Nadia comes back. As they argue, Zhenia realizes that he is in Leningrad, not Moscow. Nadia's fiancé does not believe this unbelievable story that is, nevertheless, the truth; neither does Zhenia's fiancée back in Moscow. Eventually, both fiancé(e)s run away, and a relationship develops between Nadia and Zhenia. Their emotions are largely expressed through songs they sing for each other to the guitar, examples of the individualized and lyrical use of music in this film. The next day Zhenia leaves, and Nadia follows him to Moscow.

Riazanov combined melodramatic plots with comedy and light satire of the system: *An Office Romance* (Sluzhebnyi roman, Mosfilm 1977) was about an office director (Alisa Freindlikh) falling in love with a clerk, and both are positively transformed through their feelings. *The Garage* (Garazh, Mosfilm 1979) followed a staff cooperative in a research institute for animal protection, who meet in a hall with stuffed animals. They have been informed that they will lose four of the promised garages and establish that the weakest in the meeting – who are asleep or cannot speak – will be deprived of the garage. Here it transpires that the key for the room has been lost. One member devours all the papers and thus annihilates the cooperative in legal terms. The satire on the collective points to the need for a substantial reform of a system that is utterly corrupt. In *Station for Two* (Vokzal dlia dvoikh, Mosfilm 1982), Riazanov portrays the romance between the waitress Vera (Gurchenko) and the pianist Platon Gromov (Basilashvili), who is passing by on a trip home from prison where he is serving a sentence for a crime he has not committed: his wife had caused an accident with his car. Alongside this romance Riazanov depicts, in a humorous way, the exploits of the train conductor Andrei (Mikhalkov), who controls the railway station. He knows everybody who works there, which makes it easy for him to do some illegal trading with melons. Riazanov here ventures into a bold comment on the illegal businesses that dominated the economy all over Soviet Russia.

Many films about the war dealt with the tragedy from the perspective of coming to terms with its consequences, returning to the monumentalism of the early post-war films. Examples are Bondarchuk's *They Fought for their Motherland* (Oni srazhalis' za rodinu, Mosfilm 1975), an attempt to recreate the human tragedy of *The Fate of a Man* in a monumental, colourful, and glossy epic with Vasili Shukshin in the main role, and Andrei Smirnov's *Belorussian Station* (Belorusskii vokzal,

Mosfilm 1970). This explored the fate of four soldiers and a field nurse who had said farewell in 1945. They meet again in 1970 for the funeral of Lt. Valentin Matveev. Their past, ruled by strict moral values and a clear idea of life's meaning, stands apart from the modern world that surrounds them now and which they despise. The entropy and degradation of values during the Stagnation era even goes so far as to trigger the desire for a return to the heroic past. A more popularized version of wartime was *Two Comrades Served* (Sluzhili dva tovarishcha, dir. Yevgeni Karelin, Mosfilm 1968), set in the Civil War, which used the devices of the adventure genre, with chases and traps. Two soldiers, the student Andrei Nekrasov (Yankovsky) and the mechanic Ivan Kariakin (Bykov) – representing intellectual and working class – are dispatched with a camera (seized from the enemy) to film the victory of the Reds. They fail miserably in their mission and almost perish in the exercise. As Denise Youngblood has observed, this is one of the few films dealing with the Civil War to have passed censorship in this period.[15]

A different outlook on war was presented in films of the late 1970s, such as Larisa Shepitko's *Ascent* (Voskhozhdenie, Mosfilm 1976), which is filmed in black-and-white and creates, through numerous Christian references, a parable of Jesus and Judas. The partisans Sotnikov and Rybak hide with a peasant woman during the war. Sotnikov (played by the Moscow Arts Theatre actor Boris Plotnikov, b. 1949) is ill and weak, but he gives himself up rather than betray his comrades: a true Christ-figure, he hangs on the gallows where Rybak has to perform the role of the henchman. Rybak (Vladimir Gostiukhin, b. 1946) is strong and mean, commits treason, and is caught and forced to collaborate with the Nazis. The film explores the moral choice of self-sacrifice or selfishness in a situation that ultimately beholds death for both.

In an attempt to support the filmmaker Alexei Gherman after the ban on *Trial on the Road*, the eminent writer Konstantin Simonov (1915–79) offered his script for *Twenty Days Without War* (Dvadtsat' dnei bez voiny, Lenfilm 1976), about the war journalist Lopatin (played by the clown Yuri Nikulin), who returns from Stalingrad to a film location in Tashkent where a film is being made about his war diaries. The difference between the real events and the way they appear in artistic images becomes a central issue for Gherman: the individual's recollection is elevated to form a part of truth and history. On the train Lopatin meets the pilot Stroganov, who tells him of his wife's infidelity, echoing the betrayal of Lopatin's wife, Ksenia. His narrative appears dull and undramatic through the exclusion of Lopatin's response. Lopatin visits Ksenia and her new husband, a theatre manager; at the theatre the actors turn to Lopatin in their search for dramatic accuracy for their play – a theme that also resonated in *Ivan Lapshin*. Lopatin realizes the difference between memory and its artistic representation, but also between a soldier and a non-combatant: he returns to war after a short affair with Nina (Liudmila Gurchenko of the comedy *Carnival Night*), the wardrobe manager at the theatre. The film explores the relationship between truth and memory. People make up stories of

Figure 5.6 Shepitko's *Ascent*.

heroic exploits, of reasons for husbands not writing from the front, of betrayal, yet reality is far removed from its perception by the affected participant. Reality and fiction cross when a play about the war is rehearsed while the real recruits are departing for the front. Gherman's camera again captures details and uses slow motion, while often side-tracking like the human eye, or not looking on events or characters, but peering sideways. This unfocused camerawork, later combined with soundtracks that emphasized background sounds more than the spoken word, turn Gherman's films into a demanding viewing experience.

Nikita Mikhalkov's Films, 1974–79

The 1970s also saw the rise to prominence of the director Nikita Mikhalkov (b. 1945), who had appeared as an actor before making his debut in filmmaking. His career is a controversial one, largely because of his family background: his father is Sergei Mikhalkov, a popular writer and the lyricist of the national anthem, who was highly regarded within the system. Mikhalkov's debut is an ideologically sound but stylistically innovative film that adapts successfully the genre of the western to a story about the Revolution. *At Home Among Strangers, A Stranger at Home* (Svoi sredi chukhikh, chuzhoi sredi svoikh, Mosfilm 1974) is set during the Civil War and combines the popular genre of the adventure film with elements of a detective thriller and the chases on horseback of a western. Yegor Shilov (played by the blond and blue-eyed Yuri Bogatyrev, 1947–89) accompanies a train with gold to the capital, where money is needed to purchase grain from abroad for the starving population. The train is robbed and Yegor takes it upon himself to retrieve the gold in a solitary battle against bandits and deserters. The spirit of collective work for the Revolution symbolized in the flashbacks to a happy past when he and his comrades were playing and fooling around in the fields, gives him strength and determination. Their camaraderie and trust in each other has remained unchanged, but the duties are grim and allow no space or time for distraction as shown in the black-and-white scenes. The music, a song about dreams ('The Ballad of the Ship', about generations dreaming of building a ship) underpins the theme of the hard work required to turn dreams into reality. Shilov proves to his comrades that he can be trusted and they are united at the end of the film in the same field. The film establishes the personal motivation for political expediency as a crucial element for political success, mixing personal values with the responsibility for, and duty to, the country.

The ideals of the Revolution also informed Mikhalkov's second film, *Slave of Love* (Raba liubvi, Mosfilm 1975), set in 1918, when many supporters of the Whites and former members of the bourgeoisie had moved to Southern Russia, where the fighting between Reds and Whites took place on several fronts. In 1974 Mosfilm had halted the production of the film *Unexpected Joys* (Nechaiannye radosti) because its director, Rustam Khamdamov, had departed from the script. Most of the film had been shot but not edited, and Mikhalkov was invited to peruse the footage and the script with a view to making his own film under the umbrella of the existing project. Mikhalkov rewrote the script with Alexander Adabashian and started a new film.

Slave of Love opens with a pianist accompanying the screening of a silent film entitled 'Slave of Love', starring Olga Voznesenskaya (Yelena Solovei, b. 1947, an actress who had been cast in Khamdamov's film). The film (within the film) shows a blind noblewoman (the actress Olga) playing a violin in a park, while her husband flirts with a young servant girl on the adjacent bench and tries to seduce her. The screening is interrupted by the intrusion of the Whites, led by Captain Fedotov. A man is arrested and led out of the auditorium, although he asserts that this is all a mix-up. He is beaten up and smashed into a window containing a poster of Voznesenskaya advertising her film. The frivolity of cinema is contrasted with the harsh reality of life. The theme of film and reality is extended to the juxtaposition of private and public life. A bourgeois lifestyle is portrayed on film and the film crew creates a domestic and bourgeois atmosphere in the studio. This is juxtaposed with the reality shown on documentary footage, the intrusion of the army into the screening and into the making of the film, which gradually forces the film crew out of their 'home' and removes fiction to be replaced with real life, namely the takeover of the studio by the Bolsheviks. Against this background develops Olga's fascination with the cameraman Viktor Pototsky (Rodion Nakhapetov, b. 1944, who had played the young Ulianov-Lenin in some of the 1960s films) and his underground activity as a Bolshevik, which seems to give her a new meaning in life – a life that fails to grasp the reality of political change other than through fiction. When Viktor is shot, both fiction and the fictionalized reality of a love story collapse. Mikhalkov's film offered a fine portrayal of the end of an era and established his talent in recreating the atmosphere of those 'lost times' that would be evident in his adaptations of the classics and culminate in his Oscar-winning film, *Burnt by the Sun*.

In the 1970s, Mikhalkov excelled with the adaptation of *An Unfinished Piece for a Mechanical Piano* (Neokonchennaia p'esa dlia mekhanicheskogo pianino, Mosfilm 1976), based on a little-known play by Anton Chekhov, written between 1878 and 1883 and commonly known as *Platonov* (also as *Fatherlessness* [Bezottsovshchina], published posthumously), which contains many themes of his later major plays while rather unwieldy in its dramatic form. Like Chekhov's later plays, it raises issues of a passing social order and the advent of a new period in history. Mikhalkov contrasts the old with the new order, and against this backdrop develops the meeting of Sofia (Solovei) and Platonov (Moscow Art Theatre actor Alexander Kaliagin, b. 1942), old lovers who are now both married to other partners. Sofia remembers Platonov, but fails to recognize him. They have not met since he was a student with aspirations and ambitions, which have vanished into thin air: he has become a schoolteacher without ever having graduated. Platonov introduces Sofia to his wife, Sashenka, a naive and kind woman and mother, who lacks Sofia's grace and sophistication. In an attempt to overcome his sense of inadequacy, Platonov plays the fool and enacts a comedy without people realizing this: they are first serious, then they laugh when Platonov leads them out of the game. His and other games are a mere cover for the essential loneliness and isolation of every single one of the group. Mikhalkov structured the film as a mixture of carnivalesque interludes and serious dialogue. The film took the Grand Prix at the San Sebastian Film Festival in 1977.

Mikhalkov's adaptation of the classical novel *Oblomov* (1859) by Ivan Goncharov (1812–91) became a classic in Soviet film history. The novel and film explored the lifestyle of Ilya Ilyich Oblomov, a man of middle age who is incapable of any action. He spends his time on a couch in his St Petersburg flat and lives off the income from his rundown estate, Oblomovka. His inactivity, referred to as 'Oblomovitis', diagnosed the illness that affected Russian landowners in general and of which Oblomov is an exaggerated representative. Oblomov is juxtaposed with his active and energetic friend Stolz, of German extraction, reflecting the debate between Westernizers and Slavophiles in nineteenth-century Russia.

In *A Few Days from the Life of I. I. Oblomov* (Neskol'ko dnei iz zhizni I. I. Oblomova, Mosfilm 1979) Mikhalkov cast for the role of Oblomov the audience's favourite, Oleg Tabakov (b. 1935). Oblomov is at home with his manservant Zakhar, beautifully and comically interpreted by the great actor Andrei Popov (1918–83). He is lethargic until his childhood friend Stolz (Bogatyrev) arrives and makes him pay visits, including one to Olga Ilyinskaya (Solovei). Oblomov is fascinated by Olga and agrees to spend the summer in the countryside to be close to Olga, who confesses her love to him, prompting him to leave as he is afraid of losing the comfort of habit. Oblomov marries the widow Pshenitsyna, has a son with her and dies of a weak heart, a result of obesity and lack of exercise – a part that is omitted from the film, which turns instead to the stifled family life of Stolz and Olga, who have adopted Oblomov's son, Ilyusha. Mikhalkov condemns Stolz for living a life of pretence: his activity seems to have been short-lived and he too has become lethargic and incapable of enjoying life. Oblomov never pretended to be anything other than he was: by casting a likeable and loved actor in the part of Oblomov, the viewers' sympathy lay with him.

In a series of flashbacks, Mikhalkov brings back the childhood of both protagonists to explain their character, dwelling on the responsibility of parents and society for the education of their offspring. At the end of the film the camera pans over the vast space of a Russian valley as the boy Ilyusha runs across the fields towards a river to the musical accompaniment of Rakhmaninov's *Vespers*. The green fields and woods, with a river quietly flowing through a valley, encompass Mikhalkov's favourite image that captures his ultimate view of Mother Russia, also evident in the Italian-Russian co-production of *Dark Eyes* (Oci ciornie, 1987).

Children's Films and Cartoons, 1974–79

The child and adolescent had moved into the centre of attention during the cinema of the Thaw, offering a new perspective on life: now the younger generation is tragically caught up in the Stagnation. The themes of aggression, delinquency and juvenile crime emerge in this period, showing the alienation of the younger generation from reality and their estrangement from family and society.

One of the early films on adolescence in the Stagnation era was Sergei Soloviev's *A Hundred Days After Childhood* (Sto dnei posle detstva, Mosfilm 1974), which explored the role of childhood memories of young people spending their summer in a camp where they experience their first romantic feelings for each other, with the normal complications of young love. The film consisted of a series of episodes, and the non-linearity indicated a fragmentary structure, precluding development, that would mark Soloviev's later work in the 1980s and 1990s. A similar structure of a flashback is employed in Nikolai Gubenko's *Orphans* (Podranki, Mosfilm 1976), which consists of the reminiscences of the 37-year-old Alexei Bertenev (the Lithuanian actor Juosas Budraitis, b. 1940) about his childhood and his attempt to reconstitute his real family and find his brothers. Gubenko himself had grown up in an orphanage and adopts here a structure composed of a series of flashbacks to the period before and after the war, to Bertenev's family and his life in an orphanage. Bertenev is first shown in the present, then in a record office where he learns that two of his brothers are still alive: Sergei is in prison and Denis is an architect. He visits Denis and recalls him as a child. Denis has grown up in a protected and stable family; later he has become a successful architect protective of his own son. Flashbacks show Bertenev in the orphanage, looked after by caring teachers; with his uncle and aunt; and with his sister who died after the war. Yet central to the film is the revelation of the harrowing impact of war on children's lives. One boy observes the German POWs in a nearby camp; his parents have been killed by the Germans. He makes a bomb and tries to take revenge, but blows himself up in an accident. War, deprivation and the loss of a home have left children with deep scars. *Orphans* is a first indication that not everyone had a happy Soviet childhood.

Dinara Asanova (1942–85) explored further the problems of adolescents and made an important contribution to films about young adults with *Woodpeckers Don't Get Headaches* (Ne bolit u diatla golova, Lenfilm 1974), about an adolescent boy and girl. *The Restricted Key* (Kliuch bez prava peredachi, Lenfilm 1976) was shot in a real school with model teachers (played by the professional actors Lidia Fedoseeva and Alexei Petrenko) who help the emotional development of the children. Her film *Dear, Dearest, Beloved, My Only One* (Milyi, dorogoi, liubimyi, edinstvennyi, Lenfilm 1984) is about a girl with a baby who jumps into somebody's car and asks to be taken away, claiming that she has been thrown out by her husband. It transpires that she has stolen the baby to blackmail her boyfriend, a rich suitor, because she is obsessed with having a family – which she has never had. *Tough Kids* (Patsany, Lenfilm 1983) was scripted by Yuri Klepikov (b. 1935) and set in a sports camp for young offenders led by the sportsman Pasha (Valeri Priemykhov, 1943–2000), who trusts them and treats them as equals. However, they let him down when they embark on a rampage, even though they show remorse later. The image of the model teacher and the reliance on school and education is indicative of the shift of responsibility for moral education from parents on to role models outside the family, a theme also emphasized in cartoons of the period.

Cartoons were produced by the studio Soyuzmultfilm, established in 1936, and had experienced great popularity in the 1950s when the first drawn animation films for children were released, largely based on Russian and Soviet fairy tales. In the 1960s, animators began to devise their own scripts and methods, engaging more in experimentation and developing puppet animation. Cartoons became increasingly concerned with the child's isolation in the modern world. Two major cartoon heroes of the Stagnation era were the drawn figure of Uncle Fedor and the puppet Cheburashka. The interest in puppets had been revived with Sergei Obraztsov (1901–92) and his puppet theatre in Moscow. Roman Kachanov (1921–93) and his designer Leonid Shvartsman created Cheburashka, who would soon become the emblem of the studio Soyuzmultfilm. Kachanov's films were based on Eduard Uspensky's story 'Crocodile Gena and his Friends', which he turned into four cartoons.

Cheburashka is a yellow-brown fluffy creature with large ears and rolling eyes, a mixture between a teddy bear and an orange. Just like the child isolated from the adult world of the Stagnation, Cheburashka does not belong anywhere, like any abandoned toy or a stray dog, and therefore immediately appeals to children by arousing sympathy and compassion. In the first cartoon, *Crocodile Gena* (Krokodil Gena, 1969), Cheburashka is discovered in a box of imported oranges and taken to the zoo, where she can neither be classified nor accommodated. Cheburashka becomes a window display in a toyshop, thus fulfilling her task as a Soviet citizen: to work. Cheburashka befriends the lonely crocodile Gena. Through joint efforts, Gena and Cheburashka build a home for all the homeless animals – making their contribution to the collective. In *Cheburashka* (1971), Cheburashka is not accepted into the pioneer organization: an alien has no place in society, but through hard work and determination she is accepted and becomes a pioneer. In *Cheburashka Goes to School* (Cheburashka idet v shkolu 1983), Cheburashka finds the school closed for reconstruction while the builders are playing cards. Exposing this fault in Soviet management, Cheburashka makes them finish the job so she can go to school. In every cartoon, Gena and Cheburashka expose some inefficiency of the Soviet system: they are the good citizens, who are ultimately rewarded not with a prize, but with the permission to become part of society. In this sense, the cartoons fulfil an educational function, whilst they also expose the essential loneliness of Cheburashka, whose name does not even feature in the encyclopedia (and whose gender remains undetermined).

Uspensky's stories about the village of Prostokvashino were turned into drawn cartoons by Vladimir Popov: *Three from Prostokvashino* (Troe iz Prostokvashino, 1978), *Holidays in Prostokvashino* (Kanikuly v Prostokvashino, 1980), and *Winter in Prostokvashino* (Zima v Prostokvashino, 1984). A boy with the nickname 'Uncle Fedor' adopts the stray cat Matroskin. In his attempt to find a playmate, Fedor runs not against the Soviet system, as the alien Cheburashka, but against his parents. Therefore Fedor and Matroskin leave the cramped city apartment for the village of Prostokvashino, where they join the dog Sharik and lead an alternative life in the countryside. The three form a perfect family, an alternative to Fedor's real parents, who fail to understand him, but whose authority is conventionally reinstated at the end of each series. The child guides the parents, who should listen to the children, while children are led to believe that they can fix the social unhappiness of the older generation.

Figure 5.7 Cheburashka.

This theme of isolation also informed the cartoons of other animators, including Fedor Khitruk's award-winning *Island* (Ostrov, 1974), about a man stranded on a desert island, and Yuri Norshtein, whose famous *Tale of Tales* (Skazka skazok, 1979) is a metaphor for isolation, and is composed of memories about a wartime childhood. His *The Hedgehog in the Fog* (Ezhik v tumane, 1975) is a slow-moving poetic tale of a hedgehog and bear, who meet every evening to gaze at the stars, until the hedgehog is lost in dense fog. After a night of worry and fear, the hedgehog prefers the habitual star-gazing to the scary experience of the new world, thus creating a parable for man's withdrawal from reality during the 1970s.

Maybe the most powerful films about the growing aggression caused by this sense of alienation and neglect is Rolan Bykov's *The Scarecrow* (Chuchelo, Mosfilm 1983). If the Thaw had diagnosed the problem and found a remedy, the films in the Stagnation era diagnosed the problem as incurable. *The Scarecrow* addresses the aggressive behaviour of the younger generation. The 12-year-old Lena Bessoltseva, played by pop star Alla Pugacheva's daughter Kristina Orbakaite, lives with her grandfather Nikolai Nikolaevich (the charming clown Yuri Nikulin) in a provincial town. At school, she is subjected to psychological terror in her class; only Dima Somov defends her. When the class skips a lesson to go to the movies, Dima is caught, but refuses to betray his fellow pupils, not even when another boy is suspected of instigating the truancy. Lena confesses to something she has not done, and is persecuted by the children. She is a martyr, taking the blame for others. Her suffering is quietly watched by adults, including a group of tourists in town. Bykov frequently uses dark spaces as locations to underline the gloom and bleakness of Lena's situation. The climax of her persecution lies in a scene where her peers burn Lena's effigy, in the shape of a scarecrow, in the ruins of a church. Only when Lena leaves the town does the class begin to feel remorse. The issue of fitting in with modern life, as opposed to adhering to moral values of the past, is addressed: Pugacheva's song 'Old Clocks' (*Starinnye chasy*) tells of the fact that time cannot be turned back, and that any action should be considered in terms of its consequences. Bykov's film warns of the condemnation of the weak and passive members of society, but also of the potential for aggression and indifference inherent in modern society. Stagnation films viewed the younger generation as isolated and therefore driven to violence and aggression, a theme that would move to the forefront of filmmakers' attention in glasnost cinema.

Blockbusters – Soviet Style, 1979–82

The major blockbuster of the era (attracting a record number of 87 million spectators) was the adventure movie *Pirates of the Twentieth Century* (Piraty XX veka, Gorky Studio 1980), directed by the television director Boris Durov and scripted by Stanislav Govorukhin. The film deals with the conspiracy of a gang of opium smugglers (the enemy) who seize a Soviet boat and – following the pattern of the fairy tale – the crew (the collective hero) overpower the pirates. The good Soviet sailors triumph over illegal trade and crime. The exotic setting on a boat and a remote island greatly assisted the suspense factor, offering a variation within the genre convention.

Box office hits largely drew on unusual genres for Soviet cinema's scope: the adventure film, the spy thriller and disaster movie. These films scored the highest audience numbers of the 1970s, giving some indication of the discrepancy between public taste and festival films, but also between state-commissioned films of grand production budgets and genre choices. This disparity would increase after the collapse of the industry in 1991. It is curious to note that the Mexican melodrama *Yesenia* (1970, dir. Wagner; Soviet release 1975) had 92 million viewers with its story of a gypsy woman who abducts a baby girl and is discovered when a suitor recognizes the medallion of the girl as that of a rich landowner's daughter.[16] The film shows the audience's craving for melodrama, denied to them by the state's production agenda, and it also explains the success of Menshov's melodrama *Moscow*.

Alov and Naumov's *Tehran 43* (*Tegeran-43*, Russia, Switzerland and France; Mosfilm 1981) was a spy thriller starring Alain Delon as Inspector Roche and Curd Jürgens as Maître Legrain. Set in 1943, it explored the plot of a Nazi terrorist act set to prevent the Tehran meeting of Stalin with the British and American forces. The plot is, of course, uncovered by Soviet intelligence. Alexander Mitta's *The Crew* (Ekipazh, Mosfilm 1980) was the first Soviet disaster movie, and it built the narrative in a linear manner, rather than singling out individual fates when disaster has struck. Mitta first introduces the crew at length, with their personal problems of divorce and unrequited love, before dealing with the disaster: the crew flies to a city hit by an earthquake to deliver aid, but as they take off from the damaged runway they realize that the aircraft has a technical fault.

Vladimir Menshov's *Moscow Does Not Believe in Tears* (Moskva slezam ne verit, Mosfilm 1979) was one of the last Soviet blockbusters, with 85 million viewers. Its story stretches over twenty years, from the 1950s to the 1970s. In good

Figure 5.8 Menshov's *Moscow Does Not Believe in Tears*: Katia with her newborn baby, Alexandra.

socialist style, the heroine Katia (played by Menshov's wife Vera Alentova, b. 1942) is rewarded with personal happiness only after she has made her contribution to social progress. The film combines romance and realism and impresses with the authentic re-creation of the lifestyle of the 1950s. The music of the bards Yuri Levitansky (1922–96) and Yuri Vizbor (1934–84) befits Alentova's generation, while her daughter Sasha listens to pop music on her headphones. The atmosphere of 1958 is precisely captured with the French film season, with a couple being told off for embracing in public and with the Mayakovsky Square poetry readings of Voznesensky as well as the importance of social standing and of foreign travel. Katia's suitor, Rudik (later Rodion), will not marry Katia because she is of a lower social class. His unshaken belief in the future of television is ridiculed: he calls it the 'art of tomorrow' that will change life and survive all art forms, and still says the same thing twenty years later. Katia's reward with the dream husband is at the expense of independence: she has to surrender, at least at home, to being subordinate to her man.

The film's popularity is largely due to the 'feelgood factor', which effectively shows that man can master his fate even in the most adverse circumstances. *Moscow* shows the aspiration of three girls from the provinces: Katia, who sacrifices personal happiness for the sake of social good and progress, and is rewarded with the dream man of the 1950s – Alexei Batalov's Gosha. Tonia (Raisa Riazanova, b. 1944) achieves personal happiness in a family – a safe haven in suburban Moscow, away from the centre. Liuda (Irina Muravieva, b. 1949) achieves personal happiness and advancement of social status through other men and suffers a failed marriage to a drunkard sportsman. The happy ending reclaims patriarchal rule and surrenders emancipation in this modern Cinderella story.

As Soviet cinema entered the post-Brezhnev era, it had recovered from the stalemate of the early 1970s and proven that the USSR could produce popular entertainment as well as *auteur* cinema. Slowly and steadily, a new generation of filmmakers began to emerge, who would benefit from Gorbachev's policies.

–6–

Glasnost and Before (1983–92)

Old Woman: Is this the road to the church?
Keti: This is Varlam Street. It doesn't lead to a church.
Old Woman: Then what good is it, if it doesn't lead to a church?

Repentance[1]

There's nothing worth living for, dying for.

Is it Easy to be Young?

This chapter explores one of the most vibrant periods of Soviet cinema, a time when the arts were used to promote a new agenda that signalled major reforms of a stale system and a process of lifting bans and prohibitions that made it especially appealing to Western observers. In an attempt to support Gorbachev's reforms, much of the art released and created during the period was met with great enthusiasm in the European media, with many countries organizing special events, such as 'Soviet Spring' on Channel Four, but also theatre festival and art exhibitions. Many of the films of the period derived their significance from the historical and political context, and not artistic merit alone. Therefore this chapter adopts a thematic approach that is better suited for this short period, to cover those areas that offered an innovative perspective.

The Last Years of the USSR

In the first half of the 1980s, the sense of the stagnation of the previous decade still characterized the atmosphere in Soviet culture, but politically the period witnessed a rapid succession of Soviet leaders after the death of Leonid Brezhnev in 1982. Yuri Andropov (1914–84) was in office for a little more than a year, introducing new measures against corruption. He was succeeded by Konstantin Chernenko (1911–85), who was in office for less than a year, until March 1985, and indicated his hardline course with several restrictions, such as limited university access, to increase the workforce; compulsory Russian language in the republics; and the potentially disastrous project of rerouting some Siberian rivers to Central Asia to irrigate the desert. The Afghan war continued, while the rise of the Solidarnosz movement under Lech Wałęsa in Poland in the early 1980s and the subsequent martial law in 1981 heightened further the atmosphere of oppression.

Mikhail Gorbachev (b. 1931) was elected as General Secretary of the Communist Party on 11 March 1985, and it was not until his accession to power that any real change could be noticed in the cultural sector. Gorbachev convened the first plenary session of the Central Committee in April 1985, explaining his programme of economic reforms through a decentralization of management in order to accelerate productivity (*uskorenie*). At the same time he began to implement changes in the Central Committee to the extent that, by the January 1987 plenum, over half of the Central Committee members were newly elected. During the Twenty-Seventh Party Congress in March 1986, Gorbachev further outlined his programme of glasnost (openness) and perestroika (reorganization).

Gorbachev replaced most of the hardliners in key positions in the cultural sector with more liberal officials: Vasili Zakharov was appointed Minister of Culture, succeeding Petr Demichev; in 1988 he was replaced by the actor and filmmaker Nikolai Gubenko. Boris Yeltsin took over the Moscow City Committee from Viktor Grishin; in the Central Committee the liberals Yegor Ligachev became Secretary for Ideology and Alexander Yakovlev took over the Agitprop Department. Following Khrushchev's pattern of Kremlin meetings with the intelligentsia,[2] Gorbachev invited the 'Creative Intelligentsia' to a meeting on 3 December 1986, when he encouraged a process of liberalization in the arts. A convinced communist, Gorbachev assumed he could win over the masses through the arts.

An incident of enormous scale exposed the Soviet Union's inefficiency shortly after the first signals for reforming socialism had been sent out. The explosion at the fourth reactor of the Chernobyl nuclear power station in the early hours of 26 April 1986 was first noted in a news report on 28 April in Sweden, where high radioactivity had been measured and traced back to the Ukraine. The Soviet news programme *Vremia* merely reported that an accident had occurred at Chernobyl, but that things were under control. With hindsight, it is likely that the information flow within the power structures was at fault for the 'disinformation' of the public. The Ukraine tried to conceal from Moscow the scale of the accident in the first instance, and once the centre had realized the full implications, it tried to play down the incident in order to avoid panic. Chernobyl is regarded as a watershed in Soviet news coverage, because the way in which information was delayed during the incident gave Gorbachev a lever to force the media to adopt a different approach. The media were quick to respond to this challenge. By exposing the rotten state of the Soviet system, they contributed to a much more rapid disclosure of the need for reform than Gorbachev had envisaged. Television programmes exposing areas of corruption, social degradation and collapse mushroomed after 1986.

In international terms, Gorbachev was highly regarded and elected 'Man of the Year' for *Time* magazine in 1987. At home he began to fight corruption and encouraged criticism of mismanagement, but also exposure of problems, which were so numerous that the state could hardly cope. In 1988 a law allowed the formation of cooperatives, and joint ventures and co-productions with Western countries were encouraged.

From 1987 onwards, cultural organizations were permitted budget freedom (*khozraschet*); professional artistic unions were transformed through the election of a new leadership, following the ground-breaking route of the Filmmakers' Union. Rock concerts were allowed and became widespread. Gradually, literature that had previously been published only in the West appeared in Soviet journals:[3] in 1989 the leading liberal literary journal *Novy mir* finally published Solzhenitsyn's *Gulag Archipelago* (1958–67). In the visual arts, the Seventeenth Youth Exhibition in 1986 opened a new era for the public showing of non-realist art. In July 1988 the first auction took place, organized by Sotheby's, which sold some works of the Soviet avant-garde, but also numerous conceptualist and sots-art paintings of the 1970s and 1980s. Grisha Bruskin became the best seller of the auction, where his *Fundamental Lexicon* fetched ten times over the asking price and sold for £220,000. In 1987, the physicist and dissident Andrei Sakharov was allowed to return to Moscow after seven years under house arrest and internal exile in Gorky (now Nizhny Novgorod).

In May 1987, the German Matthias Rust landed his Cessna plane on Red Square, having crossed over into Soviet airspace unnoticed by Soviet border control, exposing literally another 'hole' in the system. When Sergei Soloviev opened the Moscow International Film Festival in the Hotel Rossiya a few weeks later, he apologized to the foreign guests for having had to make the detour via Sheremetievo II (the international, northern airport) rather than landing right on the new runway of 'Sheremetievo III', as Rust had done: Red Square. The humour contained in that remark says a lot about the 'openness' that had become possible in official speeches.

By 1989, the liberalization was clearly going farther and faster than Gorbachev had anticipated. In the autumn of 1989 citizens of the GDR and Czechoslovakia sought refuge in Western embassies in Prague and Budapest, demanding political asylum. On 9 November 1989 the Berlin Wall 'fell' when people crossed the border at several checkpoints between East and West Berlin: Germany was reunited. The Velvet Revolution in Czechoslovakia brought in a democratic government and the former dissident Vaclav Havel became president.

On 12 June 1991 Boris Yeltsin was elected President of the Russian Federation – the first president of one of the constituent Soviet republics to be elected by the people. On 19 August 1991 Prime Minister Vladimir Pavlov, Defence Minister Dmitri Yazov, Minister of the Interior Boris Pugo, KGB head Vladimir Kriuchkov, and Vice-President Gennadi Yanaev formed a State Emergency Committee, the GKChP (*Gosudarstvennyi komitet po chrezvychainomu polozheniiu*). They declared that Gorbachev, who was on holiday in Foros, Crimea, was in poor health and incapable of running the country's affairs. They wanted to preserve the Soviet Union and stop the break-up that was being negotiated between Gorbachev and other heads of Soviet republics under the Union Treaty due to be signed on 20 August. At the White House – symbol of the opposition to the coup plotters – Yeltsin mounted his resistance as he stood on a tank, surrounded by the rallying crowds. The coup failed when the army refused to storm the White House. The Communist Party was abolished and on 25 December 1991 Gorbachev resigned as president of the USSR. By the end of 1991 most Soviet republics had declared independence and the USSR was disbanded. Yeltsin remained President of the Russian Federation, formerly a constituent republic of the Soviet Union and now a state in its own right. These political events changed the shape of Russia and of Europe, and they have had an enormous impact not only on the political division of the world, but also on culture and cinema.

Perestroika in the Film Industry

Lev Kulidzhanov had been secretary of the Filmmakers' Union (FU)[4] since its foundation in 1965. Since 1972 Yermash had overseen Goskino. It was time for change: Alexander Kamshalov replaced Yermash at Goskino in 1986, and the Fifth Congress of the FU, held from 13–15 May 1986 in the Kremlin, elected the filmmaker Elem Klimov, who was nominated by Alexander Yakovlev from the Central Committee, as secretary. The change at the top of the FU was thus suggested from above, just like Gorbachev's reforms in the cultural sector. Moreover, the entire secretariat was replaced, and substantially enlarged, along Gorbachev's democratic principles for a larger base.[5] Nikita Mikhalkov voiced concern about the election of a secretary like Klimov and pleaded for support of those filmmakers who had served the old system – like himself and Bondarchuk – but neither of them was elected.[6] A list of nineteen points was drawn up at the Fifth Congress, outlining the areas that required change, most urgently decentralization and a review of the bureaucracy involved in film production in connection with Goskino.[7] A Conflict Commission was established under the critic Andrei Plakhov and put in charge of reviewing banned, shelved and blocked films. Within a year the commission had 'unshelved' some 100 films and found at Gosfilmofond another 250 films that had never been released.

At Goskino there were structural changes too: Sovinfilm was relinquished in 1989 when co-production was allowed at studio level. Studios were also equipped with the right to draw up schedules and plans without Goskino's interference. In 1988 the new Cinema Centre (Kinotsentr) opened, with two cinemas, offices and the Museum of Cinema.

In parallel to the decentralization in the geopolitical arena, a plenary session of the Filmmakers' Union decided to devolve power and create unions at republican level in 1988. The constituent congress of the Russian Federation's Filmmakers' Union was held in 1990 and Igor Maslennikov was elected chairman, joined by co-chairman Sergei Soloviev. Only at this moment was the requirement of the Socialist Realist method removed from the FU's statutes.

At the Sixth Congress of the Soviet Filmmakers' Union in 1990, the membership agreed to reorganize the union as a confederation of the republican unions, and the chairman for overseeing this task was the Tajik filmmaker Dovlat Khudonazarov. As one producer commented: 'This congress was no less revolutionary than the previous one. Think about it, they elected a Tadzhik as president, and as vice-presidents, a woman and a capitalist.'[8] Thus, the FU had actually reorganized itself a year before the Soviet Union would do so on similar terms.

Within the organizations that were supervised by Goskino there was further change: Alexander Novikov was elected head of the Film Institute (VGIK). In 1989 the research institute VNIIK launched the scholarly journal *Kinovedcheskie zapiski* (Film Scholars' Notes) under its new director, the scriptwriter Ales Adamovich.

Vladimir Dostal was put in charge of the Mosfilm studio in 1987 and remained in this post until 1998. In May 1990, Mosfilm for the first time exhibited and offered its films at the Cannes market, independent of Sovexportfilm, which later claimed the right to the Mosfilm archive, but was refused. Following the introduction in 1987 of *khozraschet* and the 1988 Law on Cooperatives, the film studios were encouraged to run independent and autonomous budgets. The Association of Independent Cinema, headed by Andrei Razumovsky (Fora Film) was formed in 1990 and registered fifty-five production cooperatives, including the studios of Nikita Mikhalkov, Vasili Pichul and Sergei Soloviev.

Problems appeared on the horizon, especially with distribution: so-called KVOs (*kino-video-ob"edinenie*) were established to decentralize the distribution network. Cinemas could choose the films they wanted to screen without, however, knowing audience taste; this led on the one hand to audience polls and surveys to determine habits, and on the other to the formation in 1988 of internal film markets to sell films to cinemas. Another blow to the cinema distribution network came through the establishment of Videofilm in 1990, which allowed rampant video piracy, especially of foreign films, and this could not be hindered since the USSR had not signed the Berne Convention. Moreover, foreign films flooded the market and were much more in demand than Soviet films. This only in part had to do with the bleakness and incomprehensibility of Soviet films of the time, but more with the desire to see what had so long been forbidden fruit: American movies. Finally, another contributing factor to the demise of Soviet film was the fact that direct televised broadcasts of the Congresses of People's Deputies, with lively debates among deputies, gripped the population and scored high ratings.

The lack of experience in enabling the transition from a centralized system where production, distribution, supply and demand, sales and advertising were all handled by a single agency, to a system of independent production, distribution and sales, especially in a country with outdated technical equipment and cinemas in dire need of refurbishment and repair, would show its disastrous consequences in the 1990s, leading to a complete collapse of the infrastructure.

Looking at the films of the perestroika period is a double-edged task. On the one hand, most of these films, unshelved or new, were profoundly controversial, innovative, experimental and outstandingly daring – in the latter half of the 1980s. To the audience of the perestroika years, they were shocking in the themes – historical and contemporary – that they touched. They made sense within the context of the release of works that had not seen the light of day, whether paintings shown in the Sotheby auction, theatre productions that had been closed (a 1968 production was revived at the Taganka Theatre with the same actors – twenty years after it was banned), unshelved films, the release of albums by Vysotsky and of formerly underground rock music, or the publication of novels and historical documents, largely concerning the Stalin era. On the other hand, looking at some of these films today, they seem conventional in their choice of cinematic language, ordinary in the subject matter and its treatment, standard in terms of acting performances and acceptable in terms of directing – and often no more. Beyond the political and historical context not all of them pass the test of time.

The First Signs of Change, 1983–86

A new generation of filmmakers emerged towards the end of the Stagnation. Sergei Bodrov (b. 1948) made his first film, *Non-Professionals* (Neprofessionaly, Kazakhfilm 1985), in Kazakhstan. As many of his early films, it dealt with adolescents: a youth ensemble travels around and visits an old people's home, sharing its isolation with the old people. Karen Shakhnazarov (b. 1952) debuted with *Jazzmen* (My iz dzhaza, Mosfilm 1983), which explored the role of jazz music in the 1920s and thus reinstated its role in contemporary Soviet Russia, where it was banned as it was feared to cause 'uncontrollable' reactions. The forbidden fruit of rock music would play an important role in films in the perestroika years. The theme of the younger generation and music would become an important topic for glasnost films.

The emergence of Alexander Rogozhkin (b. 1950) as filmmaker also dates to this period. He made his debut with *For the Sake of a Few Lines* (*Radi neskol'kikh strochek*, Lenfilm 1985), which explores the fate of a military division during the Second World War when the truck with the typeset of the divisional newspaper is blown up. The typeface is scattered across the fields, and the soldiers retrieve it whilst under constant threat of attack. The realization of human loss comes to them abruptly when one of the soldiers is killed and they recognize the relative insignificance of the newspaper in the face of the war's atrocities. The individual's seemingly important task has suddenly become insignificant, echoing the loss of man's role in the history of his own country, a theme that would also characterize the glasnost films about history.

Vadim Abdrashitov (b. 1945) and scriptwriter Alexander Mindadze (b. 1949) began their collaboration in the late 1970s. In their metaphysical films they explore the 'awareness of a reality that transcends the illusory world of social conventions'.[9] *Speech for the Defence* (Slovo dlia zashchity, Mosfilm 1977) explores the court case of a girl whose inexperienced lawyer cannot defend her. In *Fox Hunt* (Okhota na lis, Mosfilm 1980) the worker Belov, who has been beaten up by two boys, visits one of them in prison, trying to establish a relationship with the convict where he could exercise forgiveness, while conducting himself in an arrogant and condescending manner. *The Train Has Stopped* (Ostanovilsia poezd, Mosfilm 1982) investigates the aftermath of a railway accident, where the investigator fails to establish responsibility as he faces a wall of lies that shields the unwillingness of people to change. All these films were imbedded in a real situation, involving crimes of some sort and pointing at the inability of the judicial system to solve the underlying problems of these 'crimes'. With *Parade of Planets* (Parad planet, Mosfilm 1984), Abdrashitov and Mindadze adopted a different style, indicating their experiment with surrealist images and fracturing the coherence of time and space. The film is an allegory of a journey into the self. Five men are called up for an army exercise, and are soon declared 'dead' in the exercise. Since they are not expected back home, they go to the village of Guskovo to kill time – and visit a city where only women live; later they swim in the river to an island, from whence they go to an old people's home where they confront the delusions of the old. They spend the night in the hay and observe a strange constellation of planets before returning home. The men, too old for the collective (the military), see their future selves as they become rejects of society. The phantom journey beyond the river makes transparent their utter isolation from society. Abdrashitov denies the spectator the possibility of differentiating between the real and the imaginary and undermines the stability of perception, thereby challenging the status quo. The films are therefore unsettling and challenging, and mark a clear departure from the visual and narrative conventions of Soviet cinema of the 1970s.

Konstantin Lopushansky, too, presented in his films an unsettling, apocalyptic vision, creating metaphors for a fading, disappearing social and global order. *Letters from a Dead Man* (Pis'ma mertvogo cheloveka, 1986) marked a new era in science fiction treatment, but also showed the culmination of the atmosphere of resignation that characterized the Stagnation era: apocalypse. The film is set in a post-nuclear world, where only the young and healthy are admitted to a bunker, where they have to shelter for thirty years. Professor Larsen (played by the popular actor and father figure, Rolan Bykov), a scientist who has won the Nobel Prize, leaves the shelter to find his wife Anna: she has been exposed to radiation and dies. A pastor who looks after orphaned children also perishes and entrusts the children to Larsen. Larsen believes that leading them into the bunker provides no solution: instead he builds a Christmas tree of metal scrap and paper to instil hope. He hides in a museum, taking some fragments of the old world along before leading the children into the unknown. The 'emigration' is not to another country, but to another world inside. Lopushansky's apocalypse may forecast the collapse of the old system, but it also

Figure 6.1 Lopushansky's *Letters from a Dead Man.*

foretells the collapse of moral value systems and the need to search for the self. Moreover, Lopushansky's apocalypse coincided with fears of nuclear disasters as seen in the haunting depiction in *The Day After* (dir. Nicholas Meyer, US 1983) and anticipated tragically the accident at Chernobyl in April 1986. He diagnosed the stagnation of a system that can only yield destruction, and indicated that hope lies only in moving on – in a rebirth, which the country was close to seeing in social and political terms.

Two films by established filmmakers signalled a novel take on the history of the Purges and the Second World War. In *My Friend Ivan Lapshin* (Moi drug Ivan Lapshin, Lenfilm 1984), Alexei Gherman Sr. adopts a documentary and authentic approach, filming a slice of life. He undermines the objectivity of perception by demonstrating that important aspects crystallize only with hindsight. This is echoed in the uneven camera movement, where the camera does not focus and does not always capture the main character within the frame, and where the dialogue is recorded without giving dominance to the speakers, so that it becomes increasingly difficult to understand the dialogue when the background noise sometimes drowns the spoken words. Thus, Gherman places the viewer in a situation where he knows and understands as little as the characters did at the time.

Figure 6.2 Gherman's *My Friend Ivan Lapshin.*

The narrator remembers his childhood based on what his father told him, whilst declaring his love for those who died fifty years ago. From the snow in a contemporary city the camera moves to the interior of an apartment where the narrator lived in his childhood, undertaking a journey into personal memory. The present is differentiated from the past by blue-green filters as opposed to the black-and-white film for the past.

Lapshin (played by Andrei Boltnev, 1946–95) is the head of the local police, who fights a gang of criminals. Life around the town is grim, with rampant theft, communal apartments, crime and prostitution. Lapshin is enamoured with the actress Natasha Adashova (acted by Muratova's discovery, the actress Nina Ruslanova) and allows her to meet a prostitute in prison so she can find an authentic key to her role as a prostitute in Pogodin's *The Aristocrats* (Aristokraty, 1935), which is due to open in the theatre: the play presents an idealized world where criminals can be reformed and prostitutes redeemed. Gherman finely explores the theme of authenticity: the artistic performance claims to be true to life, but nevertheless renders life not as it really is. In reality, crime abounds: Lapshin chases the criminal Soloviev, who escapes but whom he recaptures and shoots. He believes in the future as idealistically as the play presents a perfect society: 'We cleanse the soil, plant gardens, and will go for a walk in these orchards ourselves', has a Chekhovian resonance and echoes the belief in ideas by those people who would be strangled by the machinery they themselves helped build – alluding to the murder of Kirov, whose portrait is superseded with the effigy of Stalin on the tram with the brass band at the end of the film. Lapshin is a victim of such a belief in false ideals: the film is deliberately set at a moment in time (indicated by the portrait of Kirov at the beginning of the film, while the end of the film lingers on the portrait of Stalin) which was 'the last moment before the beginning of the great terror, a moment when it was still possible to nurture the illusion of a future, perfect world' and the film deals therefore 'not [with] the longing for the Stalin regime, rather it is nostalgia for a lost dream'.[10]

Larisa Shepitko's idea for a film about one of the many villages burnt down in Belorussia by the Germans during the war was realized by Elem Klimov with the film *Come and See* (Idi i smotri, Belarusfilm and Mosfilm, 1985). It is almost as though Klimov completed in the 1970s and 1980s the work begun by his wife – after her tragic death in a car crash en route to a film location – and then fell silent. Shot in colour, the film is based on a story by Ales Adamovich and set in 1943 near the Polish border. The teenage boy Flera (Alexei Kravchenko, b. 1969) is sent by his mother to hide with the partisans. He lingers in the woods and meets the young Glasha, and both are left behind as the partisans prepare for a German attack. As they stroll back to Flera's house, they find the entire village destroyed. Glasha, and with her the camera, catches a glimpse of bodies near a barn. Flera sets off with two other partisans across the fields; they find a cow, which is shot along with his two comrades. Flera is sheltered in the village of Perehody. When the Germans chase the villagers into a barn, Flera is allowed out through a window and escapes, watching the barn being set on fire. The partisans confront the Germans, and Flera can identify those responsible for the barn fire. He returns with the partisans to the woods. The film, with little dialogue and striking images of destruction and desolation, was a powerful visualization of the suffering that children had endured during the war. Against the violence and barbaric acts of the Germans, Flera's rifle fires only once: at an image of Hitler. Klimov's film portrays the pacifist and passive role of the teenage boy during the war, and thus reclaims the contribution of civilians and teenagers to the war effort.

Rewriting History, 1986–89

Once glasnost had showed the first effects on film production, the theme of the past was foregrounded again, this time going further in uncovering the truth about the Purges. Above all, new documentaries revealed the possibility of an open discussion of hitherto taboo topics. Documentaries on the Afghan War, on conflicts, disasters and ecological problems, appeared from 1987 onwards along with the open discussion of problems in the numerous new television programmes that appeared in the early days of glasnost, often with live studio guests or reports from remote areas, such as *Vzgliad* (View), *Dvenadtsatyi etazh* (Twelfth Floor) and *Prozhektor perestroika* (Projector of Perestroika).

Solovki Power (Vlast' Solovetskaia, 1988) by Marina Goldovskaya (b. 1941) was one such example of a courageous documentary, exploring the prison camp on the island of Solovki in the White Sea through documentary footage from a 1928 propaganda film that Goldovskaya had located in the archives. She combined this footage with interviews of survivors of the camp, including the academician Dmitri Likhachev, who had served a sentence there from 1928–32. The documentary filmmaker Semen Aranovich (1934–95) revealed footage of Anna Akhmatova's funeral and documents found in her files, in his documentary *Files on Anna Akhmatova* (Lichnoe delo Anny Akhmatovoi, 1989). In *I Served in Stalin's Bodyguard* (Ia sluzhil v okhrane tovarishcha Stalina, 1989), he used interviews with a man who remembers his time as Stalin's bodyguard to reveal the continued and unperturbed belief of the man that this service was his duty. Iosif Pasternak's *Black Square* (Chernyi kvadrat, 1988) dealt with unofficial painters and included footage of the Manege exhibition and the scandalous meeting with Khrushchev in 1962 (see Chapter 4). Thus, many documentaries addressed in the first instance the past, trying to unveil its 'hidden pages'.

However, the greatest impact in terms of lifting the veil of history was made by a Georgian film, made under Georgian Party chairman Eduard Shevardnadze's personal protection and commissioned by Georgian television – so that it was removed from Moscow's control. Tengiz Abuladze's (1924–94) *Repentance* (Pokaianie [Monanieba], Gruziafilm 1984, released 1986) became a cult film of the 1980s. It was the first feature film to address the Purges of the 1930s, even if it did so in a highly allegorical form. The film's poetic language and its complexity can partly be explained by the use of Aesopian language typical of authors treating 'forbidden' themes in the Brezhnev era, and by the school of Georgian filmmakers traditionally using a more symbolic film language.

Repentance is timeless, without any concrete, specific references to the 1930s. The location is also unspecified. The figure of Varlam Aravidze (Avtandil Makharadze, b. 1943) is a conglomerate of Chaplin, Mussolini, Hitler, Stalin and Beriya. The characters in the film extend over three generations: Aravidze (the father), Abel (the son), and Tornike (Abel's son) are set against two generations of the Baratelis: Keti's parents, Nino and Sandro, have died at the hand of Varlam Aravidze.

The film has a circular structure of unusual complexity. It begins with the 'reality' of the present: Keti is making cakes decorated with churches when she learns about Varlam Aravidze's death. As she stares at the picture in the paper, the camera captures in a subjective flash-forward what she sees in her mind's eye: she imagines Varlam Aravidze's funeral, her 'crime' – the exhumation of Aravidze's body, the reaction of the Aravidze family, her arrest, and her trial. Her true story and the motivation for her crime as revealed in the trial lead to a conflict between Abel and Tornike, which exposes Abel's double morality and eventually leads to Tornike's suicide. When Abel throws Varlam's body over the cliff, denying it eternal peace, the camera returns to Keti finishing the icing on the cake. The circle of the flash-forward is closed: there is neither change in the future nor an escape from the past, which is related in a flashback that forms a second closed circle (within the flash-forward). Yet none of this ever happened in reality: Varlam will rest in peace, and Tornike will not bear the responsibility for his family's guilt. Nobody repents in reality, and Keti does not take revenge in the reality in which she lives, where forgiveness reigns, but in her imagination. This essentially Christian message informs the reply of the old woman asking for the way: any road will lead to the church, any path will eventually lead to God, and He will pass the ultimate judgement. Structurally, Keti's imagined revenge falls within the first circle; here, she reveals the civic courage she lacks in reality. Yet Abuladze does not condemn Keti, who in her imagination also clearly sees the outcome of her revenge: she will be silenced. Her inactivity is criticized and legitimized at the same time: her action could deprive Varlam of his eternal rest, it could make the family suffer, but it would also commit Keti to a psychiatric clinic; it is legitimized on the religious level, where the judgement is left in God's hand. The film not only captures the resignation that doomed the Stagnation period, but also anticipates the reliance on religion when all other value systems fail.

The flashback into the past provides the clue for Keti's vision and her present situation, showing Keti at the age of eight, Varlam's interest in art and the friendship with the Baratelis, Sandro's arrest and Nino's torments, her final arrest and the separation from Keti. While Keti's flash-forward is highly subjective and creative,

Figure 6.3 Abuladze's *Repentance*: Keti and Tornike.

showing her as an active character, the flashback shows her and her parents as passive victims. Within the flashback, characters are only active in dreams and fables. Nino dreams that she and Sandro flee from Aravidze and hide by burying themselves in a ploughed field. Nature could save them, yet a peasant denounces them and Aravidze returns, triumphantly singing an aria in his open car. Nino's and Sandro's closeness to the soil is opposed to the artificiality of Varlam's aria. When Nino wakes up, Sandro tries to calm her with a fable about a hare who is running away; when asked why he is running, the hare says that the hunt for wolves is on, and although he is not a wolf, once caught he will have to prove the contrary. The fable, designed to show that there is no need to flee since there is no legal basis for an arrest, proves wrong: Sandro is arrested seconds later.

In the flashback the memory of the past is universal; it is part of the history everybody in court knows. The arrests, the queue for permission to send parcels, the line of women waiting for news, the search for messages on tree trunks brought back from labour camps – all form part of the collective memory of a nation and are recognized by Russian viewers: this is the past they share.

Varlam is worshipped like a god, therefore the Christian God cannot be tolerated next to him and churches must be destroyed. The church is misused for scientific purposes, but Sandro tries to save the building from destruction (a vague allusion to the destruction of the Church of Christ the Saviour). Sandro's death is paralleled with the death of Christ, by the coincidence of his death with the destruction of the church and his position of a crucified man. Christian morality is annihilated together with the individual defending it. At the present time, the church merely serves as an object for decoration on Keti's cakes.

Abuladze's film makes a worrying statement about the system, too: the guards are the same mediaeval knights both in the past (when Keti is a child) and in her visionary present actions: the system has not changed. If the system can be blamed, the individual carries no responsibility. Abel's explanation to Tornike that 'Varlam Aravidze has done nothing wrong, but such were the times' must be seen as a statement that removes guilt from the individual and refers it back to the system. Tornike rejects this perspective: he apologizes to Keti and takes the consequences for his family's guilt.

The inactivity of Keti, acting only in her imagination, is a common feature for many other films made in the glasnost and perestroika period about the Stalinist past, showing man as a helpless victim of the system, capable only of mental or intellectual resistance (a reference perhaps to the dissident movement). Films confirm that totalitarianism extends into the present, thus undermining and questioning the relationship between man and power in the present as well.

Another parable of the destructiveness of totalitarian power is Abdrashitov's *The Servant* (Sluga, Mosfilm 1989), which developed the Mephistopheles story of the sale of one's soul to the Devil. The powerful bureaucrat Andrei Gudionov (played by the Leningrad theatre actor Oleg Borisov, 1929–94, who won a Nika award for this role) subjugates everybody to his will. His driver, Pavel Kliuev, sells his soul to become a famous conductor, without enjoying music or emotionally engaging with his wife, Andrei's former mistress. The Devil returns to claim his soul: the power of a totalitarian regime is indestructible.

The documentary filmmaker Yevgeni Tsymbal's (b. 1949) short feature *Defence Counsel Sedov* (Zashchitnik Sedov, Mosfilm 1989) is set in the Stalin era, when a lawyer is forced to take on the defence of four 'enemies of the people'. As his conscience dictates, he tries to find evidence for their defence, but gets no support from the relevant organs, leading him to file a complaint – and hear that the four men are freed. Instead, however, ten officials who had been obstructive to his case have been arrested, tried and killed. The circle of destruction is never-ending and Tsymbal suggests no way out of the system: even the most loyal action offers no guarantee of justice.

Vitali Kanevsky's *Freeze, Die, Resurrect* (Zamri – umri – voskresni, Lenfilm 1989) is set in 1947 in a mining town inside the camp system, where two teenagers, Valerka and Galiya, live. Valerka has to go east and is seized by a criminal gang; Galiya goes to rescue him, but the bandits catch them again on their return. The film shows the appalling conditions in the town and the impossibility of escaping from the camp life, offering a pessimistic view of life that has no potential for change. Kanevsky (b. 1935) had himself been arrested in the 1960s and spent eight years in prison.

A mocking and surreal portrayal of the Stalin era is offered in Valeri Ogorodnikov's (1951–2006) *Prishvin's Paper Eyes* (Bumazhnye glaza Prishvina, Lenfilm 1989), which was based on a script by Irakli Kvirikadze, who had directed *The Swimmer* (see Chapter 5). The phrase 'paper eyes' alludes to the double vision facilitated by paper masks that make the newsreader seem to stare at the audience while he reads from a script. Prishvin, a television journalist, embarks on a film project about a 1949 secret service officer, but contemporary reality is mingled with the nightmares of a past that Prishvin reconstructs during his archival research. Ogorodnikov uses documentary footage, merging past and present, reality and fiction. Hitler, Mussolini and Stalin melt into one single mask of totalitarianism. In another sequence, a folk dance on Red Square cuts to Stalin on the mausoleum waving at the people as they tumble down the Odessa Steps – images from Eisenstein's *Potemkin*. The dance music turns the frantic movement of people running down the stairs into a surreal race that Stalin is watching, cheering at the people being massacred. The scene integrates also documentary footage of Nazi rallies, aligning all totalitarian regimes through a conflation of images. Stalin is responsible for the terror. His statue is dismantled in the end, and transported by helicopter across Leningrad to be deposited in the snow. The white and empty landscape symbolizes the hopelessness and aimlessness that is left after dissecting the past. The film, like many others, views the attempt at rewriting history and reorganizing it as a destructive exercise that will leave a void, and thereby predicts the collapse of the system.

Similarly surreal and fragmented is Sergei Ovcharov's (b. 1955) *It* (Ono, Lenfilm 1989), loosely based on *The History of a Town* by the nineteenth-century satirist Saltykov-Shchedrin. Ovcharov navigates the history of cinematic styles – from silent cinema to realism – of the twentieth century to illustrate different epochs and parody their leaders. The Soviet leaders are presented as a series of masks, which are ultimately interchangeable while the system remains unchanged. As in *Repentance*, Ovcharov emphasizes the indestructibility of totalitarian systems: change seems impossible. At the end of the film, IT – a planet – approaches: IT will destroy earth, which is already stifled and lethargic. Albeit playful and inventive in terms of style, Ovcharov also offers a pessimistic view on the possibility of social change in Russia. The surreal and phantasmagoric offer great visual possibilities for both Ogorodnikov and Ovcharov to depict the nightmarish atmosphere of Stalin's era, whilst also depriving the films of linear plots, reflecting the lack of logical connections in that past which, in its irrationality, remains incomprehensible.

The Stalinist past, when viewed from today's perspective, seems grotesque and almost incomprehensible to those who have not experienced it. Time travel is an attempt to bridge the gap and facilitate understanding for people's choices back then. Vladimir Khotinenko (b. 1952) made his film *Mirror for a Hero* (Zerkalo dlia geroia, Sverdlovsk Studio 1988), based on a script by Nadezhda Kozhushanaya (1952–96). The events that happened on 8 May 1949 are seen through the eyes of the young Sergei, who is transported back to a time when he was still in his mother's womb. He watches life in a small mining town, where an accident happens in the mine, where his father criticizes the boss, and where an argument leads to his arrest. Sergei lives in this world, with all the attributes of the present (watch, money, clothes), having travelled in time. The journey into the past may offer insights into the father's life, where he sacrificed his personal life to make the world a better one, and it explains the son's passivity, but it ultimately cannot resolve the divide between the father's social engagement and the son's cynical indifference towards life, reflecting the stagnation and pessimism of the time.

The year of Stalin's death preoccupied filmmakers too. Alexander Proshkin (b. 1940), who had worked on television before making his debut feature *The Cold Summer of '53* (Kholodnoe leto 53-ego, Mosfilm 1987), set his film after Stalin's death, when Beriya issued a decree that wreaked havoc on society: to free criminals and political prisoners by amnesty. As a result, crime rose sharply. In a northern village near a prison camp the freed criminals begin to terrorize the local population until two political prisoners organize resistance: Chaff ('Luzga'), the former POW Sergei Bazagin who served a sentence as 'enemy of the people' (performed by the actor and scriptwriter Valeri Priemykhov, who had played Pasha in Dinara Asanova's *Tough Kids*), and Digger ('Kopalych') – Nikolai Skorobogatov, who is an engineer accused of espionage because of foreign contacts (played by the theatre actor Anatoli Papanov, 1922–87). Their nicknames reveal the loss of identity in the camp, separating them from their past and their personal lives.

The fight between the two forces develops in the style of a western, making the film appealing to mass audiences. Digger dies in the fight, but his heroic sacrifice is ignored by his family, who still doubt his innocence for fear of their own comfort. Civic courage is an alien concept to the society of the post-Stalin era as well as the post-Stagnation period.

For Alexander Kaidanovsky, the year of Stalin's death signals the collapse of value systems for those who had believed and trusted the system. *The Kerosene Seller's Wife* (Zhena kerosinshchika, Mosfilm 1989) is set in Kaliningrad in 1953, where the twin brothers Sergei and Pavel (both played by Alexander Baluev, b. 1958) represent two ends of the political scale. Sergei is a corrupt Party official whose success has come at the expense of Pavel's career: Pavel is a surgeon who has lost his job after administering a lethal blood transfusion that Sergei had helped obtain. Since then, Pavel sells kerosene. The corrupt and irresponsible Sergei is contrasted with the 'victim', Pavel. Images of blood pervade the flashbacks of the film: blood loss – and figuratively the loss of the colour red symbolizing Soviet power – is synonymous with the loss of energy and heralds the eventual demise of both brothers: Sergei kills himself while Pavel ends up in a psychiatric hospital.

Many films tried to rewrite Soviet history in an attempt, more and more, to justify the Stagnation and the lack of perspective that doomed Gorbachev's Russia despite all the campaigns for change, trying thereby to trace the cause of the disease back to the past. Other films diagnosed the symptoms of the present – and those were terrifying symptoms.

It Is Not Easy To Be Young, 1986–88

One of the leading and most inspiring documentary filmmakers of the post-war era is the Latvian director Herz Frank (b. 1926), best known for *Ten Minutes Older* (Par desmit minutem vecaks, 1978), a film on which his student, Juris Podnieks (1950–92), held the camera. Podnieks's documentary *Is it Easy to be Young?* (Legko li byt' molodym? [Vai viegli but jaunam?], 1986) documented the demolition of a train after a rock concert in Oger, Latvia in July 1985. As the authorities had failed to lay on extra carriages, fans damaged an overcrowded train and seven people were arrested and tried, with the young Raimonds Plorins being sentenced to three years hard labour. The documentary depicted for the first time a Soviet rock concert and explored the problems of the younger generation, who were fans of the forbidden fruit of rock music, who lacked confidence, who rejected materialism, who felt they were not needed, who had no place in the society that surrounded them and could not identify with its values, who used drugs and alcohol to escape from an alienated and estranged reality, and who sought their place in life. The film did nothing outstanding by today's or Western standards, but for the Soviet Union of 1986 this was an outrageously open statement about a generation that felt superfluous to society and

Figure 6.4 Podnieks's documentary *Is it Easy to be Young?*

saw no meaning in their lives. The lyrics of rock music commented on the false ideals suggested by official culture and supported an escape into a dream world. The front men of rock bands soon became role models, ideals and heroes. The Russian rock scene had many such 'heroes' and bands to offer: Slava Butusov's Nautilus Pompilius, Boris Grebenshchikov's Aquarium, Viktor Tsoy's Kino, Konstantin Kinchev's Alisa, and Petr Mamonov's Zvuki Mu.

In the 1980s, the filmmaker Sergei Soloviev selected a course at the Moscow Film Institute, consisting of a group of students from Kazakhstan, including Rashid Nugmanov, Darejan Omirbaev, Serik Aprymov, Ardak Amirkulov, Abai Karpykov and Amir Karakulov. After graduation, these filmmakers returned to their native republic, which would soon be independent, and formed the so-called Kazakh 'New Wave'.

Playing a crucial role, both in the relationship of Russian cinema to rock music, and in terms of influence on his students, was Soloviev's *ASSA* (produced by Mosfilm's unit Krug in 1988), starring figures of the Leningrad underground movement, including the artists Sergei Bugaev and Timur Novikov, and the singers Irena Kuksenaite, Viktor Tsoy, Boris Grebenshchikov and Zhanna Aguzarova. *ASSA* (the word has no meaning but is a term used in the underground of the late 1980s) is not the first film to star rock musicians, but the first to show them in a positive light, reflecting a strong change in the perception of underground culture in general, and rock music in particular. Bananan (played by the Leningrad artist Sergei Bugaev, known as Afrika) is a peaceful and innately good character, who stands apart from the others because of his behaviour and his appearance: he wears one earring. He is juxtaposed with the Soviet official Krymov, played by the filmmaker Stanislav Govorukhin – a representative of the Establishment – who holds power over his mistress, Alika (played by Soloviev's then wife Tatiana Drubich). He may possess the power to have Bananan killed, but when Alika becomes aware of the plot, she kills Krymov. Bananan is a romantic hero, who triumphs – even if in death. In the finale, a concert by Viktor Tsoy takes place against all the rules and regulations, and the song 'I Want Change' ('Ia khochu peremen') voices the dissatisfaction with a world where happiness is possible only through escapism into a dream world. *ASSA* expresses a protest against Stagnation, and the appearance of Tsoy in this film predestined him for his role in *The Needle*. Soloviev's style is genuinely idiosyncratic: he develops dream sequences – patches of colour for Bugaev's artwork, an illustration of Krymov's book on Paul I through images from a costume drama about his murder – to endow the character with a background and to set a stylistic counterpoint. These fragments serve as simple illustrations of the characters' imagination and function like speech bubbles in a cartoon. Similarly, inter-titles with ironic keywords or phrases interrupt the narrative. Soloviev fragments and assembles sequences of images like a comic strip, thus exposing the flatness of characters and their lives. In this sense, he echoes the two-dimensionality of modern society. He ends on an optimistic note, offering a way out in the finale: the candles lit by the fans during the concert mark this visually.

Rashid Nugmanov's (b. 1954) *The Needle* (Igla, Kazakhfilm 1988) was the first film to openly address the issue of drugs. As in *ASSA*, the hero Moro is played by a rock star: Viktor Tsoy. Moro returns to his home town Alma-Ata (now Almaty) to collect debts from Spartak; he visits his former girlfriend Dina and finds she is on drugs. He tries to get her clean, taking her to a deserted *aul* (village) by the dried-up Aral Sea. When Moro discloses the dealer's identity (the freaky doctor is played by another rock star, Petr Mamonov) and prepares to leave with Dina, he is stabbed on a wintry road. However, heroes never die: Moro lives on, walking down the snow-covered road leaving red dots of blood on the white surface to the tune 'Blood Type' (Gruppa krovi). Moro's positive moral values are perpetuated as he continues to live, but only in a world of dream and escape, while the drug-dealer triumphs in reality. Nugmanov has no illusions about reality, but instils such illusions in his viewers. In this sense he follows his teacher's solution, offered in *ASSA*, where rock music offers salvation from a reality that has no room for honesty and change.

Nugmanov's film revealed the meaninglessness of life doomed by drug addiction, debt collection, and drug-dealing. If there is hope, it lies on the snow-covered road that leads to the land of illusions and dreams. *The Needle* also raised the issue of country and city: life in the city is corrupt and flawed. It is in the desert by the Aral Sea that Dina gets off drugs and finds her way back to Moro. Urban civilization

Figure 6.5 Nugmanov's *The Needle*.

may mean progress, but the future lies in a return to one's roots. Images of dryness run through the film: an empty pool, the dry autumn leaves in the park, and the dried-up Aral Sea with its stranded ship – these are images of the devastation created by Soviet mismanagement of the ecology, which echo the 'dehydration' of society: it is a world captured in static images, in which characters move between objects of the past and present, as if they were not theirs but part of a museum collection. Nugmanov cast non-professionals for the main roles, reflecting his interest in types rather than individuals, a characteristic of the Kazakh New Wave.

In Russian youth films, teenagers were often portrayed against a background of broken families, thus laying the blame for the collapse of value systems at the feet of society. Valeri Ogorodnikov's *The Burglar* (Vzlomshchik, Lenfilm 1987, script by Valeri Priemykhov) underscored the negative influence of rock music. The 13-year-old Senka returns from a concert rehearsal to find his home in disarray – the first visual sign of a broken family. His brother Kostia (the band leader Kinchev) has had a fight with their father, who has been drinking since their mother's death. Kostia rehearses with a rock band and dreams of his career, but right now a racketeer wants money for the group's synthesizer. Kostia is frustrated and angered, and in order to help, Senka steals the community club's synthesizer for him. Senka is caught and after serving his sentence, the brothers go separate ways: the family as an institution has collapsed completely, not only the bond between parents and children but also between siblings. The film paints a bleak picture of the predicament of young rock musicians, but an even bleaker picture of a society that – apart from Mafia control, racketeering and alcoholism – has not much to offer.

In his 1987 film *The Non-Professionals*, Bodrov had explored the role of rock music with a band of young people offering recitals to social organizations, but remaining largely isolated from society. Such isolation is also the theme of Karen Shakhnazarov's film *The Messenger* (Kuriier, Mosfilm 1987), where the spontaneity of break-dance stands in sharp contrast to the stifled and dull life at home. Ivan's parents are divorced, and he is failing at school. He invents a CV for himself in order to get a job as a messenger boy. His aggression and cheeky behaviour compensate for his alienation and insecurity, but he also lacks a sense of responsibility, going skateboarding instead of delivering a manuscript. At the film's end the hero is drafted into the army, and the disfigured face of a soldier who has returned from Afghanistan signals what the future holds for Ivan. If *The Burglar* led a young man to theft to forge family bonds in the absence of support at home, at work or in his club, then *The Messenger* portrays an even bleaker picture, suggesting that Ivan has no future other than within the Soviet system, and that future is a dead end.

Juvenile delinquency and aggression had already been treated in the films of the 1970s, and continued to affect the perestroika films. Prisons and labour camps replaced the camps and schools for young offenders, while the role of control and supervision was extended to the younger generation. In Abdrashitov's *Plumbum or a Dangerous Game* (Pliumbum ili opasnaia igra, Mosfilm 1985) a teenager leads a dangerous double life: he helps the police disclose criminals. The 15-year-old becomes obsessed with assignments, unable to discern reality: he is cold and so lacks emotion that he even has his father arrested, not unlike Pavlik Morozov. The modern boy scout has neither a heart, nor is he motivated by ideology: he acts out of contempt for the world around him that denies him love. Such innate aggression and evil can also be seen in Viktor Aristov's (1943–94) *Satan* (Satana, Lenfilm's Uliss and Tak-T 1991), which showed how the lack of conscience and the endurance of humiliation leads a man to crime: Vitali kills the daughter of his mistress and demands a ransom in an act of revenge for unrequited love. The aggression of children is also evident in Eldar Riazanov's *Dear Elena Sergeevna* (Dorogaia Elena Sergeevna, Mosfilm 1988), based on a play by Liudmila Razumovskaya, which deals with a group of pupils who terrorize their teacher in order to obtain exam questions.

Bodrov's *SER* (Svoboda – eto rai [Freedom is Paradise], Mosfilm 1989) centred around the 13-year-old Sasha Grigoriev, who attends a reform school. With a tattoo he identifies his motto: SER – freedom is paradise. The school is not the ideal educational institution as it had been during the Thaw, but one where a child is given no chance of change and is condemned from the outset. Sasha is a criminal, says the schoolteacher, because his grandmother has stolen cucumbers from the *kolkhoz* and served a five-year sentence. Sasha runs away when he learns that his father is in prison in Arkhangelsk. In road movie style, the film follows him: Sasha hides among cattle on a truck, he steals and begs for money, and eventually succeeds – he finds his father in solitary confinement, but is allowed an overnight visit. Sasha's father was born in prison; he tells him of a drunken attack on a policeman and that he will be released in eight years' time, and he promises that they will be together then. That hope for a future concerns an already mature Sasha; in the present, he is returned to the school. He has made the journey from Almaty to the north without engaging in any way with the land: Sasha is homeless and rootless, at ease only in 'freedom', on the road.

Khusein Erkenov (b. 1960) further investigates this theme in the film *100 Days Before the Command* (Sto dnei do prikaza, Gorky studio and Mir 1990), dealing with the daily life of army recruits, including bullying and deaths, even suicide. The disorientation of the recruits, both spatially and figuratively, is echoed in the film's composition. The perpetuation of aggression extends into adolescent life, and the army becomes a place not of discipline, but one that promotes violence and aggression even further.

Children are lonely, isolated and misunderstood, largely as a result of the breakdown of family structures and of society. The loss of the home echoes the collapse of the communist value system and anticipates the demise of the political system that would soon follow.

Corruption and *Chernukha*, 1987–90

The previous sections have shown filmmakers laying the blame on the past, offering no future for the younger generation, and charging family and society with the collapse of value systems. In turning to the present, filmmakers could not elucidate positive features here either. As Gorbachev tackled corruption, filmmakers followed suit. A fine example is Eldar Riazanov's satire on bureaucracy and corruption in his *Forgotten Melody for a Flute* (Zabytaia melodiia dlia fleity, Mosfilm 1988), where he portrays a clerk in the leisure directorate, Leonid Filimonov, as a careerist who marries only to gain promotion. Yet Riazanov adds to this satirical portrait a melodramatic line: Filimonov loves the nurse Lida who treats his cardiac condition. However, Filimonov stays with wife because of his career. When he suffers a heart attack – here Riazanov shows him in true satirical spirit at purgatory queuing for entrance to heaven – Lida resuscitates him, but then leaves. Riazanov also mocks the air of change in the administration, where promises are made but no action is taken. He also exposes the inability for change in personal life, where Filimonov fails to live according to his true feelings.

The mainstream of Russian cinema, however, largely indulged in the bleakness of life and offered neither alternative nor perspective. Filmmakers rejected their remit to act as prophets, to guide morally and aesthetically. The audiences rejected films that offered no positive outlook or spiritual guidance in the chaos, and turned instead to Latin American soap operas screened daily on Russian television. The filmmakers portrayed reality as it was, adhering to the authenticity that had once characterized the Thaw, only they showed a society about to collapse. They rejected both ideological and spiritual roles and found it difficult to establish a relationship with the outside world and with audiences.

As Gorbachev had named the decentralization of power as one of his goals, so the filmmakers directed their view away from the centre to the periphery, both at the geographical periphery (the countryside) and at the figurative periphery of society (marginal groups). The Stagnation had driven society to a complete standstill, offering no way out. As reforms were not catching on in real terms, people began to despair and insisted that this change was only temporary: 'Past experience tells us that this can all end very soon', or 'We had one Thaw and we know how that ended' were frequent comments of the time. In a rebellion against the official ideology, filmmakers made vulgarisms their prime mode of expression, replacing language as a tool of communication with curses – as did theatre and literature. Finally, the rift between the intelligentsia and the people that had already resonated in the 1970s became more obvious in the late 1980s.

Again, it was a documentary that captured best the pessimism and hopelessness of the era. Stanislav Govorukhin's documentary *This is No Way to Live* (Tak zhit' nel'zia, Mosfilm with Filmverlag der Autoren 1990) showed the moral and material collapse of the country despite all efforts of reform. The magnitude and expanse of the country are contrasted with the misery of life. Govorukhin compared social institutions, such as the police, in Russia and America; he measured the achievements of the Soviet economy (embodied in Stalin's park for the exhibition of such achievements, the VDNKh) against shopping precincts in Germany; he held up an image of Russia in terms of 'what we have' and 'what we could have'. He pointed at problems and discontent, laying the blame at the feet of politicians. Govorukhin portrayed a life worthy only of rejection, and showed all its blackness and the gloom of contemporary society, tapping into the *chernukha* (literally: making black) model of which filmmakers in the 1990s would be accused and which would be blamed for the loss of audiences in the post-Soviet era.

The key film of the period that came to represent glasnost in cinema is Vasili Pichul's *Little Vera* (Malen'kaia Vera, Gorky Studio 1988), starring newcomer Natalia Negoda (b. 1963) in the main part. She caused a furore when she became the first Soviet woman to pose for the front cover of *Playboy* in 1989. Set in an industrial town on the Black Sea, the film shows the life of a working-class family: the father, Kolia, is a truck driver; the mother works night shifts and manages the household, saving money by pickling vegetables. Vera, however, takes little interest in the household or in her parents' desire for her to continue school and hopefully have a better life. She listens to the pop singer Alla Pugacheva and to rock music,

Figure 6.6 Pichul's *Little Vera*: Vera (Natalia Negoda), on the left, with a friend.

wears a miniskirt, sports sunglasses, has her hair dyed and smokes. The parents fail to communicate with their daughter and call their doctor son from Moscow for assistance – he is their success story, although it transpires that his marriage is far from happy.

Vera has some dubious friends: she hides twenty dollars for one of them, although possession of foreign currency is illegal. She has no interest in a secure marriage to the reliable Andrei, who is about to join the navy. In this respect, Vera is a typical rebellious teenager. But she is a teenager in the Soviet Union, where not only her parents condemn her behaviour, but society and the state as well: the police clamp down on the teenagers listening to a rock concert in the park.

Vera's parents are caring and want the best for their daughter: a happy family. However, their own family life is far from perfect: the father drinks, and turns into a child that needs to be tucked up, a duty that Vera does not mind. When Vera meets Sergei, who comes from a different background (his parents work abroad), trouble appears on the horizon: Sergei has no ambitions or plans, something he shares with Vera. However, the class gap between them makes itself felt when Sergei visits Vera's home and a row escalates when the father insults Sergei, gets drunk and stabs him. Vera bails out her father with a false testimony and Sergei drops charges as well. Guilt-stricken and despairing, Vera attempts suicide, and is saved by her brother. As Vera's father is alone at home, he suffers a heart attack.

Little Vera portrays the bleakness of life in the provinces: the industrial chimneys and factory buildings loom over the opening and closing frames of the film; in this city only work counts. There is no room for life, and indeed, Vera's parents seem to be incapable of doing anything but work. The Soviet way of life has destroyed the capacity for happiness, in the old and the younger generation.

Petr Todorovsky's *Intergirl* (Interdevochka, Mosfilm with Filmstallet Sweden 1989) offers an equally bleak outlook on contemporary life. Tania Zaitseva (the young actress Yelena Yakovleva, b. 1961) is a hard-currency prostitute at night but leads a normal life during the day, when she works as a nurse. She lives with her mother, a teacher, which indicates that she has a decent family background. Then she meets the Swedish businessman Ed Larsen who proposes to her and takes her to Sweden, where she leads a comfortable but dull life. Tania wants to return to Soviet Russia despite the hardship of life there, but financial problems arise as she just keeps spending Ed's money. She cannot find a job or a role in the foreign country. Tania leaves Ed, but is killed in an accident on the way to the airport. *Intergirl* painted in dark colours the predicament of a girl who tries to have a better life; however, social mobility is not (yet) possible, and material riches do not guarantee happiness. The film also harks back to the theme of emigration, and asserts Russia's superiority over foreign lands.

The Collapse, 1987–91

Life had turned into complete stasis, despite promises of change and reform and despite the wealth of activities in the culture and media spheres. This discrepancy between promises, aspirations and dreams brought about a sense of dislocation, disorientation and weakness. On the one hand, reforms ordered from above, from the Party, were not showing effects in reality – other than verbalized protest and complaint, exposure of corruption and promise of improvements. On the other hand, the individual had both lost the trust in the system and the will – or civil courage – to take the initiative for change. Kira Muratova's film *Asthenic Syndrome* (Astenichskii sindrom, Odessa Studio 1989) became symptomatic of this climate of a social change where nothing happened. The film is in two parts, seemingly unrelated. In the first, shot in black and white, the grieving Natasha attends the funeral of her husband. She wanders around, resigns from her job as a doctor, and refuses to engage with her world; she shouts verbal abuse at people on a bus. The black-and-white film-within-a-film ends when the actress and the director meet the audience, who are appalled by the vulgarity of the film and leave the cinema. One viewer has slept and wakes at end of the film; he takes the metro home and falls asleep again: this is the English teacher Nikolai who suffers from the asthenic syndrome that manifests itself through weakness, passivity and sleepiness. Nikolai is a writer, but he cannot express himself: words seem meaningless and do not serve the purpose of communication. The weakness, lethargy and inactivity are an emblematic quality for society at large. In fact, glasnost merely exposed and uncovered the stagnation of social development and human life, and added to it the growing lack of emotion, responsibility and moral values, which ultimately led to the *chernukha* film as logical culmination and conclusion of the process begun during the Stagnation.

The feeling of dislocation is central to Sokurov's *Days of Eclipse* (Dni zatmeniia, Lenfilm 1988), a slow-moving film with a sense of endlessness. Set in the desert near the Caspian Sea and filmed through orange-yellow filters, it creates the image of a civilization on the brink of standstill. The town is a microcosm for the multi-ethnic Soviet Union, where different languages are spoken. At the same time, the town is de-centred and turns the periphery into a substitute for the absent centre. The doctor, Malianov (Alexei Ananishnov, b. 1962, who would continue to act in Sokurov's features), believes that physical health is linked to spiritual health and goes to the disease-stricken steppe settlement to observe its decay and demise. At the end, the city disappears from the field of vision, apparently annihilated by its own inactivity. Sokurov here created a powerful parable for the self-destruction of society.

A similar concern underlies Karen Shakhnazarov's (b. 1952) *Zero City* (Gorod zero, Mosfilm 1988), where the Moscow engineer Vurakin visits a provincial town and encounters a completely surreal setting. There is no way back, no return, and no escape from this world, and when Vurakin finally takes a boat out on the lake, he disappears in the mist: there is no future here either, leaving instead a sense of apocalypse.

In his debut film, Alexei Balabanov (b. 1959) diagnosed the absurdity of human existence together with a loss of the self. *Happy Days* (Schastlivye dni, SPiEF [Studio of First and Experimental Film at Lenfilm] 1991) is loosely based on Samuel Beckett's play and follows a nameless character (played by Viktor Sukhorukov, b. 1951), who is given different names by different characters: Sergei Sergeevich, Peter or Boris. He cannot remember his name, having recently been discharged from hospital after a head injury, which seems to have caused his memory loss. Viktor wanders around St Petersburg in search of a room, and of his galoshes. He rents a room, but is kicked out by the landlord once he has paid the woman who appeared to be the landlady; then he stays with a blind man and his father in a basement; finally he follows the prostitute Anna and stays in her house. However, in all these cases he sooner or later abandons his accommodation to rest on a bench in the cemetery. *Happy Days* is emblematic of the dislocation of a character, and the sense of loss – even of identity.

A more comic touch to the collapse of value systems, economies and society is evident in *Taxi Blues* (USSR/France, Lenfilm, ASK, MK2 1990), Pavel Lungin's (b. 1949) debut with cameraman Denis Yevstigneev (b. 1961). The film is set in Moscow; Ivan Shlykov is a taxi driver, who one night picks up the drunken Alesha

Seliverstov (played by rock star Petr Mamonov), an alcoholic and saxophone player (the music was written by jazz musician Vladimir Chekasin). Ivan believes in the old social order and resents perestroika, while Alesha leads a life on the margin of society. The contemporary setting of the film accurately captures the squalor of life, the queues and the vulgar language of this time. Ivan and Alesha form a comic pair: the worker and the artist, the traditionalist and the innovator. Alesha remains incorrigible, and, as representative of the bohemian intelligentsia, fails to provide a model or offer guidance in the changed world, while Ivan pragmatically adapts to the changes of perestroika. Lungin's film offers a fascinating and funny portrayal of the helplessness of the intelligentsia in the face of change, pointing not only at the rift between the classes, but also at the coming demise of the intelligentsia and the former underground movement in the 1990s.

When seen from a distance, social inactivity, immobility and stasis acquired absurd and grotesque dimensions. Thus, looking at village life through a distorted lens exposed the façade of social conventions that essentially hide the emptiness of human life. In Sergei Selianov's *Name-Day* (Den' angela, Lenfilm 1980–87), the retarded Mafusail is an onlooker on his own family, observing his alcoholic father, a war veteran with a detached, ironic and distanced view. Mafusail's elder brother is a bandit; his second brother is arrested for money forgery; and his three sisters – according to Mafusail's reductionist template – represent the attitudes of work, faith and worry. Mafusail teaches himself how to read and write – and the viewer sees the letters as he does: distorted and mirrored. Thus Selianov's camera looks at the world exclusively through the eyes of Mafusail. On his name-day, a large company gathers in the garden, leaving Mafusail disinterested. He has, however, received a present from his brother: a (forged) coin with the inscription 'Name-day', which shines in the sun. The vision of the world through a specific lens interested Selianov also in his films of the 1990s, as did the concern with folklore and tradition, reducing man to a very simple and basic set of moral values and choices. Here the boy shuns technology and sees things much more clearly than the devotees of civilization and progress. Selianov's film had an extraordinary production history: it was made at the Film Institute and later re-edited for distribution by Lenfilm. Indeed, most films of the late 1980s were produced by small companies or production units within the large studios, which reflects the devolution of power within the large studios. More films from the provincial studios (Sverdlovsk in particular) formed part of the perestroika repertoire.

Nikolai Dostal's (b. 1946) *Paradise-Cloud* (Oblako-rai, 12A and Mosfilm 1991) also has a hero who is a retarded young man – Kolia, played by the famous circus clown Andrei Zhigalov (b. 1966). He is teased and provoked by his friends into declaring his plans for the future. Tired of being asked a question to which he has no answer, he invents a story: that he will be leaving town to go to Siberia to live with a friend. His evasive response turns not into a fairy tale, but into reality; and this is not a dream that becomes true, but rather a lie. His friends urge him to depart, sell his room and his belongings, and arrange everything for him. Yet Kolia is in love with a local girl, and really wants to stay. His dreams are shattered when he leaves at the end of the film, almost against his own will, but he has to persist to the end with his lie of another life that awaits him beyond the limits of his provincial home town. Void of any direction in life, the 'hero' is forced along a path which, in reality, leads nowhere. The film's sequel, *Kolia – Rolling in the Fields* (Kolia – perekati pole, 2005), had Kolia return to his native town years later, but the film lacked the sense of dislocation explored in the first film.

The comedy genre also revealed the resistance to change in the Gorbachev years. Yuri Mamin created the grotesquely exaggerated film *The Fountain* (Fontan, Lenfilm 1988), where a rift in the wall threatens to cause an entire building to collapse. At the beginning of the film, a composer who lives in the house stands on the roof in a pilot's suit complete with wings – ready to fly off and thus realize every Soviet man's ambition. Then the film moves to the Kazakh steppe, where a herdsman patiently fills a bottle with water at a trickling source. A Soviet army vehicle stops to fill its supply canisters. As the flow is too slow, the Soviets detonate the source to create a proper well – and the trickle dries up: Mamin here comments on the exploitation of the satellite republics through the Soviet government, leaving them empty and impoverished. The Kazakh herdsman is Maya's grandfather and Maya lives with her husband in the building with the crack. The inhabitants are all absorbed in petty habits such as collecting medals, growing flowers or composing music, and their efforts to repair the rift and prevent the house from total collapse amount to the hire of three men, paid in vodka, to support the house – just like in the ancient folk belief that the world is supported by three whales. Mamin's comedy arises from exaggeration of the everyday to extreme proportions, while magic and folk beliefs play an important role in the development of the plot, allowing him to create and collate visually versatile episodes.

A superb parody, in western style, on the clash of high and low cultures is *The Man from the Boulevard des Capucines* (Chelovek s bul'vara Kaputsinov, Mosfilm 1987) by the talented comedy director, Alla Surikova. She rewrote the history of cinema in a western, with the Lumière Brothers' films representing art films, which compete against porn and violent films in a saloon. When the popular films outdo the art films, they move on – eastwards. *Boulevard des Capucines* is a fine spoof on the competition between art films and the trash that invaded the Soviet film market in the latter years of glasnost.

New Signals?

The thematic concern with a life in stasis and both ideology and value system on the verge of collapse informed the films of established directors and of the younger generation. Before the collapse of the Soviet Union a number of new directors emerged; there was also a proliferation of studios that facilitated independent production. Sergei Livnev (b. 1964) debuted with *The Miss* (Kiks, Gorky Studio, TTL and Ladia 1991), about stardom and drug addiction; Dmitri Meskhiev (b. 1963) made an adaptation of Mariengof's *The Cynics* (Tsiniki, Lenfilm Diapazon and Podmoskovie 1991); Valeri Todorovsky (b. 1962), the son of the well-known director Petr Todorovsky, wrote scripts and made his debut with *Love* (Liubov', TTL, Zodiak and Gorky Studio 1991), about the relationships between students and their girlfriends. The film historian Oleg Kovalov (b. 1950) made the *The Gardens of Scorpio* (Sady skorpiona, SPiEF 1991), using a combination of acted sequences with documentary footage, in this case of a clinic for alcoholics; Kovalov's work in montage cinema would fully develop in the 1990s. Lidia Bobrova (b. 1952) debuted with a film set in the countryside, *Oh, You Geese* (Oi, vy, gusi, SPiEF and Higher Courses for Directors 1991), where she explores the degradation of a Russian family, a portrayal that turns into a metaphor for life in Russia at large.

A further new development was the formation of the alternative movement 'CineFantom', founded in 1985 by Gleb (b. 1966) and Igor (1962–94) Aleinikov, who were joined by theatre director Boris Yukhananov (b. 1957), the necro-realist artist Yevgeni Yufit (b. 1961), and the sots-art (involving the parody of the Soviet past and Socialist Realism) artist Yevgeni Kondratiev (b. 1959). *Daddy, Father Frost has Died* (Papa, umer Ded Moroz, dir. Yufit and Vladimir Maslov, SPiEF 1991) was a horror film with ironic overtones. *Tractor Drivers II* (Traktoristy II, dir. Aleinikov Brothers, Mosfilm's Kurier 1992) parodied Pyriev's musical by removing the ideological premise and turning the plot into a spoof. Yufit made several films in necro-realist style with larger studios in the 1990s.

Finally, the period saw two films that were important as documents, but were never properly released for reasons that had nothing to do with censorship but simply with lack of proper distribution systems and production laws – problems that would become a recurrent feature in the 1990s.

Nikita Tiagunov's (1953–92) *The Leg* (Noga, 12A 1991) is a much neglected film, largely due to the untimely deaths of the filmmaker and scriptwriter (Nadezhda Kozhushanaya). The film reconstructs the events that surround a Russian tank and its crew on patrol in the Afghan mountains, culminating in the murder of the Russian soldier, Redhead (Ryzhy), by partisans. In the explosion, Martyn (Ivan Okhlobystin) sustains serious injuries and loses his leg. The narrative is not linear, however: fragments of memory about the time before recruitment, about Redhead, and about the incident that caused his injury haunt the young soldier as he convalesces in a military hospital. He gradually makes a physical recovery and is discharged, but cannot adapt to life: the memories of the happy past along with the nightmares of the war haunt him. Martyn's sarcasm and manic laughter reflect his vain and desperate attempt to integrate and the despair at his inability to do so. Tiagunov created here a powerful parable that men who have returned from the war will never be able to lead a normal life. Like Zhilin in Bodrov's *The Prisoner of the Mountains*, discussed in the next chapter, Martyn never parts with the dead. The film's special power lies in Tiagunov's skill in showing the nightmares as more terrifying experiences than the war itself. It was one of the first films to address the traumas associated with the Afghan War – a theme that would become more widespread in the 1990s.

A different story lies behind the film *Anna Karamazoff* (France/USSR, Mosfilm and Victoria Film 1991), directed by Rustam Khamdamov (b. 1944). *Anna Karamazoff* caused a stir at the Cannes Film Festival, where it was announced with great hype, while spectators and critics left the film en masse within the first twenty minutes of the screening. This 'failure' led to the film being withheld from distribution.[11] The film's aesthetic decisions, however, have been influential on many filmmakers.

Anna Karamazoff is about a woman who remains unnamed (played by Jeanne Moreau), and who in 1949 returns from prison camp to Leningrad in search of her mother. She visits various places of her past, among them a derelict house inhabited by Marie, her brother and their infantile grandmother, as Marie's parents were deported at the beginning of the war. Historically, the film addresses the devastation that the Purges had on individual lives. When the woman finds her mother's grave, the film breaks with an inter-title indicating a lapse of time. The woman has recuperated her past and continues to live in the present: she visits a cinema and sleeps through a film about an actress, who relives her film role as a saviour of Russia – a sequence consisting of a film-in-a-film inset which reconstructs Khamdamov's earlier, abandoned film *Unexpected Joys* (see Chapter 5), thus reinstating his own past as filmmaker. After leaving the cinema, the woman pursues the plan of her late friend from the prison camp, who had wanted to take revenge on a rich man. She poisons the man, who mistakes her for Anna Karamazoff – the woman from the camp. The film's lack of logic and coherence, based exclusively on visual associations, reflects well the blurring of the borderline of reality and fiction, past and present. The film emphasizes absences: the heroine has no name – she is *not* Anna Karamazoff – and this negation of her self gives the film its title. It is maybe the most powerful embodiment of emptiness and alienation, hidden beneath exceptionally rich imagery that Khamdamov created through painting, artistic *mise-en-scènes* and costumes.

Mikhalkov's *Urga* (USSR/France, Camera One, Hachette Pyramide and TriTe 1991) was the last Soviet-made film to have been entered into a major international film festival: it was screened in Venice in September 1991, where it won the Golden Lion. *Urga* explored life in Mongolia and juxtaposed oriental traditions with Western civilization. The couple Gombo and Pagma live with their three children: a baby cradled by Gombo's mother, a 6-year-old daughter Burma and her younger brother Buyin. The idyll of family life is disrupted by the intrusion of Uncle Bayartu – homeless, without family and always drunk, representing the Mongolian man corrupted by civilization; and by the Russian truck driver Sergei (played by Vladimir Gostiukhin, b. 1946, the embodiment of the Russian working-class man), whose truck gets stuck on an embankment as he has strayed from the road when falling asleep at the wheel. Sergei is a kind of Soviet popular prototype with his steel teeth, tattoos, poor speech and lack of manners. His behaviour shows how horrified he is by the traditions of the Mongolian family who leave their dead to the vultures, slaughter sheep, eat with their fingers and all live in one *yurt*.

Both Gombo and Sergei are victims of civilization: Gombo is restricted in his lifestyle with regard to the number of children the family is allowed to have, while Sergei is forced to work away from his native town. Both cultures are under threat: Sergei's child cannot find any Russian-speaking playmates, and Gombo's lifestyle is extinct by the end of the film, when the *yurt* is replaced by a factory. Mikhalkov explores the dislocation of people and the destruction of lifestyles in a more concrete manner than offered by other films of the period, which echo alienation through abstract symbols and metaphors or fragmented narratives. In this context, Mikhalkov's film is visually and structurally conservative, but remains an important contribution to the examination of the relationship between Russia and the East.

The glasnost period inherited from the Stagnation era the concern with the lack of change, but identified this as a problem inherent in the individual and his unwillingness to make changes once the state had cleared the path for reform. The preoccupation with life's bleakness, with a lack of meaning in life which had grown so strong that it inhibited people from taking action, is maybe the most common denominator of glasnost-era films – and whether this diagnosis is revealed through comedy or documentary, through prostitutes or professors as protagonists makes little difference in the overall bleak outlook offered in the face of collapse.

–7–

Post-Soviet Russian Cinema (1992–2000)

– Are you gangsters?
– No, we're Russians.

Brother 2

He is Russian – that explains many things.

Barber of Siberia

After the collapse of the Soviet empire, the issue of national identity dominated many cinematic narratives, but also many debates among filmmakers about the role of Russian cinema in society. Soviet identity had disappeared and made way for the formation of a new Russian identity. In the first instance, artists harked back to the pre-Revolutionary and Soviet past to re-establish the severed link with imperial Russia or to rewrite Soviet history – but now (as opposed to the 1980s) they did not only condemn that past. Coming to terms with the effect of Stalinism still played a major role in this debate, although the filmmakers' focus extended to historic periods beyond the 1930s. In the second instance, filmmakers investigated Russia's historical role between East and West, between Europe and Asia. As everyday life changed radically in the 1990s, the relationship between the centre and the periphery was also reassessed. A related theme was that of escape – from reality, from a collapsing society, and from a defunct economy – into other worlds, other countries or dreams. The rise of the crime film concludes this chapter, which groups films thematically. But first the political and cultural context of the Yeltsin era should be outlined.

The Yeltsin Years

On 25 December 1991, Gorbachev resigned and the Soviet Union ceased to exist. The Soviet flag was removed from the Kremlin. The new year chimed with reforms: the shock therapy proposed by Yegor Gaidar stipulated the abolition of price regulation (prices for all goods had been set by the state) on 1 January 1992. As a consequence, prices and inflation rose and the rouble plummeted, leading inflation to rise by 2,000 per cent in 1992 and 1,000 per cent in 1993. Gaidar was dismissed in December 1992 when debt accumulation led to a liquidity crisis, with salaries remaining unpaid. The situation was so bad, especially for pensioners, that Russia received humanitarian aid – a humiliating experience for Second World War veterans who were now receiving aid packets from the war enemy, Germany.

Attempts under Viktor Chernomyrdin, prime minister from 1992 until 1998, to stabilize the economy by slowing down the inflation rate were hampered by corruption, collapsing pyramid schemes and so-called 'voucher privatization', the deregulation of prices, tax evasion, money laundering, media piracy, the devaluation of the rouble and inflation, which eventually led to the crash on Black Tuesday (11 October 1994), when the rouble dropped by 27 per cent. Talking of the state of the economy, Chernomyrdin coined a phrase that has become common parlance: 'We wanted to do better, but it worked out as usual.'

As Yeltsin strengthened his presidential powers, he disbanded parliament in September 1993 and called for early elections. The parliament appointed General Rutskoy as vice-president, and on 3 October 1993 parliamentary forces attacked the television centre at Ostankino and the mayor's office. The attempted coup, led by Rutskoy and parliament speaker Ruslan Khasbulatov, was overthrown. In December 1993, elections to a federal assembly (Duma) were held and a simultaneous referendum approved the new constitution. Yeltsin had survived another major political crisis.

In 1996 Yeltsin was elected president for a second term, defeating communist leader Gennadi Ziuganov. But Yeltsin's rule continued to be shaken by conflicts and scandals over his alcohol consumption and related ill-health. The last years of the Yeltsin era were further destabilized by the rouble devaluation on 17 August 1998, as well as the rapid succession of prime ministers in an apparent attempt to find a successor for the presidency. Prime ministers changed faster than one could learn their names, as a comment during the closing ceremony of the Moscow International Film Festival in 1999 demonstrated when the host, reading Stepashin's message to the festival, pointed out his amazement that it was still the same prime minister who had opened the festival who was closing it. Stepashin was dismissed in August – only weeks after that remark – when Vladimir Putin became prime minister. On 31 December 1999 Yeltsin resigned, leaving Putin as acting president; the elections of 26 March 2000 confirmed him as president. Yeltsin had steered the country through the brisk and tumultuous transition from communism to capitalism.

The 1990s were overshadowed by wars and ethnic conflicts in the southern regions of the former Soviet empire. Autonomous regions claimed independent status within the former Soviet republics, such as Chechnya, which had been an autonomous region within the Russian Federation (RSFSR, a constituent part of the USSR). In December 1994 Russian troops were sent to Chechnya, which had not signed the treaty with the Russian Federation, claiming independence instead. By August 1996 General Lebed had negotiated an agreement with Aslan Maskhadov, and troops were withdrawn in December of that year; this military campaign is commonly known as the First Chechen War. However, the Basaev-led invasion of

Dagestan prompted the Second Chechen War, begun in 1999, and intensified by the apartment bombings in Moscow, allegedly committed by Chechen terrorists. War and terror dominated the 1990s and inflicted national and personal traumas on both sides, casting a dark shadow over debates about national unity and identity.

The loss of Soviet identity led to a sudden nostalgia for Soviet films, or rather for the economic stability and the fixed (ideological) values they represented: the comedies of Leonid Gaidai, and spy thrillers and adventure films of the Stagnation period formed the staple diet of television viewers, who craved these films (as is clear from audience ratings). Another period evoking nostalgic reminiscences was tsarist Russia. Thus, Glinka's 'Patriotic Song' became the Russian anthem, only to be replaced by the tune of the old Soviet anthem in December 2000, with revised lyrics by Sergei Mikhalkov, because it has a more uplifting rhythm than the Russian hymn. The old Russian flag was brought back, along with the coat of arms for the Russian Federation, which shows the double-headed eagle of the former Russian empire. Finally, places and streets, cities and squares were renamed, restoring their pre-Soviet names: in 1991 Leningrad became St Petersburg and Sverdlovsk changed back to Yekaterinburg. Metro stations were renamed, for example Sverdlov Square became Teatralnaya, and street names changed too: Gorky Street to Tverskaya, Kalinin Avenue to Vozdvizhenka Street, Marx Avenue to Okhotny Riad (Hunter's Row), and even Pushkin and Chekhov Streets, named to immortalize two outstanding writers, were renamed Bolshaya and Malaya Dmitrovka.

The construction plans of Moscow's mayor, Yuri Luzhkov, included a new business centre, the so-called 'City', and a third ring road. The architectural style echoed the monumentalism of the Stalin era, as Luzhkov's architects at Mosproekt coined a style of high-rises whose towers were crowned not by the star of the Stalin high-rises (the 'wedding cakes'), but by empty glass cubicles, which led to ironic comments about the replacement of an ideological symbol with an empty space. The reconstruction of the Cathedral of Christ the Saviour was a further project accomplished by Luzhkov in order to restore Moscow's past cityscape and to highlight the role of Orthodoxy in the new Russia. Finally, on 17 July 1998, the remains of the Romanov family were laid to rest in Peter-and-Paul Fortress in St Petersburg, closing another chapter in Soviet and Russian history books.

The cityscape of the capital cities changed with the influx of foreign businesses: in 1990 the first McDonald's opened on Pushkin Square in Moscow, followed by other Western restaurant and retail chains. This made Moscow's façade resemble a collage of labels and signs from a whole host of Western consumer capitals – in line with globalization – which led to questions about Russia's own identity that (as far as consumer goods were concerned) was non-existent in the early 1990s, when the domestic production of food and consumer goods had almost come to a standstill.

Chaos in the Film Industry

The new Russia's film industry experienced some major shake-ups. In the formerly state-run studios (Mosfilm, Lenfilm, Gorky Studio), a number of production units were set up; the state-managed distribution system collapsed entirely before private investors could refurbish cinemas; and the role of the producer had to be redefined after seventy years of state demand and state order.[1] In the years immediately following the collapse of the Soviet Union, the number of films produced annually doubled as money was laundered through the film industry, where almost for every film made a specially established private studio figured as production company. Then film production dropped sharply when these sources dried up in the mid-1990s. The proliferation of studios and the growing number of co-productions speak of the sudden explosion of film production in the early 1990s.

Russia's Law on Cinema underwent numerous amendments before it was passed by the Duma and approved by the president on 22 August 1996.[2] It defined the responsibilities of Goskino: conservation of the national film heritage and support of the film industry; development of the infrastructure; registration and licensing of films; assistance with the distribution and promotion of Russian cinema; higher education in film studies; maintenance of databases; and development of international relations. The law also offered limited tax breaks for organizations engaged in film production. A new law on Authors' Rights was ratified on 16 June 1995, which protected the film's authorship for director and scriptwriter, and made the prosecution of video pirates possible under the civil (but not the penal) code – i.e. a fine or payment of compensation rather than prosecution.[3] Films made between 1964 and August 1992 were deemed to be the property of the film studio where they had been produced, while films made after 1992 were the property of the director or the producer. This left the film studios in possession of the vast archive of Soviet films, which could be licensed to television to secure an income.

Toward the late 1990s, the situation began to stabilize, with the new laws taking effect. The three largest film studios came under the leadership of people from the arts. Mosfilm's director Vladimir Dostal was succeeded in 1998 by filmmaker Karen Shakhnazarov; Alexander Golutva left Lenfilm in 1997 for the post of deputy minister at Goskino,[4] and was succeeded by filmmaker Viktor Sergeev (1938–2006). The Gorky Studio was headed in 1995 by filmmaker and scriptwriter Sergei Livnev, who launched the so-called 'Low-Budget Project' programme in 1997, an initiative designed to produce cheap films that could make some profit through video and television sales. After the economic crisis, the price of video films rose only marginally, reducing the profit margin, whilst video piracy flared up. Livnev's initiative failed on economic and artistic grounds, and he resigned in 1998. Vladimir Grammatikov, director of many children's films, replaced him as head of the Gorky Studio. Thus, people from the arts rather than bureaucrats took on the responsible roles.

At the Filmmakers' Union, Sergei Soloviev was elected chairman in 1994; he was succeeded by Nikita Mikhalkov in 1997, who promised to attend to the urgent problems of the Union, namely property issues pertaining to the houses of veterans. He also promised to organize funding bodies for young filmmakers, whilst appealing to his colleagues to create films that would present a new positive hero (à la Andrei Tolstoy in his *Barber of Siberia*). None of Mikhalkov's promises have had any tangible results. Indeed, the expulsion of the Museum of Cinema from the (purpose-built) Cinema Centre (which is the property of both the FU and the Confederation of the FUs in the former Soviet republics), in order to vacate space in a property in the centre of Moscow, would appear to prove that Mikhalkov cared little about Russia's film history, while also failing to maintain the FU's venue (the House of Cinema) or its sanatoria, or indeed the medical support needed by the film veterans and largely older FU members.

Video piracy was causing the state huge losses in tax, and the industry a loss of an estimated $500 million in profit.[5] The loss in tax alone was higher than the annual budget for cinema. The rise of the illegal copying of films dates back to the late 1980s, when films could be recorded on video tapes without any fee paid to the author; moreover, video rental was levied with a tax of 70 per cent on profit and thus encouraged illegal business in the video market.

In 1991 Jack Valenti, President of the Motion Pictures Association of America (MPAA), called for a boycott of the Seventeenth Moscow Film Festival in protest against pirated American films flooding the Russian market, which were inflicting significant losses on the American industry. Pirated copies of American A-movies were often on sale in Russia before they had appeared on American screens. Valenti visited Russia again on the occasion of the Twentieth Moscow Film Festival in 1997, and addressed a conference on video piracy organized by the newly formed Russian Anti-Piracy Organization (RAPO).

In 1996, Russian film production had hit an all-time low with twenty-eight feature films. Films had no way of recouping production costs at home, since piracy dominated the sales sector almost entirely. The vicious circle meant that any Russian film, if released, could not rely on video sales to recoup production costs, while the income from theatrical release was minimal because only a few cinemas took on Russian titles; television paid a pittance for licenses as television stations catered for audience tastes by recycling the old Mosfilm archive of Soviet films. Thus, a Russian film had no chance of covering the production costs through distribution, and only (rare) foreign sales and festivals ensured some publicity for the films, which therefore relied on state funding (or sponsorship). The defunct exhibition sector and a non-existent distribution network further complicated matters. Many films of the 1990s were shown on a large screen only at the Kinotavr Open Russian Film Festival, founded by Mark Rudinshtein in an attempt to give filmmakers a platform for showing and discussing their work. It remained the only showcase for new Russian cinema for almost the entire decade, and continues in the new millennium under new management to showcase new trends in Russian cinema. In October 1996 the first refurbished cinema, fitted with Dolby Stereo System, opened in Moscow: the Kodak Kinomir (Kodak Cinema World). However, it would take several more years – well into the Putin era – for the infrastructure to recover and for Russia to become a proper film market.

The Past which We Have Lost, 1992–98

The Russia We Lost (Rossiia kotoruiu my poteriali, Mosfilm 1992) was a documentary by Stanislav Govorukhin, which harked back at the imperial past and idealized the monarchy, not without a certain nostalgia. (In rejection of this conservative view, the Russian film sidebar of the Moscow International Film Festival was titled 'The Russia We Gained' in the later 1990s.) But for the early 1990s, Govorukhin's film defined one period of the past that played an important role in culture; the second concern was the Stalin era, a period in which interest had not stopped with the collapse of the USSR. However, the films in the 1990s that addressed the 1930s explore history in a different way, dismantling the aesthetic principles and styles that covered and contradicted the horror of the period. Ivan Dykhovichny's *Moscow Parade* (Prorva, Russia/France 1992) exposed the immoral sexuality that underlies Stalinist culture. The film juxtaposes a fictional plot with documentary material in order to comment on the nature of high Stalinist culture: the disciplined parades, monumental buildings and muscle-controlled bodies are set against the decadent lifestyle of the attractive heroine Anna (played by the German musical star, Ute Lemper). Anna's husband Sasha is in charge of a parade in which Stalin's favourite horse is to appear, yet the male horse is frightened by the music and replaced by a female horse with a dildo. Gender is a façade, and sexuality part of a political power game: Sasha is impotent, whilst his wife Anna is raped by a secret service agent and later attracted to the muscular worker Gosha (Yevgeni Sidikhin), as Anna exchanges political for physical dominance.

The film features the typical landmarks of Stalinist architecture (the metro, the Agriculture Exhibition, Red Square, the river stations on the Moskva river) and undermines the façades with decadent music and dance. Dykhovichny is less concerned with politics than with the breakdown of morality in a world where only appearances matter, and with the sexual perversity of all aspects of life, almost in analogy with the political perversion. The threats to individuals remain hidden under the surface, just as they were subterranean in the 1930s.

Similarly, Sergei Livnev's *Hammer and Sickle* (Serp i molot, L-Film 1993) parodies and mocks the myth-making of Socialist Realism, whilst constructing a new myth about the Stalinist past. The film is about a state order in 1936 that the country should have more soldiers. To this end, Stalin's aide Ambrosius masterminds an experiment whereby the female tractor driver Yevdokiya Kuznetsova becomes the male construction worker Yevdokim Kuznetsov (played by the theatre actor Alexei Serebriakov, b. 1964). Yevdokim turns out to be a successful model worker in the metro construction brigade, while Ambrosius commits suicide when a change in policy leads to a condemnation of gender transformation since it 'blurs what Soviet men and women are' – an analogy to the policy changes in the 1930s and the subsequent Purges. Yevdokim marries Liza Voronina (the actress Alla Kliuka, b. 1970, who later emigrated to the US), a model *kolkhoz* worker. They literally become models for Vera Mukhina's statue of the *Worker and Collective Farmer*, and a model Soviet family when they adopt a girl, Dolores, an orphan of the Spanish Civil War. Yevdokim meets Stalin and challenges the leader's control over his life: he attacks Stalin and is shot. Paralysed and unable to speak, Yevdokim is turned into a hero once more: he has supposedly saved Stalin's life and is exhibited in a museum. His wife controls his mind (she writes his book, 'Hammer and Sickle') and she is also the master of his body, which she uses to satisfy her lust.

Hammer and Sickle challenges the assumption that the individual carries any responsibility for history: history is an artificial construct. Characters are contrived and deprived of choice. Liza and Yevdokim are artefacts, creations of a system, the model worker and peasant. The ideal Soviet man is displayed in a museum for foreign visitors and pioneers. The paralysed Kuznetsov becomes a living monument, reduced to total passivity and serving as the state's mouthpiece. Livnev resists the movement of eradicating Soviet symbolism from the map – as was evident in the name changes of the 1990s – and recreates the symbols of Stalinist culture to mock totalitarian values. Livnev's film belongs clearly with postmodernism in its fragmentation and collage of history, where history is the product of the artistic imagination.

With his Oscar-winner *Burnt by the Sun* (Utomlennye solntsem, Russia/France – TriTe 1994), Mikhalkov embraces the totalitarian past and brings it in unison with Russia's present, making the Purges part of a linear historical development. In June 1936 the NKVD officer Mitia (the popular theatre actor Oleg Menshikov, b. 1960) accepts and carries out a special assignment: the arrest of the Red Army Commander Kotov (Mikhalkov), while the latter enjoys time with his wife Marusia (the Lithuanian actress Ingeborga Dapkunaite, b. 1963) and daughter Nadia (Mikhalkov's daughter Nadia) at his in-laws' dacha near Moscow. Mitia, a family friend and Marusia's first love, spends the day with the family before taking Kotov back to Moscow in the evening. Upon his return to Moscow, Mitia commits suicide by cutting his wrists in the bath.

The film explores the marriage between two systems: the Russian intelligentsia, represented by Marusia, and Bolshevism, represented by Kotov. The alliance survives mainly because of Kotov's sexual energy and political clout, but only on the artificial island of the dacha with its old-Russian lifestyle. *Burnt by the Sun* contrasts visually and stylistically the pre-Revolutionary lifestyle of the intelligentsia outside Moscow (Marusia's father was a musician, her uncle is a historian) with that of the

Figure 7.1 Mikhalkov's *Burnt by the Sun*: Kotov (Mikhalkov), Marusia (Dapkunaite) and Nadia (Mikhalkova).

Soviet reality with its centre in Moscow (Mitia's apartment in Moscow, but also pioneers and evacuation exercises in the countryside). The film begins and ends in Moscow, the political centre, allowing the protected life of the intelligentsia only on the periphery, in a house surrounded by fences. The circular structure of time and space enhances the closed system of the film's narrative: there is no way out, either in time or space; the characters are entrapped. The detachment of the intelligentsia from the people serves at the same time as an apology for their inactivity and lack of opposition both in the past and present.

The film demonstrates the destructive power of political ideas over personal happiness. Mitia makes his decisions for personal reasons, whereas Kotov is a military man whose personal life comes second to duty. Mitia, a former White officer, has returned to a country that has destroyed his lifestyle and his happiness (by taking Marusia away). He works for a regime that threatens the remnants of that past – which are painful memories for him as he is no longer part of that world. He has no chance of recuperating his personal happiness and has finished with his life already at the beginning of the film. He relies on chance when playing Russian roulette whether he fulfils this assignment or not: if he does not arrest Kotov, then somebody else will. The system is indestructible. Kotov enjoys 'paternal' protection from Stalin but, when he realizes that Stalin is also a father figure for Mitia, who salutes the leader's effigy rising on a dirigible, Kotov cries like a child deprived of paternal love. Mitia's reaction to Stalin's portrait underlines his acceptance of his role. He is about to light a cigarette when his face contracts into a smile: he has done the job, as the leader wanted; he has played his role, and he will go – that is the only freedom he still has. Mitia is a character with many faces, skilfully displayed by Menshikov. He can adopt any role, but he has no identity. Mitia has written this role for himself, whereas Kotov is a face, a portrait in a world that venerates its idols as icons, as is beautifully underlined in a scene where Kotov is only recognized when posing in profile.

Burnt by the Sun raises the question of where the borderline lies between victim and oppressor, between the victim Kotov and the victim Mitia. Kotov is a mere executor of Stalin's political will, but acts under the illusion that he is in control; Mitia, by contrast, has tried to preserve his integrity: he acts, aware of the fact that he is a mere arm of power, an executor, an actor.

These three films close the subject of Stalinism, and they all propose a view of history that frees man from responsibility for the past. A further concern with Stalin's legacy is revealed in the cinematic interest in the 1950s in two major films of the late 1990s. Pavel Chukhrai (b. 1946), the son of filmmaker Grigori Chukhrai, addressed the post-war era, offering a nightmarish vision of the past. *The Thief* (Vor, Russia/France, 1997) opens with a young woman, Katia (a new face on the screen, Yekaterina Rednikova, b. 1973), giving birth to a baby boy, Sania, on the roadside in 1946. This scene visually extended the final shot of his father's film *Ballad of a Soldier*, where the mother overlooks the wide land in search for her lost son. Moreover, Sania's father was a soldier who died in the war – a reference to Alesha Skvortsov of the 1959 film.

The narrative voice of the adult Sania guides the spectator through the film, commenting on events from time to time. The narrator takes us on to 1952, when Sania is six years old, travelling with his mother on a train where they meet Tolian (the popular macho-type actor Vladimir Mashkov, b. 1963), a handsome officer with whom Katia falls in love. They rent a room in a cramped communal flat, and Tolian prepares for his job: to steal all the valuables from the neighbours and run away with the loot. Soon he makes Sania an accomplice to his thefts, using the agile boy to gain access to apartments. Thus they move from city to city, until Tolian is caught, arrested and sent to prison camp. Katia dies after a botched abortion, leaving Sania to grow up in an orphanage. Some six years later, Sania sees a layabout, believes him to be Tolian and shoots at him. In the final episode, Sania is a 48-year-old officer in a war zone, presumably Chechnya. He sees a beggar by the roadside, and again erroneously thinks that it is Tolian. Sania returns to his special train, taking all women and children out of the war zone.

The film focuses not just on the melodramatic line – the love story between Katia and Tolian, ending with his arrest and her death – but on the relationship between

Sania and Tolian, who are not father and son: Tolian is a substitute father who betrays the child just like Stalin betrayed his people. Tolian tries to make a tough guy out of the gentle and loving child, forcing him to behave in a more aggressive way, while Sania has visions of his natural father – a kind soldier who is waving at him. Admiring the tattoos of a tiger and of Stalin on Tolian's body, Sania idolizes him – wrongly so, he knows – but he continues to search for his false father. For his diagnosis of the long-lasting effect of betrayal, Chukhrai relies on the superb performance of the two main actors, and on the talent of Misha Filipchuk, who plays Sania.

Such a betrayal during childhood is also touched upon in another film set in 1952–3, Stalin's last year. Alexei Gherman Sr.'s *Khrustalev, My Car* (Khrustalev, mashinu!, Russia/France, Lenfilm 1998) was shown at the Cannes International Film Festival in 1998, where audiences left en masse. Later it became a favourite film of Russian critics and garnered several Nika (Russian Film Academy) awards. As in Gherman's earlier film *Ivan Lapshin*, a narrative voice accompanies the viewer through the film, where the dialogue is often inaudible against the noise of everyday life. General Klensky (played by Yuri Tsurilo, who had previously only starred as the rebel Yermak in the 1996 historical epic), a psychiatrist, is arrested during the campaign against doctors (the alleged doctors' plot, where medics were accused of poisoning Soviet officials) and raped by other convicts on the train to the prison camp. When Stalin is dying, Klensky is called upon, but it is too late: he can merely observe, together with Gherman's attentive camera, the decay and decomposition of the leader's body. Klensky returns to the camp and is released only during the Thaw. Although the film focuses on Klensky, the observing eye and ear is that of the adolescent son, who is at a loss: he cannot comprehend what happens in the world and what happens to his father. Gherman powerfully renders the sense of disorientation, leaving the viewer entangled in the events, just like people at the time who could not understand the political rights and wrongs.

History remained a preoccupation for filmmakers in other cinematic forms. An experimental and innovative approach to the past is adopted in Oleg Kovalov's montage films, *The Gardens of Scorpio* (Sady skorpiona, SPiEF-Lenfilm 1991) and *Island of the Dead* (Ostrov mertvykh, Soyuzitalofilm 1992), the latter about the film star of the silent era, Vera Kholodnaya, where Kovalov juxtaposed the life of the simple people with stardom, everyday life with culture. Another montage film was Sergei Selianov's *The Russian Idea* (Russkaia ideiia, Russia/UK – CTB 1996), for which Kovalov wrote the script and which traces the Russian idea through film fragments of the first half of the twentieth century.[6] *The Gardens of Scorpio* is a collage of fragments from around fifty documentaries and features made between 1925 and 1958. At its centre stands Alexander Razumny's 1955 film, *The Case of Lance Corporal Kochetkov* (Sluchai s efreitorom Kochetkovym), a cold-war thriller about Vasia Kochetkov (played by Vadim Grachev), who falls in love with a salesgirl. He is told that she is a spy, and that he is to play the role of the fiancé to catch her. Kovalov disrupts the story: the actor Vadim Grachev, who played Vasia, also appeared in educational reels about alcohol abuse, which Kovalov discovered in the archives. Kochetkov's exposure to secret service instruction is as hypnotic as the treatment alcoholics receive in the clinic; both Kochetkov and the alcoholics are poisoned – through a potion in tea or through vodka. The film links the overexposure to threats of espionage in everyday life as directly leading to the incapacity to lead a normal life and the succumbing to alcohol. Kovalov tries to fragment and undermine the mythical perfection of the 1950s with their polished surface.

A number of historical costume films were produced that further highlight the unfading interest in the past: they include Vladimir Krasnopolsky and Valeri Uskov's historical epic, *Yermak* (Russia/Germany 1996); Vitali Melnikov's *Tsarevich Alexei* (Russia/Poland 1997) and a biopic about Pavel I, *Poor, Poor Pavel* (Bednyi, bednyi Pavel, Lenfilm 2003), Alexander Proshkin's setting of a Pushkin story, *The Captain's Daughter* (Russkii bunt, Russia/France – NTV Profit 2000); and Gleb Panfilov's *The Romanovs. An Imperial Family* (Romanovy – Ventsenosnaia sem'ia, Studio Vera 2003). All these films showed the increasing interest in the imperial past.

Panfilov's film reinstated the figure of Nicholas II as a kind and decent family man to offset the image of his weak political leadership. However, the film that indulged endlessly in the monarchic past and fictionalized historical events on a large scale was Mikhalkov's *The Barber of Siberia* (Sibirskii tsiriul'nik, Russia/France/Italy/Czech Rep. – TriTe 1998), which tells the story of Jane Callaghan (Julia Ormond), an American woman who travels to Russia in 1885 in order to help the Irish-American inventor Douglas McCracken (Richard Harris) to secure funding for his machine, the 'barber', which is designed to cut down the Siberian forests. The theme of the exploitation of Russia's lands through the West confirmed Mikhalkov's essentially Slavophile position. McCracken, under pressure from his creditors, hires Jane – who has offered her services to men ever since she was abused as a child – to charm General Radlov (Petrenko, who had been cast as Rasputin in Klimov's film), the head of the military academy, in order to gain through him the support of Grand Duke Alexei. Jane achieves this task by pretending to be McCracken's daughter and flirting with the self-conscious and vain general until he proposes to her. But she also meets the cadet Andrei Tolstoy (Menshikov), who falls in love with her. Tolstoy has high moral values, while she continues her intrigues in order to fulfil her contract and get McCracken's papers signed by the Grand Duke: she will not sacrifice her scheme for the sake of love (if she indeed reciprocates his feelings). When Tolstoy sees Jane flirt with the general in the theatre just after she has spent the night with him, he attacks Radlov with a violin bow during a performance of *The Marriage of Figaro*, where Tolstoy plays Figaro. Radlov accuses Tolstoy of an attempt upon the Grand Duke's life, securing a promotion for himself by 'preventing a terrorist act', while Tolstoy is found guilty and sent to a prison camp in Siberia, without ever attempting to defend his actions. Ten years later, Jane is married to McCracken so that her son (Tolstoy's child) has a father. On the occasion of the launch of McCracken's invention, Jane travels to Siberia, where she finds Tolstoy's house empty as his wife Dunia (the former maid) and their children hide.

The love story is embedded in an English voiceover narration by Jane (in the Russian version this is read by Mikhalkov) who, in 1905, writes a letter to her son Andrew, a recruit at an American military base. Andrew stubbornly upholds his principles: rather than denounce Mozart, he goes for several days with a gas mask. The explanation for his stubbornness follows when Jane visits the base and shows his commander a portrait of Andrew's father, the former Russian cadet Tolstoy: 'He is Russian – that explains a lot' became the (much parodied) slogan for the film. The film includes numerous scenes that evoke the beauty of Russian life, from Shrovetide celebrations to fist fights on the ice, making this the most expensive film of the 1990s, with a budget of approximately $45 million. However, while it was well received at home, it remained commercially unsuccessful in European distribution and had no release in North America.

The Barber juxtaposes Russia and the West. Jane and McCracken represent a world that is largely deprived of spiritual values, while the Russian cadets are endowed with a sense of honour and love for the fatherland. The moral values of the young Russian cadet Tolstoy are held up as a model, aimed to help contemporary audiences value and love their fatherland. These values are characteristic of imperial Russia, so that *The Barber of Siberia* instils nostalgia in the spectator for tsarist, pre-Revolutionary Russia, related to the present through the historical event that dominated 1998: the laying to rest of the remains of the last tsar and his family, the Romanovs, in St Petersburg in July 1998.

Literary adaptations also engaged with cultural heritage, but they often took a parodic and critical approach to the originals, in line with the postmodernist deconstruction of realist narratives that affected much of the literature and visual arts of the 1990s. More conventional screen adaptations included Vasili Pichul's film on the 1920s satire *The Golden Calf*, entitled *Idiot's Dreams* (Mechty idiota, Russia/France 1993); Roman Balayan's adaptation of Leskov's *Lady Macbeth of Mtsensk* (Ledi Makbet Mtsenskogo uezda, USSR/Switzerland – Mosfilm 1989) and *First Love* (Pervaia liubov', Russia/Germany 1995), an adaptation of Turgenev's story; Alexei Sakharov's *Lady Peasant* (Baryshnia-krest'ianka, Mosfilm's Ritm 1995), based on Pushkin; Sergei Gazarov's *The Government Inspector* (Revizor, 'Nikita i Petr' 1996), starring Mikhalkov as the town's duped mayor; and Roman Kachanov's spoof on Dostoevsky's *Idiot* with the title *Down House* (Daun Khaus, Film Studio 2001). A fine example of postmodernist deconstruction is Sergei Ursuliak's *Summer Folks* (Letnie liudi, Kovsag 1995), based on Gorky's play. Ursuliak used documentary footage of an opera performance at the beginning of the century to create the temporal setting for his film. The characters emerge from this footage, as they stand to be photographed in front of the theatrical curtain, which drops to give way to the forest where the summerhouse stands and where the action develops. The characters move freely into the other space, while time bonds the summer folk with the theatre spectator of the 1910s, when the play is set. Characters are created, born in another medium. While Ursuliak links past and present, Valeri Todorovsky, in his adaptation of Nikolai Leskov's tale about the passion of a bored young wife under the title *Evenings in Moscow Suburbs* (Podmoskovnye vechera, Russia/France, 1994, known internationally as *Katya Ismailova*), sets the action in the present and thus provides a devastating analysis of the life of the 'new Russians'. Todorovsky coldly and dispassionately views Katerina's (Dapkunaite) passion, which leads her to murder. Like Leskov, he avoids psychological insights into the characters and neglects the motivation for actions. The main characters do not develop, but Katerina's beauty and eroticism is present from the start. *Katya Ismailova* is a film that would easily fit within the French *film noir*, which proves that Todorovsky is able to make a universally comprehensible film, as this was one of the many co-productions of the 1990s.

In exploring the past and cultural heritage, filmmakers avoided the present: that economic and social chaos of the Yeltsin era. When filmmakers did address the present, the theme of national identity features here too most prominently, both to assert Russia's superiority over the West and to explore sentiments of nationalism.

Russian National Identity, 1993–98

The issue of national identity stood in the forefront of films comparing Russia to the West, often in the form of eccentric comedies which echoed the topsy-turvy life of the early 1990s, containing the same grotesque and crazy features that life at the time entailed, and searching for alternatives – abroad, in the countryside, in dreams: all to little avail. The comic genre allowed comparisons of Russia and the West without sending out a seriously patriotic message and without being negative about the increasing Westernization.

Sergei Selianov's *The Time for Sorrow Has Not Yet Come* (Vremia pechali eshche ne prishlo, CTB 1995) is set in a village where there live a Russian, a Jew, a Gypsy, a Tartar and a German. When the land surveyor Methodius arrives, they are suspicious of this Soviet exercise to map the land, but Methodius is no scientist: instead he relies on pantheistic beliefs, thus undermining the Soviet myth. At the same time, the hijacking of a plane to get away to Paris ends in disaster when the plane lands on an airfield where Paris is a mere façade of cardboard buildings – another myth.

The disappointment with the West also underlies Yuri Mamin's (b. 1946) *Window on Paris* (Okno v Parizh, Russia/France – Fontan 1993), which portrays phantasmagoric journeys to Paris. The inhabitants of a communal flat in St Petersburg discover that the back of an old wardrobe opens at certain times – on to the roof of a Parisian apartment block. The inhabitants soon begin to bring back from the West what they cannot obtain at home. Russia, on the other hand, is not a place where anyone would want to live: a Russian émigré dreams of returning to St Petersburg

Figure 7.2 Sergei Selianov's *The Time for Sorrow Has Not Yet Come*: Petr Mamonov as the surveyor Methodius.

and is horrified when facing it in reality; the Parisian artist Nicole (who accidentally walks through the wardrobe) witnesses chaos and destruction in the city. But the film's hero, the music teacher Nikolai (the actor Sergei Dreiden, b. 1941, who would later play Custine in *Russian Ark*), is an exception: he is a 'bearer of spirituality and hopes of Russian culture'.[7] He appeals to his pupils to return home and help change Russia, having found in the West only the corruption of his ideals. He rejects the opportunity of staying in Paris and convinces the children to build their future in Russia, which remains – despite its chaos – a place that is preferable to the West, just as it had been for Tania in *Intergirl*.

The theatre director Dmitri Astrakhan (b. 1957) created an equally convincing message with *You Are My Only One* (Ty u menia odna, Informpressservis [Lenfilm] 1993), where Timoshin (the popular theatre actor Alexander Zbruev, b. 1938) receives a lucrative offer to work in the United States – from a girl who is in love with him. He decides to stay at home instead, in Russia, with his wife who shares with him memories of a happy Soviet past. Astrakhan's comedy *Everything Will Be OK* (Vse budet khorosho, Nikola Film 1995) took a different view of the West, albeit in a fairy-tale form. It is a Cinderella story about a poor Russian working-class family, with their daughter, the local beauty Olga. Smirnov, who emigrated to the US a long time ago, pays a visit to his home town and brings with him his son Petia, a young mathematical genius who has already won the Nobel Prize. Petia falls in love with Olga as real love can only be found in the homeland, Russia. They marry and live happily – in sunny California. Astrakhan shamelessly exaggerates the wealth and the educational standards for the émigrés, but created a film that offered a great life outside Russia, although the émigré family never forget their roots.

These films largely showed the foreign land as no alternative location for life (unless it is in the Californian dream world). In domestic settings, this patriotic sentiment (love for the homeland) turned into outright nationalism. The filmmaker Pavel Lungin, son of scriptwriter Semen Lungin, set his film *Luna Park* (Russia/France 1993) in the carnival atmosphere of the Gorky entertainment park, and against this backdrop develops the story of Andrei, who is a member of a fascist group that has set out to cleanse society of gays and Jews. Then Andrei discovers that his father – believed dead – is alive: he is a composer, and a Jew. The politically motivated protest of the youth contrasts sharply with the bohemian underground culture of the older generation, represented by the father. Unable to reconcile their worlds in Moscow, father and son leave the city for the periphery on a train, returning the image of the countryside as haven to the Soviet screen, where the centripetal movement had dominated for many years.

The anti-Semitism of the early 1990s also informed the plot of Valeri Todorovsky's *Love* (Liubov', TTL/Gorky Studio 1991), which dealt with the relationship between Sasha (played by the theatre actor Yevgeni Mironov, b. 1966) and Masha, whose parents have filed their papers to emigrate to Israel. When the visa is granted, Masha leaves despite her feelings for Sasha – and leaves behind also the memory of a racially motivated rape. In his *The Land of the Deaf* (Strana glukhikh, Gorky Studio 1998), the Mafia world serves as a backdrop for the story about Rita (Chulpan Khamatova, b. 1975, actress at the Sovremennik Theatre), dreaming of simple happiness with her boyfriend Alesha, who is a gambler and has lost the Mafia's money at the casino; unless he repays, he will be shot. Together with YaYa (Dina Korzun, b. 1971), a deaf girl, they help Alesha and survive a shoot-out between rival gangs, after which YaYa takes Rita with her into the happy land of the deaf. In a strange move, Todorovsky offers deafness as an escape from the criminal word and the reality of the 1990s.

Often films link the vision of a grotesque reality to the consumption of alcohol. Thus, Nikolai and the neighbours are drunk when they discover the window on Paris. The rise of vodka consumption in the period following the 'dry laws' of Gorbachev, limiting alcohol sale to certain shops and times, giving him the nickname 'mineral' (instead of 'general') secretary, can be explained in social terms with the inability of people to cope with reality; in artistic terms, it leads to a surprisingly lucid perception of the absurdities of the time – most perfectly illustrated in a Smirnoff vodka advert of the period, where a vodka consumer sees the guests at a party for what they really are: naked beasts.

Alexander Rogozhkin deployed this alcohol-induced vision of the world for the narratives of his films. He gained widespread popularity in Russia with *Peculiarities of the National Hunt in Autumn* (Osobennosti natsional'noi okhoty v osennii period, Lenfilm 1995), *Peculiarities of National Fishing* (Osobennosti natsional'noi rybalki, CTB 1998), and *Peculiarities of the National Hunt in Winter* (Osobennosti natsional'noi okhoty v zimnii period, ORT 2000), which all explore the Russians' notorious love for vodka as a motif for comedies of social reality. Rogozhkin merges situational comedy (bureaucrats and officials who do not behave like serious citizens and are helpless in matters of everyday life) with the typified and generalized features of the national character. The fragmentary structure, the anecdotal tone of the dialogue, and the lack of logic all replicate the incoherent speech of a drunken person.

In *Peculiarities of the National Hunt in Autumn*, a Finn who is researching the traditions of the Russian hunt from the time of the tsars to the present, joins a group of Russians – consisting of General Ivolgin (Alexei Buldakov, b. 1951), Soloveichik, policeman Semenov, and Kuzmich – in the hunt. For the Russians, the purpose of the hunt is to get drunk rather than to shoot an animal. The Finn, however, refuses to drink – while dreaming of the imperial hunting party of the nineteenth century – and thus excludes himself from the group, especially when he does the household chores and tasks normally carried out by women. The reality of the hunt coincides with neither the foreigner's imagination nor social stereotypes. What matters is not the result, but the process, the time spent in good company where alcohol effaces social and national boundaries.

In *National Fishing*, drunkenness leads the fishermen to accidentally dock on the Finnish coast. The cargo of sixteen crates of vodka is unloaded in Finland, but when Kuzmich realizes that they are outside Russia, he swiftly rushes everybody back to the boat (the idea of defecting to the 'dry' and alcohol-free Finland is plainly absurd for these characters), leaving the vodka behind – only to retrieve it with a submarine later. *Peculiarities of the National Hunt in Winter* continues the adventures of the hunters, who are visited by two inspection teams from the ministry. Rogozhkin's films have no endings, but consist of a series of gags, without a linear structure … to be continued. Rogozhkin is without doubt one of the most influential directors in the genre of comedy, bringing it back to the level that Gaidai and Riazanov achieved in the 1960s.

Figure 7.3 Rogozhkin's *Peculiarities of the National Hunt*.

Rogozhkin's characters portray the attributes of Russian national character: fun-loving, drunk and peaceful. It is on the periphery that Rogozhkin's characters subvert social order, and the periphery (or countryside) features prominently in other films of the period. Yet filmmakers no longer depict the glossy countryside of Pyriev's musicals, or the hardship of the life in the countryside where man feels alienated from the big city, as in the films of Shukshin and Muratova. Instead, the countryside harbours values of moral and spiritual strength that are endangered by the changing economic and social situation.

Centre and Periphery, 1994–2000

The countryside was no longer an idyllic place, as is most clearly shown in Konchalovsky's *Riaba Ma Poule* (Kurochka Riaba, Russia/France 1994), based on a folk tale about a hen with a golden egg, but also a sequel to *Asya's Happiness* (1968), set almost thirty years after the first film and with Asya played by a different, more extrovert actress: the popular Inna Churikova. Asya still lives in the village, however she is no longer the rebel heroine but a folk character, at one with her hen, Riaba. Asya's son brings the contemporary urban reality of racketeers and Mafia into the village, which is untouched by the changes of time. But the collective farmers know how to deal with the Mafia bosses and are by no means their victims. Konchalovsky uses clips of the earlier movie to compare past and present: Asya remembers the hard work during the late summer harvests that united and inspired the collective as she sits in her hut, alone, in winter. All that remains are memories of the past. Konchalovsky explores the aspirations to a better life, which have been disappointed in Yeltsin's Russia. The golden egg that the hen Riaba produces is a symbol of material wealth: and that, after all, it is only a figment of the imagination.

The screenplay writer Petr Lutsik (1960–2000) directed his first and only film, *Outskirts* (Okraina, Utro XXI veka 1998), a modern Russian 'western' in the style of the 1930s with reference to Barnet's film about the First World War. A community of peasants is threatened when a rich oil magnate tries to deprive them of their land. They travel to Moscow to fight for their land, and wreak a nuclear disaster on the city. Lutsik parodically illustrates the revenge of the countryside on the city for bringing about destruction.

Life in the countryside also makes characters prone to alcoholism and despair. Lidia Bobrova's *In That Land* (V toi strane, Lenfilm 1997) is set in a small village community and filmed with non-professional actors. Here alcoholism threatens the male population, leaving the women to reign over the family. Her film *Granny* (Babusia, Russia/France – Lenfilm 2003) tells about the life of the 'babusia' who raised her children, grandchildren and the neighbour's kids in a small Russian village. Bobrova views the provinces like a souvenir version of Russia, an idealized world that is preferable to the city. The children have grown up, made their careers and secured a comfortable life in the city, receiving money from the sale of Babusia's house, but leaving Babusia without an abode. None of the children seem to dispose fully of the property they 'own' or are really free to do what they want: one depends on her husband, the other on his mistress, the third lives in Moscow without a residence permit. Babusia is passed around like an unnecessary, shabby object. She is almost deprived of words, which underlines her similarity to the icon of Mary the Virgin, turning the countrywoman into a saint, capable of miracles. The peasant woman suffers and is bled to death by urbanization and modern life.

City life is also shown as corrupt. In films of the late 1990s, Moscow frequently features as a location of crime, or of wealth, excluding parts of society by choosing settings in the new Moscow shopping malls and business centres. Cameraman Denis Yevstigneev's debut as filmmaker, *Limits* (Limita, Studia 29 1994), powerfully shows the corruption in the city: Ivan and Misha have come to Moscow from the provinces in the 1970s: they were *limitchiki* – restricted to outskirts. In the 1990s they move to the centre, where Ivan makes money by hacking computer codes, while Misha works as a software developer, making encryptions for a company. One day Ivan is hired to crack a code that Misha has developed – and risks Misha's

Figure 7.4 Olga (Tatiana Drubich) and Lev in Zeldovich's *Moscow*.

life. Yevstigneev points at the disturbing egocentrism – the obsession both with self-advancement and with life in the centre – that drives these characters.

Moscow (Moskva, dir. Alexander Zeldovich, Telekino 2000) was based on a script by Vladimir Sorokin, a best-selling postmodernist writer. The film parodies themes of Chekhov's play, *Three Sisters*: the three female protagonists take their names from the heroines of the play, while the film explores what would happen if the sisters were to return to Moscow (a move that is denied to them in the play) – the 'homecoming' would turn out to be a disappointment. The sisters Masha and Olga are victims of the (sexual) corruption of the businessman Mike and his assistant Lev, who eventually takes over Mike's business and his women, in the manner in which Natasha takes over the Prozorov household (or perhaps in which the serf's son Lopakhin becomes a landowner in *The Cherry Orchard*). Moscow is a sterile and hostile place: the sights are suitable only for suicide (the ski jump on Sparrow Hills), the grave of the unknown soldier lacks meaning; the Bolshoi Theatre is a crime scene where blood is splattered over the swan-ballerina; the empty carriage of a metro train on the way to the depot serves as location for a sex scene between Lev and Olga. Yet most striking is the scene where Lev takes a map of Russia, cuts a hole into the location of Moscow and spreads the map over Masha before penetrating her through the hole in the map. Moscow, and Russia, are void of meaning.

Other Worlds, Dream Worlds 1993–2001

In the absence of meaning in the centre and the exploitation and degradation of the countryside, filmmakers exposed their characters to encounters with dream worlds, or the other world – death. Sergei Ovcharov's *Drum Rolls* (Barabaniada, Russia/France – SPiEF 1993) is an allegory for the nightmarish reality in Yeltsin's Russia. The hero (Alexander Polovtsev) – a product of the Stagnation – has no incentive or will of his own. He is a drummer: a naive, good man, a Buster Keaton-type character who gets drunk with his colleagues from the funeral orchestra. Once when they are playing, the corpse rises and leads the drummer away into another world, where objects rule: the drum Stradivarius takes command over the drummer's life. He never shows any sign of resistance, even when all his belongings are gradually taken away from him. He wanders aimlessly through Russia, exposing – in a grotesque manner – its social degradation: the homeless, the beggars, the criminals and the corrupt. The drummer who has lost orientation is a powerful symbol for Russian man.

In Vladimir Khotinenko's *Makarov* (Sverdlovsk Studio 1993), the protagonist is a creative individual, whose life is also controlled by an object: a Makarov pistol. One night the poet Alexander Sergeevich – not Pushkin – Makarov (Sergei Makovetsky, b. 1958, who would become one of the top actors in the late 1990s) returns home, having acquired a Makarov pistol, which changes his life: it deprives him of friends, family and his muse. Reality and the artificial world of literary creation overlap, as the intelligentsia is unable to survive in the nightmare that is contemporary society, which blurs lines between the real and phantasmagorical.

A detached view of death and crime appeared on screen, opposing the growing trend for crime thrillers and serials. Kira Muratova's *Three Stories* (Tri istorii, Russia/Ukraine – Profit 1997) views violence and evil as an integral part of contemporary life. The three short films are about violent deaths: the murder of a neighbour, of mothers who reject their infants, and of a handicapped grandfather. These stories reveal the crime, but no punishment. Evil is presented as an integral part of life, while images of death and dead bodies echo the morbid state of society. Muratova here collaborated with Renata Litvinova (b. 1967), who wrote one of the novellas and acted the part of Ophelia in the second novella. Litvinova, with her mannerisms of a diva, became the femme fatale of Russian cinema. Muratova's *Minor People* (Vtorostepennye liudi, Odessa Studio 2001) follows a doctor visiting a woman, Vera, when he finds a man who has collapsed on the floor, remaining there motionless. Vera and the doctor try to dispose of the body and pack it into a suitcase, which Vera deposits at the left luggage counter of the local railway station. In the meantime, the dead man's twin brother drives his boss (a gangster) through the countryside, while refusing to kill the policeman who is tied up in the boot of the car. When the boot is opened, the policeman is dead. The real death of this character passes almost as a marginal note. In the meantime, the case with the dead body is retrieved from the luggage hold and, when opened, the man is found to be still alive. Throughout the entire film the spectator follows the wrong character: the man about whom we know absolutely nothing, rather than the real victim, the policeman. Muratova misleads the spectator, making a pertinent comment on the futile concept of death. For Muratova violence is an innate part of the world, and crime part of the everyday– as is clear from *Two in One* (Dva v odnom, 2006) with one story of parental abuse (starring Litvinova) and one about a crime in the theatre.

A grotesque game with dead bodies is also at the centre of the Petersburg filmmaker Dmitri Meskhiev's *Mechanical Suite* (Mekhanicheskaia suita, 'Kinoforum 2000' 2001). Two men are sent to a remote village to collect the body of their colleague and bring it back to the city for burial. Since the proper transportation of a dead body would exceed the funds available, the two men dress the corpse and take it on the train, pretending they are lugging a drunken friend – not too far-fetched a scenario in a Russian setting. A fellow passenger causes the body to fall from the top bunk bed and, thinking he has killed the man, throws the body out of the window. The two men, suddenly in possession of a case full of money carried by the fellow passenger, who is a Mafia courier now delaying his delivery, are chased by some gangsters. Meskhiev balances the comic and the tragic, exploiting those situations with the corpse that lend themselves to slapstick comedy, whilst never losing sight of the underlying tragedy: the poverty which leads to this humiliating way of transporting the dead body in the first place.

Crime, 1997–2001

The corrupt political system led to the accumulation of wealth for some, and to extreme poverty for others; this disparity led to a rise in crime. In an age where the racketeers controlled the market, when people were shot in the streets by hit men for interfering in political games, crime soon found is way on to the screen. When filmmakers turned to the contemporary world, the *chernukha* model of the 1980s made way for the crime film, exploiting a genre that– in the alleged absence of crime in Soviet society – had not seen much screen presence in the Soviet era.

Crime series bloomed on television, led by *Streets of Broken Lights* (Ulitsy razbitykh fonarei, 1997–99), which was the first tremendously successful serial. It generated numerous sequels and was released on video under the title *Cops* (Menty). *Streets of Broken Lights* is set in St Petersburg, offering a realistic depiction of the police at work and showing the dilapidated conditions of a society where old structures have collapsed. However, the key film in terms of crime and violence is *Brother*, which also redefined the figure of the hero – no longer the ideal communist worker, the soldier of the Second World War or the honest man representing the socialism with a human face of the Stagnation era – but a killer-cum-knight.

Balabanov's *Brother* (Brat, CTB 1997) suggests a hero, Danila Bagrov (Sergei Bodrov Jr., 1971–2002), who in many ways is the product of the absurdity and chaos of the time: the film begins in provincial Russia where Danila has just returned from his army service, claiming that he has worked as a clerk in some office. It soon becomes clear that this is a myth: he has very good knowledge of firearms, and his manoeuvres are carefully planned. Danila has served in a belligerent region, probably Chechnya, and is hardened by the war.

Danila accidentally walks into the location of a video-shoot for the latest album of the rock group Nautilus Pompilius, *Wings*. The music of this group functions as a leitmotif for Danila's journey to St Petersburg, where he is sent to stay with his elder brother Viktor (Sukhorukov). Danila plays Nautilus music most of the time on his personal CD, living in the acoustic world of the group while only partly and mechanically noticing the reality that surrounds him. He has an innate sense of justice (he helps the poor), yet he has no qualms about shooting people. The ease with which Danila murders is soon extended to his personal relationships too: he is unable to discriminate between his reaction to Mafia-ruled society and to the drunken husband of his girl. He attempts to save all those who cannot defend themselves: the exploited market salesman Hoffman, the drug addict Kat, the tram driver and abused wife Sveta, and his brother whom he 'saves' from the hands of the Mafia bosses, having successfully carried out the killing which his brother was paid for in the first instance. Danila reverses the relationship of authority and respect for his elder brother and sends him back home to look after their mother, while he moves on to Moscow, the centre of crime.

Figure 7.5 Balabanov's *Brother*, played by Sergei Bodrov Jr.

Brother 2 (Brat 2, CTB 2000) develops further the theme of brotherhood, both criminal and social. The sequel takes Danila to Moscow, where his 'brother' from the Chechen war, Kostia, is killed when he tries to help his twin brother Mitia, a hockey player in the NHL, from being exploited by the American Mafia boss, Mennis. Danila and Viktor (who now works for the police in his home town – an ironic reference to the recruitment of the Russian police force) travel to Chicago to bail out Mitia. On the way, Danila 'saves' the Russian prostitute Dasha-Marilyn, makes friends with the American truck driver Ben, sleeps with the black television presenter Lisa Jeffrey, and retrieves Mitia's salary from Mennis. He may behave like a superman, but his agenda comes straight from a fairy tale: he reaches his aim by doing a few 'good deeds' on the way rather than by stubbornly following a plan. Danila again displays his innate understanding of social justice and is always ready to do a good deed: he never acts to enrich himself, but to help others. All of Danila's actions serve to punish the exploiters and rehabilitate the exploited, asserting right over wrong, and by extension Russia over America.

Balabanov used a technique of separating episodes by blackouts: Danila does not develop as a character, but reacts to a series of situations as they arise, like the threats that appear from nowhere in a computer game. Danila is responsive and quick, but he is a face, not a character with depth. This naive, boyish and innocent face of Sergei Bodrov Jr. contributed hugely to the cult status of the film and its protagonist. Bodrov represented the average young man, who was morally aloof and set his own agenda on issues of right and wrong, and who took it into his own hands to implement those principles, punishing the bad and rescuing the good. Such a Robin Hood figure not only echoes the need for order in the lawlessness of Russia in the mid-1990s, but also the need for a fairy-tale hero who acts not for personal rewards but for the good of society.

Having worked closely with Balabanov and clearly drawing inspiration from his style, Bodrov made his debut film *Sisters* (*Sestry*, CTB 2001), which continues Balabanov's theme of the modern knight: it is about two girls, Sveta (Oxana Akinshina, b. 1987, who later appeared in Lucas Moodysson's *Lilja 4ever*, 2002) and her younger half-sister, Dina. Sveta loves shooting as a sport and dreams of becoming a sniper, while Dina is a spoilt little girl who plays the violin and is the pride of her gangster daddy. Suddenly Sveta has to protect herself and Dina from some gangsters who come after Dina's father. Sisterhood, like brotherhood, involves protecting the weak from hostile reality and maintaining the child's fairy-tale world. However, in the crucial situation Sveta does not have to fire at a human target: she does not (yet) have to kill. Sergei Bodrov Jr. and his film crew, working on his second feature film *The Messenger* (Sviaznoi) in Ossetia, tragically perished after a glacier slid from the mountains into the Karmadon Gorge on 20 September 2002. The proximity between Balabanov and Bodrov can be seen in the fact that Balabanov chose in 2008 to direct Bodrov's filmscript for *Morphium*, based on Mikhail Bulgakov's play.[8]

The Afghan and Chechen Wars, 1995–2002

The war – Second World War and the Civil War – never ceased to be an important theme for Russian or Soviet cinema, but the recent wars in Afghanistan and Chechnya were explored in cinema from the mid-1990s. The Afghan War formed the backdrop for Vladimir Khotinenko's *The Muslim* (Musul'manin, VVS 1995) about the Russian soldier Nikolai (Kolia) Ivanov (the fine studio theatre actor Yevgeni Mironov) who, after seven years' captivity in Afghanistan, returns home – as a Muslim. The film is based on formal and thematic juxtapositions. Formal contrasts are achieved by the juxtaposition of sound and image (Kolia's Muslim prayer and the Russian village church in the background, followed by a sequence showing the Russian field and the Russian priest, singing); of image and image (the Russian landscape and Kolia in his Muslim outfit); and of sound and sound (Kolia's Muslim prayer and the church bells chiming in the background). The film explores not the clash of religions, but of *svoi* (one of us) and *chuzhie* (not one of us): Kolia returns to his roots, his village, a Russian village in a Russian countryside, where drinking, bribing and stealing are the order of the day. Yet he refuses to participate in these activities and excludes himself from the life to which he once belonged: his life is in a different culture and a different family in Afghanistan, where he was rescued by a man who had lost his son in the war and bought, or adopted, Kolia as a surrogate son. Kolia's exclusion is also a result of his moral values in a society that no longer has any. The film thus makes ironic comments on the theme of tolerance and the 'new' democratic order of society.

Bodrov's *Prisoner of the Mountains* (Kavkazskii plennik, Karavan 1996) offers a perspective on the war in terms of individual human loss rather than the clash of ideas or ideals. Vania Zhilin (Bodrov Jr.) is a young recruit posted to the Caucasus, whose detachment comes under attack. Together with Sasha Kostylin (Menshikov), he is taken captive by Abdul, who wants to exchange the hostages for his son who is held by the Russian military. The exchange fails since the Russians do not bring the son to the arranged meeting; Abdul tries to get the prisoners' parents to come and secure the exchange. While Zhilin's mother is on her way, the prisoners manage to run away, but they are caught when Sasha kills a shepherd to steal his rifle and a shot misfires. Sasha admits the murder and has his throat slit, while Zhilin is taken back to Abdul. In the meantime, Zhilin's mother has almost arranged an exchange of prisoners, but Abdul's son uses an opportune moment to run away, and is shot. Abdul is grieving over the loss when his daughter Dina, who has grown very fond of the kind recruit Zhilin, asks the father not to kill the captive, whom she had just been trying to let escape. Abdul takes Zhilin into the mountains and pretends to shoot him. As Abdul returns to the village, and Zhilin returns to freedom, Russian helicopters arrive to destroy the village in an act of revenge.

Bodrov shot the film in Dagestan with cameraman Pavel Lebeshev, working from a scenario written by his former student Boris Giller, who also had the idea for the

Figure 7.6 Sergei Bodrov Sr.'s *The Prisoner of the Mountains*: Oleg Menshikov and Sergei Bodrov Jr. as Kostylin and Zhilin.

film. Giller is a powerful Russian businessman, with his own film company, which produced the film at a time when production was at a low. The traditions of the Caucasian people are represented first hand, as the viewer travels with the camera around the mountain village. Abdul's daughter Dina provides the main link between the Muslim world and that of the prisoners: she explains the habits of the local people. Zhilin attempts to accept the Muslim civilization with tolerance. When Dina releases Zhilin, knowing that Abdul will kill him, he refuses to run away because he realizes that Dina would be punished. By contrast with Sasha, Zhilin does not kill, nor does he risk Dina's life. Sasha is unscrupulous in his attempts to escape from captivity; however, he takes responsibility for his actions and for the young recruit Zhilin.

Bodrov does not discriminate against any culture. The personal history of the two captives is told with the same compassion as the history of Abdul's family. The Muslims are both victims and aggressors, and so are the Russians. While Sasha resists and fights, Zhilin surrenders and survives. Neither of the soldiers has any ideals they believe in: Zhilin has his mother and others he cares for, Sasha does not. Zhilin's ability for comprehension makes him a survivor – in an idealized version of the war where soldiers are killed indiscriminately. *Prisoner of the Mountains* voices an appeal for understanding and sends a signal that bloodshed will only be followed by more bloodshed, thus offering a poignant comment on the Chechen War.

Those who return from the war are scarred for life, as Zhilin says in his final voiceover. This was also brought home by Nikita Tiagunov's *The Leg*, about a soldier sustaining an injury and losing a leg during the war, suffering from a trauma and unable to come to terms with reality (see Chapter 6). Valeri Todorovsky's *My Stepbrother Frankenstein* (Moi svodnyi brat Frankenshtein, Rekun 2004) explored the psychological wounds of the soldier Pavel, who served in Chechnya and returned physically and mentally crippled. The fear of enemy action makes it impossible for Pavel (the non-professional actor Daniil Spivakovsky) to lead a normal life, even with the support of his newly found family.

Rogozhkin's *Checkpoint* (Blokpost, CTB 1998) portrayed life at a strategically unimportant checkpoint on some southern Russian mountain road that leads to a Muslim cemetery. The lack of military strategy is reflected in the episodic structure of the film. A chronicler narrates the events as they happen: fragmented and almost anecdotal. The soldiers' routine at the checkpoint is hampered by a sniper who shoots a soldier in the end. However, the soldiers are not only attacked by the 'enemy' but also by their own: they are taken to task for a shooting in a village that was not their fault, but for which the army surrenders one of its own men to maintain the status quo. There is no sense or purpose in what the soldiers are doing, yet they bravely play their roles in an absurd war. Rogozhkin shows the everyday life and trivial events of the war without creating heroes. The soldiers have no identity, only nicknames and their private markers (ID badges) – and they have only a song about Russia to take pride in. Rogozhkin develops Bodrov's view on the lack of ideals and perspective that makes soldiers playthings of grander schemes.

Alexei Balabanov's *War* (Voina, CTB 2002) is maybe the most disturbing film about the Chechen War. The British schoolteacher Margaret (Dapkunaite), her fiancé John (Ian Kelly), the Russian soldier Ivan (Alexei Chadov, b. 1981, whom Balabanov discovered in this film) and Russian Captain Medvedev (Bodrov Jr.) are held hostage by the Chechens, whose leader Aslan Gugaev sets Ivan free for the help he has offered in computer technologies. John is released to obtain a ransom for Margaret's release. He travels back to Britain, where he fails to enlist support; together with Ivan, and a camera to capture everything to repay an advance paid by a television company, he returns to Chechnya. They free the hostages, supported heroically by Captain Medvedev. But during the operation Ivan shows no respect for civilian lives, following only the laws of war. John's filming not only puts their lives at risk on several occasions, but ultimately lands Ivan in prison for war crimes – with the camera evidence held against him. Balabanov structured the film around Ivan's narrative from his prison cell, without, however, commenting retrospectively on these events: they are all visually documented. The camera is an obtrusive and potentially dangerous tool in a war: it documents a reality that nobody wants to see, that cannot be understood visually, and that people would rather forget – of the cruelty and violence exercised by soldiers during war, which becomes compulsive. Balabanov here was ahead of his time, using a technique seen in recent films about the war in Iraq, such as Brian de Palma's *Redacted* (2007) or Paul Haggis's *In the Valley of Elah* (2007), using the hand-held or mobile phone camera to document compulsive violence in US soldiers in Iraq.

The cinema of the 1990s showed a concern with themes of national identity, and of the aspects of life in the new Russia under Yeltsin. Therefore it seems appropriate to speak of the cinema of the Yeltsin era – ranging from the massive production of films never released, to an all-time low in 1996, followed by a slow revival. The lack of a proper distribution system in post-Soviet Russia led to a breakdown of the link between director and audience, which was re-established only in the new millennium when the infrastructure was rebuilt and Russia became a major player in the global film market – at least for distribution.

–8–

Cinema in the Putin Era (2001–8)

Night Watch! Everyone step out of the Twilight!

Anton Gorodetsky in *Night Watch*

The first year of Putin's presidency was shaken by a series of tragic events, when in August 2000 the submarine *Kursk* perished, a terrorist attack rocked the Pushkin Square subway passage, and a fire destroyed the Ostankino television tower. In the following years Russia faced a number of terrorist attacks and two major hostage crises: the first during a performance of the musical *Nord-Ost* in October 2002, and the second with the siege of a school in Beslan in September 2004. Both ended with the loss of lives of many hostages after the intervention of the special forces.

The first term of Putin's presidency was also dominated by a growing state control of the media, with shares in the television channels Channel One and NTV passing from oligarchs Boris Berezovsky and Vladimir Gusinsky, who had fled Russia when accused of tax evasion, into the hands of the state-owned Gazprom-Media. Similarly, privately owned energy companies were brought back under state control, reflecting the drive of re-nationalization of the energy sector, which had been privatized during the legal chaos of the early Yeltsin years. The election of Dmitri Medvedev as president on 2 March 2008 concludes the Putin era.

This final chapter thus covers the eight years of Putin's presidency and leads up to the centenary of Russian cinema: on 15 October 1908 *Stenka Razin*, the first Russian-produced film, was screened. The chapter follows, broadly speaking, the chronological development of the period, seeing a rise in television serials, while films continued to revisit the past, before first *auteur* and later mainstream cinema returned to the level of world cinema.

The Rise of the Film Industry

Cinema in this period emerged from the shadows – initially into a twilight, but then into the limelight of international attention. As the Russian economy stabilized under Putin, the cinema sector began to grow and advanced to the fifth largest film market in the world, with box offices grossing around US$600 million in 2007.

The distribution of domestic films picked up as well. The season 2003–4 marked a breakthrough for Russian cinema, when *auteur* cinema gained the attention of international festivals with Andrei Zviagintsev's *The Return* (Vozvrashchenie) winning the Venice Golden Lion in September 2003, and Alexei Popogrebsky's and Boris Khlebnikov's *Roads to Koktebel* being named 'Best Film of 2004' by the International Film Critics' Association (FIPRESCI), while Dmitri Meskhiev's *Our Own* (Svoi) took three awards at the Moscow International Film Festival in 2004. For commercial cinema, the watershed was marked by *Night Watch* (Nochnoi Dozor, released 11 July 2004), which had a production cost of US$3.5 million and was the first film to gross in excess of US$10 million at the box office.[1]

The journey from a dilapidated system to an industry was a long one, and we can speak of profits and blockbusters only after 2004. The exhibition sector had expanded since 2002, when the first multiplex (nine screens, owned by Formula Kino) opened in central Moscow in the new shopping mall, Atrium, in front of the Kursk Railway Station. Other multiplexes followed suit and by 2005, Moscow counted 216 screens, followed by St Petersburg with fifty-nine screens and Yekaterinburg with twenty-one screens. The growth of cinema multiplexes is limited to a few exhibitors, such as Formula Kino, KinoMax, Kino Star and Cinema Park.[2] In addition, UIP ventured into the Russian market in 2005. These developments make the Russian film market a considerable player in world cinema distribution. Moreover, the national distribution network expanded vastly to cater for a growing number of exhibitors, including the distribution companies Gemini, Karo, Cascade, UIP and Central Partnership. Production rose, and with it the share of Russian films at the box office: for 20 per cent of titles released, Russian films have grossed approximately 30 per cent at the box office in 2006.

Russian film production could thus build on a developed and sophisticated infrastructure. Films are produced by independent companies, often with backing from television, although many continue to receive subsidies from Goskino or its successor, the Federal Agency for Culture and Cinematography. The major television channels, such as Channel One, Rossiya, NTV (with its – now independent – film production arm NTV-Profit), and the private channel CTC have developed powerful film production arms. The large independent studios – Sergei Selianov's CTB in St Petersburg, Igor Tolstunov's Profit, Yelena Yatsura and Sergei Melkumov's Slovo in Moscow and the production and distribution company Central Partnership (CPS) of Armen and Ruben Dishdishian – strike a sound balance between mainstream commercial cinema and *auteur* films.

Film and Television, 1999–2005

Crime serials are an ideological product of the late Yeltsin era because they reflect the chaotic conditions in Russia during that period, yet through the temporal distance they imply that these times are now over and there is order in the streets. The crime series asserts a different distribution of power, where the policeman or special agent is the winner in the fight over the gangsters, and thus reverses the real-life situation by creating the illusion of safety and stability. Many serials[3] were based on popular crime fiction: *Kamenskaya* (RTR 1999–2003) was based on the best-selling detective novels by Alexandra Marinina; *Turetsky's March* (Marsh Turetskogo, RTR 2000–2) was based on a novel by the popular detective writer Friedrich Neznansky; *The Crushing Force* (Uboinaia sila, ORT 2000–3) was based on the detective stories of Andrei Kivinov, who had scripted *Streets of Broken Lights* (see Chapter 7). *The Brigade* (Brigada, RTR 2002) was based on the novel by Alexander Belov, and is one of the last crime serials before a shift took place towards literature and history. Its popularity lies largely in its reliance on the (Soviet) model of friendship: the protagonist, Sasha Belov, returns from army service and finds that his girlfriend has left him; moreover, he has been framed for murder. His old friends try to help him overcome the corrupt and unjust structures of society in the Yeltsin years. Other serials created new popular heroes, such as *The Agent of National Security* (Agent natsional'noi bezopasnosti, TNT-NTV 1998–2001), with Mikhail Porechenkov as special agent Nikolaev; *Detective Dubrovsky's Dossier* (Dos'e detektiva Dubrovskogo, NTV 1999), starring the Lenkom Theatre's actor Nikolai Karachentsev; *Criminal Petersburg* (Banditskii Peterburg, NTV 2000–3) with veteran theatre actor Lev Borisov, as well as theatre stars Alexander Domogarov and Dmitri Pevtsov; and *The Truckers* (Dal'noboishchiki, NTV 2001), featuring the Ivan-the-Fool prototype Vladimir Gostiukhin (who played the lead role in Mikhalkov's *Urga*) and the comedian Vladimir Galkin.

Melodrama made its debut on television during the Putin era with *Poor Nastia* (Bednaia Nastia, CTC 2003). In autumn 2004, *My Beautiful Nanny* (Moia prekrasnaia niania, CTC 2004) appeared on the screens, turning Anastasia Zavorotniuk into a star overnight. The first successful sitcom was a remake of the American cult television serial *The Nanny* (1993–99), and was followed by *Not Born Beautiful* (Ne rodis' krasivoi, CTC 2006), modelled on the Latin American serial *Betty the Ugly* (Betty la Fea, Columbia 1999–2001).

Moreover, literary adaptations in the format of the mini-series flourished, especially of historical novels: Anatoli Rybakov's *Children of the Arbat* (Deti Arbata, dir. Andrei Eshpai, 2004); Fedor Dostoevsky's *The Idiot* (dir. Vladimir Bortko, 2003) was probably the first classical novel to reach the top of the best-seller lists thanks to its serialization; Mikhail Bulgakov's *Master and Margarita* (dir. Bortko, 2005); Boris Pasternak's *Doctor Zhivago* (dir. Alexander Proshkin, 2005); Nikolai Gogol's *The Case of the Dead Souls*, directed by the renowned filmmaker Pavel Lungin (Delo o mertvykh dushakh, 2005); and Alexander Solzhenitsyn's *In the First Circle* (V kruge pervom, 2006), directed by veteran filmmaker Gleb Panfilov.

Partly in the light of the imminent sixtieth anniversary of the victory over fascism in the Second World War, war drama took a prominent role in serial and film production for 2005. Serials touched on themes of war intelligence, such as *The Saboteur* (Diversant, 2004), about young intelligence officers in 1942; *Military*

Students (Kursanty, 2004), about people's effort in the winter of 1942 to sustain the defence of Stalingrad; *Red Choir* (Krasnaia kapella, 2004), about the fate of a Soviet undercover agent in Paris; and *The Man of War* (Chelovek voiny, 2005), about Soviet spies trying to undermine the German army on the western front. One of the most popular serials was *Penal Battalion* (Shtrafbat, 2004), showing how political prisoners and common criminals were deployed on the front as cannon fodder in strategic battles of the Soviet army, restoring their contribution to the war effort.

The Sixtieth Anniversary of the War Victory, 2002–6

The war also dominated feature film production, where films offered a new perspective: the war hero was perceived in a humanist tradition, a victim of war and of meaningless violence. But the enemy is also viewed as a victim of the system: the barrier between 'them' and 'us' is blurred in war films of the new millennium.

One of the first and most commercial films, which used large-scale battle scenes and pyrotechnics for the first time after the collapse of the industry, was Nikolai Lebedev's (b. 1966) *Star* (Zvezda, Mosfilm 2002), a remake of the 1949 film by Alexander Ivanov and based on a story by Emmanuil Kazakevich. It showed the work of an intelligence unit that went beyond army rules in order to complete a task. The

Figure 8.1 Rogozhkin's *Cuckoo*.

theme of individuals taking the course of events into their own hands, especially in the light of the chaos at Soviet military headquarters, had a contemporary resonance, but Lebedev underlined starkly the heroism of Soviet intelligence personnel in quite a traditional manner.

Set on the eve of Finland's withdrawal from the Second World War in September 1944, Rogozhkin's *Cuckoo* (Kukushka, CTB 2002) shows the Saami woman Anni (Anni-Kristiina Juuso), who has lived alone since her husband was drafted, sheltering a Finnish and a Russian soldier. Anni possesses an innate energy and draws her force of life from living in a symbiotic relationship with nature: she not only resuscitates the injured Russian soldier Ivan, but also performs pagan rituals, bringing back to life the Finnish soldier, Veiko, whom Ivan has shot in a rage, still seeing in him the enemy and a rival for Anni's love. Anni is strong enough to oversee death and life. The inability of the three people to understand one another (Anni speaks Saami, Veiko Finnish, and Ivan Russian) leads to comic situations: for example, Ivan's response to the question about his name is 'P'shol-ty' ('Get lost'), and this is what Veiko and Anni call him – Psholty. Anni's simple way of life, her pragmatic attitude to animosity and her sexual energy lead to a comic ending as she concludes her story from the present point of view, when she has twin boys from the two soldiers.

Such a perspective on ordinary life during the wartime was also presented in Alexei Gherman Jr.'s (b. 1976) *The Last Train* (Poslednii poezd, 2003), which focuses on two German men, a doctor and a postman, who have failed to make the right choice (or a choice) at the right time. Now they are the victims of circumstance, of politics, of regimes – and victims not of the war, but of their own predicament. Gherman's film is a manifesto about the absurdity of war, in which people can merely try to maintain their human dignity and where 'heroic deeds' lie in simple human gestures and compassion.

The theme of human dignity rather than wartime heroism is also pertinent to Dmitri Meskhiev's *Our Own* (Svoi, Slovo 2004), set in the Ukraine in August 1941. The violence and brutality of the German attack on the Soviet headquarters at the film's opening is captured in a few sequences in slow motion, which depict the horror of war in an almost documentary style as the German tanks crush the Soviet soldiers. The officer nicknamed 'Chekist' (the theatre actor Sergei Garmash, b. 1958, who became increasingly popular in film), the political commander Lifshits (the television serial star Konstantin Khabensky, b. 1972) and the sniper Mitka (Mikhail Yevlanov) manage to disguise their military rank before they surrender. They escape and hide with Mitka's father (the Ukrainian actor Bogdan Stupka, b. 1941), the village elder (Starosta) who works for the German police – who are looking for the three escaped POWs and exercise pressure on the Starosta. Meskhiev underscores that war always equals violence. The idealized image of a heroic and glorious war crowned by victory is shattered by the representation of the day-to-day reality of war. The hero might as well be Starosta, who does not turn in the soldiers, who protects his daughters, who refrains from violence, who was arrested by the Soviet regime,

Figure 8.2 Lungin's *Island.*

who sends his son back to the war, who serves the German police, and who protects his village. The final phrase of the film, when the Starosta says farewell to Mitka with the words 'Go, son, defend the motherland' is more than ironic: Meskhiev debunks the myth of the 'fatherland' for which people were ready to die and asserts that soldiers defended their country because this was their job, thus de-heroicizing military action per se.

The wartime past also preoccupied Pavel Lungin's films *Roots* (Bednye rodstvenniki, Russia/France, 2005) and *The Island* (Ostrov, Pavel Lungin Studio 2006). In *Roots*, an émigré searches for his relatives in Ukraine and, after being duped and ripped off, he uncovers the horrors of the war that almost entirely annihilated his ancestors. In *The Island*, the past haunts the main character, the priest Anatoli (Petr Mamonov): the opening sequence of the film shows how in the Second World War he failed to rescue a dying comrade in order to save his own life. The past, even distant in geographical or temporal terms, never loses its grip, but it is an individual and not a collective past that Lungin is interested in. Coming to terms with the past is essential for the development of characters, for making peace with themselves. Anatoli is an eccentric with special healing powers, but he has never forgiven himself, although it turns out that his wartime comrade was not killed after all. Even in the war, however, man should think of others and not only of himself, otherwise he carries the burden on his conscience for the rest of his life. The film's setting on an island in the far north during winter highlights the emotional coldness of the outside world, contrasted with the fire burning in Anatoli's abode.

The Soviet Past, 2003–7

The concern for the past (apart from the war, as encouraged by the anniversary) was diminished in the first decade of the twenty-first century. When the past was investigated, it was no longer the Stalin era, but instead later periods of Soviet history.

Pavel Chukhrai's *Driver for Vera* (Voditel' dlia Very, Profit 2004) is set during the Thaw. It opens in Moscow, where Viktor poses for a camera outside the Moscow State University's new building on Sparrow Hills. The film cuts from these scenes of happy life (marriage, job, future) to a morgue, where the body of Major Kraikov has undergone an autopsy after an alleged suicide. In 1962 the times are joyous; people are sporting bright dresses, carrying radios and cameras – they have acquired material wealth and enjoy life. But the 'suicide' gives reason to suspect a change in politics that has yet to surface fully.

The film unfolds the love story of Viktor, who becomes the new driver to General Serov (Bogdan Stupka), who is suspicious about Kraikov's death. Viktor is transferred to the Black Sea, where he meets Serov's daughter Vera (the Ukrainian-born Alena Babenko, b. 1972, who has since risen to a film star), a cripple who is pregnant and beyond the term to have an abortion whilst refusing to disclose the name of the father. Viktor pities Vera and marries her, but his love lacks the erotic power that is evoked by the maid Lida. When political events encroach on the personal life of the general, father and daughter are murdered while Viktor saves Vera's baby girl and leaves her with Lida. The system survives, thus re-enforcing the nightmarish vision of a never-ending state of control and violence. The film offers no happy ending, but closes with the image of Lida with the baby girl. Chukhrai reassesses the Thaw as a period of superficial relaxation that hid the clampdown which led to the ousting of Khrushchev, and thereby dismantles it as another period of Soviet history that disregarded human life.

Alexei Uchitel's *Dreaming of Space* (Kosmos kak predchuvtsvie, Rock 2005) is also set in the Thaw era and paints an equally bleak picture of the political situation, whilst offering more optimism for personal lives. Set in 1957 in a closed town in the far north, the film explores the budding relationships between the waitress Lida (Irina Pegova, b. 1978) and her sister, and two young men: the cook Konek (Mironov) and Hermann (Yevgeni Tsyganov, b. 1979), a former political prisoner who claims to be on a space programme to cover up his past and his plans to flee the Soviet Union. Once again, the Thaw era's image of space conquests, with the launch of the first satellite and the celebration of the cosmonaut Gagarin (shown in documentary footage), are only a glossy surface to the personal and emotional dramas of the period. Uchitel draws his fine actors from Moscow's studio theatres, especially the Workshop Theatre of the theatre director and teacher Petr Fomenko, who has trained some of the finest actors of the new millennium, including Pegova and Tsyganov.

Karen Shakhnazarov's *Vanished Empire* (Ischeznuvshaia imperiia, Mosfilm 2008) is set in the 1970s, the height of the Stagnation. It portrays with an almost nostalgic accuracy the illegal trade, the underground music, the pull necessary to obtain theatre or cinema tickets, and the happiness of the student generation. Sergei's carefree life comes to an end when his mother dies and his girlfriend marries his best friend. Following the footsteps of the father he never knew, Sergei becomes an archaeologist and finds fulfilment in the search for treasures and truths in the East. The Soviet empire may be vanishing, but not so the ancient history that allows us to find our roots.

The perestroika era had hardly attracted any attention from filmmakers until Abdrashitov's *Magnetic Storms* (Magnitnye buri, Mosfilm's Ark 2003), based on a script by Alexander Mindadze. For the first twenty minutes the spectator is confronted with monochrome scenes of nightly gang fights in a factory, shot in a blue-grey tint that veils the two opposed sides in a cloth of uniformity. Indeed, they are all workers at the same factory somewhere in the Urals. The fight scenes between the two groups are paced and almost choreographed, never showing any physical injury but rather concentrating on the movement – the racing steps and the beating fists. The speed with which these actions happen is reflected by the camera, which never offers an overview of the situation, muddled as it is, but captures the confusion and disorientation of those involved in the fight. The camerawork is concerned primarily with close-ups, denying the spectator (like the participants) an overview and offering very few panorama shots. This absence of an overview and the breathtakingly fast movement of the camera create a sense of dizziness for the spectator, almost like in the Dogme films shot with a hand-held camera. Abdrashitov's films are not only structurally and thematically innovative, but also visually innovative and searching.

The absence of an overview prevents an understanding of the events, which remain a backdrop: history is not man-made; it may influence events, but is no driving force. This grip of history on events that shake up human lives and pass like a thunderstorm is one explanation for the film's title, *Magnetic Storms*. The events are set in the late 1980s, when factory strikes resulted from the attempts to privatize state-owned enterprises. The workers were the (unpaid) victims in this episode of Soviet history. Against this backdrop, Abdrashitov develops a plot about a happily married couple, Marina (the theatre actress Viktoria Tolstoganova, b. 1972) and Valera (Maxim Averin, b. 1975, an actor of the Satirikon Theatre). However, the events intrude into their lives when Marina is threatened with rape and her sister Natasha, a Moscow prostitute, takes Marina with her when the latter

Figure 8.3 Balabanov's *Cargo 200*: Agniya Kuznetsova as Angelika.

realizes that she has two options: rape by the locals or prostitution in Moscow. Shortly afterwards, work resumes at the factory: economic stability has returned, but individual happiness has been destroyed. Abdrashitov paints a most accurate picture of perestroika, the desperate lives of the simple people and the loss of happiness that doomed the 1990s. In these films by Chukhrai and Abdrashitov, the past is an impasse.

Alexei Balabanov showed an engagement with the recent past in *Dead Man's Bluff* (Zhmurki, CTB 2005) and *Cargo 200* (Gruz 200, CTB 2007). *Dead Man's Bluff* shows today's businessmen as yesterday's criminals. The film is a parody of the rise of corrupt individuals to key business roles in the late 1990s, while former Mafia bosses (the main one played by Nikita Mikhalkov) are degraded to caretakers. Balabanov views society as essentially corrupt, and his characters are flatly drawn and deprived of any depth to underline that they are merely masks in a game that never ends. In *Cargo 200*, Balabanov confronts the 1980s, a time when Russian soldiers returned from Afghanistan – in coffins. The film is set in a small southern town, where Balabanov shows the aspirations and carelessness of the younger generation, the perversion of the police force, the aggression of ordinary people deprived of a meaning in life, and the pretence of the intelligentsia not to see the world for what it is. Balabanov traces evil, violence and aggression back into the late Stagnation era. Deeply rooted, it is inextricably linked to Russia's past and difficult to eradicate. In one scene, the Party chairman's young daughter Angelika (the model

Agniya Kuznetsova) loses her virginity through being raped with a bottle. In another scene she is chained to a bed by her captor, a perverse police captain, who places her next to her fiancé's corpse (which has been returned from Afghanistan) and later shoots dead on the same bed a prisoner whom he brought in to rape Angelika. Finally the policeman is himself shot in the same room, now filled with three corpses and hundreds of flies. Such scenes enraged film critics, who levelled charges of excessive violence at Balabanov and accused him of showing a past that did not resemble the truth. However, Balabanov created a powerful image of the decay and putridity of Soviet society in the 1980s, which unsettled the viewer by destroying the belief in a pure and peaceful Soviet past, showing instead Russians as passive victims of a system that eradicated human dignity long before the ideology's collapse.

The Renaissance of Auteurism, 1997–2007

Auteur cinema in Russia was associated almost exclusively with the name of Andrei Tarkovsky. Even in the twenty-first century, two of the most prominent *auteur* filmmakers, Alexander Sokurov and Andrei Zviagintsev, are referred to as 'heirs to Tarkovsky'. Indeed, few films had made a real impact at international film festivals during the 1990s, because many *auteurs* had remained silent: Alexei Gherman worked on *Khrustalev, My Car* for almost ten years; Sokurov concentrated on documentaries and returned to feature films only in 1997, while Muratova worked in now independent Ukraine. Only the end of the 1990s marks a return of these three Soviet *auteurs* to the international arena.

Sokurov embarked on a series of films about family relationships, including *Mother and Son* (Mat' i syn, Russia/Germany 1997) and *Father and Son* (Otets i syn, Germany/Russia/France/Netherlands/Italy 2003). *Father and Son* explored the pain of separation as the son leaves home. *Mother and Son* offers a slow-moving portrayal of a dying mother (the German non-professional actress, Gudrun Geyer), cradled and comforted by her son (Ananishnov), which was filmed in a manner that revealed the artificiality of nature through anamorphic shots that distort proportions, and through references to painterly compositions (largely of eighteenth- and nineteenth-century art) in the frames.

As historian and documentary filmmaker, Sokurov was predestined to work on a project that is a tetralogy about totalitarian leaders, of which three films have been completed. *The Moloch* (Molokh, Russia/Germany/Japan/Italy/Switzerland/France 1999) showed a day in Hitler's life at his residence on the Obersalzberg with his close circle. In exploring the relationship with Eva Braun, the film shows Hitler (Leonid Mozgovoy) in the most banal and everyday situations, revealing the man behind the monster. *Taurus* (Telets, Lenfilm 2001) was about Lenin's last days, while *The Sun* (Solntse, Russia/Italy/France – Proline and Nikola Film 2005) dealt with a few days in the life of the Japanese Emperor Hirohito, focusing on his private life before signing Japan's capitulation. Hirohito (the Japanese actor Issei Ogata) possesses a childlike curiosity, and the way in which he prepares for the meeting with the American General Douglas MacArthur (Robert Dawson) reveals not only his infantilism (he tries out in secret the cigarette and luxury goods that are forbidden fruit), but it makes him out as an actor, a bad imitator of Charlie Chaplin, on whose image he models himself for the photo call. In their private lives the three leaders come across as pitiful creatures, and Sokurov debunks the myths of their power.

Maybe the single most important of Sokurov's films is *Russian Ark* (Russkii kovcheg, Russia/Germany 2002), which explores Russia's national identity. The film is a unique technical feat: it is a single tracking shot lasting ninety-six minutes, filmed with a steadicam held by the director of photography Tilman Buettner, whose excellent camerawork can be seen in *Run Lola Run* (Lola rennt, dir. Tom Tykwer, 1997). The film was recorded directly in high-density digital format on to hard disk, with only the sound mastered in post-production. The filming took place on 23 December 2001, the shortest day in the year, in the Hermitage Museum in St Petersburg, leaving just four hours of daylight for filming after two days of preparation in the museum. The film creates the impression that the uninterrupted journey through 300 years of history and thirty-three rooms of the Hermitage takes just one long breath. The sensation of floating through history is achieved by a sheer technical feat.

Sokurov collapses time: there are scenes from the life of the Russian tsars in chronological order, from Peter the Great to Nicholas II, ending with the last ball in the Winter Palace in 1913. On the other hand, there are characters of different epochs, rupturing the neat chronology of the Romanov dynasty, when contemporary visitors stand next to historical characters. The journey through the space of the past is a journey through time, but the two never intersect. The Hermitage is an enclosed space that preserves the cultural heritage of the past in the 'Ark'.

Sokurov guides the viewer on the journey through the Hermitage through the character of the Marquis Astolphe de Custine (played by Sergei Dreiden, b. 1941), the French aristocrat who visited Russia in 1839 and found that it lacks a national identity, imitating Europe after having severed its bonds with Asia. Custine's comments are aggressive and cynical as he walks through the museum, engaged in a conversation with the narrator, who speaks with Sokurov's voice. The narrator is disorientated as his memory is obscured after some kind of catastrophe. Thus Sokurov lets Custine's arrogance stand unchallenged, leaving the judgement to the spectator. Sokurov seems to assume that the visual narrative is stronger than the verbal, and therefore uses his camera to impress the viewer: the eye of the camera lovingly caresses the paintings and art objects, which Custine dismisses as mere imitations. The camera pans across the rooms, focusing on details of the paintings and exploring their texture.

The final image of the film leads from the Hermitage, the 'Ark', to the sea – the Neva, a murky, foggy, grey patch of marshland that rises outside the entrance to the

Hermitage. Sokurov says farewell to Europe as he leaves the year 1913, and thus excludes the Soviet past. What remains in the Ark is the splendid past, without the horrors of the Soviet regime, but also without Russia's own art. Having severed its links with Europe, the Ark is destined to sail forever in the limbo between Europe and Asia. Russia's identity is sealed, hidden and impenetrable.

Sokurov's contribution to Russian cinema is unique: he stands in a solitary position, as his films are co-produced with Japan, Germany and other European countries. He is invited to international festivals but stands apart from the mainstream of Russian film production. His films are not uniquely Russian, but take a more universal approach, as is also clear in *Alexandra* (Russia/France – Proline 2007) – a film about a grandmother visiting her son, who serves in Chechnya. She meets a Chechen woman in the market who offers her support and takes her home, as the 70-year-old has grown tired from the walk and the heat. There is no animosity, and all people have suffered in this war. The opera singer Galina Vishnevskaya, in the role of the grandmother, endows the character with a unique civic courage that is ultimately capable of overcoming political barriers.

Andrei Zviagintsev's debut, *The Return* (Vozvrashchenie, Ren Film 2003), unexpectedly garnered two Golden Lion Awards at the International Film Festival in Venice in 2003: the Leone d'Oro and the Luigi de Laurentiis award for Best Debut. Zviagintsev never trained as a director, but is an actor by profession, and this was his debut film. Nevertheless, critics and audience unanimously hailed Zviagintsev as the 'new Tarkovsky' and compared *The Return* with *Ivan's Childhood*, which had won the Golden Lion in 1962, largely because of the religious symbolism of the film and the construction of frames that imitate the compositions of Renaissance depictions of Christ.

The Return tells the story of a father (the former studio theatre actor Konstantin Lavronenko, b.1961, in his screen debut) who returns, after twelve years of absence, to his wife and his two boys, Ivan (aged twelve) and Andrei (aged fifteen). The father takes the boys fishing, but he also has to retrieve a coffer hidden on an island. *The Return* is a journey of discovery, but the destination is the return home, thus offering a round trip that leads to physical separation and the spiritual reunion of the father and his sons. The brisk and authoritative father scares Ivan, whose aggression grows until he points a knife at his father. Shocked by his own capability for violence, Ivan runs away and climbs a makeshift observation tower. In an attempt to rescue Ivan, the father falls to his death. The children pull the body to the boat and return to the mainland; as they disembark, the boat drifts back to the open sea and sinks. *The Return* captures the boys and the father in a circular structure that offers no escape, but only returns. In this cyclical structure lies also a viable interpretation of the film: history repeats itself, but people still fail to recognize the genuine Father – Christ.

Such a religious reading is inferred by a series of painterly frames, which – unlike in Sokurov – reproduce Renaissance art. The father is first seen as a risen Christ figure straight from Andrea Mantegna's *Lamentation over Dead Christ* (1490). The first glimpse that the boys catch of him shows him lying on the bed, asleep; his body is covered with a silky blue sheet. The camera captures him from the same angle that Mantegna uses, from a position at the feet of the figure, slightly from below to allow for foreshortening (perspective). The camera then moves to an overall view of the body from above, before zooming in on the head. The sheet covers the body in exactly the same manner as in Mantegna's painting, replicating each fold. The boys stare at the image before rushing to the attic to search frantically for a picture of their father from the time before he left twelve years earlier. They find this in an old edition of the Bible, richly illustrated with etchings. However, the father in his incarnation of Christ as depicted in the Renaissance offers no guidance, nor is he a model of conduct: he never engages with the children emotionally or lovingly. For the children he is merely an image (a photo is all they will keep of him). The journey resurrects the father in order to immortalize his image.

Figure 8.4 Zviagintsev's *The Banishment.*

Zviagintsev's second film, *The Banishment* (Izgnanie, Ren Film 2007), is loosely based on William Saroyan's relatively unknown novel, *The Laughing Matter*. The film explores the relationship of a man, Alex (Lavronenko, who won the Best Actor award at the Cannes Festival for this part), who erroneously believes that his wife Vera (the Swedish actress Maria Bonnevie) had an affair and is pregnant with a child he has not fathered. He forces her to have an abortion, after which she kills herself. The film deals with disbelief and the inability to trust in others, a theme that had occurred already in *The Return*, between father and children, and which is here transferred to a relationship between adults. Zviagintsev relies on visual art to inspire his settings once again, but fails to integrate these citations coherently into the narrative, so that they protrude as artificial references to art history.

A further new direction of *auteur* cinema arose from the connection between cinema and the so-called New Drama movement that had emerged at the new millennium[4] and focused on the documentary approaches in playwriting, inspired by the verbatim technique (used to record the speech habits of marginal social groups). From New Drama, theatre and film directors took their inspiration for setting the often vulgar and violent discourse against a slow-paced, ritual action that intones everyday routine, thus reflecting the characters' essential inability to express themselves through words. A new kind of acting was required for this kind of performance, refraining from identification and psychological portrayal, dwelling instead on a detached and alienated performance. Many actors in this new line of *auteur* cinema (including Viktoria Tolstoganova, Alexander Yatsenko and Yuri Chursin) came from the two theatres at the heart of New Drama: Alexei Kazantsev's Centre for Drama and Direction, and the Moscow Art Theatre.

The most well-known exponent of this new trend is the theatre and film director Kirill Serebrennikov, who staged two plays (*Terrorism* and *Playing the Victim*) of the leading playwrights of New Drama, the Presnyakov Brothers, at the Moscow Art Theatre, and who made two films based on the Presnyakovs' plays: *Bad Bed Scenes* (Postel'nye stseny, 2005) and *Playing the Victim* (Izobrazhaia zhertvu, New People 2006). *Playing the Victim* followed the life of a young man, Valia (Yuri Chursin), in the provinces as he poses as victim for police reconstructions of crimes, which are filmed by the ever-present hand-held camera. The routine of the police work ignores the human tragedies of the police officers and the criminals, but it also leads the actor Valia to assimilate the violence he experiences in the reconstructions and commit a real, horrible crime. The film explores the relationship between re-enactment and reality, and considers re-enactment as a ritualization, and therefore normalization, of violence.

As commercial cinema rose after 2004, little room was left for experimentation. This niche was filled by the documentary movement, which eschewed the mainstream. The emergence of kinoteatr.doc, a festival held annually by the production centre for documentaries of the same name, was a significant step in advocating a new style of documentary cinema, using the hand-held camera to explore the life of marginal groups, with directors often immersing themselves in the necessary social context. The thematic 'centrality' of the periphery and of marginal groups is indicative of the alternative nature of the project, which does not rely on state subsidies.

One experiment with a more objective form of documentarism was Andrei Zaitsev's *My House* (Moi dom, 2000) in which a static camera was positioned on the windowsill of a flat in a suburban housing estate in order to capture, over the course of six months (winter, spring, summer), the same place: the back yard of a shop, which is a meeting spot. Zaitsev here removed the filmmaker from the capturing process to create a greater degree of authenticity and objectivity – although the selection of the fragments included in the film still reveals the hand of the editor. The technique of static camera shots is one of the outstanding features of the films of Boris Khlebnikov and Alexei Popogrebsky. The opening scene of Khlebnikov's *Free Floating* consists of a four-minute shot by a static camera positioned opposite the entrance to the factory where the workers arrive – inverting Louis Lumière's *Workers Leaving the Lumière Factory* (1895). The cross-fertilization of ideas between '.doc' and *auteur* cinema goes beyond the pure technical features. Khlebnikov worked with the playwright Alexander Rodionov for the script of his film *Free Floating* (Svobodnoe plavanie, Koktebel Studio 2006), drawing on the latter's experience with verbatim and documentary theatre.

Roads to Koktebel (Koktebel, Koktebel Studio 2003) is the debut film of Boris Khlebnikov (b. 1972) and Alexei Popogrebsky (b. 1972), two graduates from the Film Institute. *Koktebel* tells the story of a father (the St Petersburg theatre actor Igor Chernevich, b. 1966) and his 11-year-old son (Gleb Puskepalis) en route to Koktebel, a holiday resort in the Crimea, popular among artists in pre-Revolutionary Russia, and a superb location for gliders, who practised in the coastal upwind.

Roads to Koktebel is a road movie where the journey has a clearly defined destination for father and son: Koktebel. Yet their motives are different, and therefore their pace for the journey is different too. The father hopes to find harmony through reunion with his sister. The boy wants to visit the place of Soviet aviation achievements, which allowed man to gain an overview of the world through flight. Indeed, he claims to be able to see the world from a bird's-eye view by squinting his eyes. Yet upon arrival in Koktebel, he finds the gliders' monument in a shambles, his paper does not drift in the upwind, and there is no aunt. The director of photography Sandor Berkeshi frequently uses static camera positions, with characters walking in and out of frames, creating a comic sense of lack of focus. The camera often adopts the boy's perspective, for example when it works at the child's eye level as the boy roams the streets of Koktebel in search of his aunt, catching only views of the tourists' legs.

When the father delays the continuation of the journey, the boy despairs and runs away; he gets a lift to Koktebel – where his father rejoins him as the boy has suffered the greatest disappointment: he cannot see the world from above – and here the camera is allowed its only crane shot. Both father and son have been misled by illusions and myths, but their disappointment has brought them closer and made them realize the important thing in their lives: the understanding of each other. At last, an optimistic tone enters Russian cinematic discourse, although hope for the future – albeit a personal future – was only expressed visually, not verbally.

Khlebnikov's *Free Floating* is about the 16-year-old Lyonia (Alexander Yatsenko, b. 1977), who tries to find his place in life in his provincial Russian home town. The film is also structured like a road movie, where the stops are stations of emotional development: of learning that people cheat, of first love, and of appreciating honesty. There is no 'happy ending' in terms of the narrative, but – as in *Koktebel* – in the final scene Lyonia leaves the provincial world and enters the wide world – the vast space of the river. Popogrebsky's first solo film, *Simple Things* (Prostye veshchi, Koktebel Studio 2007), adopts a more traditional approach to filming and to the narrative. It deals with the moral dilemma of a doctor asked to terminate an old man's life, weighing ethics against materialist considerations: the doctor lives in one room of a communal apartment with his family, expecting a child and a grandchild. But he ultimately refuses to administer a lethal injection. Popogrebsky's skill clearly lies in the subtle work with actors (notably Sergei Puskepalis) and the creation of detailed interiors for contrasting worlds.

The Russian Blockbuster, 2004–8

The commercial breakthrough for Russian cinema came with Timur Bekmambetov's *Night Watch* (Nochnoi dozor, Tabbak, Bazelevs, Channel One 2004), which grossed US$16 million at the Russian box office after its release in July 2004. This represented, at the time, the largest profit ever made by a Russian film. *Night Watch* was subsequently bought by Fox Searchlight, and has been released in a number of European countries and the US. The film contains all the ingredients of an action movie while expanding the fantasy component. Occasionally it is almost simplistic in its literal citations; for example the visual rendering of the funnel (*voronka*) in the form of crows (*vorona*) is only too reminiscent of Hitchcock's horror movie *The Birds*.

Figure 8.5 Bekmambetov's *Night Watch.*

In the style of a good Hollywood movie, *Night Watch* and *Day Watch* divide characters into good and bad. Yet personal history and human errors allow characters to transgress the clearly delineated worlds of good and evil, of Gesser (Vladimir Menshov, director of the Oscar-winning *Moscow Does Not Believe in Tears* – and therefore the 'good guy') and Zawulon (Viktor Verzhbitsky). The conflict between good and evil, between the worlds of light and darkness, is set out in a historical prologue in Languedoc in 1342; this war has thus been raging for centuries. In the present world, fortune-tellers, magicians and vampires work for the evil forces, while the 'light' people work – in another very literal reference – as engineers for Gorsvet (City Light).

The film is based on Sergei Lukianenko's gripping fantasy (sci-fi) thriller trilogy; the second part of the trilogy, *Day Watch* (Dnevnoi dozor, Tabbak, Bazelevs, Channel One) was released in January 2006. *Night Watch* shows a new action hero, Anton Gorodetsky (Khabensky): a man of action who is on the side of the good – light and bright – forces, but has nevertheless an inherent flaw in his biography that gives his character a human touch. Through his actions he instils trust that there is a force (albeit not the police) that can be relied upon, that is capable of taking care of its inhabitants and protecting them from the disasters brought by the evil and dark force of Zawulon. But once upon a time Anton, too (like all of mankind), was tempted by the dark, evil world.

In August 1992 Gorodetsky wanted to revenge his wife's betrayal and to kill her unborn son. To this end, he consulted the sorceress Schulz, who was prevented from casting a spell by the forces of light. Twelve years later, Gorodetsky stands firmly on the side of 'light' and works for Gesser to protect Moscow and its inhabitants from disaster, catastrophe and evil. On a mission to save the boy Yegor, he kills one of the 'others' who have turned a girl into a vampire longing for Yegor's blood. Deprived of her prey and her beloved, she now seeks to destroy both Anton and Yegor. But here Anton's attention is distracted when he notices a woman, Svetlana, who has cursed herself and thereby brings about disaster, causing an explosion in the power plant (a chilling premonition of the power cut that struck Moscow in May 2005) and puts an aircraft at risk of crashing. When Anton finally returns from saving both Svetlana and Moscow, it emerges that Yegor has a special relationship to Anton: he is the child he wanted his wife to abort, and the boy decides to turn to the evil forces. *Day Watch* revolves around the search for a piece of chalk (located in the East) that allows Anton to turn time back and correct his mistake of 1992. *Day Watch* thus allows the character – and the viewer – to annihilate the 1990s.

Other blockbusters followed *Night Watch*, without however crossing the US$10 million mark. These included a number of sequels to successful films, such as Alexei Sidorov's *Shadowboxing* (Boi s ten'iu, CPS 2005), about the triumph of a boxer over the Mafia, even though he has to pay a price and serve a prison sentence before returning to his new-found love – and, in the sequel *Shadowboxing 2* (CPS, dir. Anton Megerdichev, 2007), to boxing. The popular film *Bimmer* (Bumer, CPS and Pygmalion 2003), directed by Petr Buslov and dealing with four friends involved in the criminal world, was followed by *Bimmer 2* in 2006, which grossed US$13 million. Finally, Timur Bekmambetov's *Irony of Fate, The Continuation* (Ironiia sud'by – prodolzhenie, Channel One and Bazelevs 2008), the sequel to Eldar Riazanov's new year hit *Irony of Fate* (1975) and relying on the film star Khabensky, became the most popular film in Russia to date with the box office grossing of almost US$50 million.

The novels by the popular writer Boris Akunin, about the investigator Ernest Fandorin, were also made into blockbusters: *Counsellor of State* (Statskii sovetnik, TriTe 2005, dir. Filipp Yankovsky), showing how Fandorin triumphs over the terrorists who endanger Russia in the 1880s, made US$7 million, while *Turkish Gambit* (Turetskii gambit, Russia/Bulgaria – TriTe and Channel One, 2005, dir. Djannik Faiziev) grossed US$18 million with a tale of Fandorin overcoming Russia's enemy in the East.

Grand-scale films with special effects and huge budgets were becoming more frequent. *Wolfhound* (Volkodav, CPS 2006), directed by Nikolai Lebedev, was one of the first fantasy films which outstanding special effects. The Afghan War epic *Company 9* (9-aia rota, Slovo 2005) showed military operations during the Afghan War in great (and costly) detail, involving the destruction of two aircraft. The film underlined the braveness of the soldiers in their fight for the Soviet fatherland, even after it has abandoned its territorial pursuits. The film was directed by Oscar-winner Sergei Bondarchuk's son, Fedor (b. 1964), and made US$23 million at the box office.

Figure 8.6 Bondarchuk's *Company 9*: Fedor Bondarchuk as Khokhol.

All these blockbusters revolve around plots that are removed in space and/or time: *Night Watch* through the historical prologue and the flashback to Anton in 1992; *Gambit* and *Counsellor* through their setting in the 1880s, both in Russia and Central Asia; *Company 9* through a geographically remote setting and the temporal distance to the Soviet regime. In all these films the heroes are victorious, but they pay for their victories and they are ready to die. The hero of Putin's cinema had become a flagship of the regime: he inspired trust in the population and reassured the viewer that Russia is a safe place.

Another recent, very encouraging development is the rise of Russian animation. After Soyuzmultfilm had been disbanded, a variety of animation studios were founded in the 1990s, the most important being the studio Pilot, of Alexander Tatarsky (1950–2007), which launched a DVD release of new cartoons, 'Mountain of Gems' (Gora samotsvetov). The Petersburg studio Melnitsa (Mill), founded by Alexander Boyarsky and Vladimir Vasenkov in 1992, hired the internationally renowned animator Konstantin Bronzit to make a full-length drawn cartoon based on the Russian folk epic *Alesha Popovich and Tugarin* (Alesha Popovich i Tugarin Zmei, CTB and Melnitsa 2004), which portrays the folk hero Alesha Popovich as a New Russian superman. His demeanour is that of the American Superman, while his use of language caricatures the incorrect language of the New Russians: Alesha's body is impressively strong, but he is dumb. Bronzit's plain images brought out the grotesque features of the characters, making the cartoon very successful. In 2008, the animated epic tale *Ilya Muromets and Robber-Nightingale* (Il'ia Muromets i Solovei-razboinik, dir. Vladimir Toropchin, CTB and Melnitsa) was released, grossing almost US$10 million at the box office – a stunning achievement for a cartoon. This gives hope for the rise of the animation industry, following the path of feature film production.

Appendix 1: Russian Films in International Festivals

This appendix surveys the Russian participation in international (A-class) film festivals and in the Academy Awards. Table A1.1 lists the Soviet or Russian nominations for the Oscar award (winners in bold typeface); Table A1.2 lists the award winners of the Moscow International Film Festival; Tables A1.3–A1.6 list the Soviet/Russian prize-winning films at Cannes, Venice, Berlin and Locarno, with main festival awards in bold.

Table A1.1 Oscar: Best Foreign Language Film

Year	*Film and Director*
1968	***War and Peace*** **(Bondarchuk)**
1969	*Brothers Karamazov* (Pyriev)
1971	*Tchaikovsky* (Talankin)
1972	*The Dawns Here Are Quiet* (Rostotsky)
1975	***Dersu Uzala*** **(with Japan)**
1978	*Wim Bim Black Ear* (Rostotsky)
1980	***Moscow Does Not Believe in Tears*** **(Menshov)**
1982	*Private Life* (Raizman)
1984	*Wartime Romance* (Todorovsky)
1992	*Urga* (Mikhalkov)
1994	***Burnt by the Sun*** **(Mikhalkov)**
1996	*Prisoner of the Mountains* (Bodrov)
1997	*The Thief* (Pavel Chukhrai)
2007	*Twelve* (Mikhalkov)

Table A1.2 Moscow Film Festival Awards

Year	*Film and Director*
1935	Lenfilm (*Chapaev*; *Maxim's Youth*; *The Peasants*)
1959	*Fate of a Man* (Bondarchuk)
1961	*Clear Sky* (Chukhrai)
	Naked Island (Kaneto Shindo, Japan)

Year	*Film and Director*
1963	*8½* (Fellini)
1965	*War and Peace* (Bondarchuk)
	Twenty Hours (Zoltán Fábri, Hungary)
1967	*The Journalist* (Gerasimov)
	Father (István Szabó, Hungary)
1969	*We'll Live till Monday* (Rostotsky)
	Lucia (Humberto Solás, Cuba); *Serafino* (Pietro Germi, Italy)
1971	*The White Bird Marked with Black* (Ilienko)
	Confessions of a Police Captain (Damiano Damiani, Italy); *Live Today, Die Tomorrow* (Kaneto Shindo, Japan)
1973	*The Sweet Word: Liberty!* (Zalakevicius)
	Affection (Ludmil Staikov, Bulgaria); *Oklahoma Crude* (Stanley Kramer, USA)
1975	*Dersu Uzala* (Akiro Kurosawa, Japan/USSR)
	The Promised Land (Andrzej Wajda, Poland); *We All Loved Each Other So Much* (Ettore Scola, Italy)
1977	*Mimino* (Daneliya)
	The Fifth Seal (Zoltán Fábri, Hungary); *Foul Play* (Juan Antonio Bardem, Spain)
1979	*Honour: Que Viva Mexico* (Eisenstein)
	Christ Stopped at Eboli (Francesco Rosi, Italy); *Seven Days in January* (Juan Antonio Bardem, Spain); *Amator* [Camera Buff] (Krzisztof Kieslowski, Poland)
1981	*Tehran 43* (Alov and Naumov, USSR with France and Switzerland)
	The Man Who Turned into Juice (João Batista de Andrade, Brazil); *The Wild Fields* (Hong Sen Nguyen, Vietnam)
1983	*Vassa* (Panfilov)
	Alsino and the Condor (Miguel Littin, Nicaragua, Cuba, Costa Rica, Mexico); *Amok* (Souheil Ben-Barka, Morocco)
1985	*Come and See* (Klimov)
	A Soldier's Story (Norman Jewison, USA); *The Descent of the Nine* (Christos Siopahas, Greece)
1987	*Interview* (Fellini, Italy)
1989	*The Icicle Thieves* (Maurizio Nichetti, Italy)
1991	*The Spotted Dog at the Edge of the Sea* (Karen Gevorkyan, USSR/Germany)
1993	*Ivan and Abraham* (Yolande Zauberman, France/Belorus)
1995	No award
1997	*Marvin's Room* (Jerry Zaks, USA)
1999	*Will to Live* (Kaneto Shindo, Japan)
2000	*Life as a Fatal Sexually Transmitted Disease* (Krzysztof Zanussi, Poland)
2001	*The Believer* (Henry Bean, USA)
2002	*Resurrection* (Taviani Brothers, Italy)
2003	*The End of the Mystery* (Miguel Hermoso, Spain)
2004	***Our Own* (Dmitri Meskhiev)**
2005	***Dreaming of Space* (Alexei Uchitel)**
2006	*About Sara* (Othman Karin, Sweden)
2007	***Travelling with Pets* (Vera Storozheva)**

Table A1.3 Cannes International Film Festival

Year	*Director and Film*	*Award*
1946	Ptushko, *The Stone Flower*	Best Colour
1951	Roshal, *Mussorgsky*	Prize for Best Art Work: production designer Nikolai Suvorov and art director Abram Veksler
1954	Yutkevich, *The Great Warrior Skanderberg*	Special Mention
1955	Vasiliev, *Shipka Heroes* (Bulgaria/USSR)	Best Director
1955	Kheifits, *The Great Family*	Acting Ensemble
1956	Yutkevich, *Othello*	Best Director
1957	Chukhrai, *Forty-First*	Special Award
1958	**Kalatozov, *The Cranes Are Flying***	**Golden Palm**
1960	Chukhrai, *Ballad of a Soldier*; Kheifits, *Lady with a Lapdog*	Participation award
1961	Solntseva, *Chronicle of Flaming Years*	Best Director
1963	Samsonov, *Optimistic Tragedy*	Best Evocation of a Revolutionary Epic
1966	Yutkevich, *Lenin in Poland* (USSR/Poland)	Best Director
1972	Tarkovsky, *Solaris*	Grand Jury Prize
1979	Konchalovsky, *Siberiade*	Grand Jury Prize
1981	Grikiavicius, *The Fact*	Best Supporting Actress: Yelena Solovei
1983	Tarkovsky, *Nostalghia*	Grand Prix for Creative Cinema
1987	Abuladze, *Repentance*	Special Grand Jury Prize
1987	Mikhalkov, *Dark Eyes*	Best Actor: Marcello Mastroianni
1990	Panfilov, *The Mother*	Artistic Contribution
1990	Lungin, *Taxi Blues* (France/Russia)	Best Director
1992	Kanevsky, *An Independent Life* (Russia/France/UK)	Jury Prize
1994	Mikhalkov, *Burnt by the Sun* (Russia/France)	Grand Jury Prize
1999	Yuri Arabov, *Moloch*	Best Screenplay
2000	Lungin, *The Wedding*	Special Mention for Acting Ensemble
2007	Zviagintsev, *The Banishment*	Best Actor: Konstantin Lavronenko

Table A1.4 Venice International Film Festival

Year	*Director and Film*	*Award*
1932	Ekk, *Road to Life*	Best Director
1934	Russian programme	Award
1946	Chiaureli, *The Oath*	Award
	Donskoy, *Unconquered*	Golden Medal
1947	Alexandrov, *Spring*	Prize for theme
	Pudovkin, *Admiral Nakhimov*	Award
1953	Ptushko, *Sadko*	Silver Lion
1955	Samsonov, *The Cricket*	Silver Lion
1957	Braun, *Malva*	Best Actress: Dzidra Ritenberg

Year	*Director and Film*	*Award*
1961	Alov and Naumov, *Peace to Him who Enters*	Special Jury Prize
1962	**Tarkovsky, *Ivan's Childhood***	**Golden Lion**
1963	Talankin, *Introduction*	Special Jury Prize
1964	Kozintsev, *Hamlet*	Special Jury Prize
1965	Todorovsky, *Faithfulness*	Best First Film
1965	Khutsiev, *I am Twenty*	Special Jury Prize
1966	Konchalovsky, *First Teacher*	Best Actress: Natalia Arinbasaeva
1982	Raizman, *Private Life*	Special Prize: Mikhail Ulianov
1984	Ioseliani, *Les Favoris de la Lune* (France)	Grand Special Jury Prize
1986	Soloviev, *Someone Else's White and the Speckled*	Grand Special Jury Prize
1988	Dykhovichny, *Black Monk*	Golden Osella for Cinematography: Vadim Yusov
1989	Ioseliani, *Et la Lumière fut* (France)	Grand Special Jury Prize
1991	**Mikhalkov, *Urga***	**Golden Lion**
1993	Khudoinazarov, *Kosh Ba Kosh* (Tajikistan, Switzerland, Russia)	Silver Lion
1996	Ioseliani, *Brigands: Chapter VII* (France)	Grand Special Jury Prize
1997	Chukhrai, *The Thief*	Italian Senate's Gold Medal
2002	Konchalovsky, *House of Fools*	Grand Special Jury Prize
2003	**Zviagintsev, *The Return***	**Golden Lion, Luigi de Laurentiis Award**
2005	Gela Babluani, *Tzameti (13)*, (France)	Luigi de Laurentiis Award
2007	Nikita Mikhalkov, *Twelve*	Luigi de Laurentiis Award

Table A1.5 Berlin International Film Festival

Year	*Director and Film*	*Award*
1975	Soloviev, *Hundred Days After Childhood*	Silver Bear – Best Director
1977	**Shepitko, *The Ascent***	**Golden Bear**
1981	Zarkhi, *Twenty-Six Days from the Life of Dostoyevsky*	Best Actor: Anatoli Solonitsyn
1983	Mikaelian, *Love by Request*	Best Actress: Yevgenia Glushenko
1984	Todorovsky, *A War Romance*	Best Actress: Inna Churikova
1985	Okeev, *The Descendant of the Snow Leopard*	Silver Bear for Outstanding Single Achievement
1986	Shengeleya, *A Young Composer's Journey*	Silver Bear – Best Director
1987	**Panfilov, *The Theme* (1979)**	**Golden Bear**
1988	Askoldov, *The Commissar* (1967)	Silver Bear – Special Jury Prize
1989	Abdrashitov, *The Servant*	Alfred Bauer Prize
1990	Muratova, *Asthenic Syndrome*	Silver Bear – Special Jury Prize
1990	Rogozhkin, *The Guard*	Alfred Bauer Prize
1991	Aristov, *Satan*	Silver Bear – Special Jury Prize
1992	Khutsiev, *Infinity*	Alfred Bauer Prize
1993	Babluani, *The Sun of the Wakeful* (Georgia)	Silver Bear for Outstanding Contribution

Year	*Director and Film*	*Award*
1994	Aranovich, *Year of the Dog* (Russia/France)	Silver Bear for Outstanding Artistic Contribution
1995	Abdrashitov, *Play for a Passenger*	Silver Bear
2002	Ioseliani, *Monday Morning* (France)	Silver Bear – Best Director

Table A1.6 Locarno International Film Festival

Year	*Director and Film*	*Award*
1946	Tisse and Moskvin, *Ivan the Terrible I*	Photography
1947	Golovnia and Lobova, *Admiral Nakhimov*	Photography
1953	Alexandrov, *Glinka*	Critics' Prize
1959	Kaplunovsky, *Captain's Daughter*	Audience Award
1960	Donskoy, *Foma Gordeev*	Best Director
1968	Yashin, *Autumn Weddings*	Debut
1969	**Panfilov, *No Path through Fire***	**Golden Leopard (by majority)**
1986	Gherman, *My Friend Ivan Lapshin*	Ernest Artaria Prize
1987	Sokurov, *Lonely Voice*	Bronze Leopard
	Tsabadze, *The Spot*	Leopard's Eye – Silver
1990	**Proskurina, *Accidental Waltz***	**Golden Leopard**
1991	Dostal, *Paradise Cloud*	Silver Leopard
1992	Omirbaev, *Kairat* (Kazakhstan)	Silver Leopard
1993	Shinarbaev, *Place on the Grey Triangular Hat* (Kazakhstan)	Golden Leopard
1993	Tsintsadze, *On the Borderline* (Georgia)	Silver Leopard

Appendix 2: Chronology of Events

Date	Cinema and Culture	History
1896		
4 May	Cinema at the Aquarium Park, St Petersburg	
14 May		Coronation of Tsar Nicholas II
1902		
2 Apr		Assassination of Dmitri Sipiagin, Interior Minister
22 Sep	Meyerhold in Kherson, *Three Sisters*	
1904		
Jan		Russo-Japanese War (until Aug 1905)
15 Jul		Assassination of Viacheslav von Plehve, Interior Minister
30 Jul		Birth of Tsarevich Alexei
1905		
9 Jan		Bloody Sunday (1905 Revolution)
19 Feb	Metropol Hotel in Moscow opens	
14–25 Jun		Uprising on battleship *Potemkin*
1906		
27 Apr		First Duma elected
9 Dec	Khanzhonkov company opens	
30 Dec	Meyerhold, *The Fairground Booth*	
1907		
28 Oct	Drankov Atelier opens	
22 Dec	Anna Pavlova dances *The Dying Swan*	
1908		
6 Sep	Tolstoy's eightieth birthday	
15 Oct	*Stenka Razin*	
1 Nov	Khanzhonkov's, *Gypsy Camp*	
23 Nov	Orion cinema in Moscow opens	
27 Nov	Film control introduced	

Date	*Cinema and Culture*	*History*
1909		
Summer	*Ballets russes* in Paris	
29 Nov	Pathé colour film *Happy-go-Lucky Merchant*	
10 Nov	Ars Cinema (Khudozhestvennyi) opens	
1910		
7 Nov	Death of Tolstoy	
	Gramophone factory near Moscow	
1911		
Feb	Fire in Bologoe cinema	
1 Sep		Assassination of Petr Stolypin (Chairman of Council of Ministers)
1 Oct	Circus opens (Nikitin Bros.)	
14 Nov	*Defence of Sevastopol* shown to the tsar	
23 Dec	Gordon Craig stages Hamlet at MAT	
1913		
16 Feb	Drankov and Taldykin, *300 Years of the Romanovs*	
14 Nov	Khanzhonkov opens cinema on Triumphal Square	
2 Dec	Futurist Theatre: *Victory over the Sun*	
26 Dec	Starewicz, *Christmas Eve*	
1914		
3 Mar	Bauer, *Child of the Big City*	
28 Jun		Murder of Franz Ferdinand
19–24 Jul		Germany, then Austria-Hungary declare war on Russia
Aug		St Petersburg becomes Petrograd
1915		
8 May	Prohibition of import of German films	
Nov	Meyerhold's *Portrait of Dorian Gray*	
1916		
Jan	'0,10' exhibition of futurist abstract art	
19 Apr	Protazanov, *Queen of Spades*	
10 May	Bauer, *Life for a Life*	
17 Dec		Murder of Rasputin
1917		
23–27 Feb		February Revolution
2 Mar		Abdication of the tsar
7–9 Mar		Arrest of imperial family

3 Apr		Lenin returns to Russia
9 Jul	Death of Yevgeni Bauer	
16 Oct	Proletkult clubs for workers	
21 Oct	Protazanov, *Satan Triumphant*	
25 Oct		October Revolution: storming of Winter Palace
Dec		Lunacharsky is head of Narkompros
Dec		Cheka (Emergency committee) established
1918		
11 Jan		Ukrainian People's Republic formed
3 Mar		Treaty of Brest-Litovsk (Russia loses territories but withdraws from the war)
4 Mar	Prohibition on cinema closures	
12 Mar		Moscow becomes capital
14 May	Protazanov, *Father Sergius*	
29 Apr		Hetmanate in Ukraine under Pavlo Skoropadsky
17 Jul	'Kinokomitet' of the Commissariat for Enlightenment (Narkompros)	Execution of imperial family in Ekaterinburg
10 Oct		New orthography introduced
Nov		Directorate of Ukraine under Symon Petlyura
18 Dec		Finnish independence
1919		
3 Feb	Death of actress Vera Kholodnaya	
27 Aug	Cinema nationalized under Narkompros	
1 Sep	Goskinoshkola (State Film School) opens	
5 Sep		Death of Chapaev
26 Dec		Campaign against illiteracy
1920		
		Azerbaijan and Armenia become Soviet republics; independence for Latvia, Lithuania and Estonia.
8 Jul		American embargo
7 Nov	Yevreinov's spectacle, *Storming of the Winter Palace*	
1921		
		Georgia becomes a Soviet republic
21 Mar		New Economic Policy introduced
28 Feb–18 Mar		Kronstadt uprising against Soviet power
13 Jul	Children's theatre of Natalia Sats opens in Moscow	
Oct	Gorky leaves Soviet Russia for Italy on health grounds	

Date	*Cinema and Culture*	*History*
1922		
	Establishment of Glavlit (Main Administration for Safeguarding State Secrets in the Press)	Campaign against the Church: arrests and executions
17 Jan	Leninist proportion: 75 per cent entertainment and 25 per cent propaganda films	
Feb		Cheka renamed GPU (State Political Directorate; from 1923 OGPU)
3 Apr		Stalin is General Secretary of the Party
25 May		Lenin suffers stroke
5 Jun	First newsreel of *Kinopravda*	
9 Jul	FEKS established	
Dec	Goskino (Central State Film and Photo Enterprise) established	
30 Dec		Formation of USSR
1923		
	Eisenstein makes *Glumov's Diary*; publishes *Montage of Attractions*	
4 Jan		Lenin's testament
6 Jul		Soviet Constitution comes into force
30 Nov	Perestiani, *Red Imps*	
1 Dec		Restriction on moves to Moscow
1924		
		Uzbekistan, Tajikistan and Turkmenistan join the USSR; Kirghiz ASSR (autonomous Soviet socialist republic) formed; USSR recognized by UK and France
21 Jan		Death of Lenin
24 Jan		Petrograd named Leningrad
31 Jan		Call for Party membership ('Leninskii prizyv')
3 Feb		Rykov is Premier
4 Jun	Sovkino (All-Russian Photo-Cinematographic Shareholding Company) formed	
1 Aug	Mezhrabpom-Rus formed (Mezhrabpomfilm from 1928)	
25 Sep	Protazanov, *Aelita* (first film after his return to Russia)	
23 Nov	First radios	
2 Dec	Zheliabuzhsky, *The Cigarette Girl from Mosselprom*	
9 Dec	Kozintsev and Trauberg, *Adventures of Oktiabrina*	
Dec		Stalin announces 'socialism in one country'

1925		
	Journal *Sovetskii ekran* launched	
28 Apr	Eisenstein, *The Strike*	
6 Nov		Yekaterinburg renamed Sverdlovsk
28 Nov	Suicide of poet Sergei Esenin	
1926		
		Grigori Zinoviev, Lev Trotsky and Lev Kamenev form an opposition to Stalin
18 Jan	Eisenstein's *Potemkin* shown at Ars Cinema	
20 Jul		Death of Felix Dzerzhinsky (Cheka founder)
11 Oct	Pudovkin *The Mother*	
Oct	Telephone exchange established	
1927		
14 Mar		Plan for hydroelectric power station Dneprostroi
15 Mar	Room, *Bed and Sofa*	
7 Nov	Moscow Youth Theatre and TRAM (Theatre of Working Youth) founded	
1928		
		First Five-Year Plan 1928–32: industrialization Kamenev and Zinoviev admit 'mistakes' and are readmitted to the Party
12 Mar	Eisenstein, *October*	
15–21 Mar	Conference on Cinema Affairs	
13 Apr	Dovzhenko, *Zvenigora*	
28 May	Return of Maxim Gorky	
10 Nov	Pudovkin, *Storm over Asia*	
1929		
	TEA jazz ensemble by Leonid Utesov	Lunacharsky dismissed; Bukharin and Rykov excluded from the Party Building of Magnitogorsk
18 Jan		Trotsky exiled to Alma-Ata
18 Mar	Kozintsev and Trauberg, *New Babylon*	
9 Apr	Vertov, *Man with a Movie Camera*	
Aug		Purges in the Academy of Sciences
15 Sep	Pilniak condemned as anti-Soviet writer	
Sep		First combine harvester
5 Oct	First sound cinema in Leningrad	
26 Oct		Destruction of Iverian Gates on Red Square (reconstructed 1995)
7 Nov	Eisenstein, *The General Line*	
Dec		Prohibition of sale of Christmas trees; no church bells

Date	*Cinema and Culture*	*History*
1930		
30 Jan		Liquidation of kulaks (campaign)
Feb	Soyuzkino formed	
6 Mar	Khudozhestvennyi (Ars) cinema equipped with sound	
8 Apr	Dovzhenko, *Earth*	
14 Apr	Suicide of Mayakovsky	
Apr	Film train departs for sixteen months	
10 Nov		New Lenin Mausoleum by Shchusev
19 Dec		Rykov replaced by Molotov as Premier
Dec	Shumiatsky is head of cinema affairs	
1931		
9 Feb	Soyuzkino factory opens in Moscow (from 1935 known as Mosfilm)	
28 Mar		Turksib railway opens
1 Jun	*Path to Life*: first sound film	
1 Jul	Soyuzkinokhronika founded	
16 Sep	Obraztsov Puppet Theatre founded	
10 Oct	Kozintsev and Trauberg, *Alone*	
7 Nov	Udarnik cinema opens	
5 Dec		Cathedral of Christ the Saviour blown up; reconstructed in 1995
1932		
1932–34		Moskva-Volga Canal construction; Dneprostroi construction
Mar	'Radist' radio factory Leningrad opens	
23 Apr	Writers' Union formed: Socialist Realism	
9 Nov		Nadezhda Allilueva (Stalin's wife) dies
27 Dec		Passport system introduced
1933		Second Five-Year Plan, 1933–37 industry and communications
25 Mar	Barnet, *Outskirts*	
20 Jun		White Sea Canal opens
12 Jul		*Cheliuskin* on Arctic expedition; crushed 13 Feb 1934
15 Jul		Uralmash industry opens
25 Nov		Korolev: rocket test
16 Nov		US–USSR enter diplomatic relations
17 Dec	First children's film: *Torn Boots*	
26 Dec		Lunacharsky dies
1934		
4 May	Dom Kino (House of Cinema) opens	
10 May		Yagoda heads secret service, OGPU

26 Jun	Savchenko, *The Accordion* (first musical)	
10 Jul		OGPU becomes NKVD (People's Commissariat for Internal Affairs)
17 Aug–1 Sep	Writers' Union Congress	
27 Oct		GULAGs (prison camps) open
7 Nov	*Chapaev*	
1 Dec		Assassination of Leningrad Party chief, Kirov
25 Dec	Alexandrov, *Jolly Fellows*	
Sep	Mosfilm, Lenfilm organized	
1935		
		VSKhV, All-Union Agriculture Exhibition, opens: building complete 1939
8–13 Jan	Cinema Workers' Union: congress	
21 Feb–2 Mar	Moscow International Film Festival	
25 Mar	Ptushko, *New Gulliver*	
1935		Trial of the Sixteen (Kamenev, Zinoviev) begins
15 May		Metro Sokolniki – Park Kultury and Okhotny Riad-Smolenskaya opens
18 May		Crash of aeroplane *Gorky*
10 Jul		Plan for the reconstruction of Moscow
19 Sep		Death of Konstantin Tsiolkovsky
17 Nov		Stalin's phrase 'Life has become better, comrades, life has become more joyous'
20 Dec	Hotel Moskva opens	
1936		
28 Jan	Attack in *Pravda* on Shostakovich for *Lady Macbeth of Mtsensk*	
9 Mar	Attack on Bulgakov's play, *Molière*, staged at the MAT	
25 Mar	First film, *The Great Citizen*, shown on television	
25 May	Alexandrov, *Circus*	
8 Jun	Soyuzdetfilm formed on the basis of Mezhrabpomfilm	
11 Jun	First colour film, *Grunia Kornakova*	
18 Jun	Death of Gorky	
27 Jun		Abortion prohibited
24 Jul		Chkalov's first flight to the east
25 Aug		Zinoviev and Kamenev executed
26 Sep		Yezhov as head of NKVD replaces Yagoda
5 Dec		Soviet Constitution revised

Date	*Cinema and Culture*	*History*
1937		
		Stars installed on Kremlin towers
Jan		Trial of the Seventeen: Radek, Piatakov, Sokolnikov
May–Nov	International Exhibition in Paris (Mukhina, *Worker and Collective Farmer*)	
Jun		Attack on Pletnev, Gorky's doctor
18–20 Jun		Flight across the Arctic to Vancouver
5 Nov	Regular evening television from Shabolovka transmitter	
10 Nov	Death of actor Nikolai Batalov	
1938		
		Third Five-Year Plan, 1938–41: armament
7 Jan	Closure of Meyerhold Theatre	
13 Mar		Russian language compulsory in all schools across USSR
17 Mar		Anschluss: Austria as ally to Nazi Germany
24 Apr	Alexandrov, *Volga-Volga*	
27 Jul		Arrest of Korolev
Jul		Third show trial: Trial of the Twenty-One – includes Bukharin, Rykov, and Yagoda; executions
Aug		Beriya replaces Yezhov as head of NKVD
7 Aug	Death of theatre director Stanislavsky	
1 Dec	Eisenstein, *Alexander Nevsky*	
15 Dec		Death of Valeri Chkalov
1939		
17 Jan		Census
18 Jan	Death in Paris of Ivan Mosjoukine	
21 Apr	Cinema Moskva installed in St Catherine's Cathedral, Leningrad	
1 May	Dovzhenko, *Shchors*	
10 Jun		Yezhov arrested and executed on 4 Feb 1940
3 Jul	Pyriev, *The Tractor Drivers*	
15 Jul	Murder of Meyerhold's wife, Zinaida Raikh	
23 Aug		Molotov-Ribbentrop Pact
1 Sep		Second World War: Germany invades Poland; Britain and France declare war on Germany
17 Sep		Soviet Army in eastern Poland; western Ukraine to USSR
30 Nov		Soviet-Finnish War (Winter War) until defeat of Russian army on 26 Dec; Soviet breakthrough 12 Feb 1940

1940		
2 Feb	Meyerhold executed	
10 Mar	Death of writer Mikhail Bulgakov	
Apr/May		NKVD shoot Polish POWs in Katyn
Jun/Jul		Ultimatum to Baltic states and annexation
21 Aug		Assassination of Trotsky
1941		
6 May		Stalin is Premier
22 Jun		Germany attacks USSR
Jul		Evacuation of Moscow
8 Aug		Stalin is Commander-in-Chief of the Army
Aug		Deportation of Volga Germans to Siberia and Kazakhstan
8 Sep		Leningrad Blockade until 18 Jan 1943
29–30 Sep		Massacre of Baby Yar
29 Nov		Zoya Kosmodemianskaya killed
1942		
12 Apr	Shulzhenko sings 'Blue Kerchief'	
4 May	*She Defended the Motherland*	
Jul 1942–Jan 1943		Siege of Stalingrad
Aug		Churchill in Moscow
Sep		Young Guard resistance in Krasnodon; executions in Feb 1943
1943		
		Patriarchate restored
28 Nov–1 Dec		Tehran conference with Roosevelt, Stalin and Churchill
1944		
1 Jan		New Soviet hymn (replaces Internationale)
24 Jan	*The Rainbow*	
Dec 1943–Apr 1944		Deportation of Kalmyks, Ingush and Chechens
1945		
16 Jan	Eisenstein, *Ivan the Terrible I*	
4–11 Feb		Yalta conference: agreement on spheres of influence in Europe
12 Apr		Roosevelt dies
25 Apr		Meeting of American and Soviet armies on the Elbe
9 May		Victory: capitulation of Germany
24 Jun		Victory Parade in Moscow
17 Jul–2 Aug		Potsdam conference: de-Nazification, demilitarization and decentralization of Germany

Date	*Cinema and Culture*	*History*
6 and 9 Aug		Nuclear bombs on Hiroshima and Nagasaki
8 Aug	Death of Protazanov	
2 Sep		Japan capitulates
26 Sep	Death of producer Khanzhonkov	
1946		
		Fourth Five-Year Plan, 1946–50: reconstruction
5 Mar		Churchill: Fulton speech ('Cold War')
18 Jun	Death of Georgi Vasiliev (*Chapaev*)	
9 Aug	Stalin criticizes Eisenstein	
4 Sep	Accusations levelled against *Great Life*	
1947		
		Zhdanov's 'cosmopolitan campaign'
24 Feb	Meeting of Stalin and Eisenstein	
Jun		Marshall Plan for the reconstruction of Germany
Jul	Chiaureli, *The Vow*	
1948		
13 Jan	Solomon Mikhoels killed in Minsk	
11 Feb	Death of Eisenstein	
2 Jun		Law on layabouts (*tuneiadtsy*)
31 Aug		Death of Zhdanov
11 Oct	*The Young Guard*	
1949		
	Closure of Jewish Theatre GOSET; closure of Pushkin Museum (Western art collection)	
5–8 Jan		COMECON formed (Council for Mutual Economic Assistance)
10 Mar	*Meeting on the Elbe*	
9 May	*Battle of Stalingrad*	
29 Aug		Soviet test nuclear bomb in the Kazakh Polygon (further tests on 24 September and 18 October 1951)
Oct		German Democratic Republic formed
4 Apr		Formation of NATO
1950		
	Tvardovsky is chief editor of *Novy Mir*	Fifth Five-Year Plan, 1951–55
19 Jan	Chiaureli, *The Fall of Berlin*	
14 Dec	Death of filmmaker Savchenko	

1951		
	Tarzan on Soviet screens	
Aug	Soviet films prevented from participating in Venice IFF	
1952		
1 Jan		2.5 million prisoners in GULAGs
10 Jul		Volga-Don Canal opens
Jul		First Soviet participation in Olympics in Helsinki
1953		
Jan		Doctors' Plot (alleged scheme of Jewish doctors to murder Soviet officials)
11 Feb		Break of Israeli-Soviet relations
5 Mar	Death of composer Prokofiev	Death of Stalin
6 Mar		Malenkov is Premier; Khrushchev First Secretary of CPSU
17 Jun		Uprising in GDR suppressed by Soviet troops
26 Jun		Arrest of Beriya
30 Jun	Death of Pudovkin	
1 Sep	Moscow State University opens on Sparrow (Lenin) Hills	
15 Oct	Radio Yunost launched	
26 Nov		Abolition of decree of 15 Feb 1947 that forbade marriage to foreigners
23 Dec		Beriya executed
31 Dec	GUM (State Department Store) opens	
1954		
		Virgin Lands campaign
12 Feb	Death of documentary filmmaker Vertov	
13 Mar		KGB (State Security Committee) replaces NKVD
1 Aug		Opening of Agriculture Exhibition
5 Aug		Abortion legalized
1 Sep		Mixed schools permitted
15–26 Dec	Second Writers' Union Congress: Fadeev replaced by Surkov	
1955		
	New Literary journals launched; Pushkin Museum reopens	Corn campaign
12 Feb		Baikonur space centre opens
8 Feb		Bulganin is Premier
Feb	Odessa Film Studio opens	

Date	*Cinema and Culture*	*History*
May–Aug	Exhibition of trophy art from Dresden Gallery before it is returned to GDR	
14 May		Formation of Warsaw Pact
25 Jul	Death of composer Dunaevsky	
15 Nov		Leningrad metro opens
Dec	Week of French Cinema	
1956		Sixth Five-Year Plan, 1956–60: living standards (lower prices; maternity leave; pension schemes; free schooling; increase in apartments) Furtseva in charge of Ideology at CC
14–25 Feb		Twentieth Party Congress
8 Mar	*The Rumiantsev Case*	
15 Apr	Sovremennik Theatre opens	
15 Oct	Chukhrai, *The Forty-First*	
21 Oct		Election of the liberal Władysław Gomułka as Party secretary in Poland
23 Oct–10 Nov		Anti-Soviet revolution in Budapest: Imre Nagy (1896–1958) is Prime Minister of Hungary
25 Oct	Death of Dovzhenko	
4 Nov		Soviet troops in Budapest
29 Dec	Riazanov, *Carnival Night*	
1957		
28 Feb–7 Mar	First Congress of Artists' Union	
25 Mar		European Economic Community (EEC) founded (Treaty of Rome)
18 May		Decision on Academy of Sciences branch in Akademgorodok, Siberia
22 May		Khrushchev's slogan: 'To catch up and overtake America'
25 May	Ukraina Hotel opens	
May		Attempt to topple Khrushchev
28 Jul–11 Aug	International Youth Festival	
29 Sep		Mayak nuclear accident near Cheliabinsk
4 Oct		Sputnik 1 launched into space
12 Oct	Kalatozov, *The Cranes Are Flying*	
Nov	*Doctor Zhivago* published in Milan	
1958		
28 Feb	Panorama cinema Mir	
Mar–Apr	Tchaikovsky competition with van Cliburn in Moscow	

27 Mar		Khrushchev is Premier
16 Jun		Nagy executed for treason
29 Jul	Mayakovsky statue erected on Triumphal Square	
25 Oct	Boris Pasternak accepts the Nobel Prize for his novel *Doctor Zhivago*	
20 Dec		'Iron Felix': monument to Dzerzhinsky
1959		
	Literary evenings at the Polytechnic Museum	Seventh Five-Year Plan, 1959–65
12 Apr	*Fate of a Man* at Udarnik cinema	
14 May	Death of filmmaker Perestiani	
18–23 May	Third Writers' Congress	
3–17 Aug	Moscow International Film Festival	
15–27 Sep		Khrushchev in the United States
1 Dec	Chukhrai, *Ballad of a Soldier*	
16 Dec	Death of filmmaker Sergei Vasiliev (*Chapaev*)	
1960		
		Furtseva is Minister of Culture (until 1974)
1 May	.	Lockheed U-2 in Soviet airspace shot down near Sverdlovsk; pilot Gary Powers arrested
4 May		New rouble
30 May	Death of the writer Boris Pasternak	
16 Jul		Swimming pool Moskva opens
23 Sep		Khrushchev at the United Nations
1961		
		Stalin removed from mausoleum
Jan		*Khrushchevki* apartment blocks launched
28 Feb	Death of cameraman Andrei Moskvin	
12 Apr		Yuri Gagarin goes into space
4 May		Law against parasitism (lack of permanent work)
9–23 Jul	Moscow International Film Festival	
13 Aug		Berlin Wall built
7 Oct		Kremlin Congress Palace opens
18 Oct	Death of cameraman Eduard Tisse	
2 Dec		Stalingrad renamed Volgograd; Stalinabad renamed Dushanbe
1962		
7 Apr	*Goluboi ogonek* musical programme on television	
9 May	Tarkovsky, *Ivan's Childhood*	
30 May	Benny Goodman in Moscow	

Date	*Cinema and Culture*	*History*
2 Jun		Strikes in Novocherkask crushed
21 Sep–11 Oct	Igor Stravinsky in Moscow	
Oct		Cuban missile crisis
6 Nov		MKAD orbital motorway around Moscow opens
11 Nov	Solzhenitsyn's *The Life of Ivan Denisovich* published with Khrushchev's permission	
1 Dec	Manege exhibition of modern art trashed by Khrushchev	
1963		
19–28 Jan	Estrada festival in Gorky	
7–8 Mar		Kremlin meetings with the intelligentsia
23 Mar	Cinema Committee under Romanov	
7–12 Jul	Moscow International Film Festival: Fellini's *Otto e mezzo* wins main prize	
18 Aug	Tvardovsky's *Terkin in the Other World* published with Khrushchev's permission	
4 Nov		Completion of New Arbat (Kalinin Prospekt)
1964		
18 Feb	Trial of Brodsky: five years' hard labour	
30 Mar	Kozintsev, *Hamlet*	
11 Apr	Daneliya, *I Walk through Moscow*	
23 Apr	Taganka Theatre founded	
14 Oct		Khrushchev ousted
23 Oct		Kosygin is Premier
1965		
8 Jan	Death of Boris Barnet	
18 Jan	Khutsiev, *I am Twenty*	
28 May	Death of filmmaker Gardin	
5–20 Jul	Moscow International Film Festival	
8 Sep	Arrest of Siniavsky and Daniel	
5 Nov	Yevgeni Urbansky dies on set in Karakum	
23–26 Nov	Congress of the Filmmakers' Union	
9 Dec		Mikoyan followed by Podgorny as Chair of Supreme Council
1966		
		Eighth Five-Year Plan, 1966–70
14 Jan		Death of rocket scientist Korolev
10–14 Feb		Trial of Siniavsky and Daniel
18 Mar	Illusion cinema opens for screenings of films from Gosfilmofond	

26 Apr		Tashkent earthquake
Dec	*Master and Margarita* published	
1967		
		Andropov is head of KGB
22 Jan		Human rights protests on Pushkin Square; arrest of Ginzburg
8 Mar		Svetlana Allilueva (Stalin's daughter) defects in India
1 Apr	Gaidai, *The Prisoner of the Caucasus*	
16 May	Open letter by Solzhenitsyn	
5–10 Jun		Arab-Israeli War (Six-Day War)
5–20 Jul	Moscow International Film Festival	
12 Jul	Death of filmmaker Ermler	
24 Aug		Aurora fast train service to Leningrad begins
30 Sep	Colour TV transmission begins	
5 Nov	Cinema Oct opens on New Arbat	
1968		
1 Jan	News programme *Vremia* launched	
8–12 Jan		Trials against dissidents: Ginzburg and Galanskov
7 Feb	Death of Ivan Pyriev	
27 Mar		Death of Gagarin
2 Jun	Solzhenitsyn's *Gulag Archipelago* completed	
29 Jul	Askeldov's *The Commissar* shelved	
21–23 Aug		Soviet troops to Prague to counter Dubcek's socialism with human face
1969		
8 Apr	Gaidai, *Diamond Arm*	
15 Apr	Oscar for *War and Peace*	
29 May		Letter to UN by Human Rights Watch
7–22 Jul	Moscow International Film Festival	
20 Jul		Apollo 11 lands on moon
26 Nov	Solzhenitsyn excluded from Writers' Union	
1970		
3 Feb	*Novy Mir* new editorial board without Tvardovsky	
29 May		Dissident Zhores Medvedev admitted to psychiatric clinic
7 Jul		Trial of dissident Natalia Gorbanevskaya
10 Aug	Death of writer Nikolai Erdman	
12 Aug		Ostverträge between USSR and FRG
8 Oct	Nobel Prize for Solzhenitsyn	

Date	*Cinema and Culture*	*History*
1971		
		Ninth Five-Year Plan, 1971–75: grain imports
20 Feb	Death of jazz musician Tsfasman	
19 Apr		First Salyut space station launched (last one launched 1982)
20 Jul–3 Aug	Moscow International Film Festival	
11 Sep		Death of Khrushchev
1 Nov	Death of Mikhail Romm	
5 Nov	Rossiya concert hall opened	
24 Dec	*Andrei Rublev* released	
29 Dec	Poet and bard Alexander Galich excluded from Writers' Union	
1972		
5 Jan	Vladimir Bukovsky arrested and sentenced to five years in prison	
May		President Nixon visits Moscow
4 Jun	Brodsky expelled from USSR	
22 Aug	Yermash is Goskino head	
1973		
		Zhores Medvedev exiled; wave of emigration to Israel
6 Mar	Death of filmmaker Ptushko	
27 Mar	Death of Mikhail Kalatozov	
11 May	Death of Grigori Kozintsev	
10–23 Jul	Moscow International Film Festival	
11 Aug	*Seventeen Moments of Spring*	
1974		
		Zakharov establishes the Moscow Human Rights Committee with Tverdokhlebov, Chalidze, and Elena Bonner
3 Jan	Death of actor Maxim Straukh	
12–13 Feb		Arrest of Solzhenitsyn and deportation
14 Jun–8 Jul	Da Vinci exhibition in Moscow	
25 Sep	Bulldozer exhibition	
2 Oct	Death of Vasili Shukshin	
24 Oct		Suicide of Furtseva
1 Nov	Suicide of scriptwriter Shpalikov	
12 Nov	Death of cameraman Urusevsky	
23 Nov		Brezhnev suffers stroke

1975		
		Demichev is Minister of Culture (until 1986)
26 Jan	Death of Liubov Orlova	
3 Jul	Central State Archive for Cinema and Photo Documentation in Krasnogorsk opens	
17 Jul	Death of actor Babochkin (Chapaev)	
10–23 Jul	Moscow International Film Festival	
28 Jul–1 Aug		Helsinki Accord on Security and Cooperation in Europe
9 Aug	Death of composer Shostakovich	
10 Oct		Sakharov receives Nobel Peace Prize
1976		Tenth Five-Year Plan, 1976–81: quality and efficiency
	Sculptor Ernst Neizvestny expelled	
1 Jan	Riazanov, *Irony of Fate*	
12 May		Helsinki Watch Group founded, headed by the nuclear physicist Yuri Orlov
14 Jul	Death of filmmaker Nikolai Ekk	
26 Jul	Death of filmmaker Abram Room	
1977		
25 Feb		Fire in Hotel Rossiya
Feb		Arrest of Helsinki Group's members
3 May	Gherman, *Twenty Days without War*	
7–21 Jul	Moscow International Film Festival	
25 Sep	Mikhalkov, *Unfinished Piece*	
7 Oct		New Soviet Constitution
1978		
		Conductor of Bolshoi, Kondrashin, seeks political asylum in Holland
		Writer Alexander Zinoviev expelled and stripped of citizenship
15 Mar		Cellist Mstislav Rostropovich and his wife Galina Vishnevskaya stripped of Soviet citizenship
10–14 Jul		Trial of dissidents Sharansky, Filatov
17 Aug	Death of actress Vera Maretskaya	
3 Sep	Melodiya record label	
17 Oct		Physicist Kapitsa receives Nobel Prize
22 Dec	Almanac *Metropol* published (*samizdat*)	
1979		
12 Jan	Death of filmmaker Stolper	

Date	*Cinema and Culture*	*History*
14–28 Aug	Moscow International Film Festival	
2 Jul	Death of Larisa Shepitko	
25 Dec		Soviet troops in Afghanistan
1980		
		Priest Gleb Yakunin condemned for anti-Soviet activity (in prison until 1987)
		Violinist Gidon Kremer seeks political asylum in Germany
		Kopelev, Voinovich and Aksenov exiled
22 Jan		Sakharov exiled to Gorky and placed under house arrest
11 Feb	*Moscow Does Not Believe in Tears*	
8 Mar	Rock festival in Tiflis	
19 May	Tarkovsky, *Stalker*	
19 Jul–3 Aug		Olympic Games in Moscow
25 Jul	Death of Vladimir Vysotsky	
30 Sep	Death of actor Anatoli Ktorov	
23 Oct		Kosygin replaced by Nikolai Tikhonov as Premier
18 Dec		Death of Kosygin
1981		
		Eleventh Five-Year Plan, 1981–85
		Solidarnosz movement in Poland: martial law
3 Mar	Death of actor Oleg Dal	
21 Mar	Death of filmmaker Donskoy	
4 Jun	Moscow-Paris exhibition	
7–21 Jul	Moscow International Film Festival	
1982		
9 Mar	Death of jazz musician Utesov	
15 Mar		Moratorium on nuclear weapons
11 Jul	Death of actor Solonitsyn	
20 Oct		Luzhniki UEFA cup match: crowd crushed
10 Nov		Death of Brezhnev
12 Nov		Andropov is General Secretary of CPSU
1983		
8 Mar		Reagan calls USSR 'empire of evil'
23 Mar		Reagan's 'Star Wars' speech
12 Jun	Death of filmmaker Alov	
16 Jun		Andropov is President of Supreme Council
7–21 Jul	Moscow International Film Festival	
1 Sep		Korean aircraft shot down by USSR
16 Dec	Death of Grigori Alexandrov	

1984		
9 Feb		Death of Andropov
13 Feb		Chernenko is General Secretary
21 Feb	Death of writer Mikhail Sholokhov	
6 Mar	Exile of theatre director Yuri Liubimov	
16 Mar		Earthquake in Uzbekistan
8 Apr		Death of Petr Kapitsa
8 May		Soviet-led boycott of Los Angeles Olympics
17 Jun	Death of singer Shulzhenko	
10 Jul	Emigration of Andrei Tarkovsky	
5 Dec	Death of writer Viktor Shklovsky	
15–21 Dec		Gorbachev in the UK
1985		
10 Mar		Death of Chernenko
11 Mar		Gorbachev confirmed as General Secretary
4 Apr	Death of filmmaker Dinara Asanova	
23 Apr	Death of film critic and historian Sergei Yutkevich	
16 May		Announcement of anti-alcohol campaign
11–12 Jun		Announcement of 'acceleration' (*uskorenie*) of scientific and technological progress
24 Jun		Announcement of perestroika
21 Jun		Yakovlev is Secretary for Propaganda in the Central Committee
28 Jun–12 Jul	Moscow International Film Festival	
16 Jul		Shevardnadze is Minister of Foreign Affairs
Aug	Twelfth International Youth Festival, Moscow	Moratorium on nuclear tests (until February 1987)
22 Aug	Death of actress Alexandra Khokhlova	
27 Sep		Tikhonov replaced by Ryzhkov (head of UralMash) as Chairman of Council of Ministers
2–5 Oct		Gorbachev on state visit to France
19–21 Nov		Reagan and Gorbachev meet in Geneva
28 Nov	Death of filmmaker Sergei Gerasimov	
24 Dec		Yeltsin replaces Grishin at Moscow Party section
1986		
		Twelfth Five-Year Plan, 1986–90: perestroika
20 Feb		Mir space station launched
25 Feb–6 Mar		Congress of the CPSU
Mar	Melodiya releases Beatles album	
26 Apr		Fire in reactor at Chernobyl

Date	*Cinema and Culture*	*History*
13–15 May	Fifth Congress of the Filmmakers' Union	
14 Aug		Law permitting cooperatives
11–12 Oct		Gorbachev meets Reagan in Reykjavik
3 Dec		Gorbachev meets with the 'Creative Intelligentsia'
23 Dec		Andrei Sakharov returns to Moscow from exile in Gorky (Nizhny Novgorod)
25 Dec	Alexei Kamshalov is head of Goskino	
29 Dec	Death of filmmaker Andrei Tarkovsky	
1987		
13 Jan	Death of actor Igor Ilyinsky	
26 Jan	Release of Abuladze's film *Repentance*, and Yuri Podnieks's documentary *Is it Easy to be Young?*	
19 Feb	Rehabilitation of Boris Pasternak	
28 Feb	Studios entitled to select theme and budget for films	
25 Mar	Death of animator Ivanov-Vano	
28 May		German aviator Matthias Rust lands a Cessna plane on Red Square
6–17 Jul	Moscow International Film Festival	
5 Aug	Death of actor Anatoli Papanov	
16 Aug	Death of actor Andrei Mironov	
11 Nov		Yeltsin removed from post as Moscow Party Chief
12 Dec	Nobel Prize for Literature to Joseph Brodsky	
1988		
5 Jan		Control of psychiatric clinics moved from Ministry of Interior to Ministry of Health
6 Feb		Nuclear test in Semipalatinsk (also 4 May)
28–29 Feb		Pogrom against Armenians in Sumgait
15 Mar	First Dali exhibition in Moscow	
2 May	Death of actor Pavel Kadochnikov	
29 May–2 Jun		Reagan in Moscow
7 Jun	First auction of modern art by Sotheby's	
29 Nov		Jamming of Radio Liberty and Radio Liberty Europe stops
7 Dec		Earthquake in Spitak, Armenia
30 Dec	Death of poet and dissident Yuli Daniel	
1989		
19 Jan	Malevich exhibition	
23 Jan		Earthquake in Tajikistan

31 Jan	First McDonald's opens in Moscow	
2 Feb	Death of actor Yuri Bogatyryov	
15 Feb		Removal of troops from Afghanistan
26 Mar		Election of delegates for the Congress of People's Deputies
May	Soviet citizenship returned to Liubimov	
25 May–9 Jun		First Congress of People's Deputies
Jun		Pogroms in Fergana
2 Jul		Death of Andrei Gromyko
4 Jul	Exhibition of Vasili Kandinsky	
7–18 Jul	Moscow International Film Festival	
9 Nov		Fall of Berlin Wall
10 Nov	Rostropovich, Vishnevskaya and Voinovich receive USSR citizenship	
2–3 Dec		Bush and Gorbachev meet in Malta
12–24 Dec		Second Congress of People's Deputies
14 Dec		Death of Andrei Sakharov
1990		
10 Feb		Pogroms in Dushanbe (Tajikistan)
11 Mar		Lithuania declares independence
12–15 Mar		Third Congress of People's Deputies elects Gorbachev as President of the USSR
16 May–2 Jun		First Congress of People's Deputies of the RSFSR
29 May		Yeltsin elected Chair of the Supreme Council of the RSFSR
2–13 Jun		Congress of the CPSU
20 Jul	Death of filmmaker Sergo Paradjanov	
13 Aug		Rehabilitation of writers Voinovich, Kopelev, Aksenov, Solzhenitsyn
15 Aug	Death of rock singer Viktor Tsoy	
23 Aug		Gorky renamed Nizhny Novgorod
22 Aug	Radio station Echo Moscow goes live	
25 Oct		Nobel Peace Prize for Gorbachev
24 Oct		Nuclear test in Novaya Zemlya
7 Nov		Attempt on Gorbachev's life
14 Nov	Death of filmmaker Leonid Trauberg	
23–5 Nov		Congress on Chechen independence
30 Nov		Double-headed eagle chosen as emblem for the Russian Federation
17–27 Dec		Fourth Congress of People's Deputies (USSR)
20 Dec		Shevardnadze resigns as Foreign Minister
27 Dec	7 Jan (Christmas) is official holiday	

Date	Cinema and Culture	History
1991		
3 Jan		Diplomatic relations re-established with Israel
7–13 Jan		Clashes in the Baltic States between Russian and national groups; Vilnius television tower seized by Russian forces
7 Mar		Gubenko is Minister of Culture
17 Mar		Referendum on USSR
28 Mar		Third Congress of People's Deputies of the RSFSR
29 Apr		Earthquake in Georgia
21–26 May		Fourth Congress of People's Deputies of the RSFSR
12 Jun		Yeltsin elected President of the RSFSR
17 Jun		Union Treaty with nine former Soviet republics
28 Jun		Union for Economic Support (SEV) disbanded
1 Jul		Warsaw Pact disbanded
10 Jul		Romanovs' remains exhumed
10–17 Jul		Fifth Congress of People's Deputies (RSFSR)
8–19 Jul	Moscow International Film Festival	
19–21 Aug		August Coup (GKChP) by Vice-President Yanaev; Kriuchkov; Pavlov; Pugo; Yazov
22 Aug		Tricolore is flag of Russia (Yeltsin)
24 Aug		Gorbachev resigns as head of CPSU; CP is prohibited
30 Aug		Nuclear polygon closed by Kazakh President Nazarbayev
5 Sep		Sverdlovsk renamed Yekaterinburg
6 Sep		Dudaev seizes power in Chechnya
7 Sep		Independence of the Baltic States Lithuania, Estonia, Latvia recognized
Autumn		Leningrad renamed St Petersburg
28 Oct–13 Nov		Yeltsin authorized by Fifth Congress of People's Deputies of the RSFSR to form a government
1 Nov		COMECON dissolves
6 Nov		Yeltsin is Premier
14 Nov		Novo-Ogarevo: union with Azerbaijan, Kazakhstan, Kyrgyzstan, Tajikistan and Turkmenistan
8 Dec		CIS Treaty at Belovezhsk: Russia, Belarus, Ukraine
25 Dec		Gorbachev resigns; Yeltsin is President of the Russian Federation

1992		
1 Jan		Economic shock therapy (Gaidai)
4 Mar	Death of actor Yevgeni Yevstigneev	
Apr		Congress of People's Deputies
8 May	Death of puppet theatre director Sergei Obraztsov	
1 Jun		Gavriil Popov succeeded by Yuri Luzhkov as Moscow's mayor
14 Dec		Chernomyrdin is PM
1993		
6 Jan	Death of dancer Rudolf Nureev	
23 Mar		Calls for impeachment of Yeltsin
25 Apr		Referendum supports Yeltsin
1–12 Jul	Moscow International Film Festival	
5 Sep	Death of spy thriller and detective writer Yulian Semenov	
21 Sep		Yeltsin dissolves parliament
3–4 Oct		Storming of White House: Rutskoy and speaker Khazbulatov oppose Yeltsin
19 Nov	Death of filmmaker Leonid Gaidai	
11 Dec		'Patriotic Song' by Glinka is new national anthem
12 Dec		Parliamentary elections: LDP 23 per cent, Vybor Rossii 15 per cent, CP 12 per cent, Union & Accord 7 per cent
12 Dec		Referendum ratifies Russian constitution
1994		
6 Mar	Death of filmmaker Tengiz Abuladze	
28 Apr	Death of actor Oleg Borisov	
23 May	*Burnt by the Sun* wins Grand Prix in Cannes	
27 May	Solzhenitsyn returns to Russia	
3 Aug	Death of actors Innokenti Smoktunovsky and Yevgeni Simonov	
26 Sep		Cathedral of Christ the Saviour to be rebuilt
20 Oct	Death of filmmaker and Oscar-winner Sergei Bondarchuk	
11 Dec	Death of filmmaker Yuli Raizman	Russian army to Chechnya
1995		
1 Mar	Murder of television presenter Vlad Listiev	
27 Mar	Oscar for Mikhalkov's *Burnt by the Sun*	
5 Apr	Tretiakov Gallery reopens after refurbishment	
25 Apr	Death of filmmaker Iosif Kheifits	
12 May	Death of actor Andrei Boltnev	

Date	*Cinema and Culture*	*History*
11 Jul		Yeltsin in hospital after heart attack
17–28 Jul	Moscow International Film Festival	
26 Oct	Iverian Gates open on Red Square	Yeltsin suffers second heart attack
Autumn	Rogozhkin, *Peculiarities of the National Hunt*	
3 Dec	Death of actor Kaidanovsky	
17 Dec		Parliamentary elections: NDR 9 per cent; CP 22 per cent; LDPR 11 per cent; Yabloko 7 per cent
1996		
28 Jan	Death of poet Joseph Brodsky	
15 Mar	Bodrov, *Prisoner of the Mountains*	
21 Apr		Death of Dudaev; succeeded by Yandarbaev
27 May		Ceasefire in Chechnya
11 Jun		Terrorist attacks on metro and buses in Moscow
16 Jun		Presidential elections: Yeltsin 35 per cent, Ziuganov 32 per cent
3 Jul		Second tour of presidential elections: Yeltsin 53 per cent (Ziuganov 40 per cent)
10 Jul	Death of musician Sergei Kurekhin	
25 Jul	Death of composer Mikhail Tariverdiev	
31 Aug		Lebed and Maskhadov sign peace accord
17 Oct		General Lebed resigns
5 Nov–23 Dec		Yeltsin has bypass operation
23 Nov	Death of composer Edison Denisov	
1 Dec		Troops withdrawn from Chechnya
1997		
1 Jan		New criminal code
27 Jan		Maskhadov elected Chechen president
25 Feb	Death of writer and dissident Siniavsky	
12 May	Release of Balabanov's *Brother*	Peace agreement with Chechnya
9 Jun	Death of actor Yevgeni Lebedev	
12 Jun	Death of poet and bard Okudzhava	
18 Jun	Death of writer and dissident Kopelev	
19–29 Jul	Moscow International Film Festival	
21 Aug	Death of clown Yuri Nikulin	
5 Nov	RAPO anti-piracy organization	
1998		
4 Jan	*Streets of Broken Lights*	
23 Mar		Kirienko replaces Chernomyrdin as PM
17 Jul		Interment of the Tsar's family in St Petersburg

3 Aug	Death of composer Alfred Schnittke	
17 Aug		'Default' (devaluation of rouble): 90-day moratorium on bank transactions
23 Aug		Chernomyrdin replaces Kirienko as interim PM
11 Sep		Primakov replaces Chernomyrdin
6 Oct	Death of actor Rolan Bykov	
Sep		Camilla Carr and John James freed from Chechen captivity (held since July 1997)

1999

20 Feb	Premiere of *The Barber of Siberia*	
18 Mar	Rogozhkin, *Checkpoint*	
29 Mar		Putin is head of FSB (Federal Security Bureau)
12 May		Stepashin replaces Primakov as PM
15 May		Impeachment against Yeltsin fails
25 Jun	Death of comedian Yevgeni Morgunov	
19–29 Jul	Moscow International Film Festival	
7 Aug		Beginning of Second Chechen campaign
9 Aug		Stepashin dismissed; succeeded by Putin (16 Aug)
31 Aug		Bomb explosion in Okhotny Ryad
8 Sep		Bomb in Moscow apartment block in Pechatniki
13 Sep		Bomb in Moscow apartment block on Kashirkoe Chausee
19 Dec		Duma elections: CP 24 per cent; Unity 23 per cent; OVR 13 per cent
31 Dec		Yeltsin resigns, leaving Putin as Acting President

2000

2 Jan	*Kamenskaya* starts on NTV	
28 Mar	Oscar to Petrov for Best Animation for *The Old Man and the Sea*	
26 Mar		Putin elected President
1 May	*Criminal Petersburg* starts on NTV	
11 May		Search of NTV offices
11 May	Balabanov, *Brother 2*	
7 May		Kasianov is PM
24 May	Death of actor and director Oleg Yefremov	
2 Jun	Death of filmmaker Mikhail Shveitser	
12 Jun		Kadyrov designated President of Chechnya
19–29 Jul	Moscow International Film Festival	
8 Aug		Bomb explosion in Pushkin Square pedestrian subway
12 Aug		Explosion on the *Kursk* submarine

Date	Cinema and Culture	History
25 Aug	Death of filmmaker and actor Valeri Priemykhov	
27 Aug		Fire on Ostankino television tower
Dec		Soviet national anthem reintroduced
2001		
4 Apr		NTV journalists strike; new management
10 May	Bodrov, *Sisters*	
21–30 Jun	Moscow International Film Festival	
28 Oct	Death of filmmaker Grigori Chukhrai	
2002		
14 Mar	Balabanov, *War*	
6 Apr	Konchalevsky, *Anti-Killer*	
9 Jun		Riots after soccer match Russia-Japan
21–30 Jun	Moscow International Film Festival	
20 Sep	Death of Bodrov Jr. and his film crew	
23–26 Oct		800 hostages at Moscow Theatre (*Nord Ost*): 120 dead
2003		
31 Mar	Baltser, *Don't Even Think*	
28 Jun	Buslov, *Bimmer*	
20–29 Jun	Moscow International Film Festival	
6 Jul		Suicide bomb at rock festival in Tushchino, Moscow
6 Sep	*The Return* wins the Golden Lion in Venice	
25 Oct		Arrest of Yukos manager Mikhail Khodorkovsky (fraud, tax evasion)
27 Oct	Death of filmmaker Elem Klimov	
25 Nov	Konchalevsky, *Anti-Killer 2*	
7 Dec		Duma elections: CP 12.5 per cent; Edinaia Rossiya 37.5 per cent; LDPR 11.5 per cent; Rodina 9 per cent
9 Dec		Suicide bomb at National Hotel, Moscow
2004		
22 Jan	KinoPark multiplex opened	
6 Feb		Terrorist attack in the Moscow metro station Avtozavodskaya
24 Feb		Putin dismisses PM Kasianov
9 Mar		PM is Mikhail Fradkov
14 Mar	Fire in the Manege exhibition hall	
14 Mar		Presidential elections: Putin 57 per cent
3 Apr	First IMAX in Moscow	
9 May		Kadyrov killed in Grozny

18–27 Jun	Moscow International Film Festival	
9 Jul		Murder of Paul Khlebnikov, Forbes Russia
11 Jul	Bekmambetov, *Night Watch*	
24 Aug		Two airliners crash as a result of terrorist attacks
1–3 Sep		Siege of School No.1 in Beslan
12 Dec	Lavrentiev, *Countdown*	
2005		
27 Feb	Faiziev, *Turkish Gambit*	
8 Mar		Aslan Maskhadov, Chechen separatist leader, killed
20 Mar	Sidorov, *Shadowboxing*	
May		Khodorkovsky sentenced
17–26 Jun	Moscow International Film Festival	
29 Sep	Bondarchuk, *Company 9*	
2006		
1 Jan	Bekmambetov, *Day Watch*	
23 Jun–2 Jul	Moscow International Film Festival	
10 Jul		Shamil Basaev killed
23 Nov		Alexander Litvinenko dies in London of polonium poisoning
7 Oct		Murder of Anna Politkovskaya
2007		
15 Feb		Ramzan Kadyrov is Chechen president
23 Apr		Death of Yeltsin
27 Apr		Death of cellist Rostropovich
21–30 Jun	Moscow International Film Festival	
14 Sep		Fradkov dismissed; Viktor Zubkov is PM
Dec		Unity Party wins with Putin as top candidate
2008		
1 Jan	Bekmambetov, *Irony of Fate 2*	
2 Mar		Election of Dmitri Medvedev as president

Notes:

- Dates used follow the old calendar until 31 Jan 1918, when Russia switched to the new style, noting that date as 14 Feb 1918.
- Names: St Petersburg became Petrograd from Aug 1914 until 24 Jan 1924, when it was named Leningrad.
- Premier: Chairman of the Council of People's Commissars until 1946; then Chairman of Council of Ministers of the USSR.

Notes

Chapter 1 The Beginnings of Russian Cinema (1908–19)

1. Pacatus (pseudonym of Maxim Gorky), 'Beglye zametki', *Nizhegorodskii listok* 4 July 1896, translated in R. Taylor and I. Christie (eds.), *The Film Factory. Russian and Soviet Cinema in Documents 1896–1939*, 1988, p. 25 (hereafter *Film Factory*).
2. Denise Youngblood, *The Magic Mirror: Moviemaking in Russia 1908–1918*, 1999, p. 10.
3. Yuri Tsivian, *Early Cinema in Russia and its Cultural Reception*, 1994, pp. 15–48.
4. Tsivian, *Early Cinema in Russia*, pp. 15–48.
5. Richard Taylor, *Film Propaganda: Soviet Russia and Nazi Germany*, 1998, p. 23.
6. A noteworthy example is that of Alexander Shiryaev, a dancer of the imperial Mariinsky Theatre and ballet teacher of the Vaganova School, who started filming dances (both acted performances and dance movements reconstructed with puppets) around 1906. These films were shown to students of the Imperial Ballet School, so they had a limited audience. For details on Shiryaev's work, see materials and documents published in *Kinovedcheskie zapiski* 67 (2004), pp. 6–101.
7. For a list see Jay Leyda, *Kino: A History of the Russian and Soviet Film*, 1960, pp. 405–6.
8. Tsivian, *Early Cinema in Russia*, pp. 83, 6.
9. Another example is *Mazeppa*, 1909, dir. Goncharov, prod. Khanzhonkov.
10. Leonid Andreev, 'Pis'mo o teatre', 10 November 1911, *Film Factory*, p. 31.
11. Vladimir Mayakovsky, 'Teatr, kinematograf, futurizm', 27 July 1913, *Film Factory*, p. 34.
12. Tsivian, *Early Cinema in Russia*, p. 146.
13. Vsevolod Meyerhold, 'V. E. Meierkhol'd o kinematografe', 31 May 1915 in *Film Factory*, p. 39.
14. Leyda argues that Russian critics who had seen Meyerhold's film and later *The Cabinet of Dr Caligari* (dir. Robert Wiene, 1920) had said that 'if it had been shown abroad it would have surpassed *Caligari*'s reputation' (Leyda, *Kino*, pp. 81–2).
15. Youngblood, *The Magic Mirror*, p. 8.
16. They also produced four series of the adventures of Anton Krechet (1916), and three parts about Vasia Churkin (1914–15).

17. Leyda, *Kino*, p. 51.
18. Leyda, *Kino*, p. 63.
19. Stanislavsky staged specially for her benefit Carlo Goldoni's *The Innkeeper's Woman* (La Locandiera).
20. Rachel Morley, 'Gender Relations in the Films of Evgenii Bauer', *Slavonic and East European Review*, 81:1 (2003), pp. 32–69; p. 37.
21. Louise McReynolds, 'The Silent Movie Melodrama: Evgenii Bauer Fashions the Heroine's Self', in Laura Engelstein and Stephanie Sandler (eds.), *Self and Story in Russian History*, 2000, pp. 120–139; p. 129.
22. McReynolds, 'The Silent Movie Melodrama', p. 130.
23. Youngblood, *The Magic Mirror*, p. 84.
24. This film is discussed in depth in Rachel Morley's 'Gender Relations in the Films of Evgenii Bauer', *Slavonic and East European Review*, 81.1 (2003), pp. 32–69 and in Morley's chapter in Beumers (ed.), *24 Frames: The Cinema of Russia and the Former Soviet Union*, 2007, pp. 13–22.
25. V. Turkin, 'Edinaia i zerkala', *Kino-Gazeta* 22 (1918) in Ivanova, V. et al. *Velikii Kinemo, 2002, p.* 322.
26. Louise McReynolds, 'Home Was Never Where The Heart Was: Domestic Dystopias in Russia's Silent Movie Melodrama', in McReynolds and Neuberger (eds.), *Imitations of Life: Two Centuries of Melodrama in Russia*, 2002, pp. 127–151; p. 144.
27. McReynolds, 'The Silent Movie Melodrama…', p. 134.
28. McReynolds 'Home Was Never…', p. 121.
29. Leyda, *Kino*, p. 119.
30. Lev Kuleshov, 'O zadachakh khudozhnika v kinematografe', *Film Factory*, p. 41.
31. The film has recently been restored and digitally mastered by Nikolai Izvolov, and provided with extensive commentary.
32. Anatoli Lunacharsky, 'Zadachi gosudarstvennogo kinodela v RSFSR', *Film Factory*, p. 47.

Chapter 2 Revolutionary Cinema, or Cinema for the Masses (1919–29)

1. 'Pochti tezisy', *Proletkino* 1–2 (1923), in *Film Factory, p.* 84; Lenin in a conversation with Anatoli Lunacharsky, in Boltyanskii, 1925, *Film Factory*, p. 57.
2. Notably with Denise Youngblood's *Movies for the Masses: Popular Cinema and Soviet Society in the 1920s*, 1992.
3. Boris Groys and Katerina Clark argue that Socialist Realism develops trends of 1920s culture rather than reverses them, as Vladimir Paperny has argued in *Culture Two*, first published in Russian in 1985 and in English as *Architecture in the Age of Stalin*, 2002.

4. Goskino renamed the pre-Revolutionary studios into first, second etc. 'Factory of Goskino': (1) Khanzhonkov; (2) Skobelev Committee (Arbeiterhilfe); (3) Ermoliev; (4) Rus; (5) Ekran; and (6) Kharitonov. Throughout the 1920s and 1930s the names of the studios in Leningrad and Moscow changed: for Leningrad, it was from 1922–25 Sevzapkino (Severno-zapadnoe oblastnoe fotokinoupravlenie); from 1925–26 Leningradkino (Leningradskii kinokhudozhestvennyi trest); from 1926–30 Sovkino Leningrad; from 1930–32 Soyuzkino Leningrad; from 1932–33 Rosfilm Leningrad; from 1933–34 Soyuzkino Leningrad; and since 1934 Lenfilm. In Moscow, it was in 1924 Goskino Factory; from 1926–30 Sovkino Moscow; from 1930–32 Soyuzkino Moscow; from 1932–33 Rosfilm Moscow; from 1933–34 Soyuzkino Moscow; from 1934 Moskinokombinat; and since 1935 – Mosfilm.
5. Miroslava Segida and Sergei Zemlianukhin, *Domashniaia sinemateka*, 1996, p. 6.
6. Kuleshov, August 1922 in *Film Factory*, pp. 72–73.
7. Denise Youngblood, *Movies for the Masses: Popular Cinema and Soviet Society in the 1920s*, 1992, p. 57 and, p. 51. In the period 1921–31 there were 944 American and 971 Soviet films.
8. Youngblood, *Movies for the Masses*, p. 20.
9. Narodnyi komitet prosveshcheniia – People's Committee for Enlightenment.
10. *Film Factory*, p. 102.
11. *Pravda* 14 July 1923, quoted in Richard Taylor, *Film Propaganda: Soviet Russia and Nazi Germany*, 1998, p. 36 n. 26.
12. The sequel films are *Savur-Mogila*, *Crime of Chiransk Princess* and *Punishment of Chiransk Princess*, and *Illan Dilli.*
13. Kuleshov, 'Amerikanshchina', *Kinofot* 25–31 August 1922, pp. 14–15 in *Film Factory*, p. 73.
14. Kuleshov, 'Amerikanshchina'.
15. Cheka (Extraordinary Committee, also VChK) established 1918 by Felix Dzerzhinsky; from 1922 (O)GPU (State Political Directorate), from 1934 NKVD (People's Commissariat for Internal Affairs) and from 1954 KGB (Committee for State Security), disbanded 1991 and reorganized into the FSB (Federal Security Service).
16. Mal'tsev, *Na pomoshch' sovetskomu kino*, Moscow, 1927; quoted in Taylor, *Film Propaganda*, p. 40.
17. Kepley, 'The origins of Soviet cinema…', in *Inside the Film Factory*, pp. 60–79; p. 76.
18. Vertov, 'Otvet na 5 voprosov', *Kino-gazeta* 21 October 1924, in Richard Taylor, *The Politics of the Soviet Cinema, 1917–1929*, 1979, p. 129 n. 29.
19. The film was remade in colour and wide-screen format in 1964; the original version was restored by the Shar studio in 1996.
20. Jeremy Hicks, *Dziga Vertov: Defining Documentary Film*, 2007, p. 65.
21. Eisenstein, 'Bela Forgets the Scissors' (1926), *Film Factory*, pp. 145–149.

22. Richard Taylor, *The Battleship Potemkin*, 2000, p. 8.
23. Eisenstein, 'Bela Forgets the Scissors' (1926), *Film Factory*, p. 147.
24. Naum Kleiman, introduction to *The Battleship Potemkin* for the BBC. This organizational principle has been refuted by Eisenstein, who claimed that the steps pre-dictated a certain movement.
25. Leyda, *Kino*, p. 195.
26. Amy Sargeant, *Vsevolod Pudovkin: Classic Films of the Soviet Avant-Garde*, 2001, p. 179.
27. Sargeant, *Vsevolod Pudovkin*, p. 70.
28. Calvin Coolidge, US president 1923–29; George Curzon, British foreign secretary 1919–24; Raymond Poincaré, French president 1913–1920.
29. Neia Zorkaia, *Portrety*, 1966, p. 167.
30. Youngblood, *Movies for the Masses*, p. 114.
31. Julian Graffy, *Bed and Sofa* (KinoFile 5), 2001, p. 66.
32. Taylor, *Film Propaganda*, p. 39.
33. See *Film Factory*, p. 423.
34. The head of script section and Sovkino consultant Vladimor Sillov, director and journalist Anatoli Ardatov, and the artist Anton Pazin were executed in 1930. Similarly Albert Slivkin, Lenfilm technical director, and Moisei Rafes of Sovkino's art department, were arrested briefly in 1929–30 and arrested again and executed in the late 1930s. See Jamie Miller, 'The Purges of Soviet Cinema 1929–1938', *Studies in Russian and Soviet Cinema*, 1.1 (2007), pp. 5–26, 12–17.
35. Youngblood, *Movies for the Masses*, p. 40.
36. Youngblood, *Movies for the Masses*, p. 13.

Chapter 3 The Purges, the Second World War and the Cold War, or How Stalin Entertained the People (1930–53)

1. Commission set up to defend Trotsky against charges levelled against him at the Moscow trials.
2. *Moscow News* was closed in 1949 when Strong was expelled from the USSR; it was re-launched in 1956 and subsequently appeared in a number of other foreign languages, and finally also in Russian.
3. For a full discussion see Alexander Prokhorov, 'Arresting Development: A Brief History of Soviet Cinema for Children and Adolescents', in Marina Balina and Larissa Rudova (eds.), *Russian Children's Literature and Culture*, London: Routledge 2008, pp. 129–52.
4. Lenfilm garnered the first prize; René Clair for *The Last Millionaire* (Le Dernier Milliardaire) the second; and Walt Disney the third.
5. 'Ever Higher', Pavel German and Yuli Khait, 1920; see von Geldern and Stites (eds.), *Mass Soviet Culture in Soviet Russia*, 1995, pp. 257–8.

6. See Gul'nara Abikeeva, *Kino Tsentral'noi Azii,* Almaty: IREX, 2001. In Kyrgyzstan, the production base in Frunze opened in 1941, and the first feature film *Saltanat*, (Pronin) was made in 1955; in Turkmenistan the Ashkhabad Studio opened in 1926 and released *White Gold* (Vladychuk) in 1929; in Uzbekistan Bukhkino was formed in 1924 and *The Rise* (Nabi Ganiev) was made in 1931; in Kazakhstan Vostokkino was set up in 1928 and *Amangeldy* (Levin) is considered the first feature film, although it was not until 1954 that a feaure film was made by a Kazakh director (*Poem about Love*, Shaken Aimanov); Tadzhikkino opened in 1930 and Kamil Yarmatov made the first feature, *The Honorary Right*, in 1932.
7. Emma Widdis, *Alexander Medvedkin*, 2005, pp. 22–34; Nikolai Izvolov had reconstructed several films for the film-train.
8. Denise Youngblood, *Soviet Cinema in the Silent Era, 1918–1935*, 1985, p. 222 and tables in *Film Factory*, pp. 423–4.
9. See Eisenstein, Pudovkin, Alexandrov 'Statement on Sound', 5 August 1928, in *Film Factory*, pp. 234–5.
10. Before the 1917 Revolution, Russian Christmas was celebrated on 25 December (7 January, New Style). Christmas was abolished in Soviet Russia in 1918 and brought back only after the collapse of the Soviet Union in 1991. However, the public wish for a celebration and festive atmosphere to give hope, especially in the bleak times of the Civil War, led the government to have Soviet 'New Year' celebrations on 1 January. This is celebrated on New Year's Eve (*novogodniaia noch'*), or the so-called Carnival Night (*karnaval'naia noch'*), when children receive presents from Father Frost and the Snow Maiden under a decorated tree. See Beumers, 'Father Frost on 31 December: Christmas and New Year in Soviet and Russian Cinema', in *Christmas in the Movies*, ed. Mark Connelly, London: I. B. Tauris, 2000, pp. 185–209.
11. VSKhV (Vsesoiuznaia sel'skokhoziaistvennaia vystavka) 1935–39; opened at the premises near Ostankino in 1939; VDNKh (Vystavka dostizhenii narodnogo khoziastva) in 1959; VVS (Vserossiiskii vystavochnyi tsentr) in 1992.
12. Richard Taylor, 'Happy Guys', in Beumers (ed.), *24 Frames: The Cinema of Russia and the Former Soviet Union*, 2007, p. 82.
13. Richard Taylor, 'The Illusion of Happiness and the Happiness of Illusion: Grigorii Aleksandrov's *The Circus*', *Slavic and East European Review* 74:4 (1996), pp. 601–620; p. 618.
14. 'Song of the Motherland', von Geldern and Stites, pp. 271–2.
15. See Richard Taylor, 'Singing on the Steppes for Stalin: Ivan Pyr'ev and the Kolkhoz Musical in Soviet Cinema', *Slavic Review*, 58:1 (1999), pp. 143–159; p. 149. Taylor suggests that Pyriev was possibly agitating against Eisenstein.
16. See Richard Taylor, 'Singing on the Steppes for Stalin: Ivan Pyr'ev and the Kolkhoz Musical in Soviet Cinema', *Slavic Review*, 58:1 (1999), pp. 143–159; p. 151.

17. Since the late eighteenth century, lacquered boxes had been made from papier mâché, which was painted with gouache or tempera before being varnished. Palekh, Mstera, Kholui and Fedoskino are the schools of lacquer box painting.
18. For a discussion and the animated sequence, see Bagrov, 'Ermler, Stalin and Animation', in *KinoKultura* 15 (2007), http://www.kinokultura.com/2007/15-bagrov.shtml (last accessed 15 August 2007).
19. *Basmachi*: led revolts against tsarist regime in 1916, and continued resistance during the 1920s.
20. *Film Factory*, pp. 334–5.
21. Eisenstein in lectures at VGIK on 12, 18, 19 March 1947, see *The Eisenstein Reader*, ed. Taylor, pp. 167–186.
22. Eisenstein quoted in Taylor, *Film Propaganda*, p. 86 (from *Selected Works*, vol. 3, pp. 118–19).
23. Shumiatskii, 'Zadachi templana 1934 goda', *Sovetskoe kino* 11 (1933), quoted in Taylor, *Film Propaganda*, p. 46.
24. For a full list, see *Iz"iatoe kino.*
25. See Catriona Kelly, *Comrade Pavlik: The Rise and Fall of a Soviet Boy Hero*, London, 2006.
26. Leyda, *Kino*, p. 306.
27. The list of those evacuated included the production units of directors such as Eisenstein, Pudovkin, Vertov, Kozintsev and Trauberg, Ermler, Room, the Vasiliev Brothers, and Barnet. The following films were made in Alma-Ata during 1942–44: Eisenstein, *Ivan the Terrible I*; Ermler, *She Defends her Motherland* (Ona zashchishchaet rodinu); Stolper, *Wait for Me* (Zhdi menia); Room, *The Invasion* (Nashestvie); Yudin, *Antosha Rybkin*; Trauberg, *The Actress* (Aktrisa); Rappoport, *Air Coachman* (Vozdushnyi izvozchik). Many films produced at TsOKS were later banned: Barnet, *A Nice Fellow* (Slavnyi mal'chik); Room, *Tonia*; Pudovkin, *Murderers go into the Street* (Ubiitsy vykhodiat na dorogu); and Kozintsev & Trauberg, *Young Fritz* (Iunyi Frits).
28. Denise Youngblood, *Russian War Films*, 2007, p. 58.
29. 'Formidable Shadows of 1947' in *Moscow News*, 7 August 1988.
30. For a complete lists see Taylor, *Film Propaganda*, pp. 212–14.
31. Evgeni Dobrenko, 'Late Stalinist Cinema and the Cold War: An Equation without Unknowns', *Modern Language Review*, 98:4 (2003), pp. 929–944.
32. For statistics see Segida, *Domashniaia sinemateka*; for lists of films banned see *Iz"iatoe kino.*
33. Segida, p. 6.
34. Taylor (*Film Propaganda*, p. 117) has pointed to anecdotal evidence that this scene is a reversal of *Potemkin*, with the superior army approaching from below, not above.
35. Taylor, 'Singing on the Steppes for Stalin', p. 143.

Chapter 4 The Thaw – New Beginnings, New Lives (1954–66)

1. During the 1960s and 1970s its status and affiliation changed several times: from 1963–65 and 1972–78 it was the State Committee of the Council of Ministers, from 1965–72 it was subordinated to the Council. In 1978 it became the State Committee for Cinematography until its liquidation in November 1991.
2. Aleksandr Galich, *Generalnaia repetitsiia*, Moscow: Sovetskii pisatel', 1991.
3. Prokhorov, 'The adolescent and the child…', p. 116–7.
4. Andrei Tarkovsky, *Sculpting in Time*, 1986, p. 17.
5. Tarkovsky, *Sculpting in Time*, pp. 63–4.
6. Jean-Paul Sartre in *Unità*, 9 October 1963, cited in 'Po povodu *Ivanova detstva*', in *Mir i fil'my Andreia Tarkovskogo*, 1991, pp. 11–21.
7. Josephine Woll, *Real Images. Soviet Cinema of the Thaw*, 2000, p. 25.
8. Woll, *Real Images*, p. 126.
9. In *Tikhookeanskii komsomolets*, quoted on *Seans: Entsiklopediia otechestvennogo kino*, http://www.russiancinema.ru/template.php?dept_id=15&e_dept_id=2&text_element_id=7197 (last accessed 8 August 2007).
10. Woll, *Real Images*, pp. 112–124.
11. Woll, *Real Images*, p. 114.
12. Other novellas were by Vladimir Semakov, Naum Trakhtenberg, Eduard Zmojro.
13. Alexander Prokhorov, 'The adolescent and the child in the cinema of the Thaw', *Studies in Russian and Soviet Cinema* 1.2 (2007), pp. 115–129; p. 126.
14. See *KinoKultura*, http://www.kinokultura.com/plus/prokat1.html.
15. Woll, *Real Images*, pp. 205–6.
16. The full title was *The Story of Asya Kliachina Who Loved But Did Not Get Married* (Istoriia Asi Kliachinoi, kotoraia liubila, da ne vyshla zamuzh) Mosfilm.
17. See Valerii Fomin, *Polka*, Moscow: NIIK 1992.
18. Tarkovsky, *Sculpting in Time*, p. 89.

Chapter 5 The Stagnation: Mainstream and *Auteur* Cinema (1967–82)

1. See Razlogov, (ed.) *Pervyi vek nashego kino*, Moscow: Lokid Press, 2006, p. 608.
2. In 1976 the Helsinki Group was headed by the nuclear physicist Yuri Orlov (b. 1924), who was arrested in 1977 and upon his release emigrated to the US. Other members of the group shared his fate: Anatoli Marchenko (1938–86) died in a camp during a hunger strike. Anatoli (Natan) Shcharansky (b. 1948) was arrested in 1978 as a member of and speaker of the *refusnik* movement (Soviet Jews who were denied the right to emigrate); he was convicted and sentenced to thirteen years in a labour camp, but was exchanged in 1986.
3. The Soviet Film Industry was largely profitable for the state during the 1960s and into the 1970s, i.e. it did not use money from the state budget.
4. Askoldov on RUSCICO release of the film. Other sources claim that the case was discussed at a Filmmakers' Union press conference (Lawton in *Kinoglasnost*).

5. Youngblood, *Russian War Films*, p. 157
6. Lawton, *Kinoglasnost*, pp. 113–14.
7. Jane Taubman, *Kira Muratova*, 2005, p. 11.
8. Gul'nara Abikeeva, *Kino Tsentral'noi Azii,* 2001.
9. John Givens, 'Vasilii Shukshin and the "Audience of Millions": *Kalina krasnaia* and the power of popular cinema', *Russian Review* 58 (1999), pp. 268–85; p. 277.
10. Gerasimov in *Iskusstvo kino* 6 (1988), p. 102.
11. Tarkovsky, *Sculpting in Time*, p. 38.
12. Tarkovsky in February 1972, quoted in *Pervyi vek nashego kino*, p. 872.
13. Tarkovsky, *Sculpting in Time*, p. 114.
14. Tarkovsky, *Sculpting in Time*, p. 117.
15. Youngblood, *Russian War Films*, pp. 150–1.
16. Neya Zorkaya, *Iskusstvo kino* 11 (1995), see Lawton, *Kinoglasnost*, p. 94

Chapter 6 Glasnost and Before (1983–92)

1. Josephine Woll and Denise Youngblood, *Repentance*, 2001, p. 73.
2. The Kremlin meetings took place on 17 December 1962 and 7–8 March 1963, and were used by Khrushchev to brief the intelligentsia about his demands on the arts (announcing the end of the Thaw).
3. Pasternak's *Doctor Zhivago* (1956), Yevgeni Zamiatin's *We* (1924), Andrei Platonov's *Chevengur* (1926–29), Leonid Grossman's *Life and Fate* (1960), Mikhail Bulgakov's satire 'The Heart of a Dog' (1925), Anna Akhmatova's 'Requiem' (1935–40), and the works of Vladimir Nabokov and Joseph Brodsky began to appear.
4. Further FU congresses took place in 1965, 1969, 1973 and 1976.
5. See Lawton, *Kinoglasnost*, p. 242 for a full list of the members of the old and new secretariat.
6. After two years at the head of the FU, Klimov took leave of absence for creative reasons (to make a film), and left filmmaker Andrei Smirnov in charge.
7. See *Iskusstvo kino* 10 (1986), pp. 121–25.
8. Lawton quoting Razumovsky: the screenwriter Maria Zvereva and Andrei Razumovsky, producer and head of the Association of Independent Cinema, were the co-chairs. Lawton, *Kinoglasnost*, p. 65.
9. Lawton, *Kinoglasnost*, p. 48.
10. Anna Lawton, *Kinoglasnost: Soviet Cinema in Our Time*, 1992, pp. 148–9.
11. The film's negative remained with the French co-producer Serge Zilberman while Mosfilm, in the rush to prepare the film for Cannes, only kept the first print of mediocre quality. The copies of the film available in Russia suffer from a deficiency in the colour scheme, while the French copy is only occasionally screened in Paris. For a discussion see Liubov' Arkus, 'Anna Karamazoff: Ischeznovenie,' *Séance* 9 (1994), pp. 104–111.

Chapter 7 Post-Soviet Russian Cinema (1992–2000)

1. Beumers, 'Cinemarket, or the Russian Film Industry in "Mission Possible"', *Europe-Asia-Studies* 51:5 (1999), pp. 871–96.
2. Federal Law on Cinema (126-FZ), *Rossiiskaia gazeta*, 29 August 1996.
3. The new Penal Code of 1997 changes this situation with article 146 (breach of authors' rights) and article 171 (illegal business).
4. Goskino was called Roskomkino until 1996, when it became a state committee, Goskino; in 2000 it was merged with the Ministry of Culture, as the department for Cinematography. It was reorganized into the Federal Agency for Culture and Cinematography in 2004. I use the name Goskino throughout this chapter to avoid confusion.
5. Sergei Soloviev at Jack Valenti's Press Conference on Anti-Piracy, Moscow, 22 July 1997. See also *Kinoglaz* 18 (1997), p. 8, which provides the following data: '120 million blank video tapes were imported in 1996; of these, 10 per cent were sold as blank tapes, while 90 per cent were purchased by video pirates. 100 million tapes were sold by video pirates, 40 million through legal video distributors. The yearly turnover of the pirate market is US$423.5 million, that of the pirate and legal market together US$700 million.'
6. The script is published in Beumers (ed.), *Russia on Reels*, 1999, pp. 12–21.
7. Karina Dobrotvorskaia, 'Uvidet' Parizh i vyzhit'', *Seans* 9 (1994), p. 85.
8. Liubov' Arkus and Konstantin Shavlovskii (eds.), *Segrei Bodrov: Sviaznoi*, St Petersburg: Seans & Amfora, 2007.

Chapter 8 Cinema in the Putin Era (2001–8)

1. Released with 300 copies, grossing a total of US$16 million through theatrical release in Russia alone. See *Screen Daily* 21 July 2004, 4 August 2004, and http://www.dozorfilm.ru.
2. The first Kino Star cinema with eleven screens opened in September 2003; a twelve-screen Kino Star opened in December 2004. The first nine-screen multiplex of Cinema Park opened in January 2004; another six-screen cinema opened in December 2004. Source: Dodona Research, *Screen International*, 24 June 2005, p. 23.
3. For a full survey of television serials see David MacFadyen, *Russian Television Today: Primetime Drama and Comedy*, New York: Routledge, 2008.
4. The movement was named after the New Drama festival initiated in 2002 by Eduard Boyakov, formerly director of the national theatre festival, Golden Mask, and currently director of the Praktika Theatre. The second edition, in September 2003, was held in conjunction with the Moscow Arts Theatre and teatr.doc; since 2006 it has moved to the auspices of the Praktika Theatre.

Bibliography

General

Reference Books

Arkus, Liubov' (ed.). *Noveishaia istoriia otechestvennogo kino 1986–2000. Kinoslovar'*. 3 vols. St Petersburg: Seans, 2001.

—— (ed.). *Noveishaia istoriia otechestvennogo kino 1986–2000. Kino i kontekst.* 4 vols. St Petersburg: Seans, 2002–5.

Iutkevich, S. (ed.). *Kinoslovar'*. Moskva: Sovietskaia Entsiklopediia, 1986.

Kudriavtsev, Sergei. *Svoe kino.* Moscow: Dubl' D, 1998.

Marshall, Herbert. *Masters of the Soviet Cinema: Crippled Creative Biographies.* London: Routledge, 1983.

Razlogov, Kirill (ed.). *Pervyi vek nashego kino,* Moscow: Lokid Press, 2006.

Taylor, Richard, with Nancy Wood, Julian Graffy, and Dina Iordanova (eds.). *The BFI Companion to Eastern European and Russian Cinema*. London: British Film Institute, 2000.

Segida Miroslava and Sergei Zemlianukhin. *Domashniaia sinemateka: otechestvennoe kino 1918–1996*. Moscow: Dubl' D, 1996.

——. *Fil'my Rossii. Igrovoe kino. 1995–2000*. Moscow: Dubl' D, 2001.

——. *Fil'my Rossii. Igrovoe kino. TV. Video. 1992–2003*. Moscow: Dubl' D, 2004.

On Russian and Soviet Cinema

Attwood, Lynne *(ed.). Red Women on the Silver Screen: Soviet Women and Cinema from the Beginning to the End of the Communist Era.* London: Pandora, 1993.

Beardow, Frank. 'Soviet Cinema, Past, Present and Future', *Rusistika* 3 (1991): 19–25.

——. 'Soviet Cinema: Coming to Terms With the Past', *Rusistika* 7 (1993): 31–36 and 8 (1993): 2–18.

——. 'Soviet Cinema: Women – Icons or Individuals?', *Rusistika* 9 (1994): 22–42 and 10 (1994): 2–13 and 11 (1995): 35–42.

——. 'Soviet Cinema – War Revisited', *Rusistika* 15 (1997): 19–34 and 16 (1997): 8–21.

Beumers, Birgit. 'Myth-Making and Myth-Taking: Lost Ideals and the War in Contemporary Russian Cinema', *Canadian Slavonic Papers* 42.1–2 (2000): 171–189.

——. 'Father Frost on 31 December: Christmas and New Year in Soviet and Russian Cinema', in Mark Connelly (ed.), *Christmas in the Movies*. London: I. B. Tauris, 2000, pp. 185–209.

——. 'Soviet and Russian Blockbusters: A Question of Genre?', *Slavic Review* 62.3 (2003): 441–454.

—— (ed.). *24 Frames: The Cinema of Russia and the Former Soviet Union*. London: Wallflower Press, 2007.

Fomin, Valerii. *Pravda skazki. Kino i traditsii fol'klora*, Moscow: Materik, 2001.

Gillespie, David. *Russian Cinema*. New York: Longman, 2003.

Golovskoy, Val and John Rimberg. *Behind the Soviet Screen*. Ann Arbor, MI: Ardis, 1986.

Horton, Andrew. *Inside Soviet Film Satire*. Cambridge: Cambridge University Press, 1993.

Hutchings, Stephen and Anat Vernitski (eds.). *Russian and Soviet Film Adaptations of Literature, 1900–2001. Screening the Word*. London: Routledge, 2005.

Kenez, Peter. *Cinema and Soviet Society, 1917–1953*. Cambridge: Cambridge University Press, 1992.

Lawton, Anna. *The Red Screen: Politics, Society, Art in Soviet Cinema*. London and New York: Routledge, 1992.

Leyda, J. *Kino: A History of the Russian and Soviet Film*. Princeton: Princeton University Press, 1960.

Rimberg, John. *The Motion Picture in the Soviet Union, 1918–1952: A Sociological Analysis*. New York: Arno Press, 1973.

Shlapentokh, Dmitry and Vladimir. *Soviet Cinematography, 1918–1991*. New York: Aldine de Gruyter, 1993.

Stites, Richard. *Russian Popular Culture. Entertainment and Society Since 1900*. Cambridge: Cambridge University Press, 1992.

Taylor, Richard. *The Poetics of Cinema*. Oxford: RPT Publications, 1982.

Taylor, Richard and Ian Christie (eds.). *The Film Factory. Russian and Soviet Cinema in Documents 1896–1939*. London and New York: Routledge, 1988.

——. *Inside the Film Factory. New Approaches to Russian and Soviet Cinema*. London and New York: Routledge, 1991.

Youngblood, Denise. *Russian War Films: On the Cinema Front, 1914–2005*. Lawrence, KS: University Press of Kansas, 2007.

Zorkaya, Neya. *The Illustrated History of the Soviet Cinema*. New York: Hippocrene Books, 1991.

Russian and Soviet Film Theory

Eagle, Herbert (ed.). *Russian Formalist Film Theory*. Ann Arbor, MI: Michigan Slavic Publications, 1981.

Eikhenbaum, Boris (ed.). *Poetika kino*. Moscow, Leningrad: Kinopechat', 1927.
Gerould, Daniel. 'Russian Formalist Theories of Melodrama', in Marcia Landy (ed.) *Imitations of Life: A Reader on Film and Television Melodrama*. Detroit, MI: Wayne State University Press, 1991.
Taylor, Richard (ed.). *The Poetics of Cinema. Russian Poetics in Translation*, 9. Oxford: RPT Publications, 1982.

Soviet and Russian Cultural Studies

Balina, Marina with Evgenii Dobrenko, Iurii Murashov (eds.). *Sovetskoe bogatstvo: Stat'i o kul'ture, literature i kino*. St Petersburg: Akademicheskii proekt, 2002.
Barker, Adele Marie (ed.). *Consuming Russia: Popular Culture, Sex, and Society Since Gorbachev*. Durham, NC: Duke University Press, 1999.
Berry, Ellen E. and Anessa Miller-Pogacar (eds.). *Re-Entering the Sign: Articulating New Russian Culture*. Ann Arbor, MI: University of Michigan Press, 1995.
Beumers, Birgit. *Popular Culture Russia!* Santa Barbara, Denver and London: ABC Clio, 2005.
Boym, Svetlana. *Common Places: Mythologies of Everyday Life in Russia*. Cambridge, MA and London: Harvard University Press, 1994.
——. *The Future of Nostalgia*. New York: Basic Books, 2001.
Clark, Katerina. *The Soviet Novel: History as Ritual*. Chicago: Chicago University Press, 1981.
Condee, Nancy (ed.). *Soviet Hieroglyphics: Visual Culture in Late Twentieth-Century Russia*. London and Bloomington: BFI/Indiana University Press, 1995.
Graffy, Julian and G. Hosking (eds.). *Culture and the Media in the USSR Today*. London: Macmillan, 1989.
Günther, Hans and Evgenii Dobrenko (eds.). *Sotsrealisticheskii kanon*. St Petersburg: Akademicheskii proekt, 2000.
——. and Sabine Hänsgen (eds.). *Sovetskaia vlast' i mediia*. St Petersburg: Akademicheskii proekt, 2006.
Hutchings, Stephen. *Russian Literary Culture and the Camera Age: The Word as Image*. London: Routledge Curzon, 2004.
James, Vaughan. *Soviet Socialist Realism: Origins and Theory*. New York: St Martin's Press, 1973.
Kelly, Catriona and David Shepherd. *Russian Cultural Studies*. Oxford: Oxford University Press, 1998.
Lahusen, Thomas (ed.). *Socialist Realism Without Shores*. Durham, NC: Duke University Press, 1997.
—— and Gene Kuperman (eds.). *Late Soviet Culture: From Perestroika to Novostroika*. Durham, NC: Duke University Press, 1993.
Miller, Frank. *Folklore for Stalin*. New York: Columbia University Press, 1990.

Robin, Regine. *Socialist Realism.* Stanford: Stanford University Press, 1992.
Stites, Richard. *Russian Popular Culture.* Cambridge: Cambridge University Press, 1992.
van Geldern, James and Richard Stites (eds.). *Mass Soviet Culture in Soviet Russia.* Bloomington: Indiana University Press, 1995.

Chronological

Pre-Revolutionary Cinema

Batalin, Viktor. *Kinokhronika v Rossii, 1896–1916gg.: Opis' kinos"emok, khraniashchikhsia v RGAKFD.* Moscow: Olma-Press, 2002.
Cherchi Usai, Paolo, et al. (eds.). *Silent Witnesses. Russian Films, 1908–1919.* Coordination by Yuri Tsivian. London: BFI, 1989.
Deriabin, A., Fomin, V., Vishnevskii, Veniamin et al. (eds.). *Letopis' Rossiiskogo kino, 1863–1929.* Moscow: Materik, 2004.
Ginzburg, Semen. *Kinematografiia dorevolutsionnoi Rossii.* Moscow: Iskusstvo, 1963.
Ivanova, V. with V. Myl'nikova, S. Skovorodnikova, Iu. Tsivian, and R. Iangirov (eds.). *Velikii Kinemo: Katalog sokhranivshikhsia igrovykh fil'mov Rossii, 1908–1919.* Moscow: Novoe literaturnoe obozrenie, 2002.
McReynolds, Louise. 'The Silent Movie Melodrama: Evgenii Bauer Fashions the Heroine's Self', in Laura Engelstein and Stephanie Sandler (eds.), *Self and Story in Russian History*, Ithaca, NY and London: Cornell University Press, 2000, pp. 120–139.
——. 'Home Was Never Where The Heart Was: Domestic Dystopias in Russia's Silent Movie Melodrama', in L. McReynolds and J. Neuberger (eds.), *Imitations of Life: Two Centuries of Melodrama in Russia*, Durham, NC and London: Duke University Press, 2002, pp. 127–151.
Morley, Rachel. 'Gender Relations in the Films of Evgenii Bauer', *Slavonic and East European Review*, 81.1 (2003): 32–69.
Sobolev, R. *Liudi i fil´my russkogo dorevoliutsionnogo kino.* Moscow: Iskusstvo, 1961.
Tsivian, Yuri. *Early Cinema in Russia and its Cultural Reception.* Chicago and London: University of Chicago Press, 1994.
—— (ed.). *Lines of Resistance: Dziga Vertov and the Twenties.* Pordenone: Le Giornate del Cinema Muto, 2005.
Vishnevskii, Veniamin, et al. (eds.). *Letopis' Rossiiskogo kino, 1863–1929.* Moscow: Materik. 2004.
Youngblood, Denise. *The Magic Mirror. Moviemaking in Russia, 1908–1918.* Madison, WI and London: University of Wisconsin Press, 1999.

Early Soviet Cinema

Aumont, Jacques. *Montage Eisenstein.* London: BFI Publishing and Bloomington, IN: Indiana University Press, 1987.

Barna, Yon. *Eisenstein.* London: Secker & Warburg, 1973.

Beumers, Birgit. 'Eisenstein: The Battleship Potemkin', in Forbes, Jill and Sarah Street (eds.) *European Cinema.* London: Palgrave, 2000, pp. 53–64.

Bordwell, David. 'The Idea of Montage in Soviet Art and Film', *Cinema Journal* 11.2 (1972): 9–17.

—— *The Cinema of Eisenstein.* Cambridge, MA and London: Harvard University Press, 1993.

Brooks, Jeffrey. 'Russian Cinema and Public Discourse, 1900–1930', *Historical Journal of Film, Radio and Television* 11.2 (1991): 141–148.

Bulgakowa, Oksana. *Sergei Eisenstein: A Biography.* Berlin and San Francisco: Potemkin Press, 2001.

Cavendish, Phil. *Soviet Mainstream Cinematography: The Silent Era.* London: UCL Arts and Humanities Publications, 2007.

Christie, Ian and Richard Taylor (eds.). *Eisenstein Rediscovered.* London: Routledge, 1993.

Eisenstein [Eizenshtein], Sergei. *Izbrannye proizvedeniia.* 6 vols. Moscow: Iskusstvo, 1964–71.

Eisenstein, Sergei. *Nonindifferent Nature.* Cambridge: Cambridge University Press, 1987.

Gillespie, David. *Early Soviet Cinema: Innovation, Ideology and Propaganda.* London: Wallflower, 2000.

Goodwin, James. *Eisenstein, Cinema and History.* Urbana and Chicago, IL: University of Illinois Press, 1993.

Graffy, Julian. *Bed and Sofa* (KinoFile 5). London: I. B. Tauris, 2001.

Hicks, Jeremy. *Dziga Vertov: Defining Documentary Film*, London: I. B. Tauris, 2007.

Iurenev, Rostislav. *Sergei Eizenshtein. Zamysli. Fil'my. Metod. Chast' pervaia: 1898–1929.* Moscow: Iskusstvo, 1985.

Kenez, Peter. *The Birth of the Propaganda State: Soviet Methods of Mass Mobilization, 1917–1929.* New York: Cambridge University Press, 1985.

Kenez, Peter. *Cinema and Soviet Society, 1917–1953.* New York: Cambridge University Press, 1992.

Kepley, Vance. 'Foreign Films on Soviet Screens, 1922–1931', *Quarterly Review of Film Studies* 4.4 (1979): 429–442.

——. 'The Workers' International Relief and the Cinema of the Left, 1921–1935', *Cinema Journal* 23.1 (1983): 7–23.

——. 'The Origins of Soviet Cinema: A Study in Industry Development', *Quarterly Review of Film Studies* 4 (1985): 22–38.

——. 'Building a National Cinema: Soviet Film Education, 1918–1934', *WideAngle* 9.3 (1987): 4–20.
——. *The End of St Petersburg* (KinoFile 10). London: I. B. Tauris, 2003.
Leyda, Jay and Zina Voynow (eds.). *Eisenstein at Work*. London: Methuen, 1985.
Liber, George. *Alexander Dovzhenko: A Life in Soviet Film*. London: BFI, 2002.
Listov, Viktor. 'Early Soviet Cinema: the Spontaneous and the Planned, 1917–1924', *Historical Journal of Film, Radio and Television* 11.2 (1991): 121–127.
——. *Rossiia. Revoliutsiia. Kinematograf: K 100-letiiu mirovogo kino*. Moscow: Materik, 1995.
—— and Elena Khokhlova (eds.). *Istoriia otechestvennogo kino: dokumenty, memuary, pis'ma*. vyp. 1. Moscow: Materik, 1996.
Mal'kova, Liliana, *Sovremennost' kak istoriia: Realizatsiia mifa v dokumental'nom kino*. Moscow: Materik, 2002.
Mayne, Judith. *Kino and the Woman Question: Feminism and Soviet Silent Cinema*. Columbus, OH: Ohio State University Press, 1989.
Michelson, Annette (ed.). *Kino-Eye: The Writings of Dziga Vertov*. Berkeley: University of California Press, 1984.
Nesbet, Anne. *Savage Junctures. Sergei Eisenstein and the Shape of Thinking*. London: I. B. Tauris, 2003.
Petric, Vlada. *Constructivism in Film: The Man With the Movie Camera*, Cambridge: Cambridge University Press, 1987.
Reeder, R. 'Agit-Prop Art: Posters, Puppets, Propaganda and Eisenstein's *Strike*', *Russian Literature Tri-Quarterly* 22 (1989): 255–78.
Roberts, Graham. *Forward Soviet. History and Non-Fiction Film in the USSR*. London: I. B. Tauris, 1999.
——. *The Man with the Movie Camera* (KinoFile 2). London: I. B. Tauris, 2000.
Sargeant, Amy. *Vsevolod Pudovkin: Classic Films of the Soviet Avant-Garde*. London: I. B. Tauris, 2001.
Seton, Marie, *Sergei M. Eisenstein. A Biography*. London: Dennis Dobson, 1978.
Taylor, Richard. *The Politics of the Soviet Cinema, 1917–1929*. Cambridge: Cambridge University Press, 1979.
——. *Film Propaganda: Soviet Russia and Nazi Germany*. London: I. B. Tauris [1979], 1998.
——. (ed.). *The Eisenstein Reader*. London: BFI, 1998.
——. *The Battleship Potemkin* (KinoFile 1). London: I. B. Tauris, 2000.
——. *October*. London: BFI, 2002.
—— (ed.). *The Eisenstein Collection*, London, New York, Calcutta: Seagull Books, 2006.
Yampolsky, Mikhail. 'Reality at Second Hand', *Historical Journal of Film, Radio and Television* 11.2 (1991): 161–171.
Yangirov, Rashit. 'Soviet Cinema in the Twenties: National Alternatives' *Historical Journal of Film, Radio and Television* 11.2 (1991): 129–139.

Youngblood, Denise. *Soviet Cinema in the Silent Era, 1918–1935*, Austin: University of Texas Press, 1985.
——. *Movies for the Masses: Popular Cinema and Soviet Society in the 1920s*, Cambridge: Cambridge University Press, 1992.
——. ' "History" on Film: the Historical Melodrama in Early Soviet Cinema', *Historical Journal of Film, Radio and Television* 11.2 (1991): 173–184.
Zorkaia, Neia, et al. (eds.). *Ekrannye iskusstva i literatura: nemoe kino.* Moscow: Nauka, 1991.

Cinema Under Stalin

Anderson, Trudy. 'Why Stalinist Musicals?' *Discourse* 17.3 (1995), 38–48.
Anon. '*Zemlia* 1930–1994', *Kinovedcheskie zapiski* 23 (1994): 103–224 [special issue].
Chernenko, Miron. *Krasnaia zvezda, zheltaia zvezda.* Vinnitsa: Globus Press, 2001.
Crofts, S. 'Ideology and Form: Soviet Socialist Realism and Chapayev', *Essays in Poetics*, II.1 (1977): 43–57.
Dobrenko, Evgeny. 'Muzyka vmesto sumbura: Narodnost' kak problema muzykal'noi kinokomedii stalinskoi epokhi', *Revue des Études slaves* 67.2–3 (1995): 407–433.
——. 'The Russia We Acquired: Russian Classics, the Stalinist Cinema, and the Past from the Revolutionary Perspective', *Russian Studies in Literature* 37.4 (2001): 61–91.
——. 'Late Stalinist Cinema and the Cold War: An Equation Without Unknowns', *Modern Language Review*, 98.4 (2003): 929–944.
——. 'Creation Myth and Myth Creation in Stalinist Cinema', *Studies in Russian and Soviet Cinema* 1.3 (2007): 239–264.
——. *Stalinist Cinema and the Production of History.* Edinburgh: Edinburgh University Press, 2008.
Dzhulai, Liudmila. *Dokumental'nyi illiuzion: Otechestvennyi kinodokumental'izm. Opyty sotsial'nogo tvorchestva.* Moscow: Materik, 2001.
Ferro, M. 'The Fiction Film and Historical Analysis,' in Paul Smith (ed.), *The Historian and Film*, Cambridge: Cambridge University Press, 1976, pp. 80–95.
Haynes, John. *New Soviet Man: Gender and Masculinity in Stalinist Soviet Cinema.* Manchester and New York: Manchester University Press, 2003.
——.'Film As Political Football: *The Goalkeeper*', *Studies in Russian and Soviet Cinema* 1.3 (2007): 283–297.
Holmgren, Beth. 'The Blue Angel and Blackface: Redeeming Entertainment in Aleksandrov's Circus', *Russian Review* 66 (2007): 5–22.
Hutchings, Stephen. 'Tchapaiev: l'homme de tous les temps, l'homme de tous les medias', *La Revue Russe* 21 (2002): 9–16.

Iurenev, Rostislav. *Sovetskoe kinoiskusstvo tridtsatykh godov.* Moscow: VGIK, 1997.

Kaganovsky, Lilya, 'The Voice of Technology and the End of Soviet Silent Film: Grigorii Kozintsev and Leonid Trauberg's *Alone*', *Studies in Russian and Soviet Cinema* 1.3 (2007): 265–281.

Kenez, Peter. 'Black and White: The War on Film', in Richard Stites (ed.) *Culture and Entertainment in Wartime Russia.* Bloomington: Indiana University Press, 1995.

——. 'Jewish Themes in Stalinist Films', *Journal of Popular Culture* 31.4 (1998): 159–169.

Kepley, V. 'Earth' in *In the Service of the State: The Cinema of Alexander Dovzhenko*, Madison, WI: University of Wisconsin Press, 1986, pp. 75–84.

——. 'Dovzhenko and Montage: Issues of Style and Narration in the Silent Films', *Journal of Ukrainian Studies*, 19.1 (1994): 29–44.

Laurent, Natacha. *L'oeil du Kremlin: cinema et censure en URSS sous Staline.* Toulouse: Privat, 2000.

Liber, George. *Alexander Dovzhenko: A Life in Soviet Film.* London: BFI, 2002.

Mamatova, Lidiia. *Kino: politika i liudi: 30-ye gody.* Moscow: Materik, 1995.

Margolit, Evgenii and Viacheslav Shmyrov. *iz"iatoe kino.* Moscow: Dubl' D, 1995.

Mar'iamov, Grigorii. *Kremlevskii tsenzor: Stalin smotrit kino.* Moscow: Kinotsentr, 1992.

Miller, Jamie. 'Soviet Cinema, 1929–41: The Development of Industry and Infrastructure', *Europe Asia Studies*, 58. 1 (2006): 103–124.

——. 'The Purges of Soviet Cinema 1929–1938', *Studies in Russian and Soviet Cinema*, 1.1 (2007): 5–26.

——. 'Educating the Filmmakers: the State Institute of Cinematography in the 1930s', *The Slavonic and East European Review*, 85.3 (2007): 462–490.

Neuberger, Joan. *Ivan the Terrible* (KinoFile 9). London: I. B. Tauris, 2003.

Prokhorov, Alexander. 'Soviet Family Melodrama of the 1940s and 1950s: From *Wait for Me* to *The Cranes Are Flying*' in Louise McReynolds and Joan Neuberger *(eds.) Imitations of Life: Two Centuries of Melodrama in Russia.* Durham, NC: Duke University Press, 2002, pp. 208–231.

——. 'Revisioning Alexandrov's Circus: Seventy Years of the Great Family, *Russian Review* 66 (2007): 1–4.

Riley, John. *Dmitri Shostakovich.* (Kino Companion 3). London: I. B. Tauris, 2005.

Salys, Rimgaila. 'Art Deco Aesthetics in Grigorii Aleksandrov's *The Circus*', *Russian Review* 66 (2007): 23–35.

Schmulevitch, Éric. *Réalisme socialiste et cinéma: Le cinéma stalinien (1928–1941).* Paris: Editions L'Harmattan, 1996.

Taylor, Richard. 'A "Cinema for the Millions": Soviet Socialist Realism and the Problem of Film Comedy', *Journal of Contemporary History* 18 (1983): 439–61.

——. 'The Illusion of Happiness and the Happiness of Illusion: Grigorii Aleksandrov's *The Circus*', *Slavic and East European Review* 74.4 (1996): 601–620.

——. 'Singing on the Steppes for Stalin: Ivan Pyr'ev and the Kolkhoz Musical in Soviet Cinema', *Slavic Review*, 58.1 (1999): 143–159.

——. 'But Eastward, Look, the Land is Brighter: Towards a Topography of Utopia in the Stalinist Musical', in Diana Holmes and Alison Smith *(eds.), 100 Years of European Cinema: Entertainment or Ideology?* Manchester: Manchester University Press, 2000, pp. 11–26.

—— and Derek Spring (eds.). *Stalinism and Soviet Cinema.* London: Routledge, 1993.

Tsivian, Yuri. *Ivan the Terrible*. London: BFI Classics, 2001.

Widdis, Emma. *Visions of a New Land: Soviet Film from the Revolution to the Second World War*. New Haven, CT: Yale University Press, 2003.

——. *Alexander Medvedkin* (Kino Companion 2). London: I. B. Tauris, 2005.

Youngblood, Denise. 'The Fate of Soviet Popular Cinema During the Stalin Revolution', *The Russian Review* 50 (1991): 148–162.

Post-war Cinema

Anninskii, Lev. *Shestidesiatniki i my.* Moscow: Souiz kinematografistov SSSR and Kinotsentr, 1991.

Andrew, Joe. 'Birth Equals Rebirth: Space, Narrative and Gender in *The Commissar*', *Studies in Russian and Soviet Cinema* 1.1 (2007): 29–44.

Baraban, Elena. 'The Fate of a Man by Sergei Bondarchuk and the Soviet Cinema of Trauma', *Slavic and East European Journal*, 51.3 (2007): 514–534.

Barta, Peter and Stephen Hutchings. 'The Train as Word-Image Intertext in the Films *Ballad of a Soldier* and *Thief, Intertexts* 6.2 (2002): 127–144.

Beumers, Birgit. *Nikita Mikhalkov* (Kino Companion 1). London: I. B. Tauris, 2005.

Bird, Robert. *Andrei Rublev.* London: BFI Classics, 2004.

DeBlasio, Alyssa. 'The New-Year Film as a Genre of Post-war Russian Cinema' *Studies in Russian and Soviet Cinema* 2.1 (2008): 43–61.

Drobashenko, S. (ed.) *Sovetskoe kino 70-e gody.* Moscow: Iskusstvo. 1984.

Dymshits, N. and Aleksandr Troshin (eds.). *Iz proshlogo v budushchee: Proverka na dorogakh*. Moscow: VNII Kinoiskusstva, 1990.

First, Joshua. 'Making Soviet Melodrama Contemporary: Conveying "Emotional Information" in the Era of Stagnation', *Studies in Russian and Soviet Cinema* 2.1 (2008): 21–42.

Fomin, Valerii. *Peresechenie parallel'nykh: Lotianu, Il'enko, Ioseliani, Mansurov, Okeev, Panfilov, Shukshin.* Moscow: Iskusstvo, 1976.

——. *Polka.* Moscow: NII Kinoiskusstva, 1992.
——. *Zapreshchenye fil'my.* (Vol. 2 of *Polka).* Moscow: NII Kinoiskusstva, 1993.
——. *Kino i vlast' : sovetskoe kino, 1965–1985 gody: dokumenty, svidetel'syva, razmyshleniya.* Moscow: Materik, 1996.
—— (ed.). *Kinematograf ottepeli: Dokumenty i svidetel'stva.* Moscow: Materik, 1998.
Gillespie, David. 'The Sounds of Music: Soundtrack and Song in Soviet Film' *Slavic Review* 62.3 (2003): 473–490.
Givens, John. 'Vasilii Shukshin and the "Audience of Millions": *Kalina krasnaia* and the Power of Popular Cinema', *Russian Review* 58 (1999): 268–285.
Goulding, Daniel J. (ed.). *Post New Wave Cinema in the Soviet Union and Eastern Europe.* Bloomington: Indiana University Press, 1989.
Graffy, Julian. 'History, Memory, Water: The Reclamation of Georgian Identity in Irakli Kvirikadze's *The Swimmer*', *Studies in Russian and Soviet Cinema* 1.3 (2007): 299–327.
Gromov, E. *Komedii i ne tol'ko komedii.* Moscow: Soiuz kinematografistov SSSR, 1989.
Hutchings, Stephen. 'Word and Image in El'dar Riazanov's "S legkym parom". Or The Irony of (Cinematic Fate)', *Essays in Poetics* 25 (2000): 236–55.
Johnson, Vida T. and Graham Petrie. *The Films of Andrei Tarkovsky: A Visual Fugue*, Bloomington: Indiana University Press, 1994.
Kozintsev, Grigorii. *King Lear: The Space of Tragedy. Diary of a Film Director.* London: Heinemann, 1977.
Le Fanu, Mark. *The Cinema of Andrei Tarkovsky.* London: BFI, 1987.
MacFadyen, David. *The Sad Comedy of El'dar Riazanov.* Montreal and London: McGill-Queen's University Press, 2003.
——. '*Moscow Does Not Believe in Tears*: From Oscar to Consolation Prize', *Studies in Russian and Soviet Cinema* 1.1 (2007): 45–67.
Mamatova, Lidiia (ed.). *Aktual'nye problemy sovetskogo kino nachala 80-kh godov.* Moscow: NII Kinoiskusstva, 1983.
Martin, Michel. *Cinéma soviétique: de Khrouchtev à Gorbatchev.* Lausanne: L'Age d'homme, 1993.
Prokhorov, Alexander. 'Soviet Family Melodrama of the 1940s and 1950s', in Louise McReynolds and Joan Neuberger (eds.), *Imitations of Life: Two Centuries of Melodrama in Russia.* Durham, NC and London: Duke University Press, 2002, pp. 208–231.
——.'Cinema of Attraction Versus Narrative Cinema: Leonid Gaidai's and El'dar Riazanov's Satires of the 1960s', *Slavic Review* 62.3 (2003): 455–472.
——.'The Adolescent and the Child in the Cinema of the Thaw', *Studies in Russian and Soviet Cinema* 1.2 (2007): 115–129.
Quart, Barbara. 'Between Mysticism and Materialism: The Films of Larisa Shepitko', *Cineaste* 16.3 (1988): 4–11.

Rifkin, Benjamin. 'The Christian Subtext in Bykov's *Čučelo*', *Slavic and East European Journal* 37.2 (1993): 178–193.

Synessiou, Natasha. *Mirror* (KinoFile 6). London: I. B. Tauris, 2001.

Tarkovskii, Andrei, *Time Within Time: The Diaries, 1970–1986*. London: Faber, 1994.

Tarkovsky, Andrey. *Sculpting in Time*, Austin: University of Texas Press, 1986.

Taubman, Jane. 'The Cinema of Kira Muratova', *Russian Review* 52 (1993): 367–381.

——. *Kira Muratova* (Kino Companion 4). London: I. B. Tauris, 2005.

Troianovskii, Vitalii (ed.). *Kinematograf ottepeli. Kniga pervaia.* Moscow: Materik, 1996.

Turovskaya, Maya. *Tarkovsky: Cinema as Poetry*. London: Faber, 1989.

Vail', Petr. '60-e: sovetskoe kino i stil' epokhi. Razmyshleniia i kommentarii', in Aleksandr Troshin (ed.) *Close-Up: Istoriko-teoreticheskii seminar vo VGIKe: Lektsii 1996–1998 gody*. Moscow: VGIK, 1999, pp. 230–233.

Vlasova, M. (ed.). *Sovetskoe kino semidesiatykh – pervoi poloviny vos'midesiatykh godov: Uchebnoe posobie*. Moscow: VGIK, 1997.

Woll, Josephine. *Real Images. Soviet Cinema of the Thaw*. London: I. B. Tauris, 2000.

——. *The Cranes Are Flying* (KinoFile 7). London: I. B. Tauris, 2003.

Youngblood, Denise. 'Andrei Rublev: The Medieval Epic as Post-Utopian History', in Vivian Sobchack (ed.), *The Persistence of History: Film, Television, and the Modern Event*. New York: Routledge, 1996, pp. 127–43.

Zorkaia, Neia. *Èl'dar Riazanov: Sbornik.* Moscow: Iskusstvo. 1974

Glasnost and Perestroika

Beardow, Frank. *Little Vera* (KinoFile 8). London: I. B. Tauris, 2003.

Boym, Svetlana. 'Post-Soviet Cinematic Nostalgia: From 'Elite Cinema' to Soap Opera', *Discourse* 17.3 (1995): 75–84.

Brashinsky, Michael and Andrew Horton (eds.). *Russian Critics on the Cinema of Glasnost*. Cambridge: Cambridge University Press, 1994.

Budiak, Liudmila. 'We Cannot Live This Way: Reflections on the State of Contemporary Soviet Film', *Film Quarterly* 44.2 (1990–91): 28–33.

Condee, Nancy. 'The Dream of Well-Being', *Sight and Sound* 12 (1997): 18–21.

Condee, Nancy and Vladimir Padunov. 'The Outposts of Official Art: Recharting Soviet Cultural History', *Framework* 34 (1987): 59–107.

Eagle, Herbert. 'Soviet Cinema Today: On the Semantic Potential of a Discredited Canon', *Michigan Quarterly Review* 28.4 (1989): 743–60.

Faraday, George. *Revolt of the Filmmakers: The Struggle for Artistic Autonomy and the Fall of the Soviet Film Industry*. University Park, PA: Pennsylvania State University Press, 2000.

Galichenko, Nicholas. *Glasnost: Soviet Cinema Responds.* Austin: University of Texas Press, 1991.

Graham, Seth. '*Chernukha* and Russian Film', *Studies in Slavic Culture* 1 (2000): 9–27.

Horton, Andrew and Michael Brashinsky. *The Zero Hour: Glasnost and Soviet Cinema in Transition.* Princeton: Princeton University Press, 1992.

Kepley, Vance (ed.). '*Contemporary Soviet Cinema'* [special issue], *WideAngle* 12.4 (1990).

Larsen, Susan. 'In Search of an Audience: The New Russian Cinema of Reconciliation' in Barker, A. (ed.) *Consuming Russia: Popular Culture, Sex, and Society since Gorbachev*. Durham, NC: Duke University Press, 1999, pp. 192–216.

——. 'Melodramatic Masculinity, National Identity, and the Stalinist Past in Post-Soviet Cinema', *Studies in Twentieth Century Literature* 24.1 (2000): 85–120.

Lawton, Anna. *Kinoglasnost: Soviet Cinema in Our Time*. Cambridge: Cambridge University Press, 1992.

Menashe, Louis. 'Moscow Believes in Tears: The Problems (and Promise?) of Russian Cinema in the Transition Period', *Cineaste* 26.3 (2001): 1017.

Plakhov, Andrei. 'Soviet Cinema into the 90s', *Sight and Sound* 2 (1989): 80–85.

Ratchford, Moira. 'Post-*Glasnost* Shock in the Russian Film Industry: The Euphoria is Past. Now Comes the Tough Part', *New Outlook* 3.1–2 (1992): 102–14.

Sandomirskaia, Irina. 'A Glossolalic Glasnost and the Retuning of the Soviet Subject: Sound Performance in Kira Muratova's *Asthenic Syndrome*', *Studies in Russian and Soviet Cinema* 2.1 (2008): 63–83.

Widdis, Emma. 'An Unmappable System: The Collapse of Public Space in Late Soviet Film', *Film Criticism* 21.2 (1996–7): 8–24.

Woll, Josephine and Denise Youngblood. *Repentance* (KinoFile 4). London: I. B. Tauris, 2001.

Youngblood, Denise. 'Repentance: Stalinist Terror and the Realism of Surrealism', in R. Rosenstone (ed.), *Film and the Construction of a New Past*, Princeton: Princeton University Press, 1995, pp. 139–154.

Zhabskii, M. (ed.). *Ispytanie konkurentsiei: Otechestvennoe kino i novoe pokolenie zritelei*. Moscow: VNII Kinoiskusstva, 1997.

Zvonkine, Eugénie. 'The Structure of the Fairy Tale in Kira Muratova's *The Sentimental Policeman*', *Studies in Russian and Soviet Cinema* 1.2 (2007): 131–145.

Post-Soviet Cinema

Beumers, Birgit 'Cinemarket, or the Russian Film Industry in "Mission Possible"', *Europe-Asia Studies* 51.5 (1999): 871–896.

——. 'Mikhalkov: The Barber of Siberia', in Forbes (ed.) *European Cinema*, London: Palgrave, 2000, pp. 195–206.

——. *Burnt by the Sun* (KinoFile 3). London: I. B. Tauris, 2000.

——. (ed.). *Russia on Reels: The Russian Idea in Post-Soviet Cinema.* London: I. B. Tauris, 1999.

—— and Vladimir Padunov (eds.). *KinoKultura*, online journal at http://www.kinokultura.com.

Gillespie, David. 'Identity and the Past in Recent Russian Cinema', in Everett, Wendy (ed.) *European Identity in Cinema.* Exeter: Exeter University Press, 1996, pp. 53–60.

——. 'Confronting Imperialism: The Ambivalence of War in Post-Soviet Film', in *Military and Society in Post-Soviet Russia*, eds. Stephen Webber and Jenny Mathers, Manchester: Manchester University Press, 2006, pp. 80–93.

Goscilo, Helena (ed.). 'Resent, Reassess, and Reinvents: The Three R's of Post-Soviet Cinema', guest edited issue of *Slavic and East European Journal* 51.2 (2007): 213–390.

Harte, Tim. 'A Visit to the Museum: Aleksandr Sokurov's Russian Ark and the Framing of the Eternal', *Slavic Review* 64.1 (2005): 43–58.

Hashamova, Yana. *Pride and Panic: Russian Imagination of the West in Post-Soviet Film.* Bristol and Chicago: Intellect Books, 2007.

Jameson, Fredric. 'History and Elegy in Sokurov', *Critical Enquiry* 33 (2006): 1–12.

Kujundzic, Dragan. 'After "After": The *Ark*ive Fever of Alexander Sokurov', *Quarterly Review of Film and Video* 21 (2004): 219–239.

Larsen, Susan. 'National Identity, Cultural Authority and the Post-Soviet Blockbuster: Nikita Mikhalkov and Aleksei Balabanov', *Slavic Review* 62.3 (2003): 491–511.

Lawton, Anna. *Imaging Russia 2000. Film and Facts.* Washington, DC: New Academia Publishing, 2004.

Livers, Keith A. 'Empty Is My Native Land: The Problem of the Absent Center in Aleksandr Zel'dovich's Moscow', *Russian Review* 64 (2005): 422–39.

Norris, Stephen. 'Tsarist Russia, *Lubok* Style: Nikita Mikhalkov's *Barber of Siberia* (1999) and Post-Soviet National Identity', *Historical Journal of Film, Radio and Television* 25.1 (2005): 101–118.

——. 'Guiding Stars: The Comet-Like Rise of the War Film in Putin's Russia', *Studies in Russian and Soviet Cinema* 1.2 (2007): 163–189.

Prokhorova, Elena. 'Can the Meeting Place Be Changed? Crime and Identity Discourse in Russian Television Series of the 1990s', *Slavic Review* 62.3 (2003): 512–524.

Stishova, Elena. *Territoriia kino: Postsovetskoe desiatiletie.* Moscow: Pomatur, 2001.

Szaniawski, Jeremi. 'Historic Space in Sokurov's *Moloch*, *Taurus* and *The Sun*', *Studies in Russian and Soviet Cinema* 1.2 (2007): 147–162.

Youngblood, Denise.'The Cosmopolitan and the Patriot: The Brothers Mikhalkov-Konchalovsky and Russian Cinema', *Historical Journal of Film, Radio & Television* 23.1 (2003): 27–41.

Animation

Asenin, S. *Mir mul'tfil'ma*. Moscow: Iskusstvo, 1986.

—— (ed.). *Mudrost vymysla*. Moscow: Iskusstvo, 1983.

Babichenko, D. (ed.). *Mastera sovetskoi mul'tiplikatsii*. Moscow: Iskusstvo, 1972.

Beumers, Birgit. 'Comforting Creatures in Children's Cartoons', in M. Balina, L. Rudova (eds.), *Reading Russian and Soviet Children's Culture*. London and New York: Routledge, 2008, pp. 153–171.

Ivanov-Vano, Ivan. *Risovannyi fil'm*. Moscow: Goskinoizdat, 1950.

——. *Kadr za kadrom*. Moscow: Iskusstvo, 1979.

Kitson, Clare. *Yuri Norstein and Tale of Tales: An Animator's Journey*. Eastleigh and Bloomington: John Libbey and Indiana University Press, 2005.

Krivulia, Natal'ia. *Labirinty animatsii*, Moscow: Graal', 2002.

MacFadyen, David. *Yellow Crocodiles and Blue Oranges*. Montreal and Kingston: McGill-Queens University Press, 2005.

Norshtein, Iurii and Francesca Iarbusova. *Skazka skazok*. Moscow: Krasnaia ploshchad', exhibition catalogue (Pushkin Museum 5 April – 29 May 2005).

Venzher, Nataliia (ed.). *Sotvorenie fil'ma*. Moscow: Soiuz kinematografistov SSSR, 1990.

Central Asian Cinema

Abikeeva, Gul'nara. *Kino Tsentral'noi Azii*. Almaty: IREX, 2001.

——. *Natsiostroitel'stvo v Kazakhstane i drugikh stranakh tsentral'noj Azii i kak etot protsess otrazhaetsia v kinematografe*. Almaty: Tsentr Tsentral'no-Aziatskoi kinematografii, 2006.

Abikeyeva, Gulnara. *The Heart of the World: Films from Central Asia*. Almaty: Tengizchevroil, Kazakhfilm, SKIF, Kino Firm, 2003.

Dömez-Colin, Gönül. 'Kazakh New Wave: Post-Perestroika, Post-Soviet Union', *Blimp: Film Magazine* 30 (1994): 12–15.

Nogerbek, Bauyrzhan. *Kino Kazakhstana*. Almaty: Natsional'nyi prodiuserskii tsentr, 1998.

Pruner, Liudmila Zebriner. 'The New Wave in Kazakh Cinema', *Slavic Review* 51.4 (1992): 791–801.

Radvanyi, Jean (ed.). *Le cinéma d'Asie centrale sovietique*. Paris: Centre Georges Pompidou, 1991.

Smailova, Tamara (ed.). *Kino Kazakhstana: Kinospravochnik*. Almaty: Zhibek Zholy, 2000.

Waller, Gregory. 'National Cinema and Film Culture in Kazakhstan', *Asian Cinema* 8.11 (1996): 39–49.

Index

Note: Page numbers in **bold** indicate illustrations.